MCSE™ Windows® 2000 Network Design

Kim Simmons
Jarret W. Buse
Todd B. Halpin

MCSE™ Windows® 2000 Network Design Exam Cram

The Coriolis Group, LLC
14455 N. Hayden Road
Suite 220
Scottsdale, Arizona 85260

(480)483-0192
FAX (480)483-0193
www.coriolis.com

Library of Congress Cataloging-in-Publication Data
Simmons, Kim.
MCSE Windows 2000 network design exam cram / by Kim Simmons, Jarret Buse, Todd Halpin.
p. cm.
Includes index
ISBN 1-57610-716-7
1. Electronic data processing personnel--Certification. 2. Microsoft software--Examinations--Study guides. 3. Computer networks--Examinations--Study guides. I. Buse, Jarret. II. Halpin, Todd. III. Title.
QA76.3 .S56 2000
005.7'13769--dc21

00-060214

Printed in the United States of America
10 9 8 7 6 5

President and CEO
Keith Weiskamp

Publisher
Steve Sayre

Acquisitions Editor
Shari Jo Hehr

Marketing Specialist
Brett Woolley

Project Editor
Karen Swartz

Production Coordinator
Wendy Littley

Cover Designer
Jesse Dunn

Layout Designer
April Nielsen

The Coriolis Group, LLC • 14455 North Hayden Road, Suite 220 • Scottsdale, Arizona 85260

ExamCram.com Connects You to the Ultimate Study Center!

Our goal has always been to provide you with the best study tools on the planet to help you achieve your certification in record time. Time is so valuable these days that none of us can afford to waste a second of it, especially when it comes to exam preparation.

Over the past few years, we've created an extensive line of *Exam Cram* and *Exam Prep* study guides, practice exams, and interactive training. To help you study even better, we have now created an e-learning and certification destination called **ExamCram.com.** (You can access the site at **www.examcram.com**.) Now, with every study product you purchase from us, you'll be connected to a large community of people like yourself who are actively studying for their certifications, developing their careers, seeking advice, and sharing their insights and stories.

I believe that the future is all about collaborative learning. Our **ExamCram.com** destination is our approach to creating a highly interactive, easily accessible collaborative environment, where you can take practice exams and discuss your experiences with others, sign up for features like "Questions of the Day," plan your certifications using our interactive planners, create your own personal study pages, and keep up with all of the latest study tips and techniques.

I hope that whatever study products you purchase from us—*Exam Cram* or *Exam Prep* study guides, *Personal Trainers*, *Personal Test Centers*, or one of our interactive Web courses—will make your studying fun and productive. Our commitment is to build the kind of learning tools that will allow you to study the way you want to, whenever you want to.

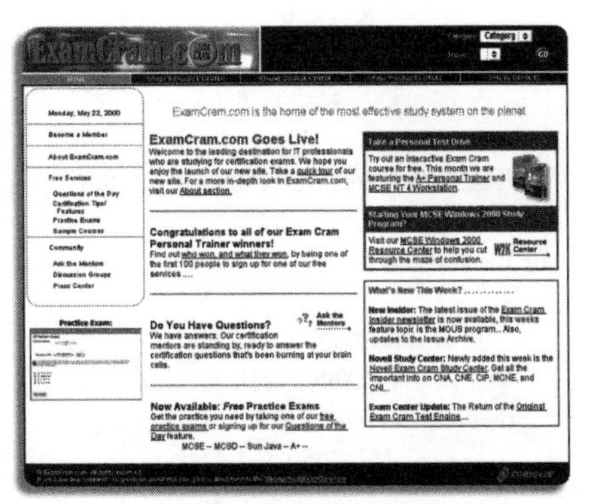

Visit ExamCram.com now to enhance your study program.

Help us continue to provide the very best certification study materials possible. Write us or email us at **learn@examcram.com** and let us know how our study products have helped you study. Tell us about new features that you'd like us to add. Send us a story about how we've helped you. We're listening!

Good luck with your certification exam and your career. Thank you for allowing us to help you achieve your goals.

Keith Weiskamp
President and CEO

Look for these other products from The Coriolis Group:

MCSE Windows 2000 Accelerated Exam Prep
By Lance Cockcroft, Erik Eckel, and Ron Kauffman

MCSE Windows 2000 Server Exam Prep
By David Johnson and Dawn Rader

MCSE Windows 2000 Professional Exam Prep
By Michael D. Stewart, James Bloomingdale, and Neall Alcott

MCSE Windows 2000 Network Exam Prep
By Tammy Smith and Sandra Smeeton

MCSE Windows 2000 Directory Services Exam Prep
By David V. Watts, Will Willis, and Tillman Strahan

MCSE Windows 2000 Security Design Exam Prep
By Richard Alan McMahon and Glen Bicking

MCSE Windows 2000 Network Design Exam Prep
By Geoffrey Alexander, Anoop Jalan, and Joseph Alexander

MCSE Migrating from NT 4 to Windows 2000 Exam Prep
By Glen Bergen, Graham Leach, and David Baldwin

MCSE Windows 2000 Directory Services Design Exam Prep
By J. Peter Bruzzese and Wayne Dipchan

MCSE Windows 2000 Core Four Exam Prep Pack

MCSE Windows 2000 Server Exam Cram
By Natasha Knight

MCSE Windows 2000 Professional Exam Cram
By Dan Balter, Dan Holme, Todd Logan, and Laurie Salmon

MCSE Windows 2000 Network Exam Cram
By Hank Carbeck, Derek Melber, and Richard Taylor

MCSE Windows 2000 Directory Services Exam Cram
By Will Willis, David V. Watts, and J. Peter Bruzzese

MCSE Windows 2000 Security Design Exam Cram
By Phillip G. Schein

MCSE Windows 2000 Directory Services Design Exam Cram
By Dennis Scheil and Diana Bartley

MCSE Windows 2000 Core Four Exam Cram Pack

and...

MCSE Windows 2000 Foundations
By James Michael Stewart and Lee Scales

I dedicate this book to my beautiful wife Cassandra and to my wonderful children Devyn, Logan, Caleb, and Miss Eilly.
—Jarret W. Buse

❧

I would like to dedicate my portions of this book to my mother Penny Lee Wade, who died on the first day of this century. She was my best friend, supporter, protector, and everything that a mother could be. Her faith and determination made everyone around her better by her mere presence. Surviving her loss are her husband and my stepfather Retired Air Force Colonel Reverend William J. Wade, my sister Jennifer Lee Kelley, and our children. I miss you mom, but you are with me every day. Thanks for looking out for your son.
—Todd B. Halpin

❧

About the Authors

Kim Simmons (MCSE, MCP+I, and MCT) includes among her 11 certifications development exams in support of her emphasis in Internet technologies. She is currently a lead instructor at Westwood College of Technology, developing and teaching a postgraduate e-commerce IT professional program. She has worked for MCI Systemhouse and EDS performing network architecture analysis and upgrade recommendations on a per project basis for outside companies. As a technical trainer teaching MCSE certification courses, she received corporate awards for being one of the top 15 and 50 trainers in the ExecuTrain Corporation national system. Before moving into technical training, Kim served in Saudi Arabia in support of the Gulf War, where she used the PATRIOT missile system to do engagement control in search of SCUD missiles.

Kim doesn't have any spare time, but she spends her off-teaching time with her three children and husband. Her goal is to develop a non-computer hobby someday.

Jarret W. Buse (MCT, MCSE+I, CCNA, CNA, A+, Network+, and i-Net+) is a technical trainer and consultant specializing in Microsoft products. He has worked with Microsoft hardware and software for the past eight years and instructs students in the use of various Microsoft products at Micro Computer Solutions in Evansville, Indiana. Now holding an Associate Degree in Programming, he is working toward Microsoft Developer Certification. He can be reached at jbuse@teammcs.com.

Todd B. Halpin (MCSE, MCT, MCP, Network+, and CCNA) has been a Network Support Technician/Engineer since 1995. He is currently employed by Micro Computer Solutions in Evansville, IN, where he is responsible for network design, implementation, and support. He is also a backup trainer for Jarret Buse. Todd provides support services for MCS clients in the Indiana, Kentucky, and Illinois areas, ranging from small mom-and-pop shops to corporate WANs. Along with co-authoring this book and providing training services, his strength is in providing his clients with solutions to challenges they face. The diversity of challenges posed by this wonderful profession cannot be equaled. "I love this game!"

Acknowledgments

Thanks to Lee Anderson and Karen Akins Swartz for being so supportive. You both made the process much easier. Thanks to Tom Gillen for copyediting and Lydia Bell for tech reviewing our work. Many thanks to the team at The Coriolis Group, including Wendy Littley for production coordination, Jesse Dunn for cover design, April Nielsen for layout design, and Brett Woolley in marketing. Eddie, thanks for understanding while I was locked away during the writing of this book. Jarret and Todd, you are the nicest guys and I wish you the best. Also to SLB, the motivation to write this book came from you.

—*Kim Simmons*

I want to thank my beautiful wife, Cassandra, for her love and support not only during the writing of this book, but also during the wonderful years we have been together. I also cherish our children and appreciate their understanding during the last few months. Devyn, Logan, Caleb, and Eilly, I could not live without you. During the writing of this book, my beautiful daughter, Eilly, was born. During her recovery, my wife dislocated her shoulders and suffered immensely for almost three weeks, and even now is still recovering from the damage done. My family's absence from me, like mine from them, was felt every minute. I will be with all of you soon and forever (especially Eilly, my little princess).

Also during this time I have appreciated the help of my mother-in-law, "Alice", for helping with the family and making me a HOT dinner every night!

I also want to thank my employer and manager for being understanding through the course of this book. Micro Computer Solutions has been a Godsend.

Thanks to my mom and dad for supporting me in all my endeavors and acknowledging my abilities to help me toward a career of my choice.

To my grandmother, this book will be Greek to you, but I think you will love it anyway.

Thanks to my great-aunt for my first computer.

Thanks to my student on Saturdays for his understanding when I cancelled class or hurried through material.

And to anyone I forgot, there is always (hopefully) a next book.

And finally, to save the best for last, thank you God for letting me get this far!

—Jarret W. Buse

I have too many to thank to list them all, so I will list the ones that need to be printed. A special thanks to Kim and Jarret for their help and support. With Kim's help in easing my writing burden, this book was completed on time. Jarret is not only a good coworker, but also a good friend, and if his four children take after their father, they will be an awesome force in this industry within a few decades. A big thanks to Kris Miller, co-owner and VP of VirtuCon, for the use of the company name, and for just being Kris.

Last, but not least, a special thanks to my wife Greta, who has the writing skills to make sure that my dyslexia was not apparent to the folks at Coriolis. Without her spelling and grammatical skills, the amount of errors would have driven the editors insane, or at a minimum, given them a nervous tick. If your child has been diagnosed with Attention Deficit Disorder or dyslexia, I encourage you to purchase a copy of *Brilliant Idiot*, by Dr. Abraham Schmitt, as told by Mary Lou Hartzler Clements, ISBN 1-56148-108-4. Don't medicate the child, educate yourself!

—Todd B. Halpin

Contents at a Glance

Table of Contents

Introduction

Welcome to *MCSE Windows 2000 Network Design Exam Cram*! Whether this is your first or your fifteenth *Exam Cram* book, you'll find information here and in Chapter 1 that will help ensure your success as you pursue knowledge, experience, and certification. This book aims to help you get ready to take—and pass—the Microsoft certification Exam 70-221, titled "Designing a Microsoft Windows 2000 Network Infrastructure." This Introduction explains Microsoft's certification programs in general and talks about how the *Exam Cram* series can help you prepare for Microsoft's Windows 2000 certification exams.

Exam Cram books help you understand and appreciate the subjects and materials you need to pass Microsoft certification exams. *Exam Cram* books are aimed strictly at test preparation and review. They do not teach you everything you need to know about a topic. Instead, we (the authors) present and dissect the questions and problems we've found that you're likely to encounter on a test. We've worked to bring together as much information as possible about Microsoft certification exams.

Nevertheless, to completely prepare yourself for any Microsoft test, we recommend that you begin by taking the Self-Assessment included in this book immediately following this Introduction. This tool will help you evaluate your knowledge base against the requirements for an MCSE under both ideal and real circumstances.

Based on what you learn from that exercise, you might decide to begin your studies with some classroom training or some background reading. On the other hand, you might decide to pick up and read one of the many study guides available from Microsoft or third-party vendors on certain topics, including The Coriolis Group's *Exam Prep* series. We also recommend that you supplement your study program with visits to **ExamCram.com** to receive additional practice questions, get advice, and track the Windows 2000 MCSE program.

We also strongly recommend that you install, configure, and fool around with the software that you'll be tested on, because nothing beats hands-on experience and familiarity when it comes to understanding the questions you're likely to encounter on a certification test. Book learning is essential, but hands-on experience is the best teacher of all!

The Microsoft Certified Professional (MCP) Program

The MCP Program currently includes the following separate tracks, each of which boasts its own special acronym (as a certification candidate, you need to have a high tolerance for alphabet soup of all kinds):

- *MCP (Microsoft Certified Professional)*—This is the least prestigious of all the certification tracks from Microsoft. Passing one of the major Microsoft exams qualifies an individual for the MCP credential. Individuals can demonstrate proficiency with additional Microsoft products by passing additional certification exams.
- *MCP+SB (Microsoft Certified Professional + Site Building)*—This certification program is designed for individuals who are planning, building, managing, and maintaining Web sites. Individuals with the MCP+SB credential will have demonstrated the ability to develop Web sites that include multimedia and searchable content and Web sites that connect to and communicate with a back-end database. It requires one MCP exam, plus two of these three exams: "70-055: Designing and Implementing Web Sites with Microsoft FrontPage 98," "70-057: Designing and Implementing Commerce Solutions with Microsoft Site Server 3.0, Commerce Edition," and "70-152: Designing and Implementing Web Solutions with Microsoft Visual InterDev 6.0."
- *MCSE (Microsoft Certified Systems Engineer)*—Anyone who has a current MCSE is warranted to possess a high level of networking expertise with Microsoft operating systems and products. This credential is designed to prepare individuals to plan, implement, maintain, and support information systems, networks, and internetworks built around Microsoft Windows 2000 and its BackOffice Server 2000 family of products.

  To obtain an MCSE, an individual must pass four core operating system exams, one optional core exam, and two elective exams. The operating system exams require individuals to prove their competence with desktop and server operating systems and networking/internetworking components.

  For Windows NT 4 MCSEs, the Accelerated exam, "70-240: Microsoft Windows 2000 Accelerated Exam for MCPs Certified on Microsoft Windows NT 4.0," is an option. This free exam covers all of the material tested in the Core Four exams. The hitch in this plan is that you can take the test only once. If you fail, you must take all four core exams to recertify. The Core Four exams are: "70-210: Installing, Configuring and Administering Microsoft Windows 2000 Professional," "70-215: Installing, Configuring and Administering Microsoft

Windows 2000 Server," "70-216: Implementing and Administering a Microsoft Windows 2000 Network Infrastructure," and "70-217: Implementing and Administering a Microsoft Windows 2000 Directory Services Infrastructure."

To fulfill the fifth core exam requirement, you can choose from three design exams: "70-219: Designing a Microsoft Windows 2000 Directory Services Infrastructure," "70-220: Designing Security for a Microsoft Windows 2000 Network," or "70-221: Designing a Microsoft Windows 2000 Network Infrastructure." You are also required to take two elective exams. An elective exam may fall in any number of subject or product areas, primarily BackOffice Server 2000 components. The two design exams that you don't select as your fifth core exam also qualify as electives. If you are on your way to becoming an MCSE and have already taken some exams, visit **www.microsoft.com/trainingandservices** for information about how to complete your MCSE certification.

In September 1999, Microsoft announced its Windows 2000 track for MCSE and also announced retirement of Windows NT 4.0 MCSE core exams on 12/31/2000. Individuals who wish to remain certified MCSEs after 12/31/2001 must "upgrade" their certifications on or before 12/31/2001. For more detailed information than is included here, visit **www.microsoft.com/trainingandservices/**.

New MCSE candidates must pass seven tests to meet the MCSE requirements. It's not uncommon for the entire process to take a year or so, and many individuals find that they must take a test more than once to pass. The primary goal of the *Exam Prep* and *Exam Cram* test preparation books is to make it possible, given proper study and preparation, to pass all Microsoft certification tests on the first try. Table 1 shows the required and elective exams for the Windows 2000 MCSE certification.

- *MCSD (Microsoft Certified Solution Developer)*—The MCSD credential reflects the skills required to create multitier, distributed, and COM-based solutions, in addition to desktop and Internet applications, using new technologies. To obtain an MCSD, an individual must demonstrate the ability to analyze and interpret user requirements; select and integrate products, platforms, tools, and technologies; design and implement code, and customize applications; and perform necessary software tests and quality assurance operations.

  To become an MCSD, you must pass a total of four exams: three core exams and one elective exam. Each candidate must choose one of these three desktop application exams—"70-016: Designing and Implementing Desktop Applications with Microsoft Visual C++ 6.0," "70-156: Designing and Implementing Desktop Applications with Microsoft Visual FoxPro 6.0," or "70-176: Designing and Implementing Desktop Applications with Microsoft

Table 1 MCSE Windows 2000 Requirements

Core

If you have not passed these 3 Windows NT 4 exams	
Exam 70-067	Implementing and Supporting Microsoft Windows NT Server 4.0
Exam 70-068	Implementing and Supporting Microsoft Windows NT Server 4.0 in the Enterprise
Exam 70-073	Microsoft Windows NT Workstation 4.0
then you must take these 4 exams	
Exam 70-210	Installing, Configuring and Administering Microsoft Windows 2000 Professional
Exam 70-215	Installing, Configuring and Administering Microsoft Windows 2000 Server
Exam 70-216	Implementing and Administering a Microsoft Windows 2000 Network Infrastructure
Exam 70-217	Implementing and Administering a Microsoft Windows 2000 Directory Services Infrastructure
If you have already passed exams 70-067, 70-068, and 70-073, you may take this exam	
Exam 70-240	Microsoft Windows 2000 Accelerated Exam for MCPs Certified on Microsoft Windows NT 4.0

5th Core Option

Choose 1 from this group	
Exam 70-219*	Designing a Microsoft Windows 2000 Directory Services Infrastructure
Exam 70-220*	Designing Security for a Microsoft Windows 2000 Network
Exam 70-221*	Designing a Microsoft Windows 2000 Network Infrastructure

Elective

Choose 2 from this group	
Exam 70-019	Designing and Implementing Data Warehouse with Microsoft SQL Server 7.0
Exam 70-219*	Designing a Microsoft Windows 2000 Directory Services Infrastructure
Exam 70-220*	Designing Security for a Microsoft Windows 2000 Network
Exam 70-221*	Designing a Microsoft Windows 2000 Network Infrastructure
Exam 70-222	Migrating from Microsoft Windows NT 4.0 to Microsoft Windows 2000
Exam 70-028	Administering Microsoft SQL Server 7.0
Exam 70-029	Designing and Implementing Databases on Microsoft SQL Server 7.0
Exam 70-080	Implementing and Supporting Microsoft Internet Explorer 5.0 by Using the Internet Explorer Administration Kit
Exam 70-081	Implementing and Supporting Microsoft Exchange Server 5.5
Exam 70-085	Implementing and Supporting Microsoft SNA Server 4.0
Exam 70-086	Implementing and Supporting Microsoft Systems Management Server 2.0
Exam 70-088	Implementing and Supporting Microsoft Proxy Server 2.0

This is not a complete listing—you can still be tested on some earlier versions of these products. However, we have included mainly the most recent versions so that you may test on these versions and thus be certified longer. We have not included any tests that are scheduled to be retired.

* The 5th Core Option exam does not double as an elective.

Visual Basic 6.0"—*plus* one of these three distributed application exams—"70-015: Designing and Implementing Distributed Applications with Microsoft Visual C++ 6.0," "70-155: Designing and Implementing Distributed Applications with Microsoft Visual FoxPro 6.0," or "70-175: Designing and Implementing Distributed Applications with Microsoft Visual Basic 6.0." The third core exam is "70-100: Analyzing Requirements and Defining Solution Architectures." Elective exams cover specific Microsoft applications and languages, including Visual Basic, C++, the Microsoft Foundation Classes, Access, SQL Server, Excel, and more.

- *MCDBA (Microsoft Certified Database Administrator)*—The MCDBA credential reflects the skills required to implement and administer Microsoft SQL Server databases. To obtain an MCDBA, an individual must demonstrate the ability to derive physical database designs, develop logical data models, create physical databases, create data services by using Transact-SQL, manage and maintain databases, configure and manage security, monitor and optimize databases, and install and configure Microsoft SQL Server.

  To become an MCDBA, you must pass a total of three core exams and one elective exam. The required core exams are "70-028: Administering Microsoft SQL Server 7.0," "70-029: Designing and Implementing Databases with Microsoft SQL Server 7.0," and "70-215: Installing, Configuring and Administering Microsoft Windows 2000 Server."

  The elective exams that you can choose from cover specific uses of SQL Server and include "70-015: Designing and Implementing Distributed Applications with Microsoft Visual C++ 6.0," "70-019: Designing and Implementing Data Warehouses with Microsoft SQL Server 7.0," "70-155: Designing and Implementing Distributed Applications with Microsoft Visual FoxPro 6.0," "70-175: Designing and Implementing Distributed Applications with Microsoft Visual Basic 6.0," and two exams that relate to Windows 2000: "70-216: Implementing and Administering a Microsoft Windows 2000 Network Infrastructure," and "70-087: Implementing and Supporting Microsoft Internet Information Server 4.0."

  If you have taken the three core Windows NT 4 exams on your path to becoming an MCSE, you qualify for the Accelerated exam (it replaces the Network Infrastructure exam requirement). The Accelerated exam covers the objectives of all four of the Windows 2000 core exams. In addition to taking the Accelerated exam, you must take only the two SQL exams—Administering and Database Design.

- *MCT (Microsoft Certified Trainer)*—Microsoft Certified Trainers are deemed able to deliver elements of the official Microsoft curriculum, based on technical knowledge and instructional ability. Thus, it is necessary for an individual seeking MCT credentials (which are granted on a course-by-course basis) to pass the related certification exam for a course and complete the official Microsoft training in the subject area, and to demonstrate an ability to teach.

This teaching skill criterion may be satisfied by proving that one has already attained training certification from Novell, Banyan, Lotus, the Santa Cruz Operation, or Cisco, or by taking a Microsoft-sanctioned workshop on instruction. Microsoft makes it clear that MCTs are important cogs in the Microsoft training channels. Instructors must be MCTs before Microsoft will allow them to teach in any of its official training channels, including Microsoft's affiliated Certified Technical Education Centers (CTECs) and its online training partner network. As of January 1, 2001, MCT candidates must also possess a current MCSE.

Microsoft has announced that the MCP+I and MCSE+I credentials will not be continued when the MCSE exams for Windows 2000 are in full swing because the skill set for the Internet portion of the program has been included in the new MCSE program. Therefore, details on these tracks are not provided here; go to **www.microsoft.com/trainingandservices/** if you need more information.

Once a Microsoft product becomes obsolete, MCPs typically have to recertify on current versions. (If individuals do not recertify, their certifications become invalid.) Because technology keeps changing and new products continually supplant old ones, this should come as no surprise. This explains why Microsoft has announced that MCSEs have 12 months past the scheduled retirement date for the Windows NT 4 exams to recertify on Windows 2000 topics. (Note that this means taking at least two exams, if not more.)

The best place to keep tabs on the MCP Program and its related certifications is on the Web. The URL for the MCP program is **www.microsoft.com/trainingandservices/**. But Microsoft's Web site changes often, so if this URL doesn't work, try using the Search tool on Microsoft's site with either "MCP" or the quoted phrase "Microsoft Certified Professional" as a search string. This will help you find the latest and most accurate information about Microsoft's certification programs.

Taking a Certification Exam

Once you've prepared for your exam, you need to register with a testing center. Each computer-based MCP exam costs $100, and if you don't pass, you may retest for an additional $100 for each additional try. In the United States and Canada, tests are administered by Prometric and by Virtual University Enterprises (VUE). Here's how you can contact them:

- *Prometric*—You can sign up for a test through the company's Web site at **www.prometric.com**. Or, you can register by phone at 800-755-3926 (within the United States or Canada) or at 410-843-8000 (outside the United States and Canada).
- *Virtual University Enterprises*—You can sign up for a test or get the phone numbers for local testing centers through the Web page at **www.vue.com/ms/**.

To sign up for a test, you must possess a valid credit card, or contact either company for mailing instructions to send them a check (in the U.S.). Only when payment is verified, or a check has cleared, can you actually register for a test.

To schedule an exam, call the number or visit either of the Web pages at least one day in advance. To cancel or reschedule an exam, you must call before 7 P.M. pacific standard time the day before the scheduled test time (or you may be charged, even if you don't appear to take the test). When you want to schedule a test, have the following information ready:

- Your name, organization, and mailing address.
- Your Microsoft Test ID. (Inside the United States, this means your Social Security number; citizens of other nations should call ahead to find out what type of identification number is required to register for a test.)
- The name and number of the exam you wish to take.
- A method of payment. (As we've already mentioned, a credit card is the most convenient method, but alternate means can be arranged in advance, if necessary.)

Once you sign up for a test, you'll be informed as to when and where the test is scheduled. Try to arrive at least 15 minutes early. You must supply two forms of identification—one of which must be a photo ID—to be admitted into the testing room.

All exams are completely closed-book. In fact, you will not be permitted to take anything with you into the testing area, but you will be furnished with a blank sheet of paper and a pen or, in some cases, an erasable plastic sheet and an erasable pen. We suggest that you immediately write down on that sheet of paper all the information you've memorized for the test. In *Exam Cram* books, this information appears on a tear-out sheet inside the front cover of each book. You will have some time to compose yourself, record this information, and take a sample orientation exam before you begin the real thing. We suggest you take the orientation test before taking your first exam, but because they're all more or less identical in layout, behavior, and controls, you probably won't need to do this more than once.

When you complete a Microsoft certification exam, the software will tell you whether you've passed or failed. If you need to retake an exam, you'll have to schedule a new test with Prometric or VUE and pay another $100.

The first time you fail a test, you can retake the test the next day. However, if you fail a second time, you must wait 14 days before retaking that test. The 14-day waiting period remains in effect for all retakes after the second failure.

Tracking MCP Status

As soon as you pass any Microsoft exam (except Networking Essentials), you'll attain Microsoft Certified Professional (MCP) status. Microsoft also generates transcripts that indicate which exams you have passed. You can view a copy of your transcript at any time by going to the MCP secured site and selecting Transcript Tool. This tool will allow you to print a copy of your current transcript and confirm your certification status.

Once you pass the necessary set of exams, you'll be certified. Official certification normally takes anywhere from six to eight weeks, so don't expect to get your credentials overnight. When the package for a qualified certification arrives, it includes a Welcome Kit that contains a number of elements (see Microsoft's Web site for other benefits of specific certifications):

- A certificate suitable for framing, along with a wallet card and lapel pin.
- A license to use the MCP logo, thereby allowing you to use the logo in advertisements, promotions, and documents, and on letterhead, business cards, and so on. Along with the license comes an MCP logo sheet, which includes camera-ready artwork. (Note: Before using any of the artwork, individuals must sign and return a licensing agreement that indicates they'll abide by its terms and conditions.)
- A subscription to *Microsoft Certified Professional Magazine*, which provides ongoing data about testing and certification activities, requirements, and changes to the program.

Many people believe that the benefits of MCP certification go well beyond the perks that Microsoft provides to newly anointed members of this elite group. We're starting to see more job listings that request or require applicants to have an MCP, MCSE, and so on, and many individuals who complete the program can qualify for increases in pay and/or responsibility. As an official recognition of hard work and broad knowledge, one of the MCP credentials is a badge of honor in many IT organizations.

How to Prepare for an Exam

Preparing for any Windows 2000 Server-related test (including "Designing a Microsoft Windows 2000 Network Infrastructure") requires that you obtain and study materials designed to provide comprehensive information about the product and its capabilities that will appear on the specific exam for which you are preparing. The following list of materials will help you study and prepare:

- The Windows 2000 Server product CD includes comprehensive online documentation and related materials; it should be a primary resource when you are preparing for the test.

- The exam preparation materials, practice tests, and self-assessment exams on the Microsoft Training & Services page at **www.microsoft.com/trainingandservices/default.asp?PageID=mcp**. The Testing Innovations link offers samples of the new question types found on the Windows 2000 MCSE exams. Find the materials, download them, and use them!

- The exam preparation advice, practice tests, questions of the day, and discussion groups on the **ExamCram.com** e-learning and certification destination Web site (**www.examcram.com**).

In addition, you'll probably find any or all of the following materials useful in your quest for Network Infrastructure Design expertise:

- *Microsoft training kits*—Microsoft Press offers training kits that specifically target Windows 2000 exams. For more information, visit **http://mspress.microsoft.com/findabook/list/series_ak.htm**.

- *Microsoft TechNet CD*—This monthly CD-based publication delivers numerous electronic titles that include coverage of Directory Services Design and related topics on the Technical Information (TechNet) CD. Its offerings include product facts, technical notes, tools and utilities, and information on how to access the Seminars Online training materials for Network Infrastructure Design. A subscription to TechNet costs $299 per year, but it is well worth the price. Visit **www.microsoft.com/technet/** and check out the information under the "TechNet Subscription" menu entry for more details.

- *White papers*—Microsoft Corporation publishes technical papers explaining the design of many of the services in Windows 2000. Often these papers are written by the engineers and designers of the service. White papers are an excellent source of information on the inner workings of a service and are often one of few sources to look at when the service is new. Visit **http://www.microsoft.com/ISN/whitepapers.asp** for a list of currently available technical white papers and links to each of them.
- *Study guides*—Several publishers—including The Coriolis Group—offer Windows 2000 titles. The Coriolis Group series includes the following:
  - *The Exam Cram series*—These books give you information about the material you need to know to pass the tests.
  - *The Exam Prep series*—These books provide a greater level of detail than the *Exam Cram* books and are designed to teach you everything you need to know from an exam perspective. Each book comes with a CD that contains interactive practice exams in a variety of testing formats.

  Together, the two series make a perfect pair.
- *Multimedia*—These Coriolis Group materials are designed to support learners of all types—whether you learn best by reading or doing:
  - *The Exam Cram Personal Trainer*—Offers a unique, personalized self-paced training course based on the exam.
  - *The Exam Cram Personal Test Center*—Features multiple test options that simulate the actual exam, including Fixed-Length, Random, Review, and Test All. Explanations of correct and incorrect answers reinforce concepts learned.
- *Classroom training*—CTECs, online partners, and third-party training companies (like Wave Technologies, Learning Tree, Data-Tech, and others) all offer classroom training on Windows 2000. These companies aim to help you prepare to pass Exam 70-221. Although such training runs upwards of $350 per day in class, most of the individuals lucky enough to partake find it to be quite worthwhile.
- *Other publications*—There's no shortage of materials available about Network Infrastructure Design. The resource sections at the end of each chapter should give you an idea of where we think you should look for further discussion.

By far, this set of required and recommended materials represents a nonpareil collection of sources and resources for Network Infrastructure Design and related topics. We anticipate that you'll find that this book belongs in this company

About this Book

Each topical *Exam Cram* chapter follows a regular structure, along with graphical cues about important or useful information. Here's the structure of a typical chapter:

- *Opening hotlists*—Each chapter begins with a list of the terms, tools, and techniques that you must learn and understand before you can be fully conversant with that chapter's subject matter. We follow the hotlists with one or two introductory paragraphs to set the stage for the rest of the chapter.
- *Topical coverage*—After the opening hotlists, each chapter covers a series of topics related to the chapter's subject title. Throughout this section, we highlight topics or concepts likely to appear on a test using a special Exam Alert layout, like this:

This is what an Exam Alert looks like. Normally, an Exam Alert stresses concepts, terms, software, or activities that are likely to relate to one or more certification test questions. For that reason, we think any information found offset in Exam Alert format is worthy of unusual attentiveness on your part. Indeed, most of the information that appears on The Cram Sheet appears as Exam Alerts within the text.

Pay close attention to material flagged as an Exam Alert; although all the information in this book pertains to what you need to know to pass the exam, we flag certain items that are really important. You'll find what appears in the meat of each chapter to be worth knowing, too, when preparing for the test. Because this book's material is very condensed, we recommend that you use this book along with other resources to achieve the maximum benefit.

In addition to the Exam Alerts, we have provided tips that will help you build a better foundation for Network Infrastructure Design knowledge. Although the information may not be on the exam, it is certainly related and will help you become a better test-taker.

This is how tips are formatted. Keep your eyes open for these, and you'll become a Network Infrastructure guru in no time!

- *Practice questions*—Although we talk about test questions and topics throughout the book, a section at the end of each chapter presents a series of mock test questions and explanations of both correct and incorrect answers.
- *Details and resources*—Every chapter ends with a section titled "Need to Know More?" This section provides direct pointers to Microsoft and third-party resources offering more details on the chapter's subject. In addition, this section

tries to rank or at least rate the quality and thoroughness of the topic's coverage by each resource. If you find a resource you like in this collection, use it, but don't feel compelled to use all the resources. On the other hand, we recommend only resources we use on a regular basis, so none of our recommendations will be a waste of your time or money (but purchasing them all at once probably represents an expense that many network administrators and would-be MCPs and MCSEs might find hard to justify).

The bulk of the book follows this chapter structure slavishly, but there are a few other elements that we'd like to point out. Chapter 16 includes a sample test that provides a good review of the material presented throughout the book to ensure you're ready for the exam. Chapter 17 is an answer key to the sample test that appears in Chapter 16. In addition, you'll find a handy glossary and an index.

Finally, the tear-out Cram Sheet attached next to the inside front cover of this *Exam Cram* book represents a condensed and compiled collection of facts and tips that we think you should memorize before taking the test. Because you can dump this information out of your head onto a piece of paper before taking the exam, you can master this information by brute force—you need to remember it only long enough to write it down when you walk into the test room. You might even want to look at it in the car or in the lobby of the testing center just before you walk in to take the test.

How to Use this Book

We've structured the topics in this book to build on one another. Therefore, some topics in later chapters make more sense after you've read earlier chapters. That's why we suggest you read this book from front to back for your initial test preparation. If you need to brush up on a topic or you have to bone up for a second try, use the index or table of contents to go straight to the topics and questions that you need to study. Beyond helping you prepare for the test, we think you'll find this book useful as a tightly focused reference to some of the most important aspects of Network Infrastructure.

Given all the book's elements and its specialized focus, we've tried to create a tool that will help you prepare for—and pass—Microsoft Exam 70-221. Please share your feedback on the book with us, especially if you have ideas about how we can improve it for future test-takers. We'll consider everything you say carefully, and we'll respond to all suggestions.

Send your questions or comments to us at **learn@examcram.com**. Please remember to include the title of the book in your message; otherwise, we'll be forced to guess which book you're writing about. And we don't like to guess—we want to *know*! Also, be sure to check out the Web pages at **www.examcram.com**, where you'll find information updates, commentary, and certification information.

Thanks, and enjoy the book!

Self-Assessment

The reason we included a Self-Assessment in this *Exam Cram* book is to help you evaluate your readiness to tackle MCSE certification. It should also help you understand what you need to know to master the topic of this book—namely, Exam 70-221, "Designing a Microsoft Windows 2000 Network Infrastructure." But before you tackle this Self-Assessment, let's talk about concerns you may face when pursuing an MCSE for Windows 2000, and what an ideal MCSE candidate might look like.

MCSEs in the Real World

In the next section, we describe an ideal MCSE candidate, knowing full well that only a few real candidates will meet this ideal. In fact, our description of that ideal candidate might seem downright scary, especially with the changes that have been made to the program to support Windows 2000. But take heart: Although the requirements to obtain an MCSE may seem formidable, they are by no means impossible to meet. However, be keenly aware that it does take time, involves some expense, and requires real effort to get through the process.

Increasing numbers of people are attaining Microsoft certifications, so the goal is within reach. You can get all the real-world motivation you need from knowing that many others have gone before, so you will be able to follow in their footsteps. If you're willing to tackle the process seriously and do what it takes to obtain the necessary experience and knowledge, you can take—and pass—all the certification tests involved in obtaining an MCSE. In fact, we've designed *Exam Preps*, the companion *Exam Crams*, *Exam Cram Personal Trainers*, and *Exam Cram Personal Test Centers* to make it as easy on you as possible to prepare for these exams. We've also greatly expanded our Web site, **www.examcram.com**, to provide a host of resources to help you prepare for the complexities of Windows 2000.

Besides MCSE, other Microsoft certifications include:

- MCSD, which is aimed at software developers and requires one specific exam, two more exams on client and distributed topics, plus a fourth elective exam drawn from a different, but limited, pool of options.

- Other Microsoft certifications, whose requirements range from one test (MCP) to several tests (MCP+SB, MCDBA).

The Ideal Windows 2000 MCSE Candidate

Just to give you some idea of what an ideal MCSE candidate is like, here are some relevant statistics about the background and experience such an individual might have. Don't worry if you don't meet these qualifications, or don't come that close—this is a far from ideal world, and where you fall short is simply where you'll have more work to do.

- Academic or professional training in network theory, concepts, and operations. This includes everything from networking media and transmission techniques through network operating systems, services, and applications.
- Three-plus years of professional networking experience, including experience with Ethernet, token ring, modems, and other networking media. This must include installation, configuration, upgrade, and troubleshooting experience.

Note: The Windows 2000 MCSE program is much more rigorous than the previous NT MCSE program; therefore, you'll really need some hands-on experience. Some of the exams require you to solve real-world case studies and network design issues, so the more hands-on experience you have, the better.

- Two-plus years in a networked environment that includes hands-on experience with Windows 2000 Server, Windows 2000 Professional, Windows NT Server, Windows NT Workstation, and Windows 95 or Windows 98. A solid understanding of each system's architecture, installation, configuration, maintenance, and troubleshooting is also essential.
- Knowledge of the various methods for installing Windows 2000, including manual and unattended installations.
- A thorough understanding of key networking protocols, addressing, and name resolution, including TCP/IP, IPX/SPX, and NetBEUI.
- A thorough understanding of NetBIOS naming, browsing, and file and print services.
- Familiarity with key Windows 2000-based TCP/IP-based services, including HTTP (Web servers), DHCP, WINS, DNS, plus familiarity with one or more of the following: Internet Information Server (IIS), Index Server, and Proxy Server.

- An understanding of how to implement security for key network data in a Windows 2000 environment.
- Working knowledge of NetWare 3.x and 4.x, including IPX/SPX frame formats, NetWare file, print, and directory services, and both Novell and Microsoft client software. Working knowledge of Microsoft's Client Service For NetWare (CSNW), Gateway Service For NetWare (GSNW), the NetWare Migration Tool (NWCONV), and the NetWare Client For Windows (NT, 95, and 98) is essential.
- A good working understanding of Active Directory. The more you work with Windows 2000, the more you'll realize that this new operating system is quite different than Windows NT. New technologies like Active Directory have really changed the way that Windows is configured and used. We recommend that you find out as much as you can about Active Directory and acquire as much experience using this technology as possible. The time you take learning about Active Directory will be time very well spent!

Fundamentally, this boils down to a bachelor's degree in computer science, plus three years' experience working in a position involving network design, installation, configuration, and maintenance. We believe that well under half of all certification candidates meet these requirements, and that, in fact, most meet less than half of these requirements—at least, when they begin the certification process. But because all the people who already have been certified have survived this ordeal, you can survive it too—especially if you heed what our Self-Assessment can tell you about what you already know and what you need to learn.

Put Yourself to the Test

The following series of questions and observations is designed to help you figure out how much work you must do to pursue Microsoft certification and what kinds of resources you may consult on your quest. Be absolutely honest in your answers, or you'll end up wasting money on exams you're not yet ready to take. There are no right or wrong answers, only steps along the path to certification. Only you can decide where you really belong in the broad spectrum of aspiring candidates.

Two things should be clear from the outset, however:

- Even a modest background in computer science will be helpful.
- Hands-on experience with Microsoft products and technologies is an essential ingredient to certification success.

Educational Background

1. Have you ever taken any computer-related classes? [Yes or No]

   If Yes, proceed to question 2; if No, proceed to question 4.

2. Have you taken any classes on computer operating systems? [Yes or No]

   If Yes, you will probably be able to handle Microsoft's architecture and system component discussions. If you're rusty, brush up on basic operating system concepts, especially virtual memory, multitasking regimes, user mode versus kernel mode operation, and general computer security topics.

   If No, consider some basic reading in this area. We strongly recommend a good general operating systems book, such as *Operating System Concepts, 5th Edition*, by Abraham Silberschatz and Peter Baer Galvin (John Wiley & Sons, 1998, ISBN 0-471-36414-2). If this title doesn't appeal to you, check out reviews for other, similar titles at your favorite online bookstore.

3. Have you taken any networking concepts or technologies classes? [Yes or No]

   If Yes, you will probably be able to handle Microsoft's networking terminology, concepts, and technologies (brace yourself for frequent departures from normal usage). If you're rusty, brush up on basic networking concepts and terminology, especially networking media, transmission types, the OSI Reference Model, and networking technologies such as Ethernet, token ring, FDDI, and WAN links.

   If No, you might want to read one or two books in this topic area. The two best books that we know of are *Computer Networks, 3rd Edition*, by Andrew S. Tanenbaum (Prentice-Hall, 1996, ISBN 0-13-349945-6) and *Computer Networks and Internets, 2nd Edition*, by Douglas E. Comer (Prentice-Hall, 1998, ISBN 0-130-83617-6).

   Skip to the next section, "Hands-on Experience."

4. Have you done any reading on operating systems or networks? [Yes or No]

   If Yes, review the requirements stated in the first paragraphs after questions 2 and 3. If you meet those requirements, move on to the next section. If No, consult the recommended reading for both topics. A strong background will help you prepare for the Microsoft exams better than just about anything else.

Hands-on Experience

The most important key to success on all of the Microsoft tests is hands-on experience, especially with Windows 2000 Server and Professional, plus the many add-on services and BackOffice components around which so many of the Microsoft certification exams revolve. If we leave you with only one realization after taking this Self-Assessment, it should be that there's no substitute for time spent installing, configuring, and using the various Microsoft products upon which you'll be tested repeatedly and in depth.

5. Have you installed, configured, and worked with:

➤ Windows 2000 Server? [Yes or No]

If Yes, make sure you understand basic concepts as covered in Exam 70-215. You should also study the TCP/IP interfaces, utilities, and services for Exam 70-216, plus implementing security features for Exam 70-220.

You can download objectives, practice exams, and other data about Microsoft exams from the Training and Certification page at **www.Microsoft.com/trainingandservices/default.asp?PageID=mcp/**. Use the " Exams" link to obtain specific exam information.

If you haven't worked with Windows 2000 Server, you must obtain one or two machines and a copy of Windows 2000 Server. Then, learn the operating system and whatever other software components on which you'll also be tested.

In fact, we recommend that you obtain two computers, each with a network interface, and set up a two-node network on which to practice. With decent Windows 2000-capable computers selling for about $500 to $600 apiece these days, this shouldn't be too much of a financial hardship. You may have to scrounge to come up with the necessary software, but if you scour the Microsoft Web site you can usually find low-cost options to obtain evaluation copies of most of the software that you'll need.

➤ Windows 2000 Professional? [Yes or No]

If Yes, make sure you understand the concepts covered in Exam 70-210.

If No, you will want to obtain a copy of Windows 2000 Professional and learn how to install, configure, and maintain it. You can use *MCSE Windows 2000 Professional Exam Cram* to guide your activities and studies, or work straight from Microsoft's test objectives if you prefer.

For any and all of these Microsoft exams, the Resource Kits for the topics involved are a good study resource. You can purchase softcover Resource Kits from Microsoft Press (search for them at **http://mspress.microsoft.com/**), but they also appear on the TechNet CDs (**www.microsoft.com/technet**). Along with *Exam Crams* and *Exam Preps*, we believe that Resource Kits are among the best tools you can use to prepare for Microsoft exams.

6. For any specific Microsoft product that is not itself an operating system (for example, SQL Server), have you installed, configured, used, and upgraded this software? [Yes or No]

   If the answer is Yes, skip to the next section. If it's No, you must get some experience. Read on for suggestions on how to do this.

   Experience is a must with any Microsoft product exam, be it something as simple as FrontPage 2000 or as challenging as SQL Server 7.0. For trial copies of other software, search Microsoft's Web site using the name of the product as your search term. Also, search for bundles like "BackOffice" or "Small Business Server."

If you have the funds, or your employer will pay your way, consider taking a class at a Certified Training and Education Center (CTEC) or at an Authorized Academic Training Partner (AATP). In addition to classroom exposure to the topic of your choice, you get a copy of the software that is the focus of your course, along with a trial version of whatever operating system it needs, with the training materials for that class.

   Before you even think about taking any Microsoft exam, make sure you've spent enough time with the related software to understand how it may be installed and configured, how to maintain such an installation, and how to troubleshoot that software when things go wrong. This will help you in the exam, and in real life!

Testing Your Exam-Readiness

Whether you attend a formal class on a specific topic to get ready for an exam or use written materials to study on your own, some preparation for the Microsoft certification exams is essential. At $100 a try, pass or fail, you want to do everything you can to pass on your first try. That's where studying comes in.

We have included a practice exam in this book, so if you don't score that well on the test, you can study more and then tackle the test again. We also have exams that you can take online through the **ExamCram.com** Web site at **www.examcram.com**. If you still don't hit a score of at least 75percent after these tests, you'll want to investigate the other practice test resources we mention in this section.

For any given subject, consider taking a class if you've tackled self-study materials, taken the test, and failed anyway. The opportunity to interact with an instructor and fellow students can make all the difference in the world, if you can afford that privilege. For information about Microsoft classes, visit the Training and Certification page at **www.microsoft.com/education/partners/ctec.asp** for Microsoft Certified Education Centers or **www.microsoft.com/aatp/default.htm** for Microsoft Authorized Training Providers.

If you can't afford to take a class, visit the Training and Certification page anyway, because it also includes pointers to free practice exams and to Microsoft Certified Professional Approved Study Guides and other self-study tools. And even if you can't afford to spend much at all, you should still invest in some low-cost practice exams from commercial vendors.

7. Have you taken a practice exam on your chosen test subject? [Yes or No]

   If Yes, and you scored 75 percent or better, you're probably ready to tackle the real thing. If your score isn't above that threshold, keep at it until you break that barrier.

   If No, obtain all the free and low-budget practice tests you can find and get to work. Keep at it until you can break the passing threshold comfortably.

When it comes to assessing your test readiness, there is no better way than to take a good-quality practice exam and pass with a score of 56 percent or better. When we're preparing ourselves, we shoot for 66-plus percent, just to leave room for the "weirdness factor" that sometimes shows up on Microsoft exams.

Assessing Readiness for Exam 70-221

In addition to the general exam-readiness information in the previous section, there are several things you can do to prepare for the Designing a Microsoft Windows 2000 Network Infrastructure exam. As you're getting ready for Exam 70-221, visit the Exam Cram Windows 2000 Resource Center at **www.examcram.com/studyresource/w2kresource/**. Another valuable resource is the Exam Cram Insider newsletter. Sign up at **www.examcram.com** or send a blank email message to **subscribe-ec@mars.coriolis.com**. We also suggest that you join an active MCSE mailing list. One of the better ones is managed by Sunbelt Software. Sign up at **www.sunbelt-software.com** (look for the Subscribe button).

You can also cruise the Web looking for "braindumps" (recollections of test topics and experiences recorded by others) to help you anticipate topics you're likely to encounter on the test. The MCSE mailing list is a good place to ask where the useful braindumps are, or you can check Shawn Gamble's list at **www.commandcentral.com**.

You can't be sure that a braindump's author can provide correct answers. Thus, use the questions to guide your studies, but don't rely on the answers in a braindump to lead you to the truth. Double-check everything you find in any braindump.

Microsoft exam mavens also recommend checking the Microsoft Knowledge Base (available on its own CD as part of the TechNet collection, or on the Microsoft Web site at **http://support.microsoft.com/support/**) for "meaningful technical support issues" that relate to your exam's topics. Although we're not sure exactly what the quoted phrase means, we have also noticed some overlap between technical support questions on particular products and troubleshooting questions on the exams for those products.

Onward, through the Fog!

Once you've assessed your readiness, undertaken the right background studies, obtained the hands-on experience that will help you understand the products and technologies at work, and reviewed the many sources of information to help you prepare for a test, you'll be ready to take a round of practice tests. When your scores come back positive enough to get you through the exam, you're ready to go after the real thing. If you follow our assessment regime, you'll not only know what you need to study, but when you're ready to make a test date at Prometric or VUE. Good luck!

Microsoft Certification Exams

Terms you'll need to understand:

- ✓ Case study
- ✓ Multiple-choice question formats
- ✓ Build-list-and-reorder question format
- ✓ Create-a-tree question format
- ✓ Drag-and-connect question format
- ✓ Select-and-place question format
- ✓ Fixed-length tests
- ✓ Simulations
- ✓ Adaptive tests
- ✓ Short-form tests

Techniques you'll need to master:

- ✓ Assessing your exam-readiness
- ✓ Answering Microsoft's varying question types
- ✓ Altering your test strategy depending on the exam format
- ✓ Practicing (to make perfect)
- ✓ Making the best use of the testing software
- ✓ Budgeting your time
- ✓ Guessing (as a last resort)

Exam taking is not something that most people anticipate eagerly, no matter how well prepared they may be. In most cases, familiarity helps offset test anxiety. In plain English, this means you probably won't be as nervous when you take your fourth or fifth Microsoft certification exam as you'll be when you take your first one.

Whether it's your first exam or your tenth, understanding the details of taking the new exams (how much time to spend on questions, the environment you'll be in, and so on) and the new exam software will help you concentrate on the material rather than on the setting. Likewise, mastering a few basic exam-taking skills should help you recognize—and perhaps even outfox—some of the tricks and snares you're bound to find in some exam questions.

This chapter, besides explaining the exam environment and software, describes some proven exam-taking strategies that you should be able to use to your advantage.

Assessing Exam-Readiness

We strongly recommend that you read through and take the Self-Assessment included with this book (it appears just before this chapter, in fact). This will help you compare your knowledge base to the requirements for obtaining an MCSE, and it will also help you identify parts of your background or experience that may be in need of improvement, enhancement, or further learning. If you get the right set of basics under your belt, obtaining Microsoft certification will be that much easier.

Once you've gone through the Self-Assessment, you can remedy those topical areas where your background or experience may not measure up to an ideal certification candidate. But you can also tackle subject matter for individual tests at the same time, so you can continue making progress while you're catching up in some areas.

Once you've worked through an *Exam Cram*, have read the supplementary materials, and have taken the practice test, you'll have a pretty clear idea of when you should be ready to take the real exam. Although we strongly recommend that you keep practicing until your scores top the 75 percent mark, 80 percent would be a good goal to give yourself some margin for error in a real exam situation (where stress will play more of a role than when you practice). Once you hit that point, you should be ready to go. But if you get through the practice exam in this book without attaining that score, you should keep taking practice tests and studying the materials until you get there. You'll find more pointers on how to study and prepare in the Self-Assessment. But now, on to the exam itself!

The Exam Situation

When you arrive at the testing center where you scheduled your exam, you'll need to sign in with an exam coordinator. He or she will ask you to show two forms of identification, one of which must be a photo ID. After you've signed in and your time slot arrives, you'll be asked to deposit any books, bags, or other items you brought with you. Then, you'll be escorted into a closed room.

All exams are completely closed book. In fact, you will not be permitted to take anything with you into the testing area, but you will be furnished with a blank sheet of paper and a pen or, in some cases, an erasable plastic sheet and an erasable pen. Before the exam, you should memorize as much of the important material as you can, so you can write that information on the blank sheet as soon as you are seated in front of the computer. You can refer to this piece of paper anytime you like during the test, but you'll have to surrender the sheet when you leave the room.

You will have some time to compose yourself, to record this information, and to take a sample orientation exam before you begin the real thing. We suggest you take the orientation test before taking your first exam, but because they're all more or less identical in layout, behavior, and controls, you probably won't need to do this more than once.

Typically, the room will be furnished with anywhere from one to half a dozen computers, and each workstation will be separated from the others by dividers designed to keep you from seeing what's happening on someone else's computer. Most test rooms feature a wall with a large picture window. This permits the exam coordinator to monitor the room, to prevent exam-takers from talking to one another, and to observe anything out of the ordinary that might go on. The exam coordinator will have preloaded the appropriate Microsoft certification exam—for this book, that's Exam 70-221—and you'll be permitted to start as soon as you're seated in front of the computer.

All Microsoft certification exams allow a certain maximum amount of time in which to complete your work (this time is indicated on the exam by an on-screen counter/clock, so you can check the time remaining whenever you like). All Microsoft certification exams are computer generated. In addition to multiple choice, you'll encounter select and place (drag and drop), create a tree (categorization and prioritization), drag and connect, and build list and reorder (list prioritization) on most exams. Although this may sound quite simple, the questions are constructed not only to check your mastery of basic facts and figures about designing a Microsoft Windows 2000 network infrastructure, but they also require you to evaluate one or more sets of circumstances or requirements.

Often, you'll be asked to give more than one answer to a question. Likewise, you might be asked to select the best or most effective solution to a problem from a range of choices, all of which technically are correct. Taking the exam is quite an adventure, and it involves real thinking. This book shows you what to expect and how to deal with the potential problems, puzzles, and predicaments.

In the next section, you'll learn more about how Microsoft test questions look and how they must be answered.

Exam Layout and Design: New Case Study Format

The format of Microsoft's Windows 2000 exams is different from that of its previous exams. For the design exams (70-219, 70-220, 70-221), each exam consists entirely of a series of case studies, and the questions can be of six types. For the Core Four exams (70-210, 70-215, 70-216, 70-217), the same six types of questions can appear, but you are not likely to encounter complex multiquestion case studies.

For design exams, each case study or "testlet" presents a detailed problem that you must read and analyze. Figure 1.1 shows an example of what a case study looks like. You must select the different tabs in the case study to view the entire case.

Following each case study is a set of questions related to the case study; these questions can be one of six types (which are discussed next). Careful attention to details provided in the case study is the key to success. Be prepared to toggle frequently between the case study and the questions as you work. Some of the case studies also include diagrams, which are called *exhibits*, that you'll need to examine closely to understand how to answer the questions.

Once you complete a case study, you can review all the questions and your answers. However, once you move on to the next case study, you may not be able to return to the previous case study and make any changes.

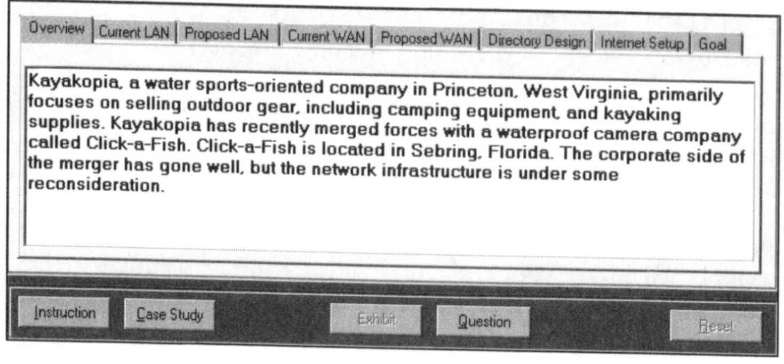

Figure 1.1 This is how case studies appear.

The six types of question formats are:

- Multiple choice, single answer
- Multiple choice, multiple answers
- Build list and reorder (list prioritization)
- Create a tree
- Drag and connect
- Select and place (drag and drop)

*Note: Exam formats may vary by test center location. Although most design exams consist entirely of a series of case studies or testlets, a test taker may occasionally encounter a strictly multiple-choice test. You may want to call the test center or visit **ExamCram.com** to see if you can find out which type of test you'll encounter.*

Multiple-Choice Question Format

Some exam questions require you to select a single answer, whereas others ask you to select multiple correct answers. The following multiple-choice question requires you to select a single correct answer. Following the question is a brief summary of each potential answer and why it is either right or wrong.

Question 1

You have three domains connected to an empty root domain under one contiguous domain name: tutu.com. This organization is formed into a forest arrangement with a secondary domain called frog.com. How many Schema Masters exist for this arrangement?

❍ a. 1

❍ b. 2

❍ c. 3

❍ d. 4

The correct answer is a because only one Schema Master is necessary for a forest arrangement. The other answers (b, c, d) are misleading because they try to make you believe that Schema Masters might be in each domain, or perhaps that you should have one for each contiguous namespaced domain.

This sample question format corresponds closely to the Microsoft certification exam format—the only difference on the exam is that questions are not followed by answer keys. To select an answer, you would position the cursor over the radio button next to the answer. Then, click the mouse button to select the answer.

Let's examine a question where one or more answers are possible. This type of question provides checkboxes rather than radio buttons for marking all appropriate selections.

Question 2

How can you seize FSMO roles? [Check all correct answers]

- ❑ a. The ntdsutil.exe utility
- ❑ b. The Replication Monitor
- ❑ c. The secedit.exe utility
- ❑ d. Active Directory Domains and FSMOs

Answers a and b are correct. You can seize roles from a server that is still running through the Replication Monitor or, in the case of a server failure, you can seize roles with the ntdsutil.exe utility. The secedit utility is used to force group policies into play; therefore, answer c is incorrect. Active Directory Domains and Trusts are a combination of truth and fiction; therefore, answer d is incorrect.

For this particular question, two answers are required. Microsoft sometimes gives partial credit for partially correct answers. For Question 2, you have to check the boxes next to items a and b to obtain credit for a correct answer. Notice that picking the right answers also means knowing why the other answers are wrong!

Build-List-and-Reorder Question Format

Questions in the build-list-and-reorder format present two lists of items—one on the left and one on the right. To answer the question, you must move items from the list on the right to the list on the left. The final list must then be reordered into a specific order.

These questions can best be characterized as "From the following list of choices, pick the choices that answer the question. Arrange the list in a certain order." To give you practice with this type of question, some questions of this type are included in this study guide. Here's an example of how they appear in this book; for a sample of how they appear on the test, see Figure 1.2.

Question 3

From the following list of famous people, pick those that have been elected President of the United States. Arrange the list in the order that they served.

Thomas Jefferson

Ben Franklin

Abe Lincoln

George Washington

Andrew Jackson

Paul Revere

The correct answer is:

George Washington

Thomas Jefferson

Andrew Jackson

Abe Lincoln

On an actual exam, the entire list of famous people would initially appear in the list on the right. You would move the four correct answers to the list on the left, and then reorder the list on the left. Notice that the answer to the question did not include all items from the initial list. However, this may not always be the case.

To move an item from the right list to the left list, first select the item by clicking on it, and then click on the Add button (left arrow). Once you move an item from one list to the other, you can move the item back by first selecting the item and then clicking on the appropriate button (either the Add button or the Remove button). Once items have been moved to the left list, you can reorder an item by selecting the item and clicking on the up or down button.

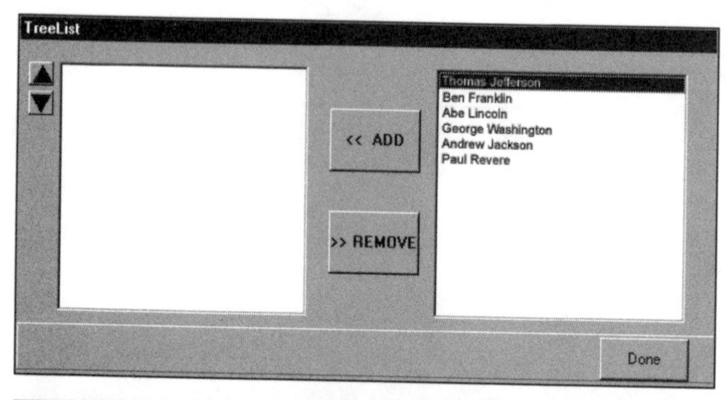

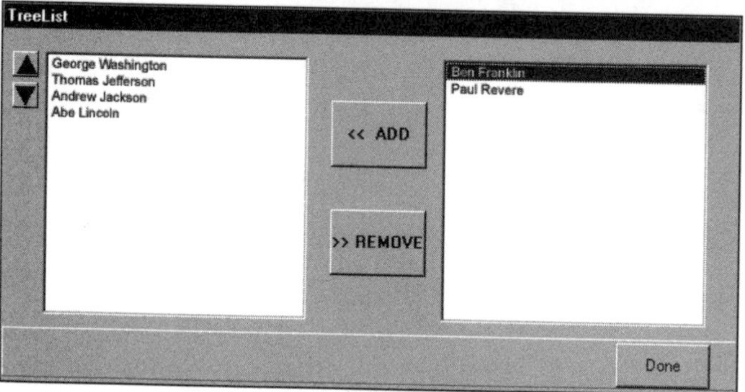

Figure 1.2 This is how build-list-and-reorder questions appear.

Create-a-Tree Question Format

Questions in the create-a-tree format also present two lists—one on the left side of the screen and one on the right side of the screen. The list on the right consists of individual items, and the list on the left consists of nodes in a tree. To answer the question, you must move items from the list on the right to the appropriate node in the tree.

These questions can best be characterized as simply a matching exercise. Items from the list on the right are placed under the appropriate category in the list on the left. Here's an example of how they appear in this book; for a sample of how they appear on the test, see Figure 1.3.

Question 4

> The calendar year is divided into four seasons:
>
> Winter
>
> Spring
>
> Summer
>
> Fall
>
> Identify the season when each of the following holidays occurs:
>
> Christmas
>
> Fourth of July
>
> Labor Day
>
> Flag Day
>
> Memorial Day
>
> Washington's Birthday
>
> Thanksgiving
>
> Easter

The correct answer is:

- Winter
    - Christmas
    - Washington's Birthday
- Spring
    - Flag Day
    - Memorial Day
    - Easter
- Summer
    - Fourth of July
    - Labor Day
- Fall
    - Thanksgiving

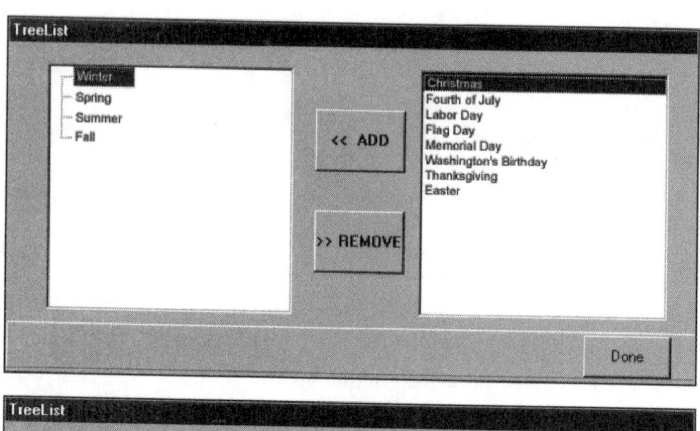

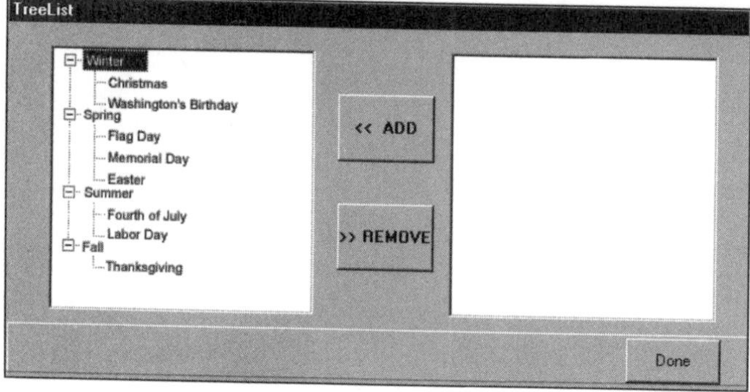

Figure 1.3 This is how create-a-tree questions appear.

In this case, all the items in the list were used. However, this may not always be the case.

To move an item from the right list to its appropriate location in the tree, you must first select the appropriate tree node by clicking on it. Then, you select the item to be moved and click on the Add button. If one or more items have been added to a tree node, the node will be displayed with a "+" icon to the left of the node name. You can click on this icon to expand the node and view the item(s) that have been added. If any item has been added to the wrong tree node, you can remove it by selecting it and clicking on the Remove button.

Drag-and-Connect Question Format

Questions in the drag-and-connect format present a group of objects and a list of "connections." To answer the question, you must move the appropriate connections between the objects.

This type of question is best described using graphics. Here's an example.

Question 5

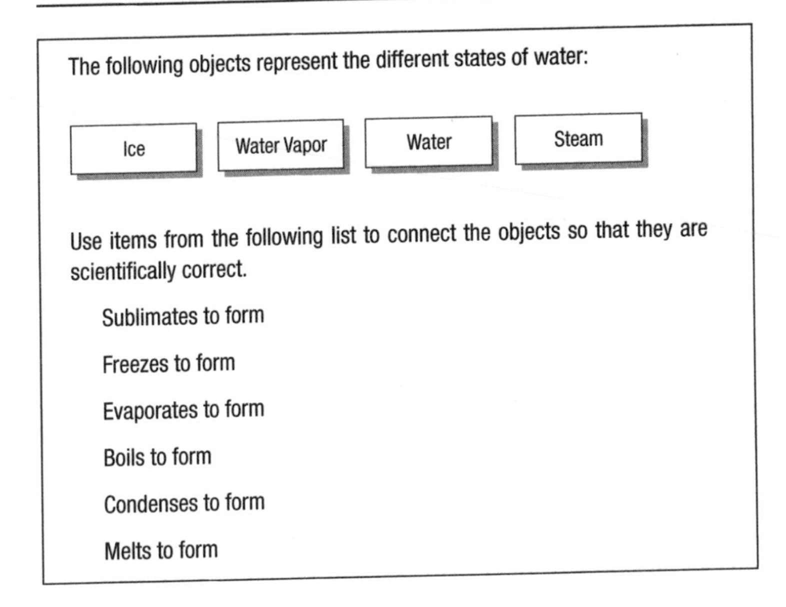

The following objects represent the different states of water:
Ice
Water Vapor
Water
Steam
Use items from the following list to connect the objects so that they are scientifically correct.
Sublimates to form
Freezes to form
Evaporates to form
Boils to form
Condenses to form
Melts to form

The correct answer is:

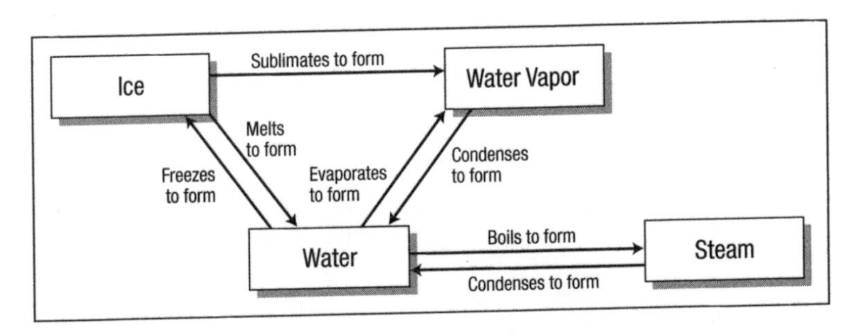

For this type of question, it's not necessary to use every object, and each connection can be used multiple times.

Select-and-Place Question Format

Questions in the select-and-place (drag-and-drop) format present a diagram with blank boxes, and a list of labels that need to be dragged to correctly fill in the blank boxes. To answer the question, you must move the labels to their appropriate positions on the diagram.

This type of question is best described using graphics. Here's an example.

Question 6

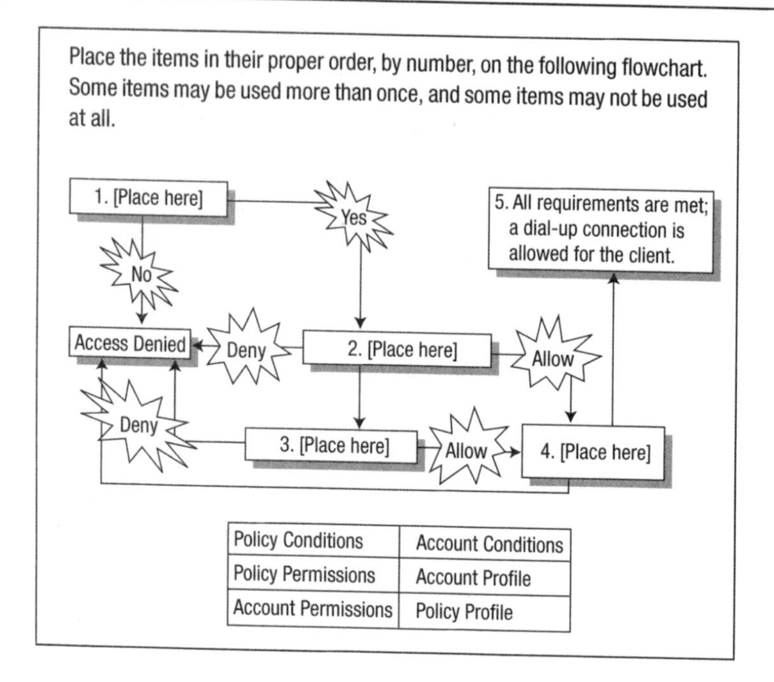

The correct answer is:

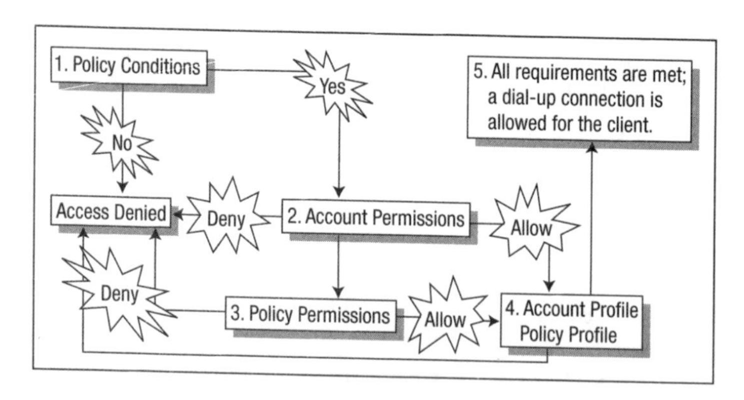

Microsoft's Testing Formats

Currently, Microsoft uses four different testing formats:

- Case study
- Fixed length
- Adaptive
- Short form

As we mentioned earlier, the case study approach is used with Microsoft's design exams, such as the one covered by this book. These exams consist of a set of case studies that you must analyze to enable you to answer questions related to the case studies. Such exams include one or more case studies (tabbed topic areas), each of which is followed by 4 to 10 questions. The question types for design exams and for Core Four Windows 2000 exams are multiple choice, build list and reorder, create a tree, drag and connect, and select and place. Depending on the test topic, some exams are totally case-based, whereas others are not.

Other Microsoft exams employ advanced testing capabilities that might not be immediately apparent. Although the questions that appear are primarily multiple choice, the logic that drives them is more complex than older Microsoft tests, which use a fixed sequence of questions, called a *fixed-length test*. Some questions employ a sophisticated user interface, which Microsoft calls a *simulation*, to test your knowledge of the software and systems under consideration in a more or less "live" environment that behaves just like the original. The Testing Innovations link at **www.microsoft.com/trainingandservices/default.asp?PageID=mcp** includes a downloadable practice simulation.

For some exams, Microsoft has turned to a well-known technique, called *adaptive testing*, to establish a test-taker's level of knowledge and product competence. Adaptive exams look the same as fixed-length exams, but they discover the level of difficulty at which an individual test-taker can correctly answer questions. Test-takers with differing levels of knowledge or ability therefore see different sets of questions; individuals with high levels of knowledge or ability are presented with a smaller set of more difficult questions, whereas individuals with lower levels of knowledge are presented with a larger set of easier questions. Two individuals may answer the same percentage of questions correctly, but the test-taker with a higher knowledge or ability level will score higher because his or her questions are worth more.

Also, the lower-level test-taker will probably answer more questions than his or her more-knowledgeable colleague. This explains why adaptive tests use ranges of values to define the number of questions and the amount of time it takes to complete the test.

Adaptive tests work by evaluating the test-taker's most recent answer. A correct answer leads to a more difficult question (and the test software's estimate of the test-taker's knowledge and ability level is raised). An incorrect answer leads to a less difficult question (and the test software's estimate of the test-taker's knowledge and ability level is lowered). This process continues until the test targets the test-taker's true ability level. The exam ends when the test-taker's level of accuracy meets a statistically acceptable value (in other words, when his or her performance demonstrates an acceptable level of knowledge and ability), or when the maximum number of items has been presented (in which case, the test-taker is almost certain to fail).

Microsoft also introduced a short-form test for its most popular tests. This test delivers 25 to 30 questions to its takers, giving them exactly 60 minutes to complete the exam. This type of exam is similar to a fixed-length test, in that it allows readers to jump ahead or return to earlier questions, and to cycle through the questions until the test is done. Microsoft does not use adaptive logic in this test, but claims that statistical analysis of the question pool is such that the 25 to 30 questions delivered during a short-form exam conclusively measure a test-taker's knowledge of the subject matter in much the same way as an adaptive test. You can think of the short-form test as a kind of "greatest hits exam" (that is, the most important questions are covered) version of an adaptive exam on the same topic.

Note: Some of the Microsoft exams can appear as a combination of adaptive and fixed-length questions.

Microsoft tests can come in any one of these forms. Whatever you encounter, you must take the test in whichever form it appears; you can't choose one form over another. If anything, it pays more to prepare thoroughly for an adaptive exam than for a fixed-length or a short-form exam: The penalties for answering incorrectly are built into the test itself on an adaptive exam, whereas the layout remains the same for a fixed-length or short-form test, no matter how many questions you answer incorrectly.

The biggest difference between an adaptive test and a fixed-length or short-form test is that on a fixed-length or short-form test, you can revisit questions after you've read them over one or more times. On an adaptive test, you must answer the question when it's presented and will have no opportunities to revisit that question thereafter.

Strategies for Different Testing Formats

Before you choose a test-taking strategy, you must know if your test is case study based, fixed length, short form, or adaptive. When you begin your exam, you'll know right away if the test is based on case studies. The interface will consist of a tabbed Window that allows you to easily navigate through the sections of the case.

If you are taking a test that is not based on case studies, the software will tell you that the test is adaptive, if in fact the version you're taking is an adaptive test. If your introductory materials fail to mention this, you're probably taking a fixed-length test (50 to 70 questions). If the total number of questions involved is 25 to 30, you're taking a short-form test. Some tests announce themselves by indicating that they will start with a set of adaptive questions, followed by fixed-length questions.

You'll be able to tell for sure if you are taking an adaptive, fixed-length, or short-form test by the first question. If it includes a checkbox that lets you mark the question for later review, you're taking a fixed-length or short-form test. If the total number of questions is 25 to 30, it's a short-form test; if more than 30, it's a fixed-length test. Adaptive test questions can be visited (and answered) only once, and they include no such checkbox.

The Case Study Exam Strategy

Most test-takers find that the case study type of test used for the design exams (70-219, 70-220, and 70-221) is the most difficult to master. When it comes to studying for a case study test, your best bet is to approach each case study as a standalone test. The biggest challenge you'll encounter is that you'll feel that you won't have enough time to get through all of the cases that are presented.

Each case provides a lot of material that you'll need to read and study before you can effectively answer the questions that follow. The trick to taking a case study exam is to first scan the case study to get the highlights. Make sure you read the overview section of the case so that you understand the context of the problem at hand. Then, quickly move on and scan the questions.

As you are scanning the questions, make mental notes to yourself so that you'll remember which sections of the case study you should focus on. Some case studies may provide a fair amount of extra information that you don't really need to answer the questions. The goal with our scanning approach is to avoid having to study and analyze material that is not completely relevant.

When studying a case, carefully read the tabbed information. It is important to answer each and every question. You will be able to toggle back and forth from case to questions, and from question to question within a case testlet. However, once you leave the case and move on, you may not be able to return to it. You may want to take notes while reading useful information so you can refer to them when you tackle the test questions. It's hard to go wrong with this strategy when taking any kind of Microsoft certification test.

The Fixed-Length and Short-Form Exam Strategy

A well-known principle when taking fixed-length or short-form exams is to first read over the entire exam from start to finish while answering only those questions you feel absolutely sure of. On subsequent passes, you can dive into more complex questions more deeply, knowing how many such questions you have left.

Fortunately, the Microsoft exam software for fixed-length and short-form tests makes the multiple-visit approach easy to implement. At the top-left corner of each question is a checkbox that permits you to mark that question for a later visit.

Note: Marking questions makes review easier, but you can return to any question by clicking the Forward or Back button repeatedly.

As you read each question, if you answer only those you're sure of and mark for review those that you're not sure of, you can keep working through a decreasing list of questions as you answer the trickier ones in order.

There's at least one potential benefit to reading the exam over completely before answering the trickier questions: Sometimes, information supplied in later questions sheds more light on earlier questions. At other times, information you read in later questions might jog your memory about network design facts, figures, or behavior that helps you answer earlier questions. Either way, you'll come out ahead if you defer those questions about which you're not absolutely sure.

Here are some question-handling strategies that apply to fixed-length and short-form tests. Use them if you have the chance:

- When returning to a question after your initial read-through, read every word again—otherwise, your mind can fall quickly into a rut. Sometimes, revisiting a question after turning your attention elsewhere lets you see something you missed, but the strong tendency is to see what you've seen before. Try to avoid that tendency at all costs.

- If you return to a question more than twice, try to articulate to yourself what you don't understand about the question, why answers don't appear to make sense, or what appears to be missing. If you chew on the subject awhile, your subconscious might provide the details you lack, or you might notice a "trick" that points to the right answer.

As you work your way through the exam, another counter that Microsoft provides will come in handy—the number of questions completed and questions outstanding. For fixed-length and short-form tests, it's wise to budget your time by making sure that you've completed one-quarter of the questions one-quarter of the way through the exam period, and three-quarters of the questions three-quarters of the way through.

If you're not finished when only five minutes remain, use that time to guess your way through any remaining questions. Remember, guessing is potentially more valuable than not answering, because blank answers are always wrong, but a guess may turn out to be right. If you don't have a clue about any of the remaining questions, pick answers at random, or choose all a's, b's, and so on. The important thing is to submit an exam for scoring that has an answer for every question.

At the very end of your exam period, you're better off guessing than leaving questions unanswered.

The Adaptive Exam Strategy

If there's one principle that applies to taking an adaptive test, it could be summed up as "Get it right the first time." You cannot elect to skip a question and move on to the next one when taking an adaptive test, because the testing software uses your answer to the current question to select whatever question it plans to present next. Nor can you return to a question once you've moved on, because the software gives you only one chance to answer the question. You can, however, take notes, because sometimes information supplied in earlier questions will shed more light on later questions.

Also, when you answer a question correctly, you are presented with a more difficult question next, to help the software gauge your level of skill and ability. When you answer a question incorrectly, you are presented with a less difficult question, and the software lowers its current estimate of your skill and ability. This continues until the program settles into a reasonably accurate estimate of what you know and can do, and takes you on average through somewhere between 15 and 30 questions as you complete the test.

The good news is that if you know your stuff, you'll probably finish most adaptive tests in 30 minutes or so. The bad news is that you must really, really know your stuff to do your best on an adaptive test. That's because some questions are so convoluted, complex, or hard to follow that you're bound to miss one or two, at a minimum, even if you do know your stuff. So the more you know, the better you'll do on an adaptive test, even accounting for the occasionally weird or unfathomable questions that appear on these exams.

Because you can't always tell in advance if a test is fixed length, short form, or adaptive, you will be best served by preparing for the exam as if it were adaptive. That way, you should be prepared to pass no matter what kind of test you take. But if you do take a fixed-length or short-form test, remember our tips from the preceding section. They should help you improve on what you could do on an adaptive test.

If you encounter a question on an adaptive test that you can't answer, you must guess an answer immediately. Because of how the software works, you may suffer for your guess on the next question if you guess right, because you'll get a more difficult question next!

Question-Handling Strategies

For those questions that take only a single answer, usually two or three of the answers will be obviously incorrect, and two of the answers will be plausible—of course, only one can be correct. Unless the answer leaps out at you (if it does, reread the question to look for a trick; sometimes those are the ones you're most likely to get wrong), begin the process of answering by eliminating those answers that are most obviously wrong.

Almost always, at least one answer out of the possible choices for a question can be eliminated immediately because it matches one of these conditions:

- The answer does not apply to the situation.
- The answer describes a nonexistent issue, an invalid option, or an imaginary state.

After you eliminate all answers that are obviously wrong, you can apply your retained knowledge to eliminate further answers. Look for items that sound correct but refer to actions, commands, or features that are not present or not available in the situation that the question describes.

If you're still faced with a blind guess among two or more potentially correct answers, reread the question. Try to picture how each of the possible remaining answers would alter the situation. Be especially sensitive to terminology; sometimes the choice of words ("remove" instead of "disable") can make the difference between a right answer and a wrong one.

Only when you've exhausted your ability to eliminate answers, but remain unclear about which of the remaining possibilities is correct, should you guess at an answer. An unanswered question offers you no points, but guessing gives you at least some chance of getting a question right; just don't be too hasty when making a blind guess.

Note: If you're taking a fixed-length or a short-form test, you can wait until the last round of reviewing marked questions (just as you're about to run out of time, or out of unanswered questions) before you start making guesses. You will have the same option within each case study testlet (but once you leave a testlet, you may not be allowed to return to it). If you're taking an adaptive test, you'll have to guess to move on to the next question if you can't figure out an answer some other way. Either way, guessing should be your technique of last resort!

Numerous questions assume that the default behavior of a particular utility is in effect. If you know the defaults and understand what they mean, this knowledge will help you cut through many Gordian knots.

Mastering the Inner Game

In the final analysis, knowledge breeds confidence, and confidence breeds success. If you study the materials in this book carefully and review all the practice questions at the end of each chapter, you should become aware of those areas where additional learning and study are required.

After you've worked your way through the book, take the practice exam in the back of the book. Taking this test will provide a reality check and help you identify areas to study further. Make sure you follow up and review materials related to the questions you miss on the practice exam before scheduling a real exam. Only when you've covered that ground and feel comfortable with the whole scope of the practice exam should you set an exam appointment. Only if you score 80 percent or better should you proceed to the real thing (otherwise, obtain some additional practice tests so you can keep trying until you hit this magic number).

If you take a practice exam and don't score at least 80 to 85 percent correct, you'll want to practice further. Microsoft provides links to practice exam providers and also offers self-assessment exams at **www.microsoft.com/trainingandservices/**. You should also check out **ExamCram.com** for downloadable practice questions.

Armed with the information in this book and with the determination to augment your knowledge, you should be able to pass the certification exam. However, you need to work at it, or you'll spend the exam fee more than once before you finally pass. If you prepare seriously, you should do well. We are confident that you can do it!

The next section covers other sources you can use to prepare for the Microsoft certification exams.

Additional Resources

A good source of information about Microsoft certification exams comes from Microsoft itself. Because its products and technologies—and the exams that go with them—change frequently, the best place to go for exam-related information is online.

If you haven't already visited the Microsoft Certified Professional site, do so right now. The MCP home page resides at **www.microsoft.com/trainingandservices** (see Figure 1.4).

Note: This page might not be there by the time you read this, or may be replaced by something new and different, because things change regularly on the Microsoft site. Should this happen, please read the sidebar titled "Coping with Change on the Web."

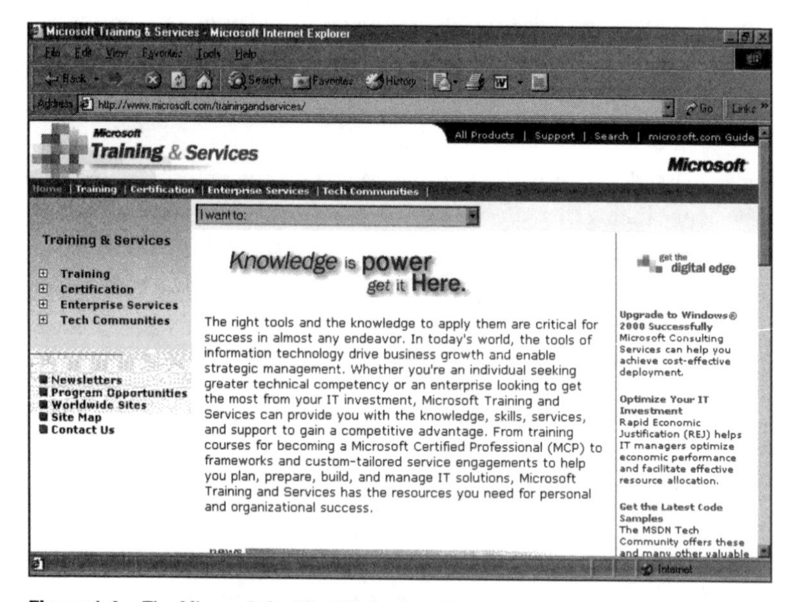

Figure 1.4 The Microsoft Certified Professional home page.

Coping with Change on the Web

Sooner or later, all the information we've shared with you about the Microsoft Certified Professional pages and the other Web-based resources mentioned throughout the rest of this book will go stale or be replaced by newer information. In some cases, the URLs you find here might lead you to their replacements; in other cases, the URLs will go nowhere, leaving you with the dreaded "404 File not found" error message. When that happens, don't give up.

There's always a way to find what you want on the Web if you're willing to invest some time and energy. Most large or complex Web sites—and Microsoft's qualifies on both counts—offer a search engine. On all of Microsoft's Web pages, a Search button appears along the top edge of the page. As long as you can get to Microsoft's site (it should stay at **www.microsoft.com** for a long time), use this tool to help you find what you need.

The more focused you can make a search request, the more likely the results will include information you can use. For example, you can search for the string

```
"training and certification"
```

to produce a lot of data about the subject in general, but if you're looking for the preparation guide for Exam 70-221, "Designing a Microsoft Windows 2000 Network Infrastructure," you'll be more likely to get there quickly if you use a search string similar to the following:

```
"Exam 70-221" AND "preparation guide"
```

Likewise, if you want to find the Training and Certification downloads, try a search string such as this:

```
"training and certification" AND "download page"
```

Finally, feel free to use general search tools—such as **www.search.com**, **www.altavista.com**, and **www.excite.com**—to look for related information. Although Microsoft offers great information about its certification exams online, there are plenty of third-party sources of information and assistance that need not follow Microsoft's party line. Therefore, if you can't find something where the book says it lives, intensify your search.

Overview

Terms you'll need to understand:

- ✓ Open Systems Interconnection (OSI) model
- ✓ Network Basic Input/Output System (NetBIOS)
- ✓ Windows Sockets (WinSock)
- ✓ Network operating system (NOS)
- ✓ Active Directory
- ✓ Domain Name Service (DNS)
- ✓ Dynamic Host Configuraion Protocol (DHCP)
- ✓ Windows Internet Naming Service (WINS)
- ✓ Virtual Private Network (VPN)
- ✓ Point-to-Point Tunneling Protocol (PPTP)
- ✓ Layer 2 Tunneling Protocol (L2TP)
- ✓ Remote Access Service (RAS)

Techniques you'll need to master:

- ✓ Using the OSI model to understand network architecture trends
- ✓ Distributing IP addresses to client computers
- ✓ Tracking the network infrastructure changes to Windows 2000
- ✓ Using encryption to allow private information to travel over the Internet securely

To design a network infrastructure, you must thoroughly understand the network architecture of the operating system. Of the many changes that Microsoft has implemented in Windows 2000, most of them involve the directory services and network architecture. This overview chapter outlines and explains the key differences between the network architectures of Windows 2000 and previous versions of Windows. The reasons for these changes—and what you need to know to understand and master them—will also be explained. Part of this explanation includes an overview of the many networking services that will be covered in later chapters of this book.

Changes in Windows 2000

Not everything has changed in Windows 2000. The operating system architecture and the handling of applications are still essentially the same as they were in Windows NT 4. But why did the directory and network architectures need such major changes? Actually, the answer is simple: Because the nature of networking has changed, vendors of operating systems have had to change—and sometimes entirely transform—their products to keep up. When PCs were first networked, the goal was to connect them only to neighboring computers. Now a desktop computer needs to be able to communicate with local computers as well as those around the world. In Windows 2000, Microsoft made some needed adjustments to support this new requirement.

The Way It Was

To fully understand the changes in the network architecture of Windows 2000, we need to examine decisions that Microsoft made years earlier regarding the networking architecture of the Windows operating system. To do this, we'll compare Microsoft's network architecture to the Open Systems Interconnection (OSI) model for networking (see Figure 2.1). The companies that make operating systems use the OSI model to divide their network architecture into components. When these components and parts are placed into the OSI model, we can compare how different operating systems access the network. Layer 5, the session layer, connects applications and services to the network, allowing two computers to link up and prepare to exchange data. The two main protocols used at this layer—NetBIOS and Sockets—each have a very different assumption of the type of network with which it is working.

Although IBM created NetBIOS, Microsoft gave it a big boost by designing its network structure and services around it. Microsoft wanted its network infrastructure to be simple and as easy to use as possible, and NetBIOS fit nicely into this plan. Computers using NetBIOS will, by default, send broadcast messages to find each other—a feature that allows computers to find and set up sessions with each other with no setup required by a network administrator.

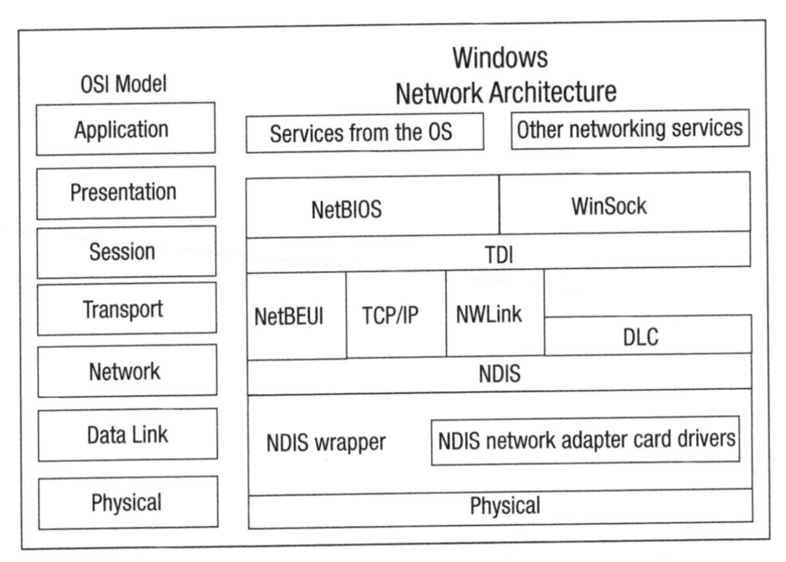

Figure 2.1 The networking structure and services of earlier versions of Windows were designed around NetBIOS at the session layer. NetBIOS works best in a local networking environment.

Previous versions of Windows use NetBIOS as the main interface to the network, and all of their services are dependent on it. If you want to access a file or send a print job, you also have to use NetBIOS, which is loaded during the install of any Windows operating system. NetBIOS is a required service that you cannot delete, except in Windows 2000. This design works best in a small, local networking environment. Broadcasts normally work over only local connections, and this limitation severely affects NetBIOS's performance over WAN connections. As networking became more important to a company's business, scalable network solutions that could grow to include all distant locations became more important. Microsoft had to adjust its strategy.

And Then Came TCP/IP

The creators of the Internet and TCP/IP went with Sockets as the session layer protocol and interface to the network. Instead of emphasizing ease of setup, the emphasis was on long-distance connections and guaranteed delivery. Because NetBIOS isn't the best tool to attain these goals, all TCP/IP and Internet services use Sockets as the interface to the network. (WinSock is short for Windows Sockets and is the implementation of Sockets in a GUI environment.) As TCP/IP and the Internet grew in popularity, Microsoft made adjustments that allowed WinSock to be used in its network architecture if a service called for it, but Microsoft-designed services stayed with NetBIOS as the only interface and session layer protocol.

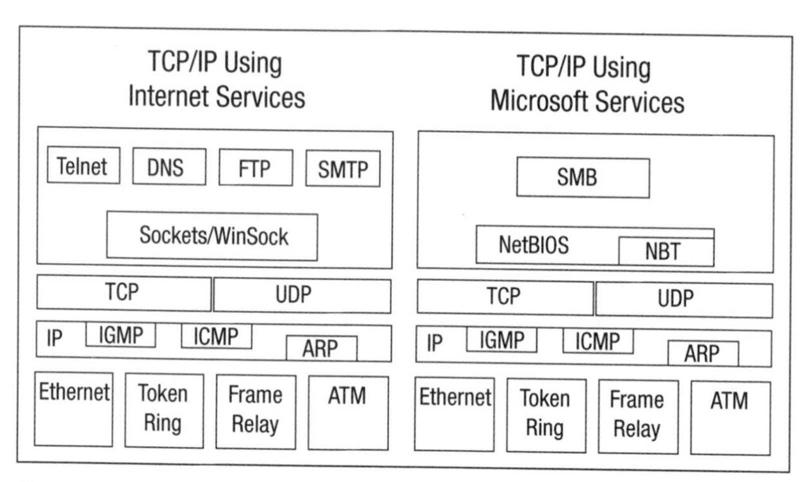

Figure 2.2 TCP/IP using Internet services is designed to use Sockets (or WinSock, in a GUI environment). TCP/IP using Microsoft services must instead use NetBIOS and the NBT protocol to access the network.

Windows' dependence on NetBIOS caused the operating system to have a dual personality in regards to its network architecture. As Figure 2.2 shows, all Internet services use Sockets or WinSock at the session layer as their interface to the network, which means that, when users wants to use an Internet service—by downloading a Web page or an FTP document or even sending email—their computers have to use WinSock. Yet, when using a Microsoft-designed service (such as connecting to a share on the local network or sending a print job through Microsoft printing services), NetBIOS is used as the session layer protocol and interface to the network.

Even TCP/IP has to make adjustments if it is loaded on a Microsoft operating system. TCP/IP normally uses Sockets at the session layer, but, because Microsoft services require NetBIOS, TCP/IP has to use an extra protocol at the session layer. This protocol is called *NetBIOS over TCP/IP* (*NetBT*), and it is needed only when TCP/IP is the transport protocol used to access Microsoft services.

The Great Name-Resolution Debate

Another problem caused by this dual network architecture concerned the naming of computers. Microsoft selected NetBIOS not only for its low administrative overhead, but also for its easy naming scheme for computers. Computer names must be unique among all other computers to which they may connect, and NetBIOS uses a different naming scheme than the Internet does. The NetBIOS namespace demonstrates that it was designed to work in a local network, because computer names can have a maximum of only 15 characters. NetBIOS also uses a flat namespace, which means that names have only one part; in essence, no middle or last names are allowed. These narrow parameters are the equivalent of declaring that all people can have only first names, that no name can have more than 15 characters, and that no name can be used more than once. This might be possible if you stay within your small hometown (a LAN), but these rules can be very limiting if you want to travel the world (a WAN).

The Internet uses the Domain Name Service (DNS) naming convention. Names are hierarchical, which means that you can have two computers named *Sales* so long as each belongs to a different Internet domain, thus making their names unique. Figures 2.3 and 2.4 illustrate the differences between these two naming conventions.

WINS, DNS, or Both?

Although computer names are handy for users, computers don't use them. Instead, they work with numbers in the form of computer addresses. A network

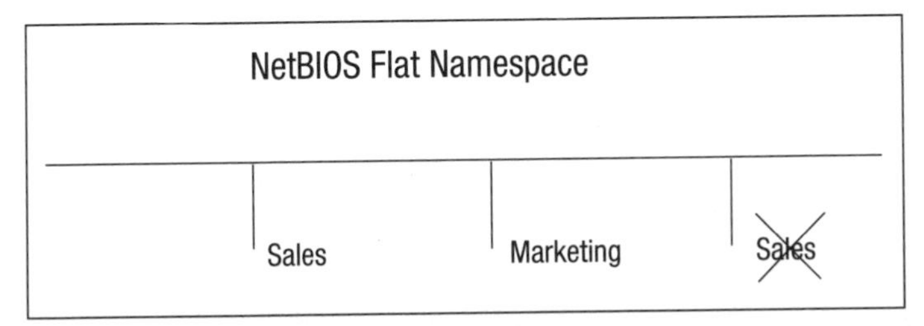

Figure 2.3 The flat namespace of NetBIOS requires that each computer have only one 15-character name to differentiate itself from all other computers. Two computers named *Sales* are not allowed in a NetBIOS environment.

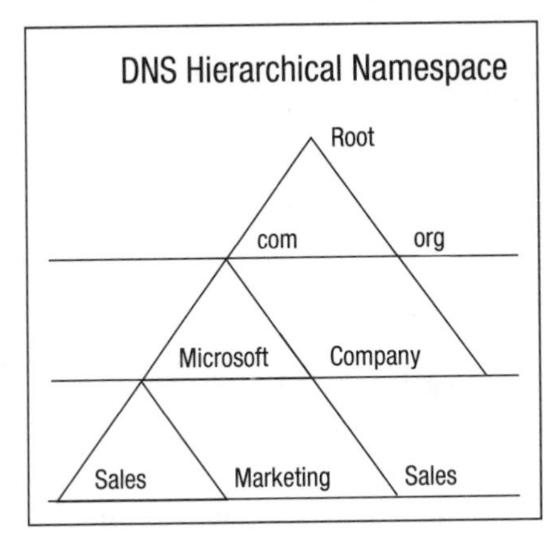

Figure 2.4 DNS uses a hierarchical naming scheme. Both the Microsoft.com and the Company.com domains can have a computer named *Sales*. Because of the hierarchy, Sales.Microsoft.com is a different computer name than Sales.Company. com.

using computer names needs to set up a name-resolution service to handle the translation of computer names to IP addresses. With name-resolution services on a network, people refer to computers by name, and the names are translated into an address. Microsoft's dual network architecture required NetBIOS computer names for its own services and DNS names for the Internet—which meant that, if you wanted to use name-resolution services on your network, you had to set up two different services: a NetBIOS naming service and an Internet name-resolution service. Windows Internet Naming Service (WINS) is Microsoft's NetBIOS naming service. It translates NetBIOS computer names to IP addresses. DNS is used to translate Internet DNS names to IP addresses. With both services on a network, one computer may have to ask WINS to resolve computer names to IP addresses when using any Microsoft service and then have to ask DNS to resolve a computer name to an IP address when using Internet services. The advantages and disadvantages of WINS and DNS should never be debated because they serve different purposes on a network. In Microsoft networking environments, prior to Windows 2000, both DNS and WINS were needed to connect to both networking types.

You may be asked how many WINS servers are required on a network. If everything has been upgraded to Windows 2000 and no other NetBIOS resources have been mentioned, then no WINS servers are needed.

Going the Way of the Internet

Starting with Windows 2000, Microsoft's dual network architectures are integrated into one. Although the dependence on NetBIOS is gone, Windows 2000 still supports NetBIOS clients, just like previous versions of Windows and Windows NT. NetBIOS support is also needed for backward compatibility with previous versions of Windows operating systems. The change is that Windows 2000 no longer needs NetBIOS for its own services. Breaking the dependence on NetBIOS is just the first of the changes necessary to bring the system into conformance with Internet standards. Windows-provided networking services have also changed.

New Service Requirements

Windows 2000 requires some services and protocols that were optional in previous versions of Windows. The nature of these services—even ones that were often used in Windows NT—have changed: TCP/IP, Dynamic Host Configuration Protocol (DHCP), DNS, and WINS all have new importance and implementations, and these changes have a dramatic impact on how you should design the network infrastructure.

Network Service Changes Required by Active Directory

Network operating systems (NOSs) are different from operating systems in that they don't just provide local control over computer hardware and software. NOSs also allow for the network and its participating computers to be controlled. Directory services refer to the way NOSs manage the network and protect access to the resources on it. Just like Window NT, Windows 2000 is an NOS, but its directory services have undergone a complete transformation—so much so that they hardly resemble the directory services provided by Windows NT. In Windows 2000, the directory services and network infrastructure changes are interrelated to the point that it is not possible to talk about one without at least mentioning the other. Windows NT requires a user account to log on to the network. These user accounts and others are saved in a database called the *Security Access Manager (SAM)*. This system works fine until an organization wants to centralize security and accounts across WAN connections. Microsoft had many ideas for how to centralize NT's directory services across an enterprise of geographically diverse locations, but all had large drawbacks. The SAM uses NetBIOS to access the network just like all other Microsoft services, which makes it difficult to operate outside of a LAN environment.

Active Directory, the name of the directory services provided by Windows 2000, stores all of the information needed to manage the network. It is much more than the database of accounts that Windows NT used: It changes the nature of your network so that it can support a much larger number of users and a greater number of resources, even if they are spread over many physical locations. If you are going to use Active Directory, be prepared for it to affect even the basic networking services.

TCP/IP

If you're going to take advantage of Active Directory, you should be aware of the many new requirements during the installation of Windows 2000. Installing the TCP/IP suite of protocols changes from an option to a requirement. Other transport protocols can be loaded for compatibility with other systems, but TCP/IP must be loaded during the installation and is the primary transport for a Windows 2000 network.

DNS

Active Directory also requires DNS in order to work correctly. Because NetBIOS names aren't required anymore, the Internet naming convention using the DNS name space is now the primary naming convention in Windows 2000, and DNS is the primary name-resolution service. Unless you disable NetBIOS, your computer will still create a NetBIOS name during installation. Because Microsoft wasn't the only company that used NetBIOS, most networks will still have some need for

NetBIOS names for backward compatibility, either with Microsoft or other systems. If your network is all Windows 2000 and even some Unix, you can turn off NetBIOS and ignore it completely. DNS is covered thoroughly in Chapter 5.

Unix and Macintosh use DNS as their name resolution service. They are not NetBIOS clients and do not use WINS.

WINS

In previous versions of Windows, WINS has an important role in the network infrastructure. NetBIOS computers, by default, broadcast to find another computer on a network. This method is quick and simple on a small network, but it causes too much traffic on the network as it grows in size. Implementing WINS on a network gives NetBIOS clients an alternative to broadcasting. With WINS, the clients make a direct request to the WINS server when they need to translate a computer name to an IP address. The WINS server directly answers the requesting computer, thereby avoiding the broadcast. Also, the direct communication between a WINS server and a client computer can work across routers and help extend the functionality of NetBIOS past a LAN environment. Implementing WINS allows Microsoft operating systems to reduce network traffic and communicate in a larger environment.

The importance of WINS has, of course, changed because NetBIOS no longer has the important role that it held in Windows NT. Nevertheless, the service is still on Microsoft's list of recommended services for the Windows 2000 environment, at least until the need for NetBIOS is completely eliminated from a network. For more information on WINS, refer to Chapter 6.

DHCP and DDNS

When using TCP/IP on a network, you must decide how the IP addresses should be distributed to the clients. The choice is between manually entering the IP address settings on each client and entering a range of addresses on a DHCP server and allowing the server to provide the addresses to the clients via the network. The choice seems simple until you consider the problem of who will update the DNS server to reflect which clients have received which specific IP address from the DHCP server. Until recently, the DNS database was a static database that contained computer names mapped to IP addresses. These database records had to be manually entered. Because DHCP assigned IP addresses in sequential order on a first-come/first-served basis, each computer could end up with a different IP address. Because the nature of DHCP is dynamic and DNS is static, the two systems did not work well together. The time saved entering IP addresses by using DHCP then caused the additional problem of how DNS would get updated.

Although Windows NT provided many suggestions to try to solve this problem, Windows 2000 actually provides a permanent solution by changing DHCP and DNS so that they communicate. Windows 2000 introduces and supports a dynamic version of DNS (DDNS). DHCP and DNS are covered thoroughly in Chapters 4 and 5.

Remote Access Connectivity

Routing and Remote Access Service (RRAS), first offered as a late add-on to Windows NT 4, is greatly expanded and offers many more options in Windows 2000. Large and small networks can select from different services that will allow them to connect with anything from dial-up lines to dedicated digital lines. Companies also have many choices that will allow them to use the Internet as a remote-connection alternative. The best part of all these services is that, regardless of your size and budget, you can find a way to connect all over the world.

Routing Improvements

As in Windows NT 4, Windows 2000 can still act as an IP, IPX, or AppleTalk router. Unlike previous versions of Windows, Windows 2000 supports Routing Information Protocol (RIP) and Open Shortest Path First (OSPF) as dynamic routing protocols (instead of just RIP), which means much larger networks can be supported. Chapter 9 details routing with Windows 2000.

Using the Internet for Connectivity

Dedicated global network connections have always been expensive to set up and maintain. Connections and lines usually have to be leased, at a premium charge, for a high-speed, dedicated, digital connection. The low-cost alternative is to allow remote access to your network through low-speed, analog telephone lines. Even with this alternative, a traveling user has to pay long-distance charges to connect to your network. A low-cost and possibly high-speed alternative is to use the Internet for remote connections. A remote user can make a local call to a nationwide or global ISP, and, whether they are two or 2,000 miles from your network, the connection will have no long-distance charges. The obvious drawback to this solution is that, because the Internet is intended for public use, it is not a secure medium for the transmission of private company information.

For a public network such as the Internet to maintain information security, the information must be altered for transmission. Encryption renders information useless and unreadable to those who may capture and look at the packets. Encryption can be used to change just username and passwords for secure authentication, or it can be used to protect all of the information including the data itself. Internet standards groups are working to make available more encryption solutions to allow the Internet to act as a Virtual Private Network (VPN). Until then, encryption allows users to protect their information so that the Internet acts as if it were a private network solution, but without the considerable cost of actual private dedicated lines.

Changes in VPN Implementation

Windows 2000 has simplified the implementation of VPNs. Now you can set up a VPN with a wizard that walks you through the process. Also, in Windows 2000, you can choose which encryption protocols to use, such as Point-to-Point Tunneling Protocol (PPTP), which is available in Windows NT, and Layer 2 Tunneling Protocol (L2TP). PPTP is the only choice if you must communicate over a VPN with previous versions of Windows, because it's all that clients other than Windows 2000 can use. The major difference between the two protocols is that PPTP uses a Microsoft-proprietary encryption protocol, whereas L2TP is an open Internet standard and uses IPSec (another open Internet standard protocol) as its encryption protocol. When creating a VPN with Windows 2000, L2TP is considered to have greater security, although PPTP has backward compatibility. Having both choices allows for flexibility. For more information on VPN setup, refer to Chapters 9 and 11.

Improved Authentication

Remote Authentication Dial-In User Service (RADIUS) allows your ISP to authenticate your users using their Windows 2000 user account. RADIUS is implemented as part of a larger service, Internet Authentication Service (IAS). Together, IAS and RADIUS allow you to control and manage remote connections coming into your network. In Chapter 12, you will learn to integrate RADIUS into a dial-up or VPN solution.

NAT and Proxy Server

Encrypting your data is not the only way to make an Internet connection secure. Connecting to the Internet is safer when your client computers remain anonymous. Both NAT (Network Address Translation) and Proxy Server allow this anonymity by making all Internet requests for them. A NAT or proxy server usually has at least two network interfaces: one connected to the local network and one connected to the Internet. Client computers make their Internet request to the local NAT or proxy server. The NAT or proxy server protects the internal network by allowing only its own computer and IP address to be exposed to the Internet. The difference between the services is in the size of network that they support. NAT not only provides Internet connections, but it is also a substitute for WINS, DNS, and DHCP. It is somewhat of an all-in-one solution for Internet connectivity on a small network. Proxy Server can be scaled up for much larger networks, but sticks just to protecting and helping Internet connections. NAT and Proxy Server are covered individually in Chapters 7 and 8.

Designing Network Services

This chapter provided an overview of the services included in the Windows 2000 network architecture. It explained what changes you will see in Windows 2000 networking and why those changes were necessary. The most changes occurred to the services that connect and integrate your network with the Internet. Some of these services have been a part of the Microsoft network infrastructure for some time, whereas others are providing new support and connectivity that were not included in previous Microsoft architectures.

Designing a network infrastructure requires a full understanding of each service and how it fits with the rest. Many of the services you will learn about provide the best and most secure solution when implemented together. Also, some services are best suited to networks of a certain size. In this book, each service will be explained in detail so that you gain an understanding of each individually. Then you will learn how to integrate the services so that you will be ready for the exam.

Practice Questions

Question 1

What purpose does the protocol NetBT serve on a network?

- ❍ a. To allow TCP/IP to use NetBIOS
- ❍ b. To allow TCP/IP to use Sockets
- ❍ c. To allow TCP/IP to access the Internet
- ❍ d. To tunnel through the Internet

Answer a is correct. NetBT stands for *NetBIOS over TCP/IP*. Usually, TCP/IP uses Sockets as its interface, but previous versions of Microsoft Windows forced TCP/IP to use NetBIOS to access the network instead. NetBT is a protocol at the session layer of the OSI model and is used when TCP/IP uses NetBIOS to access the network. Because sockets are normally used when accessing the Internet, NetBT is not needed in this case. Tunneling through the Internet requires encryption and does not need NetBT.

Question 2

Which service is not required on a Windows 2000 network when using Active Directory?

- ❍ a. WINS
- ❍ b. DNS
- ❍ c. Sockets
- ❍ d. TCP/IP

Answer a is correct. DNS, Sockets, and TCP/IP are all required when using Active Directory on a Windows 2000 network. WINS is not required because NetBIOS is no longer a requirement, and WINS translates NetBIOS computer names into IP addresses.

Question 3

Which protocols can be used to create a VPN on a Windows 2000 network? [Check all correct answers]

- ❑ a. L2TP
- ❑ b. DES
- ❑ c. PPTP
- ❑ d. SSL

Answers a and c are correct. Both PPTP and L2TP can be used to create encrypted packets over the Internet and create a Virtual Private Network on a Windows 2000 network. DES is an authentication encryption protocol and encrypts only the username and password. SSL is used to encrypt services over the Internet, but it does not create an end-to-end encrypted connecion for the entire session.

Question 4

Which services can now communicate with and update DNS? [Check all correct answers]

- ❑ a. VPN
- ❑ b. NAT
- ❑ c. RRAS
- ❑ d. DHCP

Answer d is correct. DHCP can now update the DNS database on behalf of DNS clients. The other services are used to make remote and Internet connections more secure and do not communicate with DNS.

Question 5

The networking changes in Windows 2000 most affect which layer of the OSI model?

- ❍ a. Application
- ❍ b. Presentation
- ❍ c. Session
- ❍ d. Transport
- ❍ e. Network
- ❍ f. Data link
- ❍ g. Physical

Answer c is correct. Microsoft ended its dependence on NetBIOS at the session layer, which affected all of its proprietary networking services. WinSock, a version of Sockets, is now the primary, session-layer protocol used in its network infrastructure.

Question 6

Which VPN protocol uses a proprietary encryption protocol?

- ❍ a. IPSec
- ❍ b. PPTP
- ❍ c. L2TP
- ❍ d. DES

Answer b is correct. PPTP uses a proprietary encryption protocol while L2TP uses IPSec, a protocol that is an open Internet standard. DES also uses a standard encryption protocol.

Question 7

Why would NAT be used on a network? [Check all correct answers]

- ❑ a. To provide IP addressing services to client computers
- ❑ b. To provide remote access to client computers accessing the network
- ❑ c. To provide name-resolution services to client computers
- ❑ d. To protect client computers trying to access the Internet

Answers a, c, and d are correct. On a small network, NAT provides all the services needed to access the Internet. NAT can act as a substitute proxy, WINS, DNS, and DHCP server. NAT does not provide remote access services.

Question 8

Which routing protocols does Windows 2000 routing support? [Check all correct answers]

- ❑ a. EIGRP
- ❑ b. EGP
- ❑ c. OSPF
- ❑ d. RIP

Answers c and d are correct. Windows 2000 routing supports only RIP and OSPF, thus providing routing solutions for both small and large networks.

Question 9

The hierarchical name space used on the Internet is called what?

- ❍ a. DNS
- ❍ b. dotted decimal notation
- ❍ c. WINS
- ❍ d. NAT

Answer a is correct. DNS stands for *Domain Name System* or *Service* and uses a hierarchical naming system that more easily allows unique names. Dotted decimal notation refers to the way IP addresses are written. WINS is a NetBIOS naming service, and NAT is a networking service in Windows 2000.

Question 10

Which services use more than one network interface to protect an internal network from an external one? [Check all correct answers]

- ❑ a. NAT
- ❑ b. DNS
- ❑ c. DHCP
- ❑ d. WINS
- ❑ e. Proxy Server

Answers a and e are correct. NAT and Proxy Server make requests directly to the Internet for client computers. When used at the edge of a network, two interfaces allow each service to protect the internal network. They receive client requests from one interface before sending out a separate request to the Internet on the other network interface. DNS, DHCP, and WINS are for use on an internal network and do not provide services that protect clients from Internet connections.

Need to Know More?

Smith, David. *Managing Windows 2000 Network Services.* Syngress Media, Rockland, MD, 2000. ISBN 1-92899-406-7. This book focuses on network services, including the implementation and overview of the services.

RFC 2136 Dynamic Updates in the Domain Name Service (DNS UPDATE). **http://ietf.org/rfc/rfc2136.txt?number=2136**. This RFC explains the implementation of DDNS and how the DDNS database is dynamically updated.

RFC 1631 The IP Network Address Translator (NAT) **http://ietf.org/rfc/rfc1631.txt?number=1631**. Since NAT is a new service, there isn't much information on how it works. This RFC describes the open Intenet standard for the NAT service.

Search the TechNet CD (or its online version through **www.microsoft.com/support**) and the Windows 2000 Server Resource Kit CD using the keywords "DDNS", "VPN", "WINS", "RRAS", and "Active Directory".

TCP/IP Networking Solutions

Terms you'll need to understand:

- ✓ The Open Systems Inteconnections (OSI) model
- ✓ Transmission Control Protocol/Internet Protocol (TCP/IP) addressing
- ✓ Private and public networks
- ✓ IP Filtering
- ✓ Internet Protocol Security (IPSec)
- ✓ Bandwidth management using Quality of Service (QoS)

Techniques you'll need to master:

- ✓ Subnetting
- ✓ Making a network secure with IPSec
- ✓ Guaranteeing delivery with QoS

In this chapter, you'll learn about the TCP/IP protocol suite and its many components. You'll become familiar with subnetting a TCP/IP network. We'll discuss the enhancements made to the Windows 2000 implementation of the TCP/IP protocol suite and look at examples of scenerios where these enhancements can be best utilized. We'll also cover security and bandwidth reservations that are available with the Windows 2000 implementation of the TCP/IP protocol suite.

TCP/IP History and Review

The development of the Transmission Control Protocol/Internet Protocol (TCP/IP) was funded by the United States Government's Advanced Research Projects Agency (ARPA) in the 1960s and 1970s. In the mid-1970s, ARPA connected its research sites at universities and research facilities into the world's first packet-switching network, *ARPANET*. Its success drew the interest of other research organizations that combined efforts to transform ARPANET technologies to a standard suite of protocols. In the late 1970s, the Transport Control Protocol (TCP) and the Internet Protocol (IP) were born. Since that time, advancements have been made to the TCP/IP suite, which is also known as the *TCP/IP stack*. These enhancements are developed through a process called the Request for Comments (RFCs) and proposals are approved by the Internet Architecture Board (IAB).

Internet administration is handled by a private organization, the Internet Network Information Center (INTERNIC), which is responsible for the maintenance and distribution of RFCs, as well as top-level administration that makes this network what it is today. The Internet Engineering Task Force (IETF), at **www.ietf.org**, posts the RFCs. With the explosion of the Internet in the mid-1990s, TCP/IP has quickly become the protocol of choice, as well as necessity.

The role of the TCP/IP protocol suite has changed with the release of Windows 2000. With the incorporation of Active Directory and Dynamic DNS (DDNS), TCP/IP is now required. The reason for this change relates to Microsoft's desire to fully integrate Internet functionality into the entire software line. Other protocols, such as IPX/SPX and NetBEUI, are still available for Win9x and Windows for Workgroups connectivity, but have taken a legacy support role. Windows 2000 uses TCP/IP to interoperate with other vendor-based networks (like Unix, Linux, IBM Mainframe, and Novell NetWare) for authentication file and print services, information replication, and connectivity.

The OSI Model

The TCP/IP stack is a suite of protocols that allows the creation of a logical peer network by binding a 32-bit binary address to the physical address (MAC address) of the network interface card (NIC). The Windows 2000 implementation of the TCP/IP stack corresponds to the seven layers of the Open Systems Interconnections (OSI) model, with the Windows 2000 TCP/IP model spanning several layers of the OSI model (see Figure 3.1). The OSI model was designed to provide a standard for vendors to develop integration with protocol suites that provides easy interoperability with competing networks.

Each layer of the OSI model performs a specific task when receiving data from a host. Lower layers of the OSI model receive data, perform modifications, and pass the modified data to the layer directly above. When the application needs to send data, the process is reversed in the same manner.

Physical Layer

Networks function by sending and receiving binary data streams across a physical medium. Although the physical medium normally consist of wire (such as twisted pair, coaxial cable, and fiber optic), wireless media are not excluded. Wireless technologies can utilize radio waves or infrared and laser light to transmit data. The physical layer describes a set of rules that the transmission of data must abide by to transmit on these different types of physical media.

Data Link Layer

The data link layer assembles the bits into recognizable data called *frames*. Once the physical layer has received the bits, they are passed upward to the data link layer. This layer packages the bits into a frame, which contains the destination

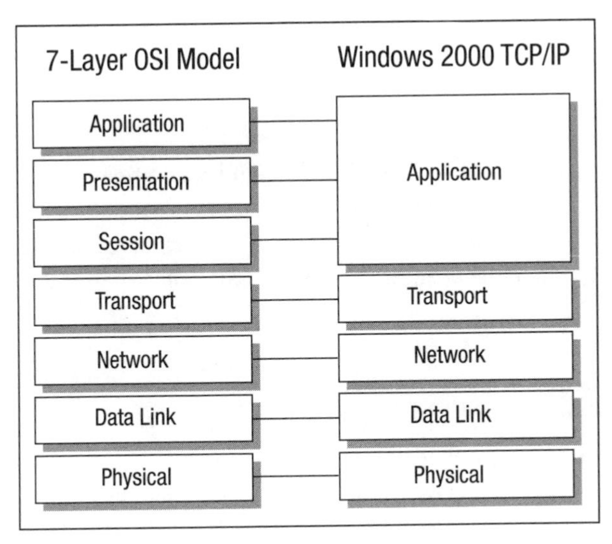

Figure 3.1 The OSI layer and the associated Microsoft implementation of the TCP/IP protocol.

address, the sender's address, the information type, the data itself, and an error-detection checksum. Even though the frame contains a destination address, protocols that reside in this layer are not routable. Although the checksum that is included in the frame will provide error-checking on the received data, it does not guarantee that all of the requested data has been received.

Network Layer

Network-layer protocols provide addressing, routing, and traffic management for transmissions among nodes. The network layer resolves the address forwarded by the data link layer. Traffic management is achieved by prioritization that is now a part of the Quality of Service (QoS). Certain types of data are given priority over others to assure the best possible performance of the message.

Transport Layer

The transport-layer protocols are responsible for making sure that the data was received without errors. It reassembles messages that were subdivided into the intended size by segment sequencing. During this process, an attached sequencing number is used to aid in the regeneration of the original message. This layer also informs the sender that the data has been received.

Session Layer

The session layer defines the management of individual network sessions. It establishes, maintains, and ends sessions between nodes. Basic network services, including login or file transfer, object locking, and data check points are used to create a session. Session-layer protocols are very reliable and can increase throughput.

Presentation Layer

The Presentation layer provides standards for encoding and encryption across a network. This layer acts as a negotiator for the rest of the protocol stack, and it is responsible for making the protocol stack network independent, meaning that communication between competing operating systems is accomplished by utilizing standard encoding.

Application Layer

The application layer is the top layer of the OSI model. However, it does not refer to desktop applications, but rather the connection between services. The Application Program Interface (API) uses this layer to access program utilities such as file and print services.

TCP/IP Addressing

Any device that is connected to a TCP/IP network uses a 32-bit logical address (such as 192.168.2.1) and is called a *host*. The TCP/IP address of the host must be unique in the network. This host address is combined with a subnet mask to separate the host address and the network address. In the above example, the host had a TCP/IP address of 192.168.2.1. If the subnet address were 255.255.0.0, the network address would be 192.168.0.0. Class-based TCP/IP has been reserved for the logical organization of networks, and classes have been defined by the conversion of the TCP/IP address to its 32-bit binary equivalent. Table 3.1 lists examples of class-based IP addresses and their binary 32-bit equivalents.

Subnet Masks

The subnet mask designates which portion of the 32-bit TCP/IP address relates to network identification and which portion relates to the actual host ID. When a host requires information from another host, the destination TCP/IP address is compared to the sender's address and subnet mask through a process called *anding*. If the network addresses (the portion of the IP address that designates the network number) match, the resolution request is sent to the local network. If the network number is not equal, the resolution request is sent to the default gateway.

Variable Length Subnet Mask

The variable length subnet mask (VLSM) is a method to further divide a subnet. An existing subnet mask is subdivided in a hierarchical fashion by using routers that support Routing Information Protocol (RIP) for IP2, or Open Shortest Path First (OSPF). VLSM allows administrators to eliminate unused IP addresses and to create additional network addresses as needed.

Supernetting

Supernetting is used to combine two or more small subnets, thus allowing companies to lease Class C addresses and combine the network addresses to meet the required number of host IDs. Supernetting requires routers that support RIP for IP2, OSPF, or BGP (Border Gateway Protocol). CIDR (Classless Interdomain Routing) supports supernetting and is described in more detail in RFC 1519.

Table 3.1 Class-based addresses and their binary equivalents.

Address Range	Binary Equivalent	Subnet Mask	Class
1-127	00000001-01111111	255.0.0.0	A
128-191	10000000-10111111	255.255.0.0	B
192-223	11000000-11011111	255.255.255.0	C

Addressing Schemes for Private and Public Networks

In the past, the main reasons for using TCP/IP included the ability to scale the network to better optimize the infrastructure with routing and Internet connectivity. Now with Windows 2000, the reason is simple: It is required. However, effective routing and Internet connectivity should be the design goals. The two major Internet connectivity strategies are *public* and *private*.

Public Networks

If you have a large number of hosts that need to be addressed via the Internet, a public network may be needed. Most companies opt for private networks due to the monetary, administrative, and security overhead.

During your planning, you will need one registered TCP/IP address for each host and two for each router. Additional addresses for future growth will also need to be considered. In most instances, this will become a large and very expensive undertaking. Another important factor will be possible security holes. You can protect your public network from attack with packet-filtering routers and firewalls. Because TCP/IP uses many ports to transmit data between hosts, it will be important to disable any unused ports on the packet-filtering routers to prevent someone from getting to sensitive areas of your network.

Private Networks

If you have a small number of hosts that need to be addressed via the Internet, a private network will be to your advantage. A private network normally uses one Internet connection and registered TCP/IP address to provide its users with full functionality. An IP proxy, such as Microsoft Proxy Server 2.0, is a good way to provide access for your users while reducing the possibility of unauthorized access to your network. In most cases, an IP proxy is also used for caching purposes, which increases the speed with which Web pages are displayed. As with a public network, private networks use packet-filtering routing and firewalls to secure the network from unauthorized access. With a private network, the TCP/IP addresses of your internal network are not limited by the availability of leases through your ISP or InterNic, because they are not directly accessed from the Internet. For a listing of private TCP/IP addresses that are not routed by the Internet, refer to RFC 1918.

Designing Your TCP/IP Network

When you are designing a TCP/IP scheme for your network, you will need to consider the number of hosts needed, the physical groupings of the hosts due to location, logical groupings, redundancy of WAN links, and infrastructure capacity.

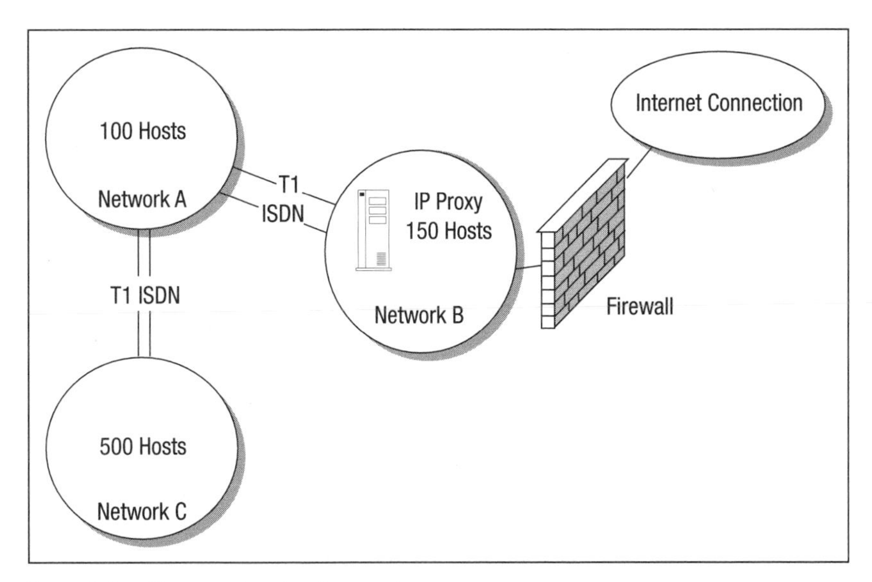

Figure 3.2 The example network scenario.

Let's say that you are a network engineer for a company with three geographical locations connected by T1 links, as illustrated in Figure 3.2.

For redundancy, you also have a dual-channel, ISDN, dial-on-demand connection for each location. The corporate office (Network A) has 100 hosts in a large high-rise office building that houses the marketing department and executive offices. The production plant (Network B) has 150 hosts, and the distribution warehouse (Network C) has 500 hosts. You decide to use a Class B addressing scheme of 192.168.0.0 for your network. This will provide you with one subnet and 65,534 hosts. What you really want is one subnet for Network A and one for Network B. To break up the traffic in Network C, you decide that your current routers and switches should have a maximum of 200 hosts. You do not expect any large increases of hosts in any of your locations, but, to ensure that you are well prepared, an additional subnet is planned at each location. With this in mind, you need to calculate a subnet mask that will allow you to divide your network into eight segments. The easiest way to arrive at a solution is the equation (x^y) equals or exceeds the required subnet amount.

You can use the scientific view on your Windows calculator and the exponent button to calculate this equation. The base, or *X*, will always equal 2, because a binary number has only two places—0 or 1. The *Y* is your variable. In this instance, your answer will be 4. This will allow 14 subnets. You will need four binary bits to achieve your appropriate subnet mask as shown in the following calculations:

(2^4)=16-2=14 available subnets

(2^{12})=4096-2=4094 available hosts

These calculations illustrate that, for this subnet mask, you will need a 32-bit binary number of 11111111.11111111.11110000.00000000 or a dotted decimal of 255.255.240.0. This will allow 12 bits for host addresses, or 4,094 hosts per subnet. The first subnet address will be 192.168.32.0 and will continue in increments of 16 until reaching 192.168.240.0.

In Figure 3.2, the Internet connection was installed at Network B, where a proxy server and firewall provides Internet access and security for authorized users. You will need two routers at each location for the WAN links to the other sites. If the WAN link between Network A and Network B goes down, the redundant ISDN connection will be utilized. This is determined by the cost-metric setting for each gateway set from within the advanced properties of the TCP/IP protocol. By setting the cost-metric value higher on the ISDN connection, it will be utilized only when the T1 connection is unavailable.

Due to the amount of users at Network C, three subnets will be implemented—which means that, besides the routers needed for the WAN links, two additional routers will be needed to connect the internal subnets. In most cases, this can be implemented by geographical location within a building. For example, you might separate by different floors of the building, wings, or departments.

IP Configuration

In a Windows 2000 environment, you can automate the TCP/IP configuration in several ways, all of which greatly reduce the overhead of a TCP/IP network. Although manual allocation is not the best way to configure your hosts in most cases, certain pieces do require manual allocation: routers, DHCP servers, WINS servers, and non-Microsoft hosts that do not support DHCP/BOOTP.

DHCP

Dynamic Host Configuration Protocol (DHCP) manager is a database of available TCP/IP addresses that are dynamically assigned to the DHCP client during its boot cycle. The available addresses for the client are created in a scope from within the DHCP manager. By right-clicking on the default scope and choosing properties, you can make changes to the scope, such as reservations or exclusions. The host retains this address for a certain period, which is known as the *lease*.

Note: Automatic Private IP Addressing assigns a unique IP address if no manual or BOOTP/DHCP configuration is available. Some brands of network cards do not support DHCP and require BOOTP for autoconfiguration. If this arises, you will need to configure DHCP to assign addresses to both client types.

Automatic Private IP Addressing

Windows 2000 and Windows 98 support IP autoconfiguration, or Automatic Private IP Addressing, a new feature that uses discovery packets to assign a unique IP address if no manual or BOOTP/DHCP configuration is available. The discovery will assign an unused host address within the Class B network address of 169.254.0.0. You can assign a unique IP address to your NIC using the "LINKLOCAL Network" IP address space. Like 127.0.0.0 and 192.168.0.0, this is a private address and will require a private network with an IP proxy to access the Internet. This new feature has come under criticism for extending the boot time by several seconds. Despite this negative response by some people in the industry, it allows a client to access some resources if a DHCP server becomes disabled in a strictly TCP/IP environment.

TCP Performance Enhancements

The Windows 2000 implimentation of the TCP/IP protocol stack has been ehanced to support several new features. It is important to remember that this is Microsoft's implementation of the stack, and some of these enhancements are not new to the industry as a whole. New enhancements to the TCP/IP stack are made by the IETF, and it is up to the software vendors to incorporate them into their operating systems. Windows 2000 has several enhancements to its TCP/IP stack compared to Windows NT 4.

Increased TCP Window Size

Windows 2000 has a little performance tuning to support network paths, such as fiber-optic or high-capacity packet satellite channels, known as the "long, fat pipe." Networks containing these types of connections are referred as *LFN* or *elephan(t)*. This is explained in detail in RFC 1323. With these large-capacity connections, performance is degraded by the TCP window size. With this larger window size, the host can send more packets without receiving an acknowledgment, which allows administrators to optimize the servers on both sides of this type of WAN connection.

TCP Selective Acknowledgment (SACK)

TCP Selective Acknowledgment (SACK) complements the larger window size by allowing TCP to request a retransmit of only those packets that have not been received within a window. Currently, when a window fills and a bad packet is detected, a retransmit message is sent for all packets to the left of the damaged packet in the TCP window, causing the retransmission of even those packets that have been successfully received. With the implementation of SACK, all packets will be read and only the damaged packets retransmitted. If you have an increased window size, the benefits from this are quite evident. For additional information on SACK, refer to RFC 2018.

Internet Control Message Protocol (ICMP)

Internet Control Message Protocol (ICMP) is another TCP performance enhancement supported by the Windows 2000 TCP/IP stack that will be well received by administrators in a WAN environment. Before a host can send data outside of its subnet, a gateway must be established. In the past, Windows NT 4 used the default gateway address listed in the TCP/IP Properties page for a designated adapter. With ICMP, the gateway can be discovered without an entry using router discovery messages called *router advertisements* and *router solicitations*. Routers will periodically advertise from each interface and announce its IP address. A host can discover the address of the router on its local subnet by listening for this advertisement. When an attached host boots up, it can ask for an advertisement. If it does not receive one, it will retransmit the solicitation. Any router that becomes available will then be designated as the gateway. This enhancement has the opportunity to become one of the most time-saving features in networking. For additional information on ICMP, refer to RFC 1256.

Disabling NetBIOS over TCP/IP (NetBT)

Windows 2000 allows you to disable NetBIOS over TCP/IP (NetBT), although for only those hosts in specialized roles that are accessed by DNS for name resolution and registration. Examples of these hosts are proxy servers and firewalls. See Chapter 6 for an in-depth discussion of this procedure.

Security

With the growing concern over security, it makes sense that Microsoft included several new utilities to help administrators secure their network. Since the beginning of 2000, we have seen an increased interest in Internet security by corporations and the U.S. Government in direct response to denial-of-service attacks and email worm viruses. The U.S. Government has gone so far as to appoint a council to search out new talent for protecting its resources from hackers.

Filtering IP Traffic

In the past, routers and firewalls have been used to keep unwanted and malicious traffic from entering your network. With the Windows 2000 implementation of the TCP/IP protocol, traffic filtering is now possible at the Application layer of the OSI model. The filtering is actually done by specialized portions of the operating system and not at the Network layer of the TCP/IP stack. Figure 3.3 shows the Filtering Properties window.

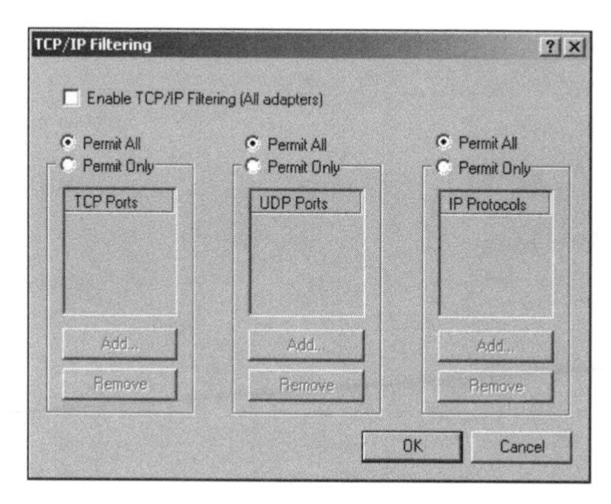

Figure 3.3 The TCP/IP Filtering Properties window.

You can use these filters on a host-by-host basis to block the delivery of any IP packets that do not conform to preset criteria. Exceptions are filtering by the following packet types: TCP, UDP, ICMP, or IGMP. For example, you can set a filter to block inbound FTP packets to port 25 that are not sent from a certain host. However, if the allowed host has forwarded a packet from a host that you would not like to enter your system, the filter cannot be applied. This is because the incoming packet has the source address of the allowed host.

Securing TCP/IP Traffic with IPSec

The Windows 2000 implementation of the TCP/IP stack has been enhanced to include support for the new protocol, IPSec. Windows 9x and other clients will require third-party software to connect with Windows 2000 hosts that require mandatory secure communications. IPSec provides data integrity and data encryption in your Windows 2000 network. IPSec is CPU-intensive, and different security levels of IPSec can degrade system performance. Use your hardware capacity and security needs to decide on an encryption level. Too much encryption and too little hardware can result in long days of monitoring your network resources. Figure 3.4 shows the TCP/IP Security window.

Predefined IPSec Policies

IPSec uses a protocol called ISAKMP/Oakley, which allows the receiver to verify the sender's identity using X.509 digital certificates and then sets up a trusted session after authentication. For two hosts to communicate using IPSec, communication policies must be established to tell the IPSec hosts how they will interface and establish a trust. The process that calculates a security association (SA) between the hosts is called the *Internet Key Exchange*, or *IKE*. The SA controls the encryption between the hosts on a session basis and is recalculated based on the quantity of the data and the session time. The following are predefined policies:

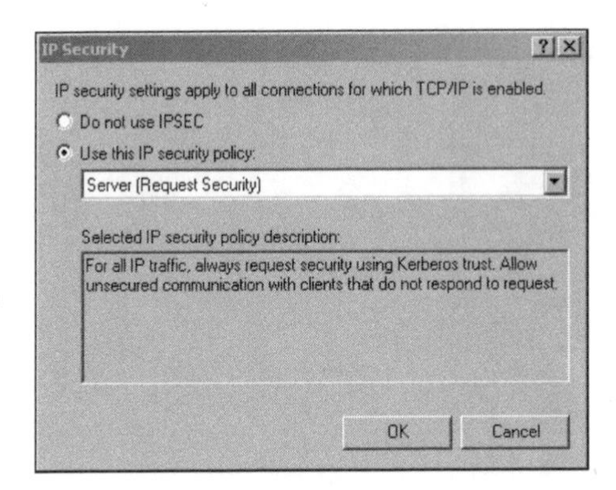

Figure 3.4 The TCP/IP Security window.

- *Client policy*—For hosts that use IPSec only when they are requested to by another host. With this setting, the host computer can respond to requests to communicate with IPSec-secured communications.
- *Server policy*—For hosts that can accept both secured and unsecured traffic. When a host establishes a session with the sender, a request for secured communications is sent. If the sender responds with an SA, the communications between the hosts will be secured. If the host fails to respond, the communications will continue, but they will not be secured using IPSec.
- *Secure Server policy*—For hosts that require secured communication. Any requests to send using unsecured communications are rejected.

IPSec Data Integrity and Data Encryption in Windows 2000 Networks

Data integrity is the ability to allow only certain hosts to communicate. It is attained by using an authentication header (AH) that is inserted after an IP header and before the other information being authenticated.

Data encryption uses encapsulation security and payload (ESP) to provide both data-integrity authentication and data encryption. This means that an AH is not used, or rather, that the ESP provides the same service as the AH, while also providing encryption services to the packet. ESP provides confidentiality and integrity by encrypting data to be protected and placing the encrypted data in the data portion of the IP.

IPSec Authentication Protocols

IPSec uses two protocols to authenticate hosts: Message Digest 5 (MD5) and the Secure Hash Algorithm (SHA).

- *MD5*—An authentication algorithm that has been proposed as the default authentication option in IPv6. When enabled, the MD5 protocol operates over the entire data packet, including the header, to provide 128-bit authentication with random keys. For more information, refer to RFC 1321.

- *SHA*—A 160-bit authenticator to provide data-origin authentication. The key must ensure that unique keys are allocated and distributed only to the hosts participating in the secured communication. For more information, refer to RFC 2404.

IPSec Encryption Algorithms

IPSec uses the Data Encryption Standard (DES), which describes data encryption from 40-bit DES (needed for secure communication with hosts in France) to 128-bit Triple DES (3DES). Communications scrambled in 56-bit DES (meaning the key to descramble the message has 56 elements) have 70 quadrillion possible keys. Despite this huge number of possible keys, it does not take long to break. In fact, during a contest in February, 1998, a team of programmers broke a 56-bit DES key in 39 days, about a third of the time it took a similar team the year before. Although Triple DES is much more secure, it is a processor-intensive protocol, and, the more bits in the encryption algorithm, the more processor time is used.

Note: The U.S. Government still restricts the export of 128-bit key encryption on the grounds that it could be used by criminals to mask their activities.

Internet Key Exchange Protocol (IKE)

The Internet Key Exchange protocol, formerly known as ISAKMP/Oakley, is a tool for negotiating the terms of the communication before a secure session can begin. These communication security parameters include which encryption algorithms are to be used, the duration of the encryption, and the encryption key. The negotiation process is automatic and secure to allow scaling to the Internet.

When a session between two hosts is established, only those hosts know the security key used. The Internet Security Association and Key Management Protocol (ISAKMP) and the Oakley key-generation protocol create an SA between the hosts. Then Oakley authenticates, and the session can begin. Table 3.2 lists the securtiy peer authentication methods used by IKE to create a session between two IPSec enabled hosts.

Table 3.2 Security peer authentication methods.

Security Association	Usage
Kerbose version 5	Default authentication for trusted domain members
Public key certificates	The Internet and remote connections
Preshared keys	Windows 9X and other clients using third-party software

Routing IPSec

IPSec protocols use specific ports and protocol numbers that can be seamlessly routed if they are configured. You will need to enable your routers, firewalls, gateways, and proxy servers to accept the following protocols on these ports:

- IPSec Header Traffic Protocol ID 51 (0×33)
- IPSec ESP Protocol ID 50 (0×32)

Quality of Service (QoS)

QoS provides a routing mechanism that can guarantee delivery of data for a certain application. Paths for traffic flows are determined based on some knowledge of resource availability in the network, as well as the QoS requirements (needed amount of bandwidth) for the flows. QoS-based routing allows the determination of a path that has a good chance of accommodating the requested QoS. The Windows 2000 implementation of QoS provides bandwidth reservations and priority levels for the data flows based on the user, application, or QoS policies.

Routing deployed in today's Internet is focused on connectivity. The current Internet routing protocols, OSPF and RIP, use shortest-path routing. These opportunistic protocols optimize routing paths based on a hop count. In other words, they choose the best path from point A to point B based on how many routers they will use to get to the destination. They do not allow alternate paths based on available bandwidth. Opportunistic routing will shift from one path to another if a shorter path (one with fewer hops) becomes available. This shifting of paths can produce delays and "jitters" in data-intense applications such as realtime audio and video.

It is important to remember that for QoS to be fully utilized, all routers between the communication hosts must be QoS aware.

QoS Components

QoS employs several components to set up a data-delivery system for network traffic, which utilizes the available subnet bandwidth. These components each perform a specific role in the creation of the data stream.

- *Generic QoS (GQoS)*—An abstract interface that allows application programmers to specify or request bandwidth based on their application or media.
- *RSVP SP (Rsvp.dll) (Resource Reservation Protocol Service Provider)*—Accesses the RSVP.exe.

- *RSVP (Resource Reservation Protocol)*—A signaling component of QoS. It is not dependent on media, which allows the protocol to facilitate end-to-end communications.
- *Traffic Control (Traffic.dll)*—Regulates data by using QoS-defined parameters. Traffic control is called on by the GQoS API.
- *Generic Packet Classifier (Msgpc.sys)*—Determines the class of the packet.
- *QoS Packet Scheduler (Psched.sys)*—Enforces the parameters of the traffic flow.
- *QoS Admission Control Service (QoS ACS)*—Is the central point that allows or denies requests for bandwidth. The QoS ACS service is not required on each network segment; however, high-traffic areas are better served by having a local QoS ACS.
- *Local Policy Module (Msidlpm.dll)*—Is responsible for providing a policy-enforcement point and policy-decision point. The QoS ACS uses this module to examine the user's name from the RSVP message and to compare it to the admission control policy located in the Windows 2000 Active Directory.

Putting It All Together

A QoS-enabled client sends a request for service. The QoS-aware application calls the RSVP SP. The RSVP SP calls the RSVP service to request the necessary bandwidth. Then a RSVP message is sent to the QoS ACS server requesting the necessary reservation needed by the application. The QoS ACS verifies the available bandwidth resources and then calls the LPM and compares the user policy with the permissions set in the Windows 2000 Active Directory.

After the permissions have been verified with Active Directory, the QoS ACS grants the request and allocates the available bandwidth. The QoS ACS then passes the message to the receiving host. During this process, QoS-enabled routers are informed of the bandwidth reservation. The routers cache this information and wait for the RSVP message to be returned from the receiving host. The receiving host receives the message and retransmits back to the sender a message that it is ready to receive the data.

When the receiver's message passes through the routers, it is compared to the request sent by the sender and the use of the requested bandwidth is now granted. Throughout this process, the message traffic is sent by best effort until the sender receives its returned request. Now the sender's Traffic Control module classifies, marks, and schedules the packets using the Generic Packet Classifier and QoS Packet Scheduler. For more information, see RFC 2386.It is important to remember that QoS sessions do not begin until the sending host has received its request back from the receiving host. Until the requesting host receives the message, the message is sent by best effort.

Practice Questions

Case Study

VirtuCon is a manufacturer of hi-tech equipment, based in Carson City, Nevada. It has a manufacturing plant in Indianapolis, IN, and a distribution facility in Louisville, KY. The corporate offices in Carson City have 150 hosts. The manufacturing plant in Indianapolis has 300 hosts, and the distribution center has 250 hosts. The network infrastructure was designed in 1995 and needs upgrades. The management staff has assigned you to design the proposed upgrades, utilizing as much of the existing equipment as possible.

Current WAN Structure

VirtuCon is currently using Windows NT 4 servers at all locations. The client workstations are currently running Windows 95 and Windows NT 4 workstation.

The hubs and switches at all locations are autosensing 10/100. The network cards in client and server machines have been replaced in the past year and are also 10/100. The current hub switches and routers will effectively support 200 hosts per subnet.

VirtuCon has doubled in size since its network's installation in 1995. The projected growth over the next 5 years is 20 percent

Proposed WAN Upgrades

VirtuCon's management staff would like to upgrade its network to provide fail over redundancy of its WAN links and to provide better security for sensitive data transferred between locations. It also wants your design to take into consideration a realtime job management database that is located at the Carson City office and is accessed through WAN Links.

Most of the hosts are 166MHz Pentium computers with 16MB of RAM and a 1.6GB hard drive. Management has approved the upgrade of all client machines to PIII class machines with 128MB of RAM and 12GB hard drives. All clients and servers will be upgraded to Windows 2000.

The decisions you make for the upgrades should incorporate the current network state and the expected five-year growth plan with the most economical solutions.

Current WAN Connectivity

The locations have 168Kbps fractional T-1 connections from Carson City to Indianapolis and from Indianapolis to Louisville. The routers have been replaced in the past year and are QoS aware.

Proposed WAN Connetivity

The Carson City site should have a failover 128Kbps ISDN connection with the Indianapolis office. The Indianapolis office should have a failover ISDN connection with the Louisville office. These connections should be dial-on-demand, since the provider bills VirtuCon a monthly carrying fee for the service. If the connection is used, VirtuCon will also be charged for the connection time. Your solution should take this into account and provide automatic connection and disconnection, should the failover link be used.

All clients and servers will be upgraded to Windows 2000.

Directory Design Commentary

VirtuCon's current password policies will be duplicated on the Windows 2000 servers.

Current Internet Positioning

VirtuCon currently accesses the Internet from all locations using a single leased IP address at the Indianapolis location. This location has an IP Proxy and firewall to protect the network and provide access.

A Web-hosting firm hosts the company Web site. The firewall server at the Indianapolis site provides all remote employees with a Web-based email client for remote access to email.

Future Internet Plans

Eventually, VirtuCon would like to host its own site and provide remote users with Web-based access to the job database.

Company Goal with the Proposed Upgrade

VirtuCon has put you in charge of designing and managing the implementation. Your goal is to incorporate all of the previously mentioned requirements and implement the most cost-effective design.

You have a small support staff, so automatic responses to variations in the network infrastructure will provide the best support to the clients.

Question 1

Considering the case study, which subnet mask will provide the proper amount of logical network segments and give the maximum amount of available hosts using a Class C network address?

- ❍ a. 255.255.255.0
- ❍ b. 255.255.248.0
- ❍ c. 255.255.0.0
- ❍ d. None of the above

Answer b is correct. Considering the hosts at each location, the projected growth, and the existing hardware's ability to effectively support 200 hosts, 5 subnets will be needed. This will require a subnet mast of 255.255.248.0. Both answers a and c do not allow you to break down the address range into logical networks.

Question 2

Considering the case study, which of the following options will provide failover redundancy for the WAN connections listed? [Choose all that apply]

- ❑ a. Third-party software will be needed to manage the links
- ❑ b. The ISDN router/modem will need to be configured to dial out if it sensed that the fractional T-1 became disabled
- ❑ c. You need to add the IP address of the router for the fractional T-1 and the ISDN connection as default gateways
- ❑ d. You need to set the cost metric of the fractional T-1 to 1 and the cost metric of the ISDN router/modem to 40

Answers c and d are correct. The cost metric setting provides additional links that can be utilized if the primary link is not available. When the link is restored, this setting would direct clients to reconnect to the T-1 connection and drop the ISDN connection. Third-party software will provide the connection when needed; however, it will also require an additional purchase.

Question 3

Considering the case study, what could you implement to secure communications between the hosts at all locations?

- ❍ a. IPSec
- ❍ b. QoS
- ❍ c. DHCP
- ❍ d. SNMP

Answer a is correct. With the Windows 2000 implementation of the TCP/IP stack, support for the IPSec protocols has been added. This protocol provides encryption between hosts on a network. QoS provides a routing mechanism that can guarantee delivery of data for a certain application. DHCP is used to automatically assign IP addresses to DHCP and BOOTP clients. SNMP is a component of the TCP/IP suite that allows the remote monitoring and management of network resources.

Question 4

Considering the case study, which predefined security level should you implement on your Windows 2000 hosts?

- ❍ a. Client
- ❍ b. Sever
- ❍ c. Secured Server
- ❍ d. 128-bit triple DES

Answer c is correct. To allow hosts to communicate only with other hosts using IPSec secured connections, Secured Server is the proper predefined security level. All communications from hosts using unsecured communications will be rejected. This will provide the most secure connections between hosts. The Server policy is for hosts that can accept both secured and unsecured traffic, the Client policy is for hosts that use IPSec only when they are requested to by another host. 128-bit triple DES is an encryption standard.

Question 5

Considering the case study, what configurations will need to be made to the routers to allow IPSec to be seamlessly routed through the network? [Choose all that apply]

- ❑ a. Enable Port 21 to accept SMB packets
- ❑ b. Enable IPSec ESP Protocol ID 50 (0x32)
- ❑ c. IPSec Header Traffic Protocol ID 51 (0x33)
- ❑ d. Do nothing—if routers support RIP for IP, then no configuration is necessary

Answers b and c are correct. To allow IPSec to be seamlessly routed through the network, you must enable IPSec ESP Protocol ID 50 (0×32) and IPSec Header Traffic Protocol ID 51 (0×33). Port 21 is used mainly for FTP communications.

Question 6

Considering the case study, what best describes the type of addressing scheme for the network?

- ❍ a. Public
- ❍ b. Secured
- ❍ c. QoS enabled
- ❍ d. Private

Answer d is correct. Since all of the hosts access the Internet through an IP Proxy at one location, the network would be considered private. Private networks employ IP proxies to provide Internet access by using a single IP address. A public network would require that each host would have a registered IP address. All networks need to be secured from tampering. QoS enabled does not describe the type of addressing scheme for the network.

Question 7

Considering the case study, place the QoS ACS server in the most logical place in the following diagram.

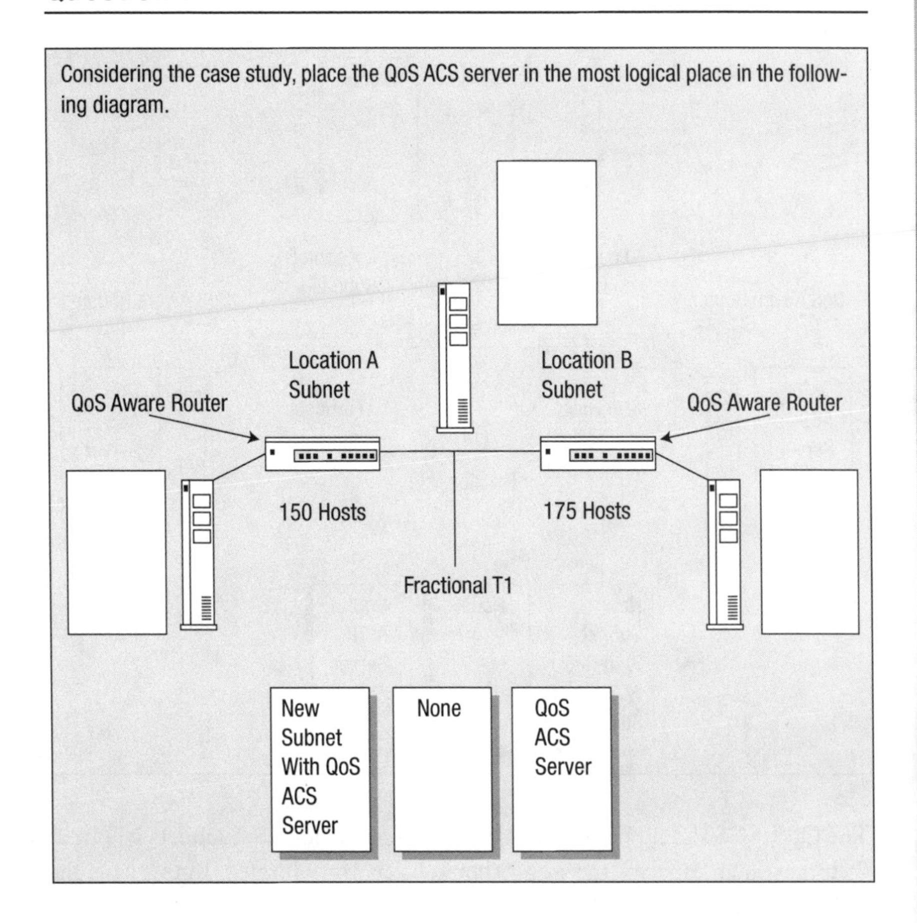

The answer is:

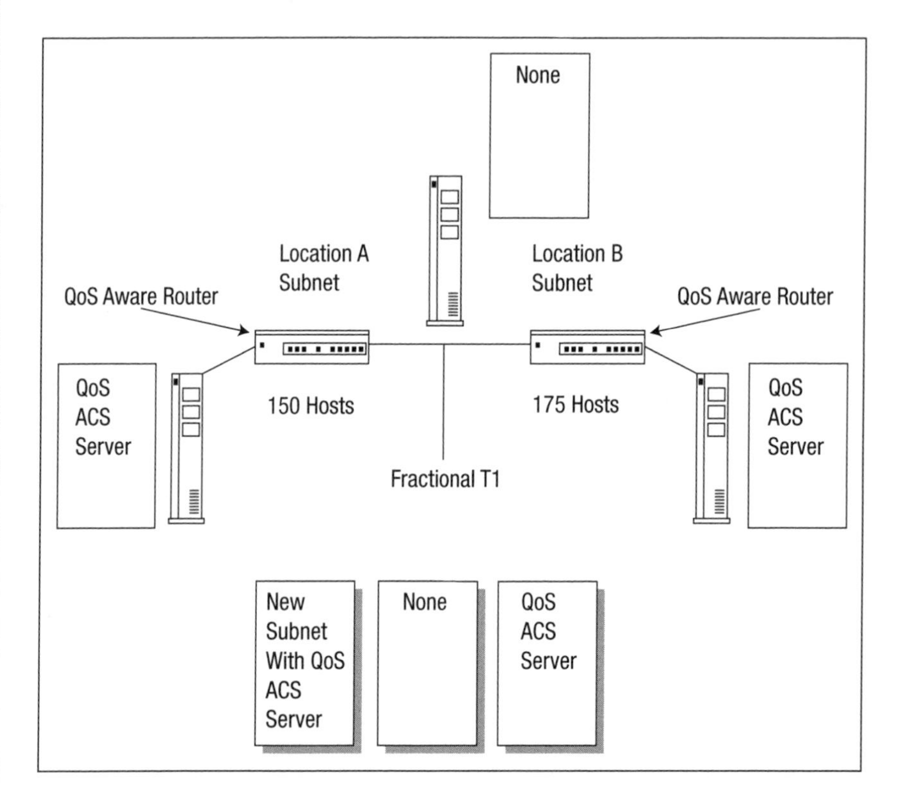

The QoS ACS should be centrally located. Since none of the subnets will be at their maximum capacity, the server should be centrally located. In this case, the QoS ACS server will be placed in the Indianapolis location. If either Carson City or Louisville becomes unavailable or is required to use the redundant ISDN link, the unaffected location will continue to access the QoS ACS server with the best possible bandwidth.

Question 8

Considering the case study, when would a host at the Carson City location be able to establish a QoS session with a host at the Louisville location?

- ❍ a. When the router at the Carson City location cached a reservation for bandwidth
- ❍ b. When routers at Carson City and Indianapolis had cached a reservation for bandwidth
- ❍ c. When routers at Carson City, Indianapolis, and Louisville had cached a reservation for bandwidth
- ❍ d. When the request was returned to the sending host at the Carson City location

Answer c is correct. A QoS sender must receive its request message back from the receiving host before a QoS session can begin. A bandwidth allocation is cached at each router alone the path between the two hosts during the session creation.

Question 9

Considering the case study, on which WAN links could the increased TCP/IP window size be employed?

- ❍ a. On any T1 connection where the QoS ACS resides
- ❍ b. On the T1 connection where the QoS ACS does not reside
- ❍ c. On any ISDN connection
- ❍ d. None of the above

Answer d is correct. The increased TCP/IP window size is only beneficial with a high-speed connection, such as fiber optic or satellite connections. T1 and ISDN lines are unable to benefit from the window size because the data transfer rates are slow compared to fiber optic and microwave.

Question 10

Considering the case study, on which server should the IPSec Secure Server be located?

- ❍ a. At location A
- ❍ b. At location B
- ❍ c. At location C
- ❍ d. None of the above

Answer d is correct. The Secured Server is a predefined security policy that must be set in the advanced properties on each host on the Windows 2000 network. A sever to security is not utilized. QoS uses an ACS or Access Control Server to allocate bandwidth and authenticate users.

Need to Know More?

Comer, Douglas. *Internetworking with TCP/IP Vol. I: Principles, Protocols, and Architecture*. Prentice Hall. Upper Saddle River, NJ, 2000. ISBN 0-13018-380-6. A great reference for learning about TCP/IP, this book is respected for its clarity and accessibility.

Microsoft Online Knowledge base, Article ID: Q244910 Description of Reservation State in RSVP.

RFC 1519. Classless Inter-Domain Routing (CIDR). **www.ietf.org/rfc/rfc1519.txt?number=1519**. This RFC gives detailed information on classless inter-domain routing, or CIDR. It is in-depth but can be tough to follow.

RFC 1918. Address Allocation for Private Internets. **www.ietf.org/rfc/rfc1918.txt?number=1918.** This RFC outiles public and private adressing, and gives examples of their utilization. An extremely good RFC.

RFC 2018. TCP Selective Acknowledgment Options. **www.ietf.org/rfc/rfc2018.txt?number=2018.** This RFC deals with the TCP/IP SAC protocol. A very in-depth article that will also explain the benefits of a bigger TCP window size.

RFC 1256. ICMP Router Discovery Messages. **www.ietf.org/rfc/rfc1256.txt?number=1256.** This RFC outlines the ICMP router discovery message and how it is used by routers to automatically assign a default gateway to hosts on a TCP/IP network.

RFC 2404. The Use of HMAC-SHA-1-96 within ESP and AH. **www.ietf.org/rfc/rfc2404.txt?number=2404.** This RFC covers the authentication headers and encryption standards used by IPSec.

DHCP Design

Terms you'll need to understand:

- ✓ Dynamic Host Configuration Protocol (DHCP)
- ✓ DHCP Relay Agent
- ✓ Scope
- ✓ Superscope
- ✓ Boot Protocol (BOOTP)
- ✓ Vendor options
- ✓ Multicast

Techniques you'll need to master:

- ✓ Using vendor options
- ✓ Securing DHCP
- ✓ Making DHCP services redundant
- ✓ Improving DHCP performance

In this chapter, you'll learn how to implement the Dynamic Host Configuration Protocol (DHCP) in a Windows 2000 network infrastructure. You'll learn how to use DHCP services to design a network to enhance Windows 2000 in a networking environment. These designs will decrease your administrative duties for the Windows 2000 TCP/IP while keeping your network secure.

DHCP Overview

The DHCP service is used on TCP/IP networks to automate IP addressing and TCP/IP optional parameters rather than manually assigning IP addresses.

Manually assigning each computer in a TCP/IP network a unique IP address would require an administrator to visit each computer, enter a unique IP address for it, and keep track of the addresses as they are assigned so as to avoid duplicating any of the already used IP addresses. The DHCP service is configured to use a range, or *scope*, of addresses. Once IP addresses are assigned from this range, they are immediately and automatically excluded from being assigned to any other computer by the DHCP server. If you assign a collection of scopes for a network, this is defined as a *superscope*.

If two computers have the same IP address, the second one that attempts to initialize TCP/IP will not be able to initialize the protocol. If other protocols are bound on the computer, the computer will use those. Until a valid TCP/IP address is used, the two systems will show a conflict and only one system's TCP/IP protocol will initialize at a time.

When a computer is started that has DHCP Client Service enabled, the following occurs:

1. The client sends a broadcast to the network asking for a DHCP server (where the DHCP server services are installed and a scope is assigned).
2. The DHCP server receives the broadcast and returns to the client a broadcast offering an IP address.
3. The client accepts or rejects the offer; if the offer is accepted, an acknowledgment broadcast is sent back.
4. The DHCP server marks the address as being active so that no other computer can have the same one, and then the DHCP server broadcasts a final acknowledgment to give the client final permission to use the assigned IP address.
5. The client starts the TCP/IP service with the newly assigned address.

If multiple DHCP servers are available, they all send an offer for an IP address. The client accepts the first offer, and, when it sends the broadcast back to accept, the other DHCP servers will withdraw their unaccepted offers.

The DHCP server must be permanently assigned a static IP address that is excluded from the scope so that it cannot be assigned to another computer.

Other optional parameters that can be configured are the default Domain Name Service (DNS) servers, Windows Internet Name Service (WINS) servers, gateways, vendor-specific options, multicast address allocation, and lease time.

These options are not the only services that DHCP can configure on the client computer, but they are the ones that are most important when designing a network infrastructure. For a more detailed list, search the Windows 2000 help file "DHCP Options Reference".

Vendor-Specific Option Categories

The vendor-specific options are divided into two types: user-specific and vendor-specific. They are defined in RFC 2132.

You should take note that the vendor-specific options are not all supported on earlier versions of NT DHCP Client and non-Microsoft DHCP clients.

User-Specific Options

The user-specific options are used for clients needing common DHCP configurations, such as IP subnet addresses, WINS server, DNS server, gateways, and so on.

These options can be useful for a group of people in one building who need different DHCP scope options than people in another building who require another set of DHCP scope options. Thus, the two buildings can share a single DHCP server.

This option is used only in Windows 2000 based systems.

Vendor-Specific Options

The vendor-specific options are used for systems that are running Windows 2000 or Windows 98. For instance, one set of DHCP options can be used for everyone running Windows 2000, and another set of DHCP options for those using Windows 98.

This flexibility is useful for a company that requires Windows 2000 on all desktop systems but wants Windows 98 on all laptop systems. The DHCP options will be able to specify that the Windows 98 systems have different options for being able to use Routing and Remote Access Services (RRAS) for mobile users who are dialing into the company's network.

Some of the various vendor-specific options are:

- *Release DHCP lease on shutdown*—Allows the IP addresses to be reused when a system is shut down, rather than waiting for the lease to expire. This feature allows a scope to include more available addresses. For example, if someone leaves on vacation for a week and the lease time is set to three days, that IP address is available immediately when the system is shut down rather than after three days.
- *Disable NetBIOS over TCP/IP*—Forces the Windows 2000 systems to use DNS rather than WINS and thus reduces some network traffic. Windows 2000 is designed more around DNS than WINS. Address resolution is quicker, because there is no waiting for the WINS request to time out in the absence of a WINS server.
- *Default router metric base*—Specifies the default metric for the gateways. The metric determines which gateway is faster than another. For example, if Gateway A has a metric of 100 and Gateway B has a metric of 500, Gateway A will be used before Gateway B (unless it is unavailable).

Multicast Address Dynamic Client Allocation Protocol (MADCAP)

DHCP services also help assign multicast addresses, which are used for the simultaneous transmission of information (such as streaming video) from one PC to multiple PCs. To implement MADCAP on a network, you need a server that is running DHCP services and the Site Server ILS service. Once these are installed and running, a MADCAP scope is set and activated. Any application needing a multicast address can then request one from the DHCP server just as a system requests a standard IP address. The address that is requested by all systems for a multicast broadcast are given the same IP address. (They must already have an existing Class A, B, or C address.) All systems with the same multicast address are listed as a multicast group to receive multicast broadcasts.

Make sure your routers allow the multicast addresses to pass through and not be filtered out when the presentation will span more than one network.

Note: For a DHCP server to offer IP addresses for multicast, it must first be authorized (which is described later in this chapter under "Active Directory Integration").

To set up a Multicast scope, in the DHCP Administrator, right-click on the DHCP server to be used as the multicast server and select New Multicast Scope as shown in Figure 4.1. You then follow the wizard to set up the multicast scopes. The wizard allows you to specify a range of addresses to assign for multicast from 224.0.0.0 to 239.255.255.255 (Class D addresses), as shown in Figure 4.2.

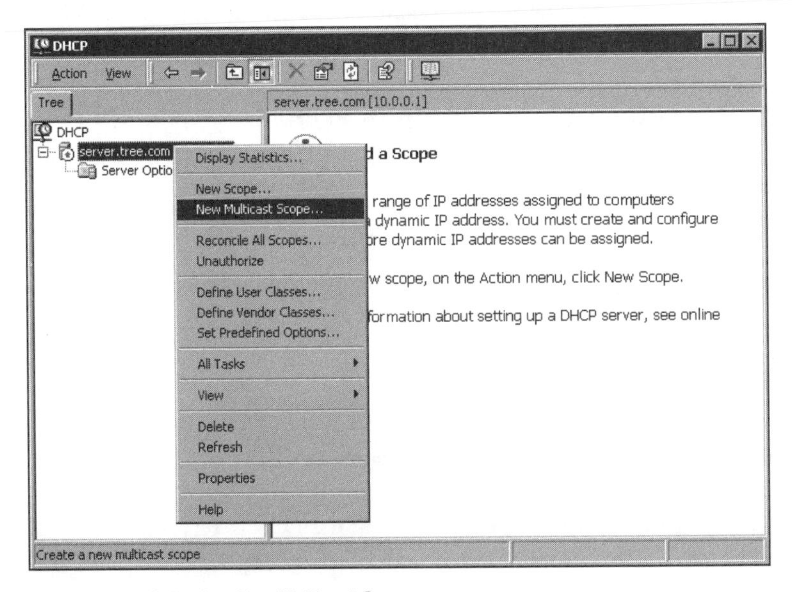

Figure 4.1 Selecting New Multicast Scope.

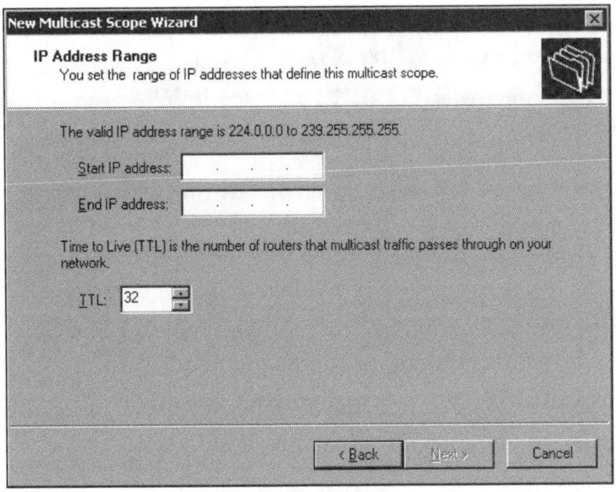

New Multicast Scope Wizard

IP Address Range
You set the range of IP addresses that define this multicast scope.

The valid IP address range is 224.0.0.0 to 239.255.255.255

Start IP address:

End IP address:

Time to Live (TTL) is the number of routers that multicast traffic passes through on your network.

TTL: 32

< Back | Next > | Cancel

Figure 4.2 Multicast range selection.

Lease Time

The lease time is how long an IP address and options are valid before the DHCP client must request a new IP address or renew the lease on the one it has.

Leases allow a network to retain as much of its scope of IP addresses as possible. For instance, a computer with an assigned IP address is removed from the network. Because the database shows that the absent computer still retains ownership of the IP address, that address cannot be reused. A lease, however, causes this ownership to either be renewed or to expire after a set amount of time (Windows 2000 has a default of eight days).

DHCP Integration with Windows 2000

DHCP integrates well with Windows 2000 because DHCP is used for medium- to large-based networks. (Even though DHCP can be used for small businesses, the full benefits are better realized in larger networks.)

DHCP can integrate with a few different Windows 2000 services to make the network more robust and more secure, with less administrative overhead.

DNS Integration

DHCP in Windows 2000 integrates with DNS to allow DHCP to automatically update the DNS table when DHCP assigns an IP address. This includes non-Microsoft DHCP clients as well as Microsoft DHCP clients. The DHCP service handles the DNS updates, which is set at the DHCP server by selecting the Always Update DNS option located under Properties on the DNS tab and shown in Figure 4.3.

Once this option is enabled, any client receiving an address from the DHCP server will have its address updated in the DNS tables automatically. It will update the Forward (A Record) and Reverse (PTR Record) lookup tables (if they exist). This makes DNS dynamic instead of static, as it was in Windows NT 4 and previous versions.

If the DHCP server is a Windows 2000 server, it can update the records of non-Active Directory DNS servers. This does include non-Windows systems and older Windows DNS servers.

Active Directory Integration

Integrating DHCP in Active Directory allows more security by preventing rogue servers from issuing IP addresses to systems on the network. If a DHCP server is not authorized, the services will not start on a Windows 2000 server.

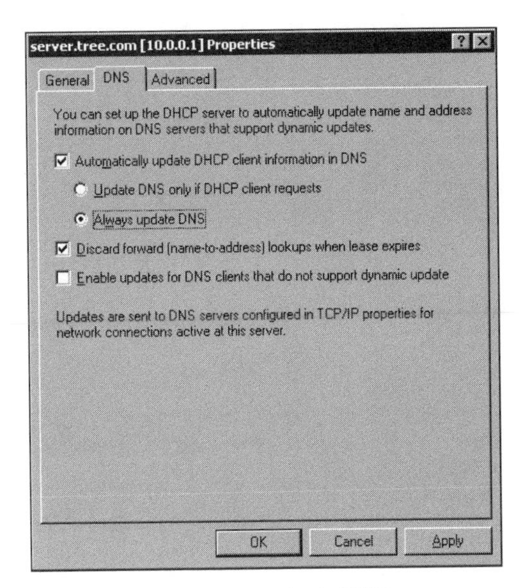

Figure 4.3 DNS update option in DHCP.

Keep in mind that DHCP services on a Windows 2000 server should be authorized in Active Directory. An authorized DHCP server is one that can answer requests for IP addresses. IP address offers from unauthorized DHCP servers will not be accepted.

Authorizing a DHCP server does require that Active Directory is installed and that you have a domain controller operating. Active Directory will not function in a workgroup.

When using Active Directory, the Windows 2000-based DHCP clients will request a list of DHCP servers that are authorized from the Active Directory. Non-Windows 2000 DHCP clients will request an IP address from authorized and unauthorized DHCP servers.

The built-in group DHCP Administrators has access to DHCP Manager, and the built-in group DHCP Users has read-only permission to access the DHCP Manager. Using built-in groups allows an administrator to assign a specialized administrator to administer DHCP scope and options, thus keeping the DHCP management secure.

In a network using strictly Windows 2000-based DHCP clients and authorized DHCP servers, the issuing of IP addresses can be more secure. To keep it secure, the DHCP services request access to the Active Directory authorized list when starting and every five minutes thereafter, which prevents the DHCP server service from running when it has lost its authority.

Routing and Remote Access Integration

This integration allows remote systems connecting to a RRAS to use DHCP to obtain IP addresses. The number of incoming ports will determine the number of initial IP addresses the RAS server requests from the DHCP server. If a DHCP server has a modem pool with 9 modems set for incoming calls, the RAS server gets 10 addresses from the DHCP server for use: 1 for itself and 9 for the connected users through the 9 modems. If the clients are connecting from the Internet, the RAS server receives an initial 11 addresses: 1 for itself and 10 for the first 10 users to connect. After that, it gets more addresses in blocks of 10, if it needs them.

When using DHCP with routing and remote access services, decrease the lease expiration time to make the IP addresses available sooner, because most remote access users will not be online for extended periods of time.

If the RAS server also has DHCP Relay Agent, it can get the IP addressing options from the DHCP server. (DHCP Relay Agent is a service that answers the DCHP requests from DHCP clients and forwards the request to the configured DHCP server.) If the DHCP client is on a routed network that is not BOOTP-enabled (that is, connected by a router that does not pass DHCP requests to the other subnet, but instead filters them out), any DHCP client will not be able to communicate with the DHCP server. On the other hand, if the routers are BOOTP-enabled, the requests and offers pass through the router to the other subnets. This basically means that, on a routed network that does not support BOOTP, one must use DHCP Relay Agent.

Designing a LAN DHCP Service

In a single nonrouted network, one DHCP server is sufficient for thousands of DHCP clients. But DHCP can be hard disk-intensive, and Redundant Array of Independent Disks (RAID) implementations should be beneficial. An administrator can use Performance Monitor to watch for bottlenecks when more client systems are added to the network.

Note: Performance Monitor is located in the Administrative Tools under the heading Performance.

Set up one scope on the DHCP server to offer IP addresses to the DHCP clients. If you want to use multiple DHCP servers for redundancy (for example, when one server fails, you will still want DHCP services active on your network), you would divide the scope in two and place half on each DHCP server.

Just make sure that one-half of the scope is sufficient for your whole network, which may be necessary if one server's downtime is longer than the lease expiration.

In a single LAN, depending on how static the configuration is, the default expiration time should be extended. If the IP addressing options are being changed often for testing, the lease time should be shortened until the testing is completed.

Designing WAN DHCP Services

When dealing with a WAN or a routed network, broadcasts (which are essential to the function of DHCP services) are not allowed to cross the router barrier. If BOOTP is enabled on the routers, then only the DHCP broadcasts are allowed to cross the router barrier (not all broadcasts). If a subnet is joined to a subnet with a DHCP server by a router without BOOTP, that subnet must have DHCP Relay Agent.

In a WAN, DHCP servers must be accessible by all DHCP clients. Depending on whether the routers are configured with BOOTP and if there is enough server hardware to manage DHCP server load will determine whether one or multiple DHCP servers should be implemented.

One DHCP Server in a WAN

Because the DHCP server will need to be accessed by all DHCP clients on every subnet of the WAN, the best performance can be achieved by placing the DHCP server in the subnet with the greatest number of DHCP clients. This will keep the majority of the DHCP requests on the local subnet.

If DHCP Relay Agent is used on other subnets that are not BOOTP-enabled, the majority of the DHCP requests from clients and the relay agents will still be local. The relay agents will direct their requests to the DHCP server directly and not by broadcasts. (This prevents DHCP requests from flooding all of the subnets with requests from other subnets.)

Multiple DHCP Servers in a WAN

If the DHCP client requests overwhelm the hardware capabilities of a DHCP server or bandwidth of a network, multiple DHCP servers should be used. Also, if subnets are connected with unreliable connection paths, the subnet that may or may not be able to contact the other subnet should have its own local DHCP server.

Multiple DHCP servers should also be used to accommodate the growth of the network for more-scalable WAN expansion.

Designing DHCP High Availability

To make sure that DHCP is always available to issue IP addresses to systems on a network, the DHCP service must be functioning somewhere on a network at all times and be accessible by all systems. You can ensure such an availability of DHCP services in two ways: clustered DHCP servers and multiple DHCP servers.

Clustered DHCP Server

DHCP is a cluster-aware service that will function on clustered servers. Setting up a cluster requires two computers of almost identical hardware and configuration. Clusters also require a high-speed connection between the two for fast communications, which allows one system to take over in case the other fails, an event known as a *failover*.

Note: During a failover, all of the cluster-aware services automatically start on the second server in the cluster. The interruption should cause no loss of data or downtime.

Cluster servers support more failover services than just DHCP. Cluster servers can failover such services as Exchange, SQL, IIS, and some third-party software services.

Multiple DHCP Servers

Using multiple DHCP servers can assure that one DHCP server is always online. The problem is that each DHCP server may be issuing addressing for two or more different subnets.

The rule here is 80/20: Assign 80 percent of the IP addresses to a scope for the DHCP server in that subnet, and assign the other 20 percent of the scope to the DHCP server on the other subnet (and vice versa). If one DHCP server fails, the other DHCP server can still issue some IP addresses for the other subnet, plus almost all of its own. The 20 percent for the remote subnet should not be exhausted before an administrator has time to fix the DHCP server that failed (unless the lease time is too small or the server needs major repairs to bring back online).

Enhancing DHCP Performance

Enhancing DHCP performance improves the server's response to DHCP clients. It also reduces the TCP/IP initialization time, which will let the clients start faster.

Hardware Implementation

The hardware can be improved by implementing any of the following options:

- Faster CPU (or multiple CPUs)
- More memory

- Faster network interface cards (NICs) for faster transmissions
- Faster disk subsystems
- Putting the DHCP server on a subnet of highest system location (the one with most users)
- DHCP servers on every side of a WAN link

Software Implementation

The software can be improved by implementing any of the following options:

- Share scopes (the 80/20 rule).
- Modify lease expiration. (If the expiration is set to a lesser time frame, the DHCP will be contacted more often to renew leases, which causes more overhead. On the other hand, if the expiration time is increased too much, the DHCP server will have less of a load, but some IP addresses will be unavailable until the lease time expires.)

Practice Questions

Case Study

Current LAN/Network Structure

2Market currently has two subnets. One subnet is for the IT department. All servers are located on the IT department subnet so that the servers can be kept in a locked and restricted room, and for backup and restore purposes. The other subnet is composed of the rest of the 2Market network. This subnet has roughly 600 TCP/IP devices (computers, printers, and so on).

Proposed LAN/Network Structure

2Market would like to isolate the sales department on its own subnet.

Current WAN Connectivity

None at the current time.

Proposed WAN Connectivity

2Market would like its traveling sales force to be able to dial in remotely to the sales subnet.

DHCP Design Commentary

The IT department has its own addressing scheme for its subnet. The current DHCP server is a member server that is also hosting an SQL database.

IT Manager

The IT department needs to keep all servers containing data in the locked server room. If a server does not need to be backed up during the daily backup routine, it can be outside the server room.

The IT department's subnet is isolated from the rest of the network by an older router that does not support BOOTP. New equipment will be purchased to isolate the sales department.

Sales Manager

The sales department needs to be accessible to sales reps so that they can enter orders and check on order status when out of town. The department needs to be isolated from the rest of the network to minimize traffic. Any servers it may use for external accessibility will not store any data. The sales department consists of 75 employees, who are currently part of the main subnet.

Current Internet Positioning

2Market is registered as **2Market.com**. 2Market does not currently sell mechandise on its Web site.

Future Internet Plans

No changes are proposed at the current time.

Question 1

Implementing the least number of servers, how many DHCP servers and relay agents are needed?

- ❍ a. 1 DHCP server, 1 relay agent
- ❍ b. 1 DHCP server, 2 relay agents
- ❍ c. 2 DHCP servers, 1 relay agent
- ❍ d. 2 DHCP servers, 2 relay agents

The answer is a. Since the IT department is already using a DHCP server that has data on it and cannot be moved and the router is non-BOOTP enabled, a relay agent is needed for the other two subnets, which will be divided by a newer router (with BOOTP).

Question 2

In the current configuration with all of the required scopes, what is the least number of DHCP servers that can be implemented to support this design?

- ❍ a. 1
- ❍ b. 2
- ❍ c. 3
- ❍ d. 4

The answer is a. One scope will be created for the IT department and another for the rest of the network. Since multiple scopes can reside on one DHCP server one server is sufficient for company needs. Two or more DHCP servers would just add fault tolerance for the DHCP services.

Question 3

If there were no specifications on server security, what options would be available for setting up redundancy on the DHCP servers? [Choose all that apply]

- ❑ a. Subnet the network.
- ❑ b. Install a second DHCP server.
- ❑ c. Use the 80/20 rule.
- ❑ d. Cluster the DHCP server.

The answers are b, c, and d. Installing a second DHCP server and using the 80/20 rule would allow the network to remain functional if one server failed. The 80/20 rule places 80 percent of a subnet's addresses on one server and the other 20 percent on another. On the IT subnet without BOOTP, clustering the DHCP server would make DHCP redundant on the IT subnet.

Question 4

2Market currently uses a Unix server as the DNS server. Without replacing the Unix server, how can you enable a DHCP server to work with the DNS server? [Choose all that apply]

- ❑ a. Enable dynamic DNS updates for systems that do not support dynamic updates
- ❑ b. Unplug the Unix server
- ❑ c. Make the Unix server a secondary DNS server to the Windows 2000 DNS primary server
- ❑ d. Do nothing

The answers are a and c. Enabling dynamic updates on a Windows 2000 DHCP server will let it automatically update the DNS services on the Unix server. If the Unix server is a secondary DNS server to the Windows 2000 DNS servers, it will receive a copy of the DNS database from the Windows 2000 DNS servers. Answer b is incorrect because the owners do not want the Unix boxes replaced. Answer d will have no effect because the Unix server will not receive any updates.

Question 5

If all computers in the 2Market network are running Windows 2000, and the laptops (which are not being upgraded) for the sales department are running Windows 98, what can be done to enable different configurations for local and remote users? [Choose all that apply]

- ❑ a. Employ user options
- ❑ b. Employ Multicast scope
- ❑ c. Disable DHCP
- ❑ d. Employ vendor options

The answers are a and d. The Windows 2000 clients can employ user options, and the Windows 98 and 2000 clients can use vendor options. Multicast scopes are used when multicasting. Disabling DHCP would have adverse effects on the current configuration.

Question 6

If, to improve performance, the DHCP server were moved to the non-IT and non-Sales subnets and a DHCP Relay Agent were placed on the IT subnet, would this new design be functional? Yes or no?

- ❍ a. Yes
- ❍ b. No

The answer is a, yes. DHCP Relay Agent will allow the IT department to receive DHCP addresses. The other router is BOOTP enabled, so the DHCP server will be accessible by all DHCP clients.

Question 7

In the current configuration, how does DHCP Relay Agent contact the DHCP server for a lease?

- ❍ a. Through broadcasts
- ❍ b. By querying the DHCP server using its IP address
- ❍ c. By submitting a specialized packet to the router
- ❍ d. By getting an address from its own assigned scope

The answer is b. When DHCP Relay Agent is installed, the IP address of the DHCP server is manually configured. Thus, Relay Agent can send a request packet directly to the DHCP server instead of using a broadcast, which will not cross the non-BOOTP enabled router. Relay Agent sends a standard TCP/IP packet to the router that is addressed with the DHCP server's IP address. No specialized packets are used. Relay Agent has no configured scopes; only the DHCP server has scopes.

Question 8

The president of 2Market wants to have a monthly or quarterly update sent over the network to all employees at once by video. What option would be used?

- ❍ a. User options
- ❍ b. Multicast scopes
- ❍ c. Gateways
- ❍ d. Vendor options

The answer is b. Video streaming to computers is called multicasting, and a multicast scope is required to assign multicast addresses.

Question 9

How would you design the network? Place each label in its appropriate position on the diagram. Options are used only once, and not all options will be used.

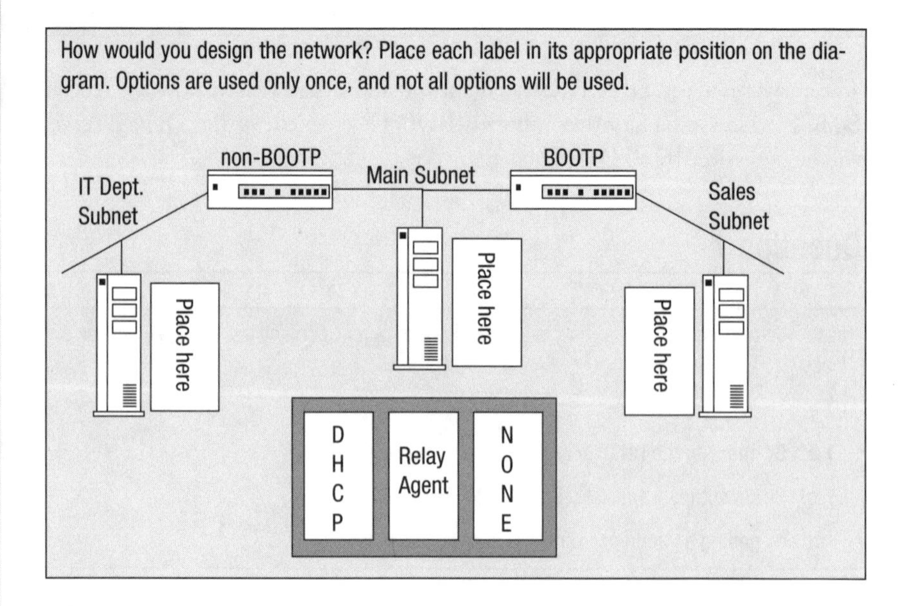

The answer is:

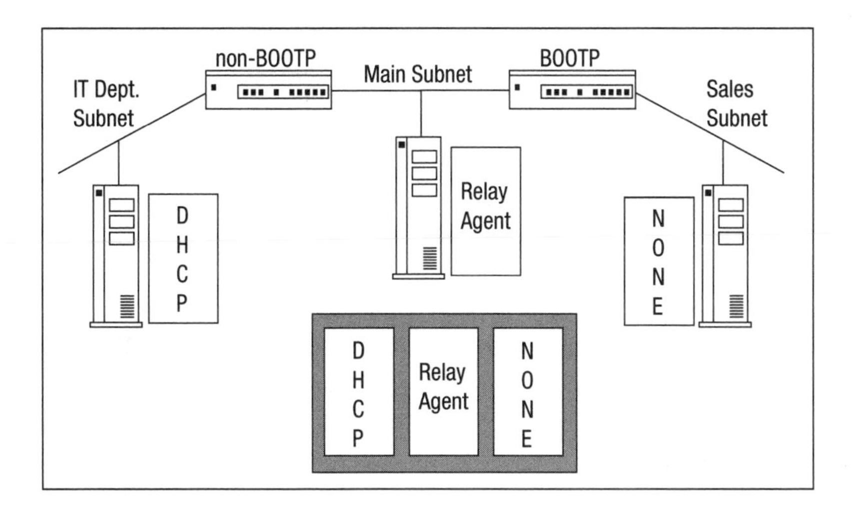

The DHCP server is used on the IT subnet since it has data on it. A relay agent would be used for the remaining subnets (preferably placed on the main subnet since there are more DHCP clients).

Question 10

In the proposed network configuration, the sales department will have a RAS server. It wants to implement 15 dial-in connections from the local phone company. How many total addresses will the RAS server require?

- ❍ a. 11
- ❍ b. 15
- ❍ c. 16
- ❍ d. 18

The answer is c. A RAS server using dial-in connections will request one address for its network interface and one for every dial-in connection, which would equal 16.

Need to Know More?

Novosel, Gary, Kurt Hudson, and James Michael Stewart. *MCSE TCP/IP Exam Cram 3E*. The Coriolis Group, Scottsdale, AZ, 2000. ISBN 1-57610-677-2. Guide to TCP/IP for Windows NT 4.

Parker, Timothy. *TCP/IP Unleashed*. Sams Publishing, Indianapolis, IN, 1996. ISBN 0-672-30603-4. Chapter 31, "DHCP and WINS", has extensive information on DHCP, configuration, and options.

Search the TechNet CD (or its online version through **www.microsoft.com**) and the *Windows NT Server Resource Kit* CD using the keyword "DHCP". Also see the Windows 2000 Server or Advanced Server help.

DNS

Terms you'll need to understand:

- ✓ Domain Name System (DNS) namespace
- ✓ Berkeley Internet Naming Domain (BIND)
- ✓ Request for Comment (RFC)
- ✓ Zone
- ✓ Screened subnets
- ✓ Resolver
- ✓ Forwarder
- ✓ Slave
- ✓ Zone delegation

Techniques you'll need to master:

- ✓ Mapping out your network to view connections
- ✓ Implementing DNS name resolution with recursion and iteration
- ✓ Working with different versions of DNS
- ✓ Integrating DNS with Active Directory in Windows 2000

Designing an effective Domain Name System (DNS) solution can be difficult simply because it has grown so complicated over the past few years. The DNS service now has more than 10 Requests for Comments that define the service. This difficulty is compounded by the fact that different operating systems can have their own version of DNS. Although the basics of the DNS service remain the same, its importance in the network infrastructure has grown: DNS is now the primary name-resolution service in Windows 2000. Also, DNS is a required service for most network configurations in Windows 2000.

Design Issues for DNS

Because of the difference in domains between Windows NT and Windows 2000, many networks may require a redesign of—or at least additions to—the DNS namespace. In Windows 2000, the nature of a Microsoft directory services domain has changed. In Windows NT, the domains used NetBIOS names instead of DNS. Because the NT and DNS domains used separate naming systems, many companies had two unrelated naming conventions: one for NT domains and one for DNS domains. Windows 2000 uses DNS as its primary name-resolution service because its directory services no longer need NetBIOS—and therefore no longer need NetBIOS names.

The Importance of a Network Diagram

Before you start designing a DNS solution for a network, you should have an overview of what the network looks like. Because the features available in DNS have grown more complicated, DNS needs to be designed from a high level to ensure availability, security, and optimized performance. It also must be robust enough to handle the added traffic from Windows 2000 clients. Most networks have a network diagram, even though it may date back to when the network was first installed. You don't need a complicated or professionally designed diagram; in fact, a simple one will be much easier to work from. Figure 5.1 serves as an example.

You will add more to this diagram as your DNS system develops, but, to get started, you need to include only the following elements:

- Local area network (LAN) locations
- Number of clients at each LAN location
- Wide area network (WAN) connections
    - Speed of WAN connections
    - Type of connectivity device (such as router, bridge, or switch)

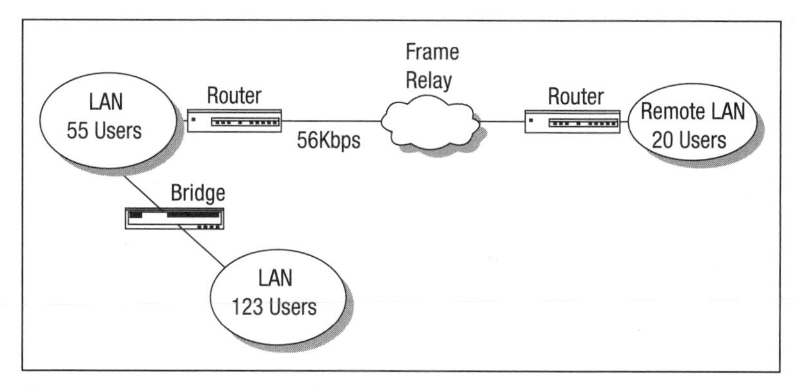

Figure 5.1 A simple drawing of a network and connections, including concentrations of users.

Documenting Your DNS Server Types

Even if a DNS system is currently in place (as is the case in most networks today), any updates or modifications to the network infrastructure call for another look at the DNS system currently in place. Keep this in mind because the changes in the directory services for Windows 2000 put a heavier burden on your DNS system. Also, DNS now has features that optimize network usage and add security. So, you must redesign the current system to take advantage of these features.

The Different Faces of DNS

The Windows 2000 DNS Server is capable of implementing DNS in three different ways: a Berkeley Internet Naming Domain (BIND), Windows NT 4, or Windows 2000 DNS Server. This flexibility allows it to more easily integrate with other types of DNS servers and clients. Because it can interact with down-level clients and servers, Windows 2000 DNS Server does not require that the whole environment be upgraded whenever it is added to an existing DNS system.

A Request for Comment (RFC) is a document that outlines standards for Internet services. Currently, Windows 2000 supports 8 of the 10 RFCs that define the DNS service. (The Windows NT 4 DNS Server supported only two.) Of course, compliance with an RFC does not mean that a DNS server stays within the bounds of the RFC. BIND, Windows NT 4, and Windows 2000 DNS servers all have features outside of the RFCs that they support.

The BIND standard is the most common standard for the implementation of a DNS server. BIND allows DNS servers to communicate and resolve hostnames among themselves even if they are running on different operating systems. Microsoft's DNS servers are automatically BIND-compliant when installed. However, when developing the code for its first DNS server in Windows NT 4, Microsoft decided to write its own code instead of adopting the BIND code. The company had different ideas for extra features that it wanted to include in its own DNS server, and writing its own code was the easiest way to do this. Microsoft's extra features are mainly DNS-to-WINS resolution in Windows NT 4 DNS and Active Directory integration in Windows 2000 DNS.

BIND Compliance

BIND exists in different versions. The DNS service in Windows NT 4 most closely follows the standard for BIND version 4.9.6. This version and Windows NT support only static updates to the DNS database, which means its database does not accept updates from another service. Also, BIND 4.9.6 and Windows NT DNS service use full-zone transfers. Zones and zone transfers will be covered later in this chapter. When a primary DNS server replicates its database to a secondary server, the full database—not just the updates—is copied over.

BIND 8.1.2 has many features in common with Windows 2000 DNS. Both support dynamic updates to the DNS database, and both support incremental instead of full-zone transfers. Although your non-Microsoft DNS servers can be integrated into your DNS structure, you will need to check the version of BIND that they support to find what features will be supported.

Adding to Your Network Diagram

Because different versions of DNS servers support different features, you must overlay the locations and types of DNS servers onto your network diagram. This overlay allows you to see what types of features you can implement, and it also reveals if your current DNS servers need to be upgraded.

Additions to your DNS network diagram include:

- Overlay of current DNS infrastructure
    - Locations of current DNS servers
    - Type of DNS server (such as Windows NT 4, non-Windows DNS servers)
    - BIND version of non-Windows DNS servers

Documenting Your DNS Client Types

Now that you have documented your DNS server operating systems, you need to note the operating systems of your DNS clients. You don't need to write each client onto the diagram because DNS servers can provide down-level services. Noting client types will help you to see your administrative overhead for the DNS system that you are designing. All you have to do is to put your clients into one of three categories: non-Microsoft, Windows 2000, and Microsoft clients that are not Windows 2000.

Windows 2000 clients and BIND 8.1.2 clients support dynamic updates to the DNS database, thus eliminating the need for a person to update records in the DNS database (and thus easing a large administrative burden if you are using DHCP on your network). Previous Windows and non-Microsoft clients supporting BIND 4.9.6 will not be able to directly update the DNS database. However, if they are DHCP clients, the Windows 2000 DHCP server can be set to send the updated DNS records to the DNS server instead.

So, the last information for the network diagram is:

- Operating system of DNS clients
- BIND version of non-Windows DNS clients
- Preferred and alternate DNS server for each computer

Marking the preferred and alternate servers for each client will show how the DNS service load is balanced. Ensuring a balanced load will help the performance of the DNS servers on the network. Seeing the preferred and alternate DNS servers will also allow the service designer to better distribute clients to new DNS servers that are added to the design of the DNS system.

Note: Because DNS and Active Directory both use the DNS namespace, you must first decide how to integrate the namespace for the two services. This section of the book refers only to DNS namespace issues, which is not the same as Active Directory-integrated zones. Active Directory integration changes the features that DNS can support in Windows 2000, and this topic is discussed later in the chapter.

Integration of Active Directory and DNS

Now that you have a complete and usable network diagram, you must design DNS to integrate with any DNS or Active Directory services that already exist in the network. A network's previous configuration can affect the DNS design in Windows 2000 because the naming convention for Active Directory has changed. Four categories describe the different possible configurations from which a network can start, and each requires a different approach:

- You have no previous DNS configuration (or you are willing to start over).
- Active Directory and DNS will use the same namespace.
- Active Directory and DNS namespace will not overlap.
- Active Directory will integrate with non-Microsoft DNS servers.

Active Directory requires DNS as its name-resolution service and will not install without a DNS server on the network. Because Active Directory uses DNS namespace rules, you must decide when Active Directory is implemented on a network whether DNS and Active Directory will use the same namespace.

No DNS or Starting Over

The ideal situation is to have no previous DNS configuration or to be able to start over and design a new DNS system and namespace. In this case, you could install the first DNS server during the upgrade to Active Directory on your network. Starting over is a possibility for a Windows NT 4 network that implemented Microsoft DNS servers and used DNS-to-WINS resolution. In such a case, the DNS service may not have been greatly developed. However, it is not necessary to start over when implementing Active Directory on a Windows 2000 network. Most networks are more heterogeneous and could have non-Microsoft DNS servers. Keeping the old DNS system in place and integrating with Windows 2000 simply requires more decisions before implementing.

Same Namespace

Another easy answer to Active Directory implementation is to use the same DNS namespace for Active Directory and DNS. In this case, a Windows 2000 server has to be the root DNS server for the domain. This root DNS server would be authoritative for the domain. In this scenario the root server must be a Windows 2000 DNS server, but other DNS servers can be Windows NT 4 and non-Windows, BIND-compliant DNS servers. These other DNS servers can be integrated into the Active Directory DNS system.

Different Namespace

DNS does not have to be redesigned or changed when implementing Active Directory in Windows 2000. Active Directory can be implemented as a subdomain in the current DNS infrastructure. In this configuration, some or even none of the DNS servers need to be on an Active Directory server. If no Active Directory servers are used in the DNS infrastructure, the only restriction is that Windows NT 4 cannot be used as the root DNS server for Active Directory. Active Directory requires DNS servers that support service (SRV) records, and BIND-compliant DNS servers that support versions 4.9.6 and 8.1.2 and up support SRV records. SRV records are used to register network services in DNS. One way that Windows 2000 computers use SRV record queries in DNS is to locate a domain controller for a network logon. DNS record types are covered later in this chapter.

Integration with non-Microsoft DNS Servers

It is important to remember that Active Directory can be integrated with non-Microsoft DNS servers. For test purposes, non-Microsoft DNS servers do not have to be changed to the Microsoft DNS service. In order for this scenario to work, you must install a Windows 2000 standalone server. Then, you need to install DNS on the Windows 2000 server and create a secondary zone to an existing primary zone. Your final step will be to implement Active Directory, which you'll achieve by promoting a Windows 2000 server to a domain controller. You did not change the existing DNS infrastructure or namespace and you still fulfilled the requirements for having DNS in an Active Directory environment.

In the preceding case, the existing primary DNS server must support SRV records. SRV records are supported by BIND-compliant servers 4.9.6 and above. Active Directory must have DNS servers that support SRV records. Record types are covered later in this chapter.

Zones

The next step in designing a DNS system is to determine which type of zone works best for the network. A DNS database is only authoritative for some records. This authority over records is established by creating a zone. A zone file contains the database of resource records for a DNS server. DNS zones and domains do not have to be equal. In fact, a zone can contain more than one domain as long as the domains are contiguous in the DNS namespace. For example, a zone can contain records from the domain sales.Microsoft.com and east.sales.Microsoft.com. The root domain would be sales.Microsoft.com, and records for east.sales. Microsoft.com could be included in the zone. However, one zone created for records from inside.sales.Microsoft.com as the root could not contain records from outside.sales.Microsoft.com. These two subdomains are not contiguous with each other.

A zone database file is named after its root domain with the addition of the ".dns" extension. So, sales.Microsoft.com would have a zone file named "sales.Microsoft.com.dns" by default.

Configuring a zone is not required for a DNS server to work. A DNS server with no configured zones is referred to as a *caching-only* DNS server. Later in the chapter we will discuss how to improve performance by adding caching-only servers to a DNS design.

Zone Types

When creating a zone, it must be defined as either a standard primary, standard secondary, or Active Directory-integrated zone. A primary zone is said to be authoritative because it is where the records for the zone were created. A secondary zone is simply a copy of a primary zone's database received through a zone transfer. Any zone that is set up to transfer to a secondary zone is considered to be a master zone. Master zones can be primary, secondary, or Active Directory-integrated zones. If the master zone is unavailable or the network connection is down, the secondary will not receive the update. This is referred to as a single point of failure. Active Directory-integrated zones use Windows 2000 Active Directory services to update other DNS servers. How DNS zone information is transferred between DNS servers is the main difference between using standard and Active Directory-integrated zones. Microsoft recommends using Active Directory-integrated zones on Windows 2000 DNS domain controllers, because the transfer of DNS information is included in normal Active Directory updates. This is beneficial to your network for two reasons. First, DNS will not be transferred as a separate service on the network, which can lower network traffic. Second, all Active Directory-integrated DNS servers will accept updates from other domain controller DNS servers. Active Directory-integrated zones eliminate the need for primary and secondary DNS server roles and so eliminate the single point of failure that can occur in a standard DNS zone.

The downside of Active Directory-integrated zones is that they must be Windows 2000 domain controllers. However, Active Directory-integrated zones can work with standard DNS zones. Active Directory-integrated zones can be set up as master zones for standard secondary zones in non-Windows 2000 DNS servers. This means that you can have some Active Directory-integrated zones in your DNS infrastructure mixed in with standard zones in Windows NT 4 and non-Microsoft DNS servers. Also, zones can be changed from standard to Active Directory-integrated and back, which allows a flexible DNS design that can be upgraded to Active Directory-integrated zones in stages.

Resource Records

Zones contain resource records. Although mappings of hostnames to IP addresses is the most common type of DNS resource record, a DNS database can actually contain many types of records. Table 5.1 lists often-used resource records and their purposes.

How to Get Records into Your Zone File

Windows 2000 DNS server supports dynamic and static updates to the DNS database. Until fairly recently, administrators had to update the DNS database manually. (This is called a *static update* because it is performed manually by a person instead of automatically by the system.) Outside of RFC compliance, Windows NT 4 added an extra feature that served as a workaround for static updates. It allowed DNS to ask WINS when it did not have the resource record. Because WINS is a dynamically updated name-resolution service, it gave the DNS database the appearance of being dynamic. This feature is still available in Windows 2000 DNS, but Windows 2000 DNS also allows for true dynamic

Table 5.1 Common resource records and their purposes.

Resource Record Name	Purpose of Record
SOA (Start of Authority)	Identifies the zone as the primary name server and therefore the best source of records for the zone. The first record created in a zone.
NS (Name Server)	Identifies the DNS server as authoritative for the domain. Can be the primary or secondary server.
A (Address)	Host record containing mappings of hostname to IP address.
PTR (Pointer)	Used for reverse lookups in which a client has an IP address and needs to find the domain name.
SRV (Service Location)	Allows a domain controller to register available services in DNS. Clients can then query DNS to locate services like domain controllers on the network. Required record in an Active Directory-integrated zone and in a DNS server supporting Windows 2000 domain controllers.
MX (Mail Exchanger)	Used to locate a mail server on the network.
WINS and WINS-R	Used by DNS to integrate with WINS. The WINS record is for WINS forward lookups, and the WINS-R record is for reverse WINS lookups. Microsoft DNS in versions NT 4 and 2000 are the only DNS servers that support WINS lookup by a DNS server. Other DNS servers do not support the WINS and WINS-R resource records.

updates. DNS can now communicate with the DHCP server and Windows 2000 clients for updates. So, your choices for record additions to your DNS zone file are manual, DNS passing queries to WINS, or dynamic updates from Windows 2000 clients or the DHCP server.

Designing for Dynamic Updates

Dynamic updates are the recommended configuration for DHCP and DNS because of the lowered administrative and query overhead. Even in a mixed environment, Dynamic DNS (DDNS) can still be set up. The default setting for both Windows 2000 DHCP server and DNS clients is for the DNS client to update its own A record. By default, the DHCP server updates the PTR record for even DHCP clients. (Although this is the default setting, the DHCP server can be set up to update both records.)

Designing a Secure DNS System

When implementing changes that are new to DNS, security becomes an issue. In a static DNS environment, only the administrator of the DNS database handled DNS records. Now, because the records can be updated over network connections, impersonation can be a problem. Also, security within a local network isn't a big concern when transferring zones, but DNS works over WAN connections. Zone transfers can even take place over the Internet through Virutal Private Networks (VPNs). Some of the new features in the DNS service help alleviate these security issues.

Using Access Control Lists (ACLs) in DNS

Dynamic updates to the DNS server reduce the administrative overhead of the DNS service. They also allow for DNS and DHCP services to finally work well together on a network. Windows 2000 and BIND-compliant 8.1.2 DNS clients and servers support dynamic updates to DNS, which is referred to as DDNS. As we mentioned, one security problem with dynamic updates is the impersonation of a DNS client, which could reveal IP information or, even worse, change the zone database file.

Windows 2000 DNS server introduces Secure Dynamic Update to make dynamic updates secure. With Secure Dynamic Update, access control lists (ACLs) are used to check the permissions of DNS clients when they update their DNS records. Upon first registration, a permission is set on a DNS record that allows the record to be changed from only the originating client's computer account. Any other client trying to update the record is denied permission to make the change.

Secure Dynamic Update is available only in Active Directory-integrated zones and is enabled by default when an Active Directory-integrated zone is created.

Screened Subnets

Because DNS works as a distributed service, each domain is responsible for providing its own DNS database for the Internet's use. So, users from the Internet may need access to the DNS database on your local network. A screened subnet is created by setting up firewalls between a private network and a public network, such as the Internet. A firewall protects the private network by stopping all incoming connections except those specifically allowed. Any information in your network that needs to be accessed by external clients via the Internet is vulnerable to attack. To protect the internal network, this information needs to be separated from it. A separate DNS server containing only those records that are needed by Internet clients can be separated from the internal network with a screened subnet. As shown in Figure 5.2, a screened subnet protects the DNS server from Internet use by placing it between two firewalls. The second firewall protects the internal network not only from the Internet but also from the users of the DNS server.

However, using firewalls to protect the DNS server and the internal network may not be enough. Because the DNS server in the screened subnet is vulnerable

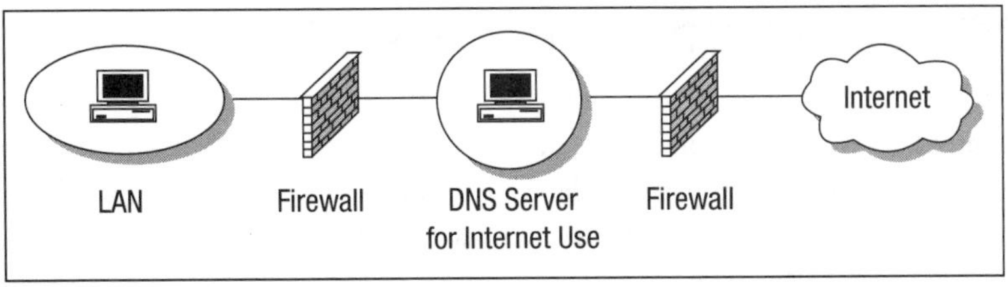

Figure 5.2 Example of a screened subnet.

to attack, more steps need to be taken to protect it. Using a separate namespace from your internal network can help. A DNS server for use on the Internet should contain only that information that is needed on the Internet and should never contain information about internal resources. Also, it is best not to use Active Directory-integrated zones on a screened subnet. Because Active directory-integrated zones can be implemented on only Windows 2000 domain controllers, this leaves valuable information open to attack. Standard secondary servers are best to use in this situation, because they have a read-only zone database file. Secondary servers accept updates from only their master server.

Encrypting Zone Transfers

If the screened subnet DNS server is a secondary, it gets its information from a master server in the internal network. Although the zone transfer is the only data coming from the internal network, even that can present a security risk. A good way to minimize this risk is to encrypt the zone transfer, and this best done by implementing a VPN with IPSec encryption.

Forwarding, Forwarder, and Slave Servers

You can protect the internal network through the use of forwarding, forwarder, and slave servers. The internal DNS server and the DNS server in the screened subnet actually can fill all three roles. The point of using these types of servers is to keep the IP address of the internal DNS server hidden from the Internet. First, have the internal DNS server forward queries that it cannot resolve internally to the DNS server in the screened subnet. At this point, the internal DNS server becomes the forwarding DNS server, and the screened subnet DNS server becomes the forwarder. By default, DNS servers that do not receive a complete response from their forwarder start to perform their own queries to complete the name resolution. Allowing the internal DNS server to make its own queries compromises it. To avoid this, make the internal DNS server a slave to its forwarder, thus forcing it to accept the answer from the forwarder and keeping it from performing its own queries.

Increasing DNS Performance

Security usually degrades performance on a network, but part of the features enhancements in Windows 2000 can increase performance and availability. Even if a DNS infrastructure is already in place, the implementation of Windows 2000 and Active Directory causes not just Internet services but nearly all network services to use DNS as the primary name-resolution service. This places a substantial new burden on the existing DNS system. New and existing DNS infrastructures need to be designed or redesigned to increase client availability and optimize performance.

One DNS Server per Location

One DNS server can support many clients. In earlier Windows environments DNS resolution may have even taken place over a WAN connection because use of the service was only needed for Internet services. Now that the importance of DNS has changed, it is better to place at least one DNS server per LAN location and to avoid DNS resolution over WAN links. DNS resolution will cause a lot more traffic in a Windows 2000 network, and additional DNS servers will be needed to handle the extra load.

Zone Delegation

DNS databases are parsed, read top to bottom, like many reference files on the network. Reducing the file size increases performance for clients making queries. Zone delegation is simply the process of creating more DNS zone files so that they will each have fewer entries and therefore have quicker responses when queried. Creating more domains is one way to increase zone files, but, because zones and domains are not equal, it is not the only way. Four to five subdomains down from a second-level domain are all that is recommended.

In a Windows NT 4 environment, administrators were encouraged to have high-level DNS servers only and then to pass DNS queries to WINS. Zone delegation and the creation of more zone files are ideal for this environment.

Load Balance Client Requests

Increasing zone transfers and copying a database file to secondary zones is another way to create more zones. One primary zone can send a transfer to more than one secondary, and secondary zones can also be master zones performing zone transfers. Increasing the number of secondary zones makes them available on more servers for load balancing. In Figure 5.4, DNS1 is a primary DNS zone. DNS1 does a zone transfer to DNS2 making DNS1 the master server for the zone transfer and making DNS2 a secondary zone. DNS2 then is set up to do a zone transfer to DNS3. For this zone transfer DNS2 is the master. DNS3 is still considered to be a secondary zone because it contains a copy of the zone instead of the original database file.

Creating more DNS servers and zones allows administrators to change the preferred and alternate DNS servers for clients on different parts of the network. Because implementing Windows 2000 and Active Directory results in more DNS requests, DNS client requests should be spread over more DNS servers and zones. The network diagram should be used to see if clients are evenly spread over the available DNS servers. The diagram will also show where another DNS server may be needed to lighten the query load on existing servers.

Use Caching-Only Servers

Although the DNS service has no zones configured when it is first loaded, it can still act as a DNS server. A DNS server with no configured zones is referred to as a *caching-only* DNS server, and such servers can increase performance by working as forwarders. Internal DNS servers can pass their requests on to the caching-only DNS server, which then can pass it out to the Internet and perform the needed queries. The caching-only server will cache the resolved query for, by default, 60 minutes. If it receives another query, it may be able to resolve it through cache instead of having to perform queries.

You can also use caching-only DNS servers in your internal network. The service can be added to an existing server without causing too much of a performance drain on its current services. Adding a caching-only server can increase the number of DNS servers available to the whole network and add to the performance of the DNS system.

Practice Questions

Case Study

The Bongo Drum Company is based in Kalamazoo, MI, and has 300 hosts divided into 2 subnets. The corporate office is located in Kalamazoo and has 45 hosts. The manufacturing plant in Little Rock has 28 hosts.

Current WAN Structure

The network has two locations.

Proposed WAN Structure

The company is growing and the addition of another location is planned in Mobile, AL.

Current WAN Connectivity

Currently, two locations are connected through a 56Kbps modem.

Proposed WAN Connectivity

While planning for the addition of a third location, the company is looking into using the Internet as a connection between its different locations. This seems to be the least expensive alternative for connecting all locations.

Current Internet Usage

The company uses an ISP to provide company employees with connections to the Internet.

Proposed Internet Plans

The company would like to create a Web site and needs to provide a way to allow Internet users to connect to the Web site while keeping the private network secure.

Company Windows 2000 Goal

The client computers have already been upgraded to Windows 2000 Professional. Although the servers are still a mix of Windows NT 4 and Unix, the plan is to upgrade the NT 4 servers to Windows 2000 Server using Active Directory for directory services. Figure 5.3 shows the company's network with the proposed Internet Connection.

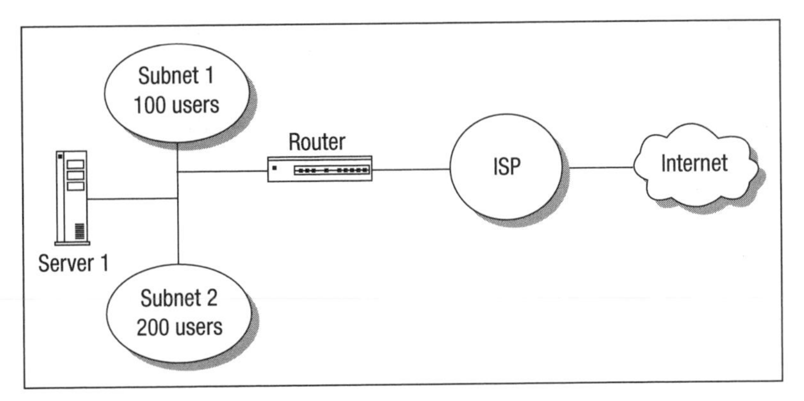

Figure 5.3 A domain with four subdomains.

Question 1

The company is planning an upgrade to a Windows 2000 network that uses Active Directory services. Active Directory requires a DNS server on the network. Currently, Unix DNS servers are providing DNS services to the network. Since the current DNS infrastructure is working well, many at the company do not want to change it or add any DNS servers to it. What is the easiest way to accommodate their wishes and still upgrade to Active Directory? [Check all correct answers]

- ❑ a. This is not possible.
- ❑ b. Set up a local DNS server on a Windows 2000 server before promoting to a domain controller.
- ❑ c. Install DNS during the promotion of the Windows 2000 server to a domain controller.
- ❑ d. Make the DNS a secondary zone to an existing primary zone.
- ❑ e. Create a new DNS subdomain for the Active Directory DNS.

Answers b and d are correct. Windows 2000 using Active Directory requires the DNS service. However, since Windows 2000 Active Directory uses an RFC compliant DNS service, it can work with any DNS server that is RFC compliant. It does not have to interact with a Microsoft DNS server. If it is decided that the current DNS structure should not be changed, a secondary zone needs to be created. If DNS is not yet installed on a Windows 2000 server when it is promoted to a domain controller, then the domain controller will install the DNS service locally and automatically create an Active Directory-integrated zone.

Question 2

While adding Active Directory to the network, an administrator installs a DNS server locally while a Windows 2000 server is upgrading to a domain controller. What type of zone was created by default?

❍ a. Master

❍ b. Primary

❍ c. Secondary

❍ d. Active Directory-integrated

Answer d is correct. When upgrading a Windows 2000 server to a domain controller, Active Directory services require a DNS server. If during the upgrade you elect to install the DNS service locally on the domain controller, it will automatically create an Active Directory-integrated zone.

Question 3

Now that the network has an Active Directory-integrated zone, what features will that zone support that are not supported by other types of DNS zones and servers? [Check all correct answers]

❑ a. Dynamic updates

❑ b. SRV record support

❑ c. Secure Dynamic Updates

❑ d. DHCP Server integration

Answer c is correct. All of these services are supported by a Windows 2000 DNS Active Directory-integrated zone, but most of these services are also supported by BIND DNS servers. Dynamic updates and incremental zone transfers are supported starting in BIND version 8.1.2 compliant servers. SRV record support began in BIND version 4.9.6. The only service not yet supported by other DNS servers is Secure Dynamic Updates.

Question 4

After implementing Active Directory, the company wants to set up DNS so that the internal DNS server resolves queries for internal computers, and Internet queries are directed to the ISP's DNS server. How can this set be up?

- ❍ a. Make your internal DNS server a slave to the ISP's DNS server.
- ❍ b. Set the clients' preferred DNS server to the internal DNS server and the alternate to the ISP's DNS server.
- ❍ c. Make the internal DNS server a forwarder for the ISP's DNS server.
- ❍ d. Make the internal DNS server a master to the ISP's DNS server.

Answer a is correct. You need to stop the internal DNS server from making queries on the Internet. Making the ISP's DNS server an alternate for the clients will work only if the internal DNS server is not responding to the client request. By default, the internal DNS server will attempt to make queries on the Internet. The only way to block that action is to make the internal DNS server a slave to the ISP's server. First, you will set the internal DNS server to forward queries to the ISP's DNS server. In this case the internal DNS server is the forwarding server, and the ISP's DNS server is the forwarder. This is why c is not the correct answer. To make the internal DNS server a slave to the ISP's DNS server, you would not allow the internal DNS server to make its own queries if the ISP's DNS server returns a "host not found" response to the forwarded query.

Question 5

Users in subnet 2 are complaining of slow connections to internal resources. An administrator finds that the problem is slow name resolution. Without adding another DNS server, what can be done to help resolve this problem?

- ❍ a. Use WINS resolution.
- ❍ b. Implement dynamic updates to the DNS server.
- ❍ c. Create a separate zone for subnet 2.
- ❍ d. Use reverse lookups.

Answer c is correct. Without installing a new local DNS server the only answer that will help optimize DNS traffic is to create separate zones in the DNS server for subnets 1 and 2. Each zone file will be smaller and therefore be read more quickly to resolve client requests. WINS resolution will make no difference, because Windows 2000 Professional clients are using DNS instead of WINS. Dynamic updates are implemented by default on a Windows 2000 DNS client, and reverse lookups will slow down the network even more. Also, reverse lookups are used by security services and applications and not by individual DNS clients.

Question 6

The company is ready to add another remote location to the network and wants to use the Internet as the WAN connection. The location will have 10 users, and the decision is made to give them their own DNS server. An administrator wants to set up a zone transfer between locations but is concerned about internal DNS information getting out on the Internet. How can this be set up in a secure manner? [Check all correct answers]

- ❑ a. Set up SSL for the transfer.
- ❑ b. Set up a VPN using IPSec for encryption.
- ❑ c. Set up Secure Dynamic Update.
- ❑ d. Make the internal DNS server a master to the remote DNS server.

Answers b and d are correct. First, make the internal DNS server a master to the remote DNS server. This will cause a zone transfer from the internal DNS server to the remote DNS server, making the remote DNS server a secondary zone to the internal DNS server. To protect the information sent between the internal and remote networks, you need to set up a VPN using IPSec as the encryption protocol. SSL is used to encrypt Web pages in a Web site, and Secure Dynamic Update deals with dynamic updates to the DNS server from DNS clients. SSL does not deal with zone transfers, and it does not encrypt information.

Question 7

The company is ready to deploy its new Web site and decides to have an ISP host the Web site. However, it also decides to discontinue DNS services with the ISP and provide its own DNS services to incoming Internet client requests. How can this be set up while still protecting the internal network from attack?

- ❍ a. Do nothing. Your VPN with IPSec will protect your internal network.
- ❍ b. Add another DNS server for Internet clients, and make it a slave to the internal DNS server.
- ❍ c. Add another DNS server for Internet clients, and implement Secure Dynamic Updates.
- ❍ d. Create a screened subnet with a separate Internet DNS server between two firewalls.

Answer d is correct. Your VPN encryption is only protecting information transfer between your remote office and your internal network. Adding another DNS server is necessary, but placing the new DNS server in a screened subnet is the best way to protect the internal network. The internal DNS server needs to be a slave to the Internet DNS server instead of the other way around. Secure Dynamic Update is for updates to the DNS database and does not protect against queries.

Question 8

When implemented, the Internet DNS server was created as an Active Directory-integrated zone. Now the design of the DNS service calls for that zone to be a standard primary zone. Is this possible?

❍ a. Yes

❍ b. No

Answer a is correct. Zones can be changed from Active Directory-integrated to standard and can even be changed back again.

Question 9

Users are complaining about slow loading Web pages. After troubleshooting, an administrator decides the problem is slow name resolution. The decision is made to add two more DNS servers, which will make one DNS server for each subnet. What other changes need to be made?

❍ a. Configure the new DNS servers as forwarders to each other.

❍ b. Change the preferred DNS server for each client.

❍ c. Configure the Internet DNS server as a forwarder for each new DNS server.

❍ d. Configure each new DNS server as a caching-only server.

Answer b is correct. Changing the preferred DNS server for each subnet will direct traffic to the new DNS servers. Answers a and c will not reduce traffic or speed up query response. Caching-only servers help DNS performance when used in conjunction with DNS servers that are supporting zones.

Question 10

To give DNS performance an added boost, a caching-only DNS server will be added to the network. What is the best location for this new server?

❍ a. Inside the screened subnet

❍ b. Inside subnet 1

❍ c. Inside subnet 2

❍ d. Inside subnet 3

Answer a is correct. The original problem was slow loading Web pages, which means the DNS server in the screened subnet needs help handling queries.

Need to Know More?

Scheil, Dennis and Diana Bartley. *MCSE Windows 2000 Directory Services Design Exam Cram*. The Coriolis Group, Scottsdale, AZ, October 2000. ISBN 1-57610-714-0. A good source for background information on DNS and its implementation.

Shinder, Debra Littlejohn, Thomas Shinder, and Tony Hinkle. *Managing Windows 2000 Network Services*. Syngress Media, Inc., Rockland, MA, 2000. ISBN 1-92899-406-7. This book provides background on the networking services described in this chapter and shows dialog boxes for implementation hints.

www.microsoft.com/windows2000/library/howitworks/communications/nameadrmgmt/w2kdns.asp. *Windows 2000 DNS*. Microsoft Corporation, Redmond, WA, 1999. This Microsoft white paper describes the changes to the Windows 2000 implementation of DNS.

www.microsoft.com/ntserver/nts/deployment/planguide/dnswp.asp. *DNS and Microsoft Windows NT 4.0*. Microsoft Corporation, Redmond, WA, 1996. This Microsoft white paper explains its implementation of DNS in Windows NT 4.

Search the TechNet CD (or its online version through **www.microsoft.com**) and the *Windows NT Server Resource Kit* CD using the keywords "DDNS", "DNS", "Active Directory-integrated zone", and "DNS namespace".

6

WINS Design

Terms you'll need to understand:

- ✓ Network Basic Input/Output System (NetBIOS) namespace
- ✓ NetBIOS name server (NBNS)
- ✓ Windows Sockets (WinSock)
- ✓ Replication partners
- ✓ Spoke-and-hub design
- ✓ Convergence time
- ✓ Persistent connections
- ✓ Push replication
- ✓ Pull replication
- ✓ Tombstoning

Techniques you'll need to master:

- ✓ Understanding the architecture of Windows Internet Naming Service (WINS)
- ✓ Working with WINS name registration and resolution
- ✓ Designing an effective WINS replication strategy
- ✓ Protecting WINS traffic when using public networks
- ✓ Removing the WINS service from a network

Windows Internet Naming Service (WINS) translates computer names into IP addresses, just like Domain Name Service (DNS) does. The difference between the two services is the type of names that they translate into IP addresses: DNS translates Internet domain names, and WINS translates Network Basic Input/Output System (NetBIOS) names. (Chapter 2 provides an overview of the OSI model and the session-layer changes in Windows 2000.)

Until Windows 2000, Microsoft built its network infrastructure around NetBIOS, which caused a dual personality in its network architecture: If you wanted to use Internet services, you needed DNS for name resolution; if you wanted to use Microsoft services—such as sending a local print job—you needed WINS.

In Windows 2000, the dependence on NetBIOS is gone. Microsoft redesigned all of its core network services to use Windows Sockets (WinSock)—just like the Internet does—as the interface to the network instead of NetBIOS. In fact, in a purely Windows 2000 environment, NetBIOS and the use of NetBIOS names can be turned off completely. Yet, Microsoft still recommends the use of WINS in the Windows 2000 environment for the sake of backward compatibility. It is a time-consuming task to make a complete transformation to an all Windows 2000 environment. Also, some legacy applications may use NetBIOS instead of WinSock. Although NetBIOS went from a required service to a legacy service in one upgrade, WINS is still needed to support legacy clients and applications. Without WINS, the impact on a network can be severe.

WINS Basics

Until NetBIOS is no longer used in your network, you must understand why WINS is necessary for NetBIOS clients. Basically, NetBIOS just doesn't work as well as WinSock in a large network environment. The NetBIOS default name resolution—combined with the namespace that defines the rules for NetBIOS names—causes problems for networks with many nodes. By default, the design of NetBIOS works best in a small networking environment, and WINS allows NetBIOS clients to work in environments larger than just a LAN.

The NetBIOS Namespace

The NetBIOS namespace limits the size of the network on which it can be used. A namespace sets rules for naming computers. The NetBIOS namespace allows only 15 characters for a computer's name. Because each computer name must be unique from all others with which it communicates, you'll find that the possible permutations of a 15-character set are quickly exhausted in a network with tens of thousands of nodes, particularly if you keep the names friendly so that users can easily remember them.

Broadcasts on a Network

A limited namespace is not all that plagues NetBIOS computers on a large network. NetBIOS computers use broadcasting as the default method for resolving names to IP addresses. The problem is that broadcasts do not work well in a large network environment, because a broadcast is just that: a broadcast of a network packet that is not specifically aimed at one computer. Specifically addressed packets are much easier for a networked computer to see if they are intended for it or a different computer on the network. With a specifically addressed packet, a computer can quickly see if it should ignore or process the packet further to find out what data the packet contains.

If you receive mail addressed to you, you open it. If the mail is addressed to someone else, you don't need to be concerned with it. On the other hand, if you receive junk mail addressed to "occupant," you can be fairly sure it's not important and so you discard it. Broadcasts are like junk mail in that they are addressed to no computer in particular. But, because computers cannot throw away a broadcast without reading it the way you do junk mail, each computer must process the packet to find out if it contains data for that computer. It's easy to see how broadcast traffic clogs each computer's network adapter as it tries to process packets that it would be able to ignore if they were specifically addressed to another computer.

WINS reduces broadcasts by giving NetBIOS clients another method of name resolution. Instead of sending a broadcast when trying to locate another computer's IP address, the WINS client can send a directly addressed packet to the WINS server.

Routers and Broadcasts

The other bonus of using WINS instead of broadcasts for name resolution is that it allows name-resolution packets to pass through routers. Figure 6.1 shows how one network that adds a router—placing nodes on each side of the router—actually creates two separate networks. The router filters traffic by allowing only those packets addressed for the other side to pass through. Routers block broadcast

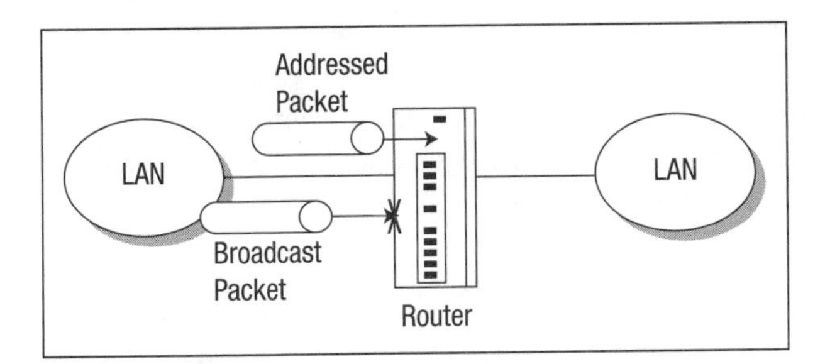

Figure 6.1 A router will allow a packet specifically addressed to a computer in the other part of the network through, but the router will block the NetBIOS broadcast with no specific address.

traffic, by default, by not allowing packets to pass through unless they are specifically addressed for the other side. Because packets sent to and from the WINS server are specifically addressed, the router allows them to pass through.

To fix the broadcast problem for NetBIOS clients, a NetBIOS name server (NBNS) is needed. WINS is Microsoft's version of an NBNS. WINS is still needed until all NetBIOS-dependent clients and applications are replaced on a network. Removing WINS prematurely will cause previous version of Windows and any other NetBIOS clients to resort back to broadcasts for name resolution.

WINS-Provided Services

The design of WINS has always been dynamic and this, of course, has not changed in Windows 2000 WINS. The WINS client software is automatically installed when TCP/IP is installed on a Windows client. The only other setting that is needed for a Microsoft WINS client to work is the IP address of a WINS server. The WINS server IP address can be entered manually or be handed out to the clients by the DHCP server. Once the client has the IP address of the WINS server, it uses the WINS service automatically and broadcasts only if other name-resolution methods (like WINS) fail.

During boot up, a WINS client registers its names with WINS. This registration happens automatically with no intervention from the user or network administrator. A client computer can actually make five or more registrations, not because it has that many computer names but because the WINS service registers more than just generic computer names. WINS registers computer names based on the services that they provide to the network. All Windows 2000 computers will register a computer name for each of the workstation, server, and messenger services as well as the username. Also, a client computer will register as a member of a domain. A domain controller can make 8 to 10 registrations to WINS because it provides more services to the network than a client system does. WINS differentiates between registrations by looking at the 16th character of a NetBIOS name. And this is the reason that NetBIOS computer names can have only 15 characters: The 16th character is reserved to identify the service for which the client is registering. This makes WINS more versatile for the network. A WINS client can query WINS for the IP address of a domain controller or ask for a member of a certain domain or even a username instead of a computer name. All are registered and tracked in the WINS database.

Placing and Configuring WINS Servers

Just like other network services, WINS needs to be designed on paper to create an effective and problem-free WINS solution. Because of the nature of WINS resolution, the placement of servers and the configuration of replication partners can make large differences in the performance of the service.

WINS Name-Resolution Process

Like DNS clients, WINS clients use a query to ask the WINS server for a name-to-IP address translation. The WINS server, like the DNS server, checks its local database of name-to-IP address mappings to resolve the query. But the similarities between the query processes for each end there. DNS servers were designed to work in a WAN environment. To accommodate a large number of computers, the DNS system allows for DNS servers to refer queries to other DNS servers in order to completely resolve them. This procedure is referred to as a *partitioned database.* Figure 6.2 shows an example of a how a partitioned database works in a WAN environment. When referring to the DNS system, it is assumed that different DNS servers will have only a portion of the DNS entries and that no one DNS server will have all of the possible entries throughout the network on which it is working. Partitioning the DNS database is explained in detail in Chapter 5 of this book.

Because NetBIOS names are limited to 15 characters, the service was not designed to assume a partitioned database. A WINS server is expected to resolve the query, and it does not ask other WINS servers for help. This means that one WINS server must have all possible answers for the entire network in its local database that maps names to IP addresses. Figure 6.3 shows that a WINS server needs to contain all possible records to answer any query.

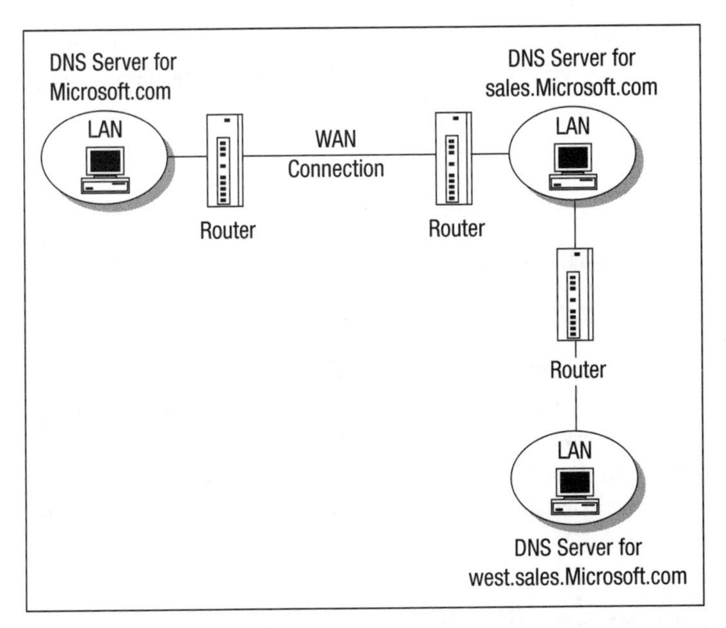

Figure 6.2 The DNS database for Microsoft.com needs to contain records only for its own domain. The DNS servers for sales.Microsoft.com and west.sales.Microsoft.com also need to contain records only for their own domains. Each DNS database can refer queries for records that reside in a different portion of the database—on another server—to that other server.

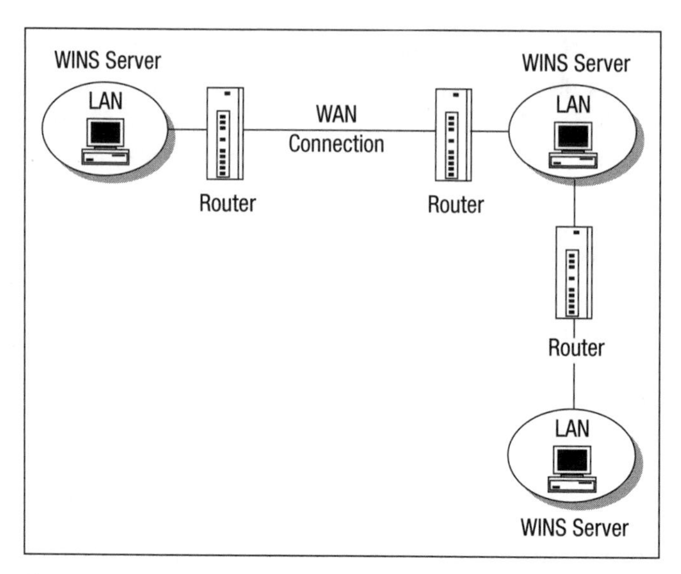

Figure 6.3 In the same network configuration as Figure 6.2, all WINS servers must contain all records possible in the entire network. They cannot contain only those records for the LAN on which they reside.

A Network Diagram

Because good designs start from a high level, a network diagram is essential when designing any network service. You should include the following items in your network diagram when planning for WINS:

- LAN locations
- WAN connections, including speed of each connection
- Number of users at each location
- Location of current WINS servers

When designing a service, you must also plan for capacity. You must note concentrations of users so that their queries can be spread out among different WINS servers. Because WINS servers do not refer queries to each other, you'll first need to work out a plan for the replication of WINS records between the servers. This plan will determine the placement of the WINS server as well as the replication relationships.

Future Plans for the Network

Before designing begins, you must ask the question: What will the need for WINS be in six months? A year? If a network is migrating from legacy Windows systems to an all Windows 2000 environment, how long will the migration take?

Are any legacy applications needed that also use NetBIOS? If an analysis of the network shows that a full migration will be completed in one year, then add a plan to disable NetBIOS over TCP/IP on your network and decommission your WINS servers. You can find details for what steps to include in this process at the end of this chapter.

How Many WINS Servers Are Needed?

A frequent mistake of WINS designs is the implementation of too many WINS servers. One WINS server can support 10,000 clients, and this capability should be used as part of your design. Even if one physical location has fewer than 10,000 clients, a backup WINS server should be implemented to provide fault tolerance, in case one goes down or a network connection becomes unavailable. Remember that adding this second WINS server is only for fault tolerance: Only one WINS server is required if there are fewer than 10,000 WINS clients and fault tolerance is not an issue. If WINS resolution is not performing well, then the answer may be to upgrade the hardware of the existing WINS server rather than to add more servers. Adding more WINS servers just adds more replication traffic to the network.

Unlike DNS, WINS does not come with guidelines to place a server at each physical location. The placement decision rests on many different factors such as the bandwidth availability between locations and the number of clients on either side of the connection. The biggest factor is how much the WINS server will be used. Remember that a connection between two Windows 2000 computers does not need WINS. For this connection, DNS is the primary name-resolution service. However, connections between legacy Windows systems and Windows 2000 will need WINS. How much traffic does WINS generate? To calculate how much traffic you can expect, you must first understand the different types of WINS traffic.

WINS Traffic

Although WINS generates very little traffic when compared to other services on the network, even a small amount of traffic can have a big impact when designing a service to use WAN connections. Traffic from the WINS service can be of four different types: registrations, queries, refreshes, and releases. Table 6.1 details the four types.

Even though Windows 2000 clients do not use WINS by default, they will need to use WINS when connecting to a NetBIOS resource. Because all Microsoft client operating systems—even Windows 2000 computers—are WINS clients by default, they will register, renew, and release their NetBIOS names also by default. Until WINS is not needed on the network, this traffic will still be on the network.

Table 6.1 The four types of WINS traffic.

Type	When Traffic Occurs	Description
Registration	Boot up	A WINS client registers its records and gets them created and added to the WINS database. This is the most traffic generated by WINS. It generates two packets per service registered.
Query	Connecting to NetBIOS resource	A NetBIOS client connecting to a NetBIOS resource queries the WINS server for a name-to-IP address mapping. Queries can also be made to contact a domain controller or other needed resource on the network. This traffic is just two packets per query.
Refresh	By default, every three days	Because WINS registration is dynamic, WINS clients need to renew their registrations to keep the WINS database from getting out of date. The default renewal interval is six days. WINS clients refresh their registrations by default at 50% of the renewal interval. This traffic is just two packets per refresh.
Release	Shutdown	Part of the shutdown procedure is for a client to release its registered names from the WINS database. If a client loses power suddenly and does not go through shutdown, then the names can remain in the WINS database even though they are no longer valid. This generates as much traffic as a registration with two packets per name released.

Spoke-and-Hub Design

Client-to-server traffic is not the only type of traffic that the WINS service generates. Because WINS servers must have the answer when queried by a client, replication of WINS records is the most important factor in WINS server placement. The servers must replicate their records to each other so that each database contains the records of every WINS client on the network. Server-to-server traffic is generated when WINS servers replicate changes to the database to each other. Because only changes are replicated, each replication event is usually small. The only design that accomplishes this replication without causing unnecessary stress on the network is the spoke and hub. It keeps the WINS database up to date and correct.

One Physical Location

If only one physical location needs to be supported, the WINS design can be kept very simple. Because only one WINS server is needed per 10,000 WINS clients, one physical location may allow for a low number of WINS servers. Even if there are fewer than 10,000 WINS clients, at least one other WINS server will be needed for fault tolerance. Replication is simple to set up with just two WINS servers: The WINS servers will simply replicate to each other.

In a large, single-location environment with more than 10,000 clients, you may need more than two WINS servers. Using an example of 50,000 users, Figure 6.4 shows the spoke-and-hub design needed to set up WINS replication correctly. One WINS server is designated as the hub for replication purposes. In the diagram, WINS1 is the hub. The rest of the WINS servers are configured to replicate to the WINS1 hub. These WINS servers are the spokes, just like spokes in a wheel join at the hub. The spoke-and-hub configuration allows WINS1 (the hub) to gather the changes from the other WINS servers and to replicate these changes out to its replication partners (the spokes) in the least amount of time.

Adjusting for WAN Locations

In a WAN network environment, the spoke-and-hub design still needs to be used. The design is just as simple as it is for a single-location network. Each physical location should be set up as Figure 6.4 shows, with one WINS server chosen as the hub and the rest of the servers serving as spokes. In a multiple-location network, each of the individual hubs will become part of a spoke-and-hub design for the WAN environment. One hub server for a physical location will be chosen as the hub for the WAN. Each of the other local hub servers will then serve as spokes to the WAN hub. Figure 6.5 shows an example of the spoke-and-hub configuration for a WAN environment. WINS1Sea is the hub for the Seattle location as well as for the entire WAN environment. WINS1Den is the hub for the Denver location and a spoke for the WAN environment. WINS1Atl is the

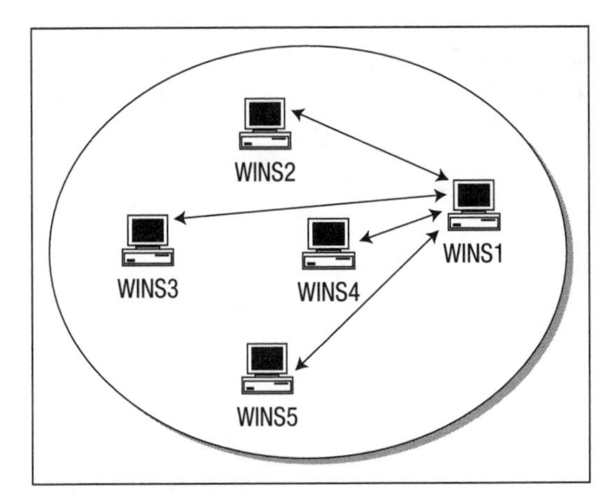

Figure 6.4 Spoke-and-hub design for a single physical location.

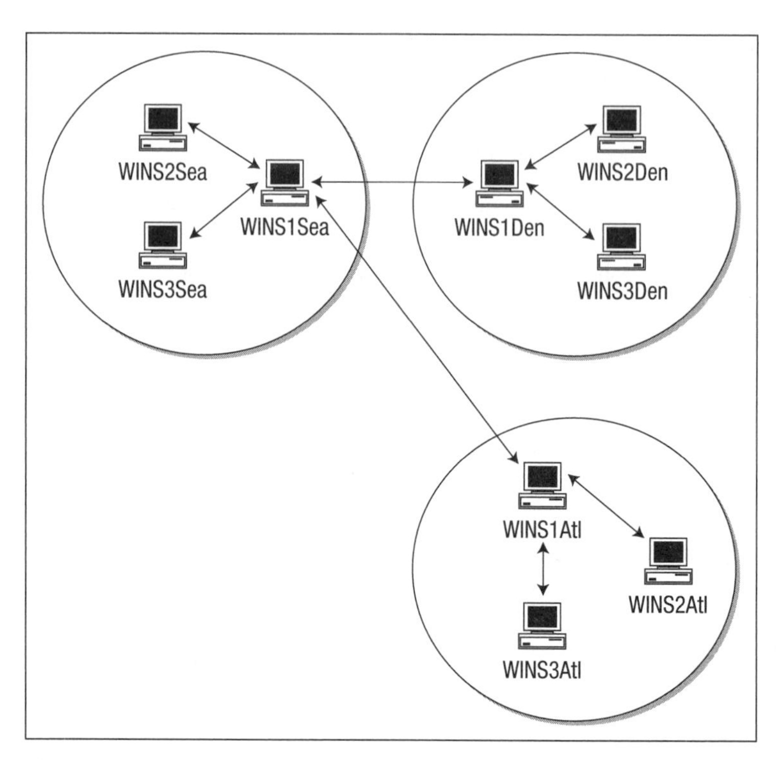

Figure 6.5 Spoke-and-hub design for multiple physical locations.

hub for the Atlanta environment and a spoke for the WAN environment. This design allows for replication of the WINS database throughout the WAN without causing unnecessary traffic or delays getting the changes out.

Understanding WINS Replication

Designing WINS database replication is the biggest factor in determining where to place the WINS server(s). But replication involves more than just placing the servers in the right location. Because WINS replication sends only changes to the database (and only to its configured replication partners), configuring these partners and their relationships also plays an important role in keeping the WINS database current.

Convergence Time

Convergence time is the time it takes to replicate a change to the WINS database throughout the enterprise. How long a designer is willing to wait for convergence has an enormous impact on a WINS design. Part of an effective WINS solution is calculating the convergence time and trying to minimize it. The convergence time is calculated with a worst-case scenario in mind, as if a change just misses a replication interval each time it reaches a new WINS server. But, before you can calculate the convergence time, you need to understand replication times and the types of replications.

Push and Pull Replication

Setting up a spoke-and-hub relationship between WINS servers involves not only the designation of spokes and hubs, but also the configuration of the servers as replication partners. WINS servers replicate their records to each other through a push or pull method. Each partner uses a different method—push or pull—to cause a replication event. A push method uses a certain number of changes as its interval. When configuring a push partner, you can set the number of changes that trigger a replication. A new feature in Windows 2000 WINS is the allowance of persistent connections. This means that the session set up for communication between replication partners does not close when the replication is complete. Maintaining an open session reduces the network overhead of replication. Because of persistent connections, the update count for a push partner can be set to zero, which causes every change to be sent immediately. With persistent connections, the session remains open between replication partners, and the only network traffic is the actual replication information. Microsoft recommends that push partners be configured with zero as the update interval, if persistent connections are being used.

Pull partners use a set amount of time for a replication interval instead of a specified number of changes. This is the recommended setting if WAN servers are separated by a slow or heavily used WAN link. Because WAN connections usually are short on available bandwidth, a pull relationship allows control over when the replication occurs. The amount of time between pull replications should be set based upon two factors: the amount of time that you're willing to wait for convergence and the amount of available bandwidth between WAN connections.

The recommended setting for WINS servers at the same physical location is to configure them as both push and pull partners. Doing so increases the consistency in the WINS database. This relationship is referred to as a push/pull relationship.

Automatic discovery is a feature that allows WINS servers to automatically discover replication partners. Do not use this feature on a network with more than three WINS servers. Because automatic discovery configures replication partners in a push/pull relationship, it does not configure a spoke-and-hub relationship that would be needed in a large WINS environment. Automatic discovery is best only for small networks with high-speed LAN connections, in which a push/pull relationship among all WINS servers is appropriate.

Calculating Convergence Time

Now that you've placed all the servers and configured all the relationships, you can calculate the convergence time. Figure 6.6 uses the setting in Figure 6.5 with replication relationships configured between servers. Because convergence time is based on a worst-case scenario, you'll use the pull interval to calculate it. The WINS servers within the LANs are using a pull interval of 15 minutes, which sends a change to the hub server in the LAN every 15 minutes. Because of the spoke-and-hub configuration of replication partners, the convergence time within the LAN is kept to 30 minutes: 15 minutes to send the change to the hub server and 15 minutes to send that change out to the other spoke servers.

To calculate convergence time for the WAN, we must add the time it takes to pull a change across the enterprise. Figure 6.7 shows a WAN environment with three locations. Atlanta and Denver are configured as spokes to the Seattle WINS server to keep WAN convergence time to a minimum. Because the WAN pull replication time is set to 60 minutes, a change coming from a WAN server would take two hours to be replicated out to the whole enterprise. The LAN pull time is again 15 minutes. Add 15 minutes for the change to come from a LAN server and 15 minutes for it to be replicated to a local WINS server from its hub. This results in a total of two hours and 30 minutes for the network convergence time.

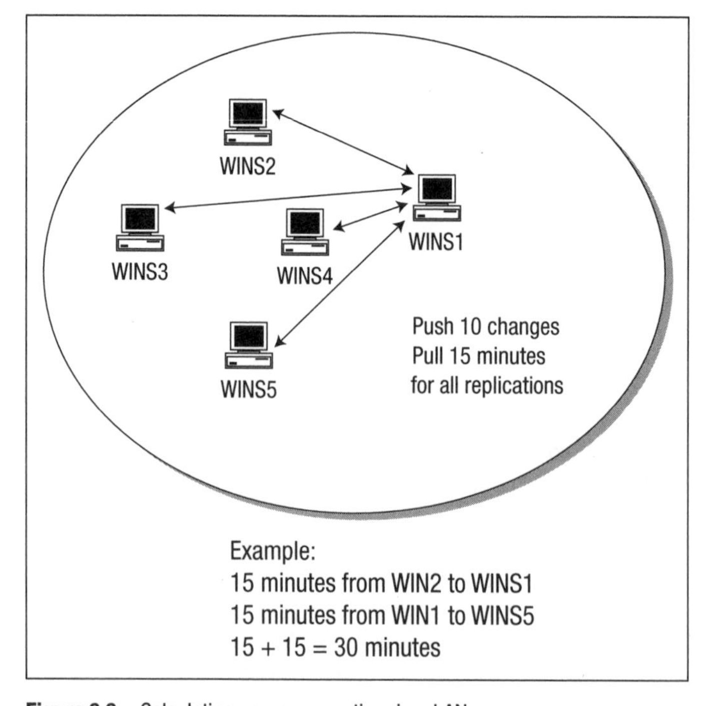

Figure 6.6 Calculating convergence time in a LAN.

Taking WINS off the Network

If the plan is to go to an all Windows 2000 environment, a good WINS design should consider the eventual removal of NetBIOS from the network. Once all of the NetBIOS clients are replaced, NetBIOS can be disabled and the WINS servers can be decommissioned.

Disabling NetBIOS on the Network

After all of the NetBIOS dependent clients are removed (or replaced with Windows 2000 clients), NetBIOS needs to be disabled on the network. The Windows 2000 clients were originally configured as WINS clients, and you have two ways to change this: manually and by using DHCP. To make the change manually, you must remove the IP address of the primary and all secondary WINS servers from the network settings of each client. This is a large task if all clients are manually configured for IP addresses and for WINS. Another, much easier method is to use DHCP. First, remove the WINS options 44 and 46 that configure WINS clients to use WINS and to give the IP addresses of the WINS primary and secondary servers. In addition, the Windows 2000 DHCP server has an option number 1 that disables the use of NetBIOS over TCP/IP (NetBT) on the network. Use this option in a Windows 2000 network in which all of the clients have been upgraded and NetBIOS is no longer needed on a network. DHCP is covered thoroughly in Chapter 4 of this book.

Decommissioning the WINS Servers

The last step in removing NetBIOS and all related services from a network is to decommission the WINS servers. It will be much easier on the network and the administrator if this is done correctly. Microsoft recommends using the manual tombstoning feature of Windows 2000 WINS to delete and tombstone the WINS records before removing the WINS service from the server. Doing so lets the other WINS servers know to remove the records from their databases rather than trying to replicate them back.

Practice Questions

Case Study

The Widgets Company is based in Seattle, WA. It has a manufacturing plant in Denver, CO, and a distribution facility in Atlanta, GA. Each facility has its own separate IT department. The corporate offices are located in Seattle and have 210 hosts. The manufacturing plant in Denver has 205 hosts, and the distribution center in Atlanta has 56 hosts. The company is currently upgrading to Windows 2000 but lacks expertise in this operating system.

Current WAN Structure

The company's network has three locations.

Proposed WAN Structure

No additional locations are planned.

Current WAN Connectivity

Currently all locations are connected through a 56Kbps Frame Relay connection.

Proposed WAN Connectivity

No upgrades are planned to increase the bandwidth of the current connections. The company is hoping to design the network services so that they will work with the current available bandwidth.

Current State of Network Administration

The IT department has three separate divisions in each physical location. The network is divided into three Windows NT 4 domains with no trust relationships configured. Each location is separate and distinct from the others.

Future Plans for Network Administration

Since the network is being upgraded to Windows 2000, the decision has been made to create one Active Directory domain with Windows 2000. The IT department will be centralized in Seattle at the corporate headquarters. Individual administrators will provide support at each of the remote locations, but most services will be centralized in Seattle. The centralization of the IT department will take at least eight months to complete.

Company Windows 2000 Goal

The client computers are in the process of being upgraded from Windows NT 4 Workstation to Windows 2000 Professional. Although the servers are still using Windows NT 4, the plan is to upgrade the NT 4 servers to Windows 2000 servers.

Question 1

A network administrator for the Seattle network decides that he will not need WINS since the network is being upgraded to Windows 2000. He decides to not install the service on the Seattle network. He also decides that now is a good time to disable NetBIOS on his network. What is the quickest way to accomplish this?

- ❍ a. Use DHCP with option 44, 46, and 1
- ❍ b. Use DHCP without option 44 or 46
- ❍ c. Use DHCP without option 44 or 46, but add option 1
- ❍ d. Do not use DHCP

Answer c is correct. Using DHCP is the quickest way to disable NetBIOS on a network. Because option 44 and 46 are used to set up WINS clients on the network, these options should not be used. Option 1, which is Microsoft specific, disables NBT on the network.

Question 2

Now that NetBIOS has been disabled on the Seattle network, what problems might occur over the next six months as the clients get upgraded to Windows 2000? [Check all correct answers]

- ❑ a. Slow network connections
- ❑ b. Increased broadcast traffic on the network
- ❑ c. Clients unable to connect to resources on their local subnet
- ❑ d. Clients unable to connect to resources outside of their local subnet

Answers a, b, and d are correct. Because the network administrator has upgraded only the servers, all of the clients are still Windows NT 4 workstations and thus dependent on NetBIOS, which they use to access file and print services. Without WINS, the clients will be forced to broadcast to find resources. Although this allows the clients to connect to local resources, it will not work for resources outside of the local subnet.

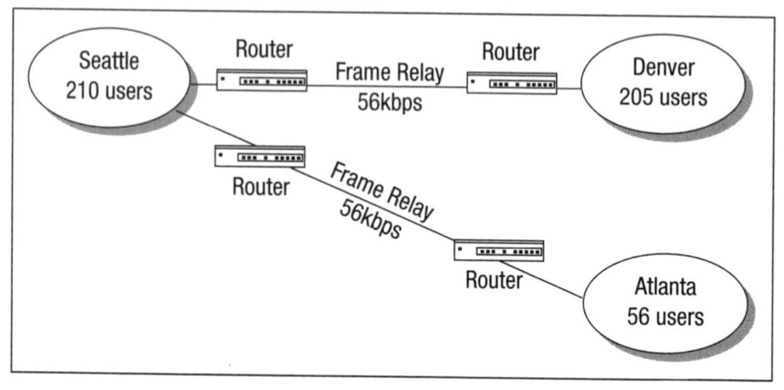

Figure 6.9 Diagram for Questions 3 and 4.

Question 3

It has been decided that a WINS solution is needed for the entire network. Based on Figure 6.9, how many WINS servers are required?

❍ a. One

❍ b. Two

❍ c. Three

❍ d. Four

Answer a is correct. This is a tricky question because the focus for WINS design is often on fault tolerance and performance. Because one WINS server can support 10,000 clients, one server is all that is required. A question like this may be asked because designers tend to overdo it when implementing WINS and add too many WINS servers.

Question 4

It is decided that WINS must be available 24 hours a day. Based on the diagram in Figure 6.9, how many WINS servers are required for the network?

❍ a. One

❍ b. Two

❍ c. Three

❍ d. Four

Answer b is correct. If WINS must be available at all times, another WINS server is needed. Even though there is a WAN connection, there's no requirement or recommendation for a WINS server to be placed on either side of a WAN link. No more than two WINS servers are needed.

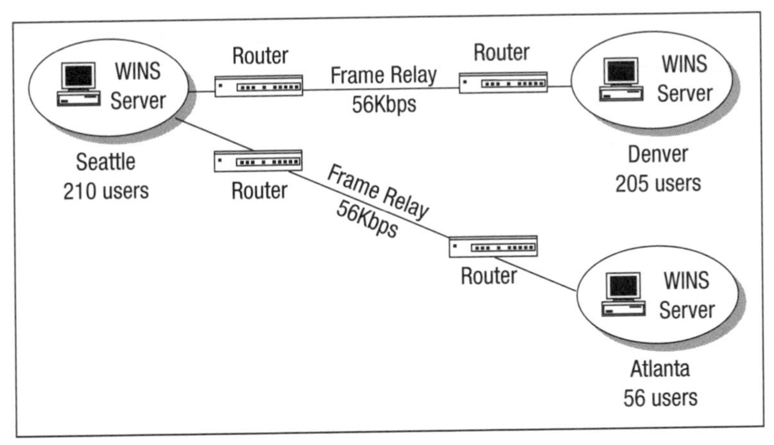

Figure 6.10 Diagram for Questions 5, 6, and 7.

Question 5

As shown in Fiure 6.10, the WINS service is set up by adding WINS servers to each location according to the following diagram. Each client's primary WINS server is configured as the local WINS server on the client's LAN. Replication between the new WINS servers is not configured. How will this affect access to the network? [Check all correct answers]

- ❑ a. Clients will not be able to access remote resources.
- ❑ b. Clients will be able access remote resources.
- ❑ c. Clients will be able to access local resources.
- ❑ d. Clients will not be able to access local resources.

Answers a and c are correct. Without replication configured between the WINS servers, each WINS server will have only the entries of the local LAN. When a client asks for a remote resource outside of the LAN, the record will not exist in the local WINS server.

Question 6

Replication needs to be configured between the WINS servers on the network. On the diagram in Figure 6.10, draw the best configuration for replication for this network.

The answer is:

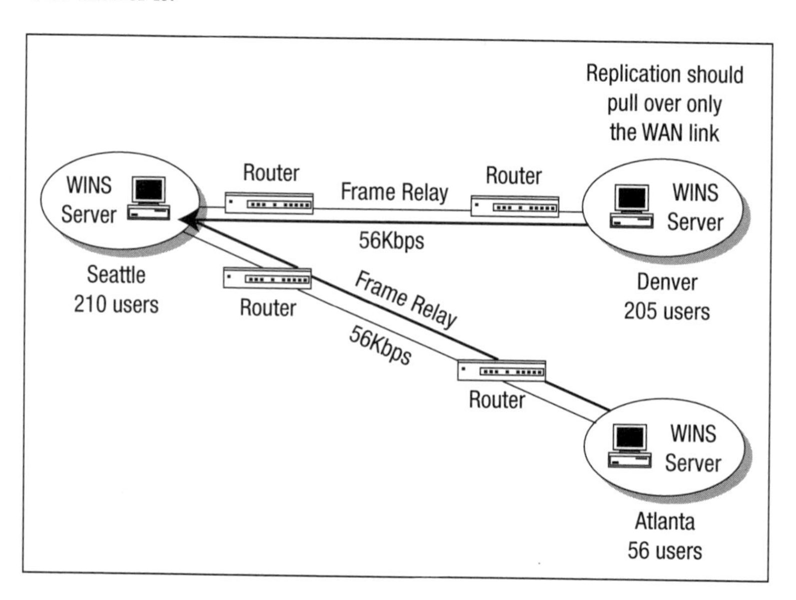

Replication needs to be set up with a spoke-and-hub design. Designate one server as the hub server and the rest of the WINS servers as spoke servers. Set up replication only from spoke to hub.

Question 7

In the diagram in Figure 6.10, which server must be designated as the hub server?

- ❍ a. WINS1
- ❍ b. WINS2
- ❍ c. WINS3
- ❍ d. It does not matter
- ❍ e. All of the WINS servers

Answer d is correct. Only one WINS server is needed as a hub, and any WINS server can be designated as the hub server.

Question 8

One morning, at the Seattle network an administrator removes a WINS record from the WINS database, but that afternoon, while in the WINS console, she sees that the record is back. Why?

❍ a. Replication added the record back to the database.

❍ b. Tombstoning brought the record back to the database.

❍ c. Restoring from backup brought the record back to the database.

❍ d. The WINS server is corrupted.

Answer a is correct. Records that are manually deleted can show back up, because they are replicated back from replication partners. The record will come back if it is not tombstoned before deleting it. A corrupt server and a backup restore did not happen in this scenario.

Question 9

How can the problem from the previous question be fixed? [Check all correct answers]

❑ a. Delete the record again.

❑ b. Turn off replication.

❑ c. Delete WINS database and restore from backup.

❑ d. Manually tombstone the record.

Answers a and d are correct. When a record is manually deleted, it must also be manually tombstoned. Doing so deletes the record from the databases of replication partners, thus preventing the record from being replicated back to the original server. Just deleting the record again will cause the record to come back in the next replication. Replication is a needed service for a WAN location. The same problem will occur if the WINS database is restored from backup.

Question 10

Why is spoke-and-hub the recommended configuration for WINS replication? [Check all correct answers]

- ❑ a. To keep the WINS database from becoming corrupted
- ❑ b. To keep convergence time to minimum
- ❑ c. To keep the WINS replication traffic low
- ❑ d. To keep deleted records from reappearing in the database

Answers a, b, and c are correct. The spoke-and-hub configuration for replication helps to keep the WINS database from becoming corrupted. Also, with spoke-and-hub the replication of a record can be traced and timed to ensure that it is replicated out to other WINS servers in the least amount of time. WINS replication traffic is only from spoke to hub and hub back to spoke which keeps WINS replication traffic low. Deleted records can only be kept from coming back by tombstoning them. WINS replication configuration does not affect the need for tombstoning a record when it needs to be deleted from the system.

Need to Know More?

www.microsoft.com/NTServer/nts/techdetails/techspecs/WINSwp98.asp *Microsoft Windows NT 4.0 Windows Internet Naming Service (WINS) Architecture and Capacity Planning.* Microsoft Corporation, Redmond, WA, 1996. This Microsoft white paper explains its implementation of WINS in Windows NT 4. This paper contains more about convergence time and Windows basics than does the Windows 2000 WINS paper.

www.microsoft.com/WINDOWS2000/library/howitworks/communications/nameadrmgmt/wins.asp *Microsoft Windows 2000 Windows Internet Naming Service (WINS) Overview.* Microsoft Corporation, Redmond, WA, 1999. This Microsoft white paper focuses mostly on the changes in the Windows 2000 implementation of WINS.

Read the WINS help available on a Windows 2000 server that has the WINS service loaded. "Understanding WINS," "Planning WINS networks," and "Migrating from WINS to DNS" contain many hard-to-find hints and advice.

Search the TechNet CD (or its online version through **support.microsoft.com/directory**) using the keywords "WINS," "WINS convergence," "WINS replication," "tombstoning," and "disabling NetBIOS."

NAT Protocol Design

Terms you'll need to understand:

- ✓ Network address Translation (NAT)
- ✓ Public network
- ✓ Private network

Techniques you'll need to master:

- ✓ Implementing NAT
- ✓ Making NAT secure
- ✓ Improving NAT performance

This chapter introduces you to the implementation of the Network Address Translation (NAT) in a Windows 2000 network infrastructure. You'll learn about the NAT protocol and how to use it to design a network that enhances and makes secure the Windows 2000 operating system.

NAT Overview

Network Address Translation (NAT) is the protocol used to hide the TCP/IP settings of a private network from a public network. A private network is what a company uses internally (with all of its associated hardware such as the cabling, hubs, and routers within the company's buildings). The public network is the Internet, which spans the globe and to which everyone is able to connect.

NAT was originally implemented on routers as a hardware solution to the problem of the dwindling stock of numbers that were available for IP addresses. Now, the NAT service is included with Windows 2000 servers to function as a NAT router.

A problem arises when a private company wants to enable access from its private network to the Internet: The connection allows anyone on the Internet to determine the TCP/IP configuration for the business's internal network. The private network is thus open to persons who may try to illegally access the company's data or equipment.

NAT also allows a company to use unregistered IP addresses within the internal network and to have only a few registered IP addresses for access to the Internet. If private and public IP addresses exist in a one-to-one ratio, IP Routing can be used. However, NAT is used if the IP addresses on the private network outnumber the few registered public addresses—a many-to-few ratio and no enhanced Internet access performance is needed (in this case Proxy should be used, see Chapter 8).

In Windows 2000, NAT can be implemented only under the Routing and Remote Access that is covered in Chapter 9.

NAT Implementation

Implementing NAT is a little more complex than DHCP or DNS. Because NAT handles both DHCP and DNS resolution, it incorporates a little of both services.

Understanding NAT's function is the most important issue in designing a Windows 2000 network infrastructure. Understanding NAT's function will let you determine where to place NAT and how to make it secure. The main issue is when to use NAT or when to use Proxy Server or IP Forwarding for different design issues.

Installing NAT

To install NAT, open Routing And Remote Access under Administrative Tools on the Start menu. Right click on the server name in the left pane:

1. Select Configure And Enable Routing And Remote Access.
2. Select Next from the Configure And Enable Routing And Remote Access Wizard.
3. Select Internet Connection Server from the list as shown in Figure 7.1.
4. Choose Set Up A Router With The Network Address Translation (NAT) Routing Protocol as shown in Figure 7.2.

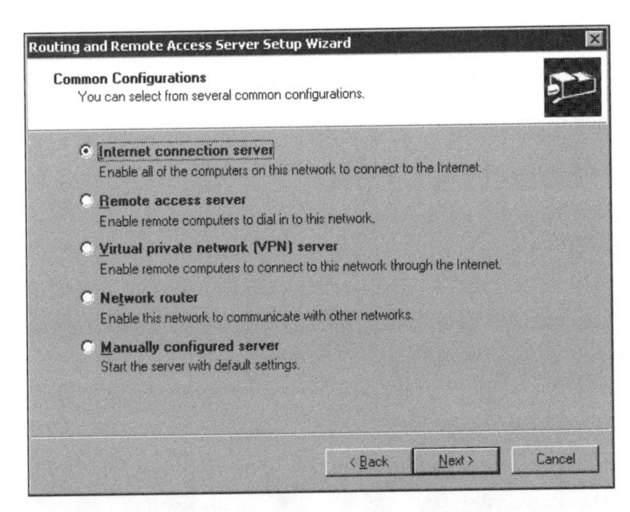

Figure 7.1 Routing and Remote Access configurations.

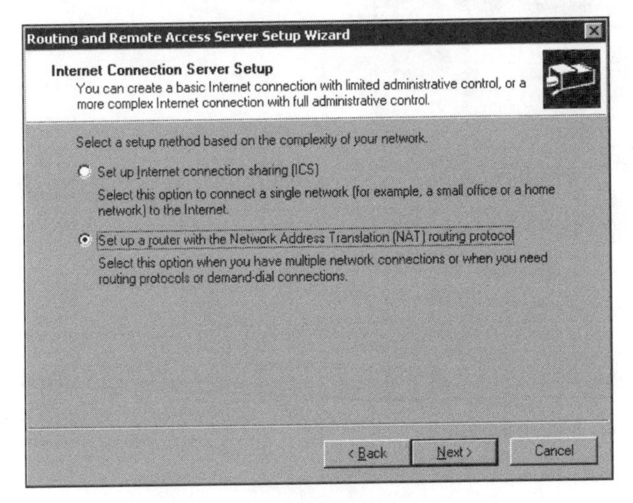

Figure 7.2 Internet server connection setup.

5. Select the type of connection to the Internet such as a modem, in a multi-homed computer, or a device for demand-dial access. (This can also be a Virtual Private Network, or VPN, as discussed later in this chapter.)

Note: Modems and modem banks must be configured for demand-dial connections.

Configuring NAT

Once the wizard finishes the setup, select server name in the left pane and IP Routing in the right pane in the Routing and Remote Access Microsoft Management Console (MMC), and then:

1. Right-click on Network Address Translation.
2. Select Properties.
3. From the dialog box that appears, select the Address Assignment tab, as shown in Figure 7.3.

Here is where you'll assign an IP address scheme for your private network.

The DHCP and DHCP Relay Agent Services cannot be running on the same network. NAT will offer IP addresses to the DHCP clients. The DNS and default gateway address is the IP address for the network card in the NAT system that is connected to the private network. Because NAT doesn't have a relay agent, it doesn't function on a routed network.

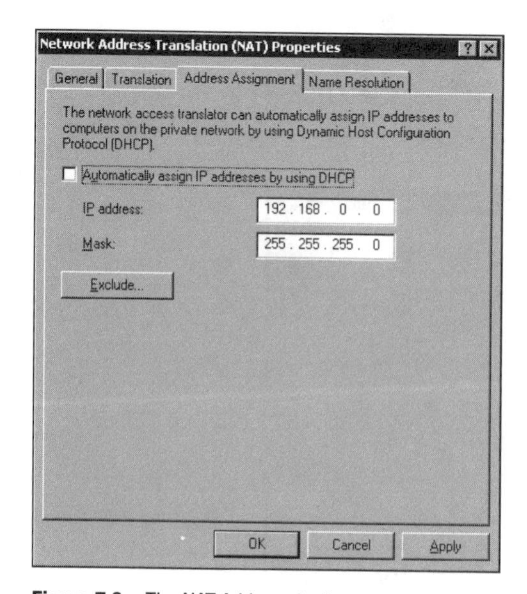

Figure 7.3 The NAT Address Assignment tab.

Addresses can also be used from the Automatic Private IP Addressing (APIPA). The interface on the private-network side is assigned an APIPA address.

Select the Automatically Assign Ip Addresses By Using DHCP checkbox and configure the IP scope. Select the Exclude button to enter exclusions for the scope. You can also specify to resolve DNS names through the NAT system by forwarding the request to a private or public DNS server. (This is accomplished under the Name Resolution tab.) However, this will not allow a separate DNS to handle name resolution directly; the NAT server must forward it acting as a DNS proxy.

On a NAT network, the NAT system will replace the DHCP services. The network cannot be routed, so DHCP relay agents cannot be used either. The DNS service is handled differently as noted under "NAT and DNS".

For private networks, one of the following address ranges must be used for NAT.

- *Class A*—10.0.0.0 - 10.255.255.255
- *Class B*—172.16.0.0 - 172.31.255.255
- *Class C*—192.168.0.0 - 192.168.255.255

NAT does not support multiple or multicast scopes.

NAT in Action

Once all options are configured and in place, a user in your private network should be able to connect to the Internet. The IP address shown to the public should be a NAT public address and not a NAT private address. When a user starts his or her computer, it receives a private IP address that allows it to communicate with other systems in the private (business) network. When using an application to access the Internet (the public network), the computer is assigned a public address from NAT. When a request is sent from the user's system to the default gateway (NAT system), the TCP/IP header information that has the user's source IP address is removed and replaced with the user's assigned NAT address (the public address). When a packet is received from the Internet for the private network, the NAT router table is parsed for the public address and matches it to the private address. The TCP/IP header is then changed once more to put the private address back in the destination address.

Not only does NAT change the header information, it also recalculates the checksum to reset its value if needed so that the packets do not appear to be corrupted.

In most cases, the private network, from NAT's viewpoint, comprises not only IP addresses but also port numbers. Multiple client systems will have the same public address but are kept separate by unique port numbers assigned by NAT. This is how a business can have many private IP addresses to its few Internet addresses. This implementation is different from Proxy Server, in that Proxy Server uses only one public address (and IP Routing uses a one-to-one ratio of IP addresses).

Integrating NAT into Existing Networks

When integrating NAT into an existing network, the following items must be resolved:

- DHCP servers must be disabled.
- Client computers must be configured to request DHCP-assigned addresses.
- NAT supports only the IP protocol. (TCP/IP must be running.)
- NAT cannot translate the following protocols:
  - SNMP
  - COM/DCOM
  - LDAP

The NAT server should be placed between the public and private networks to maintain security. NAT can use a standard modem, ISDN, and so on to connect to a public network, or another private network.

Note: To be able to communicate with private systems, the public network interface must have an IP address and a subnet mask that is functional on the private network. The public interface should be assigned the IP address and subnet mask given by the InterNIC or ISP.

NAT can be used to integrate one network into an existing one, and serve as the connection point, for example, between two offices. Let's say both networks have Routing and Remote Access installed and enabled. One system has NAT, and the other is configured to accept incoming connections. The default gateway and DNS server IP address for a network should be configured to the IP address of the private network interface of the local Routing and Remote Access server as shown in Figure 7.4.

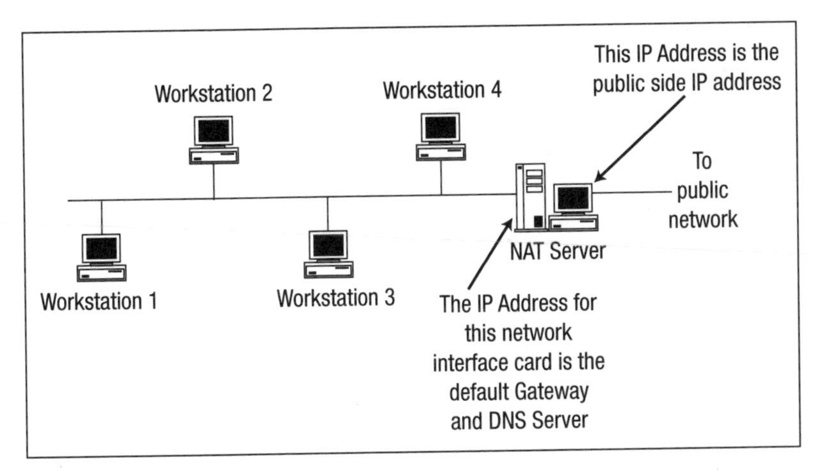

Figure 7.4 NAT network diagram

NAT and DNS

DNS servers cannot be used on the private network. Requests are sent to the NAT server which then resolves the request if it is a private system name. The DNS server IP address option is entered as the IP address of the NAT server on the clients.

If a business's DNS server is not resolved by NAT on the private network, the NAT server will be configured with the address of a DNS server on the public network. These options are shown in Figure 7.5.

NAT has a variety of security features, which can be implemented independently or together for higher security restrictions. A security "fault" in NAT is that all security is set as a whole and not for an individual user; other security options must be used to implement individual security. (See "VPN Security" for individual settings.)

Routing and Remote Access Security for NAT

Security can be implemented by the Routing and Remote Access Service filters to permit or prevent packets coming into any network interface on the NAT server.

NAT Interface Security

Filters can be applied to the private or public interface on the NAT server to allow or disallow packets to pass the specified interface.

A filter on the private network interface will block any packets attempting to pass from the public network to the private network. Also, a filter on the public interface will prevent anyone on the private network from accessing the Internet.

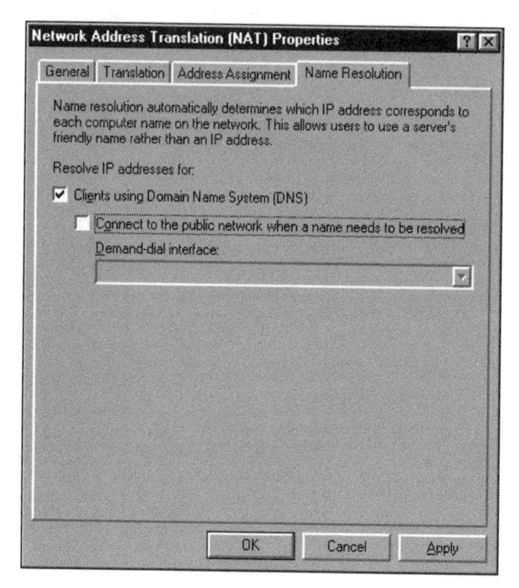

Figure 7.5 DNS configuration in NAT security

Be careful that the public and private interface filters do not contradict each other. A conflict could prevent IP traffic from exiting or entering the private network through the NAT server.

Filters are basically rules that can be set to allow/disallow packets to pass the interface based on the source IP address, the destination IP address, and the IP port numbers—all of which can be used either independently or together. Combining them makes a more secure filter.

Filters can also be applied to the demand-dial connections (such as modems and ISDN). But these demand-dial filters cannot be used in conjunction with NAT, as they will be disregarded.

NAT's default security setting is to disallow public network requests to access the private network. Depending upon a business's needs, this default security may have to be changed.

Single IP Address

If the business has only one usable IP address from the InterNIC or ISP, then every computer accessing the Internet will appear to be using the same IP address, but through different ports.

Port mappings must be defined so that ports are available for address translations. An IP address and a port together define a socket. When the NAT server receives a packet from the public network with a certain socket, NAT knows which socket matches to which system, and so retranslates the packet to send it to the proper system. Every resource shared on the private network must have a port mapping for it to be accessed from the public network (if it is to be accessed from the public network).

If the available addresses are in a one-to-many ratio and access performance needs to be enhanced, the solution is to use Proxy Server (as described in Chapter 8).

Multiple IP Addresses

If the business has more than one usable IP address from the InterNIC or ISP, you can make a scope of usable addresses with ports.

Remember to reserve some of the scope if private network resources are to be shared on the public network.

If enough addresses are available, each public address may have one private address (a one-to-one ratio of public to private). Instead of using NAT in this situation, it may be easier to use IP Forwarding. The addresses are not translated back and forth from public to private, and the implementation is simpler (there is no security to hide the TCP/IP configuration of the private network).

VPN Security

Virtual Private Network (VPN) is used when you need to implement security on a user-by-user basis. You can use VPN if you need tighter security for individual users.

VPN on NAT can support Point-to-Point Tunneling Protocol (PPTP) for authentication and encryption. With authentication, access to resources can be allowed or disallowed to a user.

Because of NAT's translations of the TCP/IP header for the addresses, encrypting the packet causes NAT to be unable to do the job it was intended to do. In these cases in which encryption such as L2TP and IPSec must be used, you should use some means other than NAT.

Performance

Performance depends upon a few different factors. To see where you can improve the performance, you should monitor the hardware, the software, and the connections to and from the networks.

Because the NAT system connects to a public network (usually the Internet), the connection between the NAT server and the public network should be able to handle the necessary traffic to and from the private network. Multiple connections to the public network may be required. (Having multiple connections also provides redundancy if one connection fails). The connections can also be upgraded to a faster type, such as replacing modems with an ISDN or T-1 connection.

Connecting to the public network can be slow, and the time that the NAT server takes to connect to the public network can be reduced by having a consistent connection. This way, the connection will be always available when it is needed, thus allowing users immediate access. Users won't have to wait for the NAT server to reconnect to the public network whenever it disconnects or times out.

Another performance boost can be obtained from upgrading the actual server hardware. Monitoring the processor, memory, and hard disk access in a NAT server can reveal bottlenecks that can be remedied with a simple hardware upgrade. Even the network cards can cause such a bottleneck if too much traffic is generated through or to the NAT server. Use Windows 2000's Performance Monitor to monitor specific resources to determine if they are slowing traffic.

Practice Questions

Case Study

Current LAN/Network Structure

2Market currently has 10 servers that are set up for their various data storage and network services, such as SQL, Exchange, SMS, and various application and file servers. Additionally, there are:

- ➤ 50 Windows 95 workstations
- ➤ 50 Windows 98 workstations
- ➤ 20 Windows NT 4 workstations
- ➤ 75 Windows 2000 Professional workstations
- ➤ 10 Network printers

The network is not subnetted at all. The network is using a Class A address.

Proposed LAN/Network Structure

2Market proposes no network changes other than a Windows 2000 Server with two interface cards, one connected to the LAN and one connected to the Internet. There are 25 IP addresses that must be reserved on the private network for servers, network printers, and some future additions of servers and network printers.

Current WAN Connectivity

None at the current time.

Proposed WAN Connectivity

None at the current time.

Current Internet Positioning

2Market has leased the following IP address from the InterNIC: 38.187.128.40. The company's domain name is 2Market.com. 2Market will not host its own Web site. Any Internet connections from 2Market will be used strictly for Internet access by the employees.

Future Internet Plans

No new IP addresses will be leased from the InterNIC. All employees need access to the Internet. No company policy is currently in place to specify which browser type is preferred. No individual security settings are required. Sales personnel must be able to access customer Web sites and to send email to customers and perspective clients. Internet access performance is not an issue, although security is a major concern. The private network must remain secure at all times.

Question 1

What would be the main reason to implement NAT?

❍ a. To confuse the administrator

❍ b. To hide public addresses from the private network

❍ c. To improve Internet performance

❍ d. To hide private addresses from the public network

The answer is d. Answer b is in the wrong order: private addresses are hidden from the public network. Answer c is implemented by Proxy Server. Answer a is obviously incorrect.

Question 2

In the scenario, which services must be installed on the Windows 2000 Server that will provide NAT? [Check all correct answers]

❑ a. DHCP

❑ b. FTP

❑ c. WINS

❑ d. DHCP Relay Agent

❑ e. DNS

❑ f. Routing and Remote Access

❑ g. WWW

The correct answer is f. Routing and Remote Access is required for NAT to function. Answers a and d cannot be implemented with NAT at all. Answers b, c, and g are not necessary to the function of NAT. Although answer e could be implemented, it should be a separate system for the sake of performance or to use a DNS server from the public network.

Question 3

In the case study, if a packet's source is the public network and its destination is the private network, what is its route? Place the choices in the correct order. Not all choices will be used.

Private network computer system

Public network interface

Private interface filter

Proxy server

Public network computer system

DNS server

WINS server

Private network interface

DHCP relay agent

IP header translation

Public interface filter

The correct order is:

Public network computer system

Public network interface

Public interface filter

IP header translation

Private interface filter

Private network interface

Private network computer system

Question 4

Click on the appropriate button to install NAT in the Routing And Remote Access Server Setup Wizard:

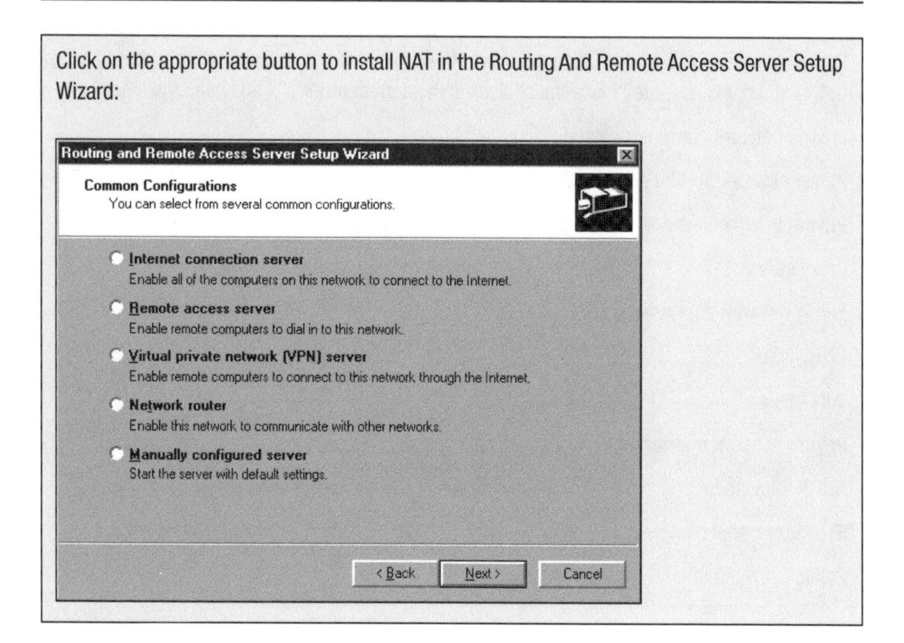

The answer is:

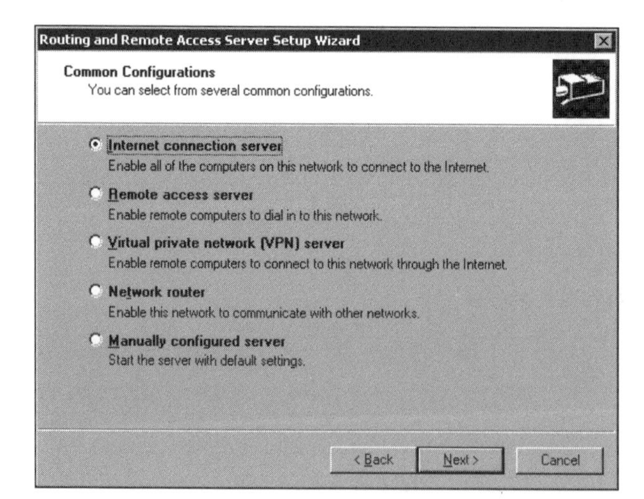

Question 5

In the case study, can the IP address for the private interface be assigned by a DHCP server?

❍ a. Yes

❍ b. No

The answer is b, No. NAT functions as a DHCP server. DHCP cannot be running on the same network. And, as with a DHCP server, the NAT server must be configured with a static IP address.

Question 6

In the case study, if the NAT server were connecting to a branch office instead of the Internet, which of the following protocols could be used? [Check all correct answers]

❑ a. IPX/SPX

❑ b. NetBEUI

❑ c. TCP/IP

❑ d. AppleTalk

The only correct answer is c. NAT is a service of the Windows 2000 TCP/IP protocol suite, and it functions with only TCP/IP in Windows 2000. None of the other protocols will function with NAT.

Question 7

In the proposed network, NAT can forward DNS requests to which of the following? [Check all correct answers]

❑ a. DNS server on the public network

❑ b. WINS server on the public network

❑ c. Your boss's Windows 98 laptop

❑ d. WINS server on the public network

❑ e. DNS server on the private network

The correct answers are a and e. NAT can forward DNS requests from the client computers to a public or private DNS server. In NAT, DNS requests are forwarded only to DNS servers and not to any other service, such as WINS or

DHCP, nor to any computer unable to run DNS services, such as client computers (which is where the requests are usually initiated).

Question 8

To implement security features on the Windows 2000 NAT server in the case study, what option can be used?

- a. IP addresses
- b. Filters
- c. Subnet mask
- d. A lock with no key

The answer is b. Filters are applied to determine the source addresses, destination addresses, and ports of packets that are allowed or not allowed to pass through the interface. All interfaces on the NAT system that will use TCP/IP must have an IP address and subnet mask to be usable by TCP/IP. Although this allows them to function, it does not work as a security feature. A lock and key has no validity.

Question 9

In the case study, the design will improve public network performance?

- a. True
- b. False

The answer is b, false. NAT will not improve Internet access. Its function is to hide the private network from the public network. This scenario should implement Proxy Server, which does improve access

Question 10

In the case study, the IT manager of 2Market wants to implement more security. He has no understanding of NAT and gives you a list of security measures. Which of the following will not work? [Check all correct answers]

- ❑ a. PPTP
- ❑ b. IPSec
- ❑ c. Filters
- ❑ d. L2TP

The answers are b and d. Answer a is used with NAT for VPNs. Answer c is NAT's main security implementation. Answers b and d use encryption to encrypt the header, and NAT cannot translate the header to replace the IP address.

Need to Know More?

Microsoft Corporation. *Microsoft Windows 2000 Server Resource Kit*. Microsoft Press, Redmond, WA, 2000. ISBN 1-57231-805-8. The kit consists of seven books and a CD-ROM. Each book contains comprehensive information about the respective area that it covers.

Search the TechNet CD (or its online version through **www.microsoft.com**) and the *Windows NT Server Resource Kit* CD using the keyword "NAT". Also, see the Windows 2000 Server or Advanced Server help.

ftp://ftp.isi.edu/in-notes/rfc1631.txt. Search for RFC 1597 and 1631 for more information on network address translation.

8

Microsoft Proxy Server 2.0

Terms you'll need to understand:

- ✓ Proxy
- ✓ Firewall
- ✓ Local Address Table (LAT)
- ✓ Socks
- ✓ Passive caching
- ✓ Active caching
- ✓ Cache Array Routing Protocol (CARP)
- ✓ Domain filtering
- ✓ Demilitarized Zone (DMZ)
- ✓ Packet filtering
- ✓ Chaining
- ✓ Reverse proxying
- ✓ CERN

Techniques you'll need to master:

- ✓ Differentiating a proxy server from a firewall
- ✓ Integrating multiple proxy servers into a network
- ✓ Determining when to set up proxy chains and arrays
- ✓ Learning requirements for proxy client and server setup

An integral part of designing a network infrastructure is the connection of the internal network to external networks, such as the Internet. Because the Internet is designed for public use, connecting an internal network provides an opening that can be exploited by anyone with Internet access. Because each external connection poses a potential security risk, it's difficult to protect a large number of computers on a network when they all have Internet access. Individual Internet access for each networked computer leaves the entire network vulnerable at every connection. Also, client computers that send information over the Internet can become vulnerable by simply making connections to Internet servers.

By acting as a gateway between internal and external networks, Microsoft Proxy Server reduces the risks that are inherent in connecting an internal network to the Internet. In this book, we often discuss screened subnets as part of the design of many of the network services in Windows 2000. Proxy Server allows a network to create screened subnets and to separate their internal network from external, and possibly unsafe, connections.

What Does a Proxy Server Do?

A "proxy" is something that acts as a replacement or stand-in for something else, and a proxy server acts as a gateway for the computers on the network that need to make an Internet connection. A proxy server serves as the single connection to the Internet and, as such, it protects an internal network from the Internet while, at the same time, controlling access to the Internet. This dual function solves both of the major problems associated with computer networks accessing the Internet: the vulnerability of each Internet connection and the difficulty in controlling the Internet access of individual computers.

A proxy server is the only computer actually connected to the Internet, and the computers on the internal network make their Internet requests to it. The proxy server then goes out onto the Internet to fulfill the request and return it to the client. Only the IP address and information of the proxy server is exposed to the Internet, thus protecting the internal network and lessening the risk of external connections.

Understanding Internet Connections

When a client makes a request for information on the Internet, a connection must be made between the client and the Internet server even before the requested data can be sent. This connection works at the session layer of the Open Systems Interconnection (OSI) model. (For more information on the OSI model and the session layer, refer to Chapter 2 of this book.) First, the client needs the

IP address of the Internet server to find the server on the Internet, but this does not complete the connection between the two computers. Because an Internet server can provide many services to the Internet, the client must also have a port number to complete the connection. Ports are better understood if they are thought of as doorways into the server. Just as a building can have many doorways that lead to its different areas, an Internet server can have many ports leading to the different services that it provides. Ports allow Internet servers to simultaneously provide many different services, each of which is assigned to a different port number. The IP address gets you to the server, and the port number gets you inside to the needed information. Just like a building address won't be of any real use if the door is locked, an IP address won't help a client make a connection to the server if the port is closed and not accepting the connection.

Ports

The port number is included in the uniform resource locater (URL) of a Web site. A URL specifies the format of a Web address, as in **http://www.microsoft.com**. Although users don't normally enter the port number nor even realize that it is needed, the port number is supposed to follow the Internet server name or IP address in this way: **http://www.microsoft.com:80**. If a user does not enter a port number in the URL, then the client will default to a port number that is usually used by the protocol in the URL. The protocol used by the Web service, HTTP, defaults to port 80. The Internet actually has more than 65,000 different port numbers, but only the first 1,023 are designated as well-known ports. Many of these are assigned to services on the Internet. The rest are open for any use.

Setting up the Connection

The IP address and the port number together form the socket. If the port is open, the socket is formed and the connection is successful. Once the port is open and the connection is made, the requested data is still not sent to the client until the client and server exchange information. This information is called *header information* because it is included in the header of the data packets that are sent between clients and servers. Although the header information can vary, it usually includes a client's IP address and other information about the client, such as the type of browser and the Web address from which the client made the new connection. This information is intended for the server's use, but it can make the client vulnerable. Providing Internet connections for users also leaves the clients on the network vulnerable. Protecting information such as your internal network's IP addresses is an important security issue. Figure 8.1 shows closed and open ports, one making a connection and the other refusing a connection.

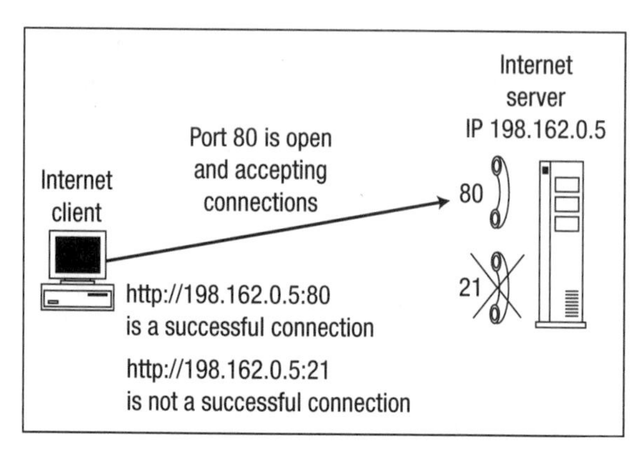

Figure 8.1 Internet connection from client to server using IP address and port number to form socket connection. Port 21 is closed and the connection cannot be made.

Protecting the Network

Although designing a proxy server solution for a network can involve several proxy servers in different roles, the basic role of the proxy server remains the protection of the internal network from the Internet. The proxy server at the edge of the network needs at least two network interfaces: one connected to the internal network and one connected to the Internet. It is important that no IP packets are routed or forwarded between the two interfaces. Instead of the proxy forwarding a client request to the Internet, it reformulates the request so that the origin of the request is not included in packets sent to the Internet. The request is reformulated so that a new request from the proxy server goes out to the Internet. The Internet server returns the requested information to the proxy server, which then sends that information to the original requesting client.

A Proxy vs. a Firewall

Although a proxy server and a firewall are both intended to protect the internal network, they are not the same. A proxy server makes Internet requests for internal computers, and a firewall protects the internal network by blocking packets coming in from the Internet. As explained earlier, Internet computers make connections by using sockets, which are formed with the IP address and the port. A firewall protects the internal network by closing ports and not allowing requests coming from the Internet to make a connection. The request makes it to the server at the IP address, but the port is closed and thus doesn't accept connections. Proxies and firewalls are easily confused, because proxy servers often have firewall capabilities. Microsoft Proxy Server provides both proxy and firewall capabilities. Figure 8.2 shows a proxy server acting as a gateway for outgoing requests and a firewall protecting the internal network by blocking incoming packets.

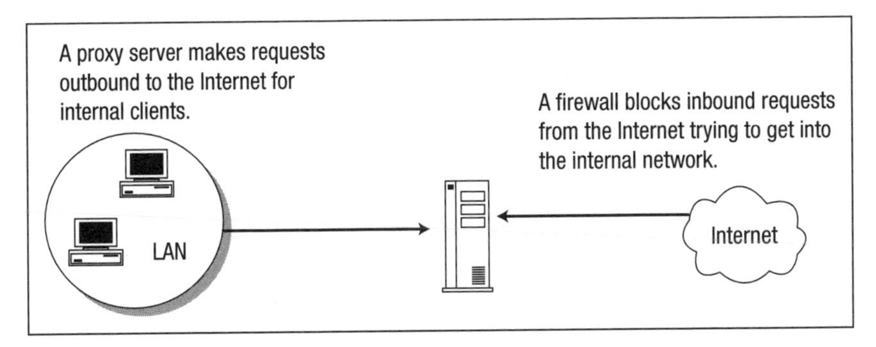
A proxy server makes requests outbound to the Internet for internal clients.
A firewall blocks inbound requests from the Internet trying to get into the internal network.
LAN
Internet

Figure 8.2 Proxy and firewall services serve different purposes on a network.

Microsoft Proxy Server

Proxy Server's current version is 2.0, and has been since 1996. Although the version number has remained the same, Proxy Server has had to adjust as the software on which it runs has changed. For Proxy Server to run, it must be loaded on a Microsoft server operating system, either Windows NT or Windows 2000. Also, Proxy Server runs within Microsoft's Internet Information Server (IIS), and is administered within the IIS administration tool, Internet Services Manager. Internet Services Manger runs within the Microsoft Management Console (MMC). During the time that Proxy Server has been available, IIS has updated from version 3 to version 5. Proxy Server is compatible with all of these versions of IIS.

Proxy Server Software

Proxy Server is a component of BackOffice 4.0 and 4.5, and, although it isn't included on the Windows 2000 Server or Advanced Server CD, it does appear in exam 70-221 Designing a Windows 2000 Networking Infrastructure. It's included on the exam because it is assumed that Internet connections will be included in your network. Microsoft believes that Internet connections are no longer an option, but a necessity in the design of a Windows 2000 network. Because Proxy Server protects your internal network from the vulnerability of Internet connections, it is also considered a necessity for all but the smallest of networks.

Note: Even the smallest of networks need protection from Internet connections. However, proxy services can be provided to small networks with the Network Address Translation (NAT) service. Understanding and implementing NAT is the subject of Chapter 7 of this book.

Microsoft Proxy Server 2.0 and Windows 2000

To install Proxy Server on Windows 2000, IIS must first be loaded. IIS version 5.0 comes with Windows 2000 and can be loaded during or after installation of the operating system. Microsoft has created a special installation file for Proxy Server when it is loaded on Windows 2000. This file can be downloaded from **www.microsoft.com/proxy**. This file does not contain the Proxy Server software: It's simply a program that ensures the correct installation of Proxy Server under Windows 2000. When you run it, you'll be prompted for the BackOffice disk that contains Proxy Server software.

Microsoft's Proxy Server provides both proxy and firewall capabilities. Its default configuration closes all incoming ports so that no connections can be made by incoming requests from the Internet. Packet filters allow some ports to be opened. Configuring packet filters is covered later in this chapter.

The Local Address Table (LAT)

The LAT is very important in the performance of Proxy Server, because the LAT is used to determine whether an IP address is on the internal or external network. The LAT needs to contain all of the IP address ranges from the internal network. When a computer needs to make a connection, it consults the LAT to see if the address is internal or external. If the LAT contains the address, it resides on the internal network and a direct connection can be used. If the address is not on the LAT, then the address is assumed to be external to the network. The packet then needs to be sent to the proxy server to get to its destination. The LAT is created during the installation of Proxy Server, and the server on which Proxy Server is being installed uses its internal routing table to start populating the LAT with IP addresses. An administrator needs to check to make sure that the LAT is correct to prevent packets from being sent to the Internet when they are meant for internal resources.

Services Provided by Proxy Server

There's more to providing proxy services than just retrieving Web pages for internal clients. A proxy server also helps connect Web applications between the client and the Internet server. Often, a Web site provides more than just Web pages for its users. If it provides videos, games, or any other services, these are usually provided by a Web application. A proxy server providing Web pages to internal clients is called a *Web proxy*. A proxy server also needs to provide connections to different types of clients for Web applications. Microsoft Proxy Server is a Web proxy, but it also provides two other proxy services to a network for Web applications: WinSock proxy and Socks proxy. WinSock proxy connects Windows clients to Internet application servers, and Socks does the same for non-Windows clients like Macintosh and Unix.

Note: Although Socks is often written in all uppercase, it is not an acronym and the letters do not stand for anything. The term Socks is derived from sockets. To find out more about Socks, visit www.socks.nec.com.Microsoft Proxy Server supports Socks version 4.3a. This version of Socks does not support UDP connections. Web applications like RealAudio that use UDP as the transport protocol will not work with the Socks proxy service using Microsoft Proxy Server.

Transparency

Like most proxy servers, Microsoft Proxy Server is not a fully transparent proxy server. It *is* transparent in that the user, when typing in the URL for the Web destination, does not see that the request is being made through a proxy server. It is *not* transparent in that the client computer is aware that it needs to make its request to the proxy server instead of trying to make a direct connection to the Internet.

Improved Performance

A client connecting to the Internet tries to improve performance by caching Web pages on its local hard disk, because it's faster to read Web pages from the local disk than retrieving them from the Internet. Caching for Web pages actually is just storing Web pages on the hard disk. Proxy Server tries to improve Internet performance by allowing all clients to benefit from a centralized Web cache. A client requesting an often-accessed Web page can benefit on the first connection if the page already resides in the Proxy Server cache. Caching is affected by how often Web documents change. Documents that change often require more updates while in cache, and Proxy Server checks how often a Web page is updated to decide how often to update its cache. Proxy Server provides both passive and active caching services for the internal network, and each has a different method for updating cached objects.

Passive caching caches information only when it is requested from client computers. When a Web page is requested, Proxy Server retrieves the page from the Internet and stores it in cache. When another client asks for the same Web page, the request can be filled from the Proxy Server's cache. Because the proxy server cache fulfills the request, instead of reformulating it and forwarding it on to the Internet, internal network performance is improved and traffic on the external connection to the Internet is reduced. To keep the cached information from growing stale, each page is assigned a Time To Live (TTL) when it is cached. If the TTL expires by the time another client requests it, then the proxy server may need to go out to the Internet and refresh the document. However, by default, active instead of passive caching is enabled in Proxy Server.

Active caching does not wait for a document to be requested before it is refreshed in the cache. Active caching automatically refreshes documents that are often used by clients on the internal network or that have frequently updated content.

To ensure that active caching does not create a drag on Proxy performance or the network, it is set to update when Proxy Server is not busy and during times of low network traffic. Active caching adds to performance by updating the cache during times of low Internet traffic, so that it is refreshed and ready for times of high traffic.

Caching Limitations

Caching is only for the Web proxy service. WinSock and Socks are proxy services for only Web application connections and do not cache information. Also, not all Web documents can be cached. Dynamic content contained on Active Server pages and from server-side applications (such as connections to a database or search pages) must receive an update from the server every time the page is accessed. These pages cannot be cached. Also, secure pages encrypted with SSL are not cached by default, because these pages usually contain sensitive information that is meant for only a few individuals. Caching does not help performance for these types of Web pages. Also, caching requires a lot of hard disk space: a minimum of 100MB plus 500K for each client that will be supported by the cache.

Also, information in Web pages can be dated. The header of a Web document can contain information on whether or not the information expires and, if it does expire, how long the information is good before it needs to be updated. Administrators of a Web site can set this information at the Web server, and each page can have a different setting based on its content. Although some information expires immediately (this information cannot be cached), other information can last from 30 minutes to 30 days. The setting depends upon the time sensitivity of the information contained in the page.

Optimizing Cache Settings

Cache settings should be set to provide the highest hit ratio possible. A hit ratio for cache shows what percentage of client requests are serviced from cache rather than forwarded to the Internet to retrieve the page. When trying to increase the cache hit ratio, consider the factors that affect it: active data, users not asking for same pages, and low Web use (information goes stale before it can be used from cache). Also, because secure Web data cannot be cached, users accessing sensitive information can affect cache hits. Regardless of how cache is set up or refreshed, certain Web usage will make it impossible to configure high cache hit ratios.

Proxy Arrays

An array is a set of proxy servers that are designated to work as a single logical unit. Arrays provide fault tolerance and bigger caches for internal clients. If one server in an array goes down, the others can continue. Also, each individual proxy server in an array will add its cache size to the array's cache. The caching protocol used by Microsoft Proxy Server allows the cache on each member of the array to act as if it is one large cache instead of a number of smaller caches. To join proxy servers to the same array, they must belong to the same Active Directory domain and site. Both the fault tolerance and improved cache performance make arrays an important alternative in a proxy design.

Cache Array Routing Protocol (CARP)

A problem in setting up an array of proxy servers is that the cache, although it is supposed to act as if it is a single logical cache, still physically exists on different proxy servers. Originally arrays would query each other for cached objects, but this method degrades performance as the array grows larger. Also, the cache on each member of the array could contain redundant objects. The Cache Array Routing Protocol (CARP) uses an algorithm to spread the cache, without redundancy, across the array. CARP's algorithm calculates a score for each requested URL before placing it in cache, and clients use this same scoring system to determine on which member of the array the requested URL is most likely cached. By default, other members of the array will be checked according to the next highest score for the object before the request is forwarded on to the Internet to be fulfilled. The algorithm adjusts automatically when members are added to or removed from the array. CARP allows arrays to grow more efficient as members are added, although 20 proxy servers are considered to be the maximum in one array.

Security Services Provided by Proxy Server

Even though it works to improve Internet performance, Proxy Server is really set up for security. Most of the services it provides are for the security of the internal network. Because a proxy server acts as a gateway for Internet connections, controls can be placed on these connections, and these controls can be as fine as which services are available, which users can use these services, and which sites users can access.

For Outbound Access

Proxy Server allows administrators to control user access to the Internet. An administrator can set the server so that only certain users or groups of users are allowed access to Internet services. The administrator can even set which Internet sites can and cannot be accessed.

Active Directory Integration

Not everyone on the internal network may need all services provided on the Internet. Proxy Server integrates with Active Directory services provided in Windows 2000 by allowing the administrator to set whom may use Internet services.

For example, the Sales group may need to use the FTP service, but doesn't need to access the Web. Although most users are usually provided access to all Internet services, this control is included in Proxy Server.

Domain Filters

Besides controlling who can use Internet services, Proxy Server can be set to control what Internet sites are accessed. A company may decide that only a company intranet site should be accessed and block access to all other sites, or a company may decide to block access to certain sites while allowing access to all others.

Controlling Inbound Access

By controlling inbound traffic, Proxy Server is, in effect, acting as a firewall for the network. Because Proxy Server is a gateway for all Internet traffic, it can even watch for attacks by evaluating inbound traffic. For example, Proxy Server is aware of such attacks as those that try to overwhelm the network with packets or spoofed packets that have been altered.

When firewalls create a network separate from the internal network and the external (Internet) network, this new network can be called a screened subnet or a demilitarized zone (DMZ). Information is placed in the DMZ when clients coming in from the Internet need the information. By placing the information in the DMZ the internal network is protected from Internet access, yet Internet clients can still get to the needed information.

A screened subnet and a DMZ are the same thing. Some Microsoft literature refers to screened subnets and some refers to DMZs. It is important to understand that they are the same.

Packet Filters

After installing Proxy Server and connecting it to an external interface, no packets from the Internet are allowed, by default, into the internal network. This is because packet filtering closes all inbound ports to prevent external computers from connecting to internal computers. Packet filters can be implemented on only the external interface to the Internet. Because port access can be outbound or inbound, packet filters actually apply to traffic coming from internal and external sources. Because all ports are closed by default, an administrator needs to create exceptions that will allow some ports to be opened to provide services to the network. Once a packet filter exception is configured, it applies to all three services that Proxy Server provides.

Packet filters can be dynamic or static. A static filter is either open or closed at all times. For example, an outbound request for a Web page would need to use port 80. A static filter would leave port 80 open for outbound connections at all times. A dynamic packet filter would close port 80 until it was needed for an outbound request. It would then open the port for the request, closing it when the request was completed. Dynamic filters are used by default in Proxy Server.

Preparing a Network for Proxy Server

Before Proxy Server can be incorporated into a network, planning must be completed and changes may be needed to prepare the network. One issue that needs to be resolved is IP addressing. Clients that currently have a direct connection to the Internet also must have valid IP addresses for the Internet. Because each IP address used on the Internet must be unique, the use of IP addresses on the Internet must be controlled. An administrator of a network can obtain valid IP addresses directly from the controlling organization or from an Internet Service Provider (ISP). Obtaining a block of IP addresses is not as inexpensive as it once was, and Proxy Server can save a company money. A company that decides to obtain a block of IP addresses directly must contact the American Registry of Internet Numbers (ARIN) at **www.arin.net**. However, this is not a cheap method: The smallest block of IP addresses available to lease is 4,096, and that will cost you $2,500 per year. A smaller block of IP addresses can be obtained from an ISP.

Note: Until the end of 1997, IP addresses for use on the Internet were obtained from Network Solutions, Inc. (InterNIC). Control of IP addressing has now been passed to Regional Internet Registries (RIR). The entire world is divided into three regions for the purpose of contolling the allocation of IP addresses for Internet use. The three RIRs each control the assignment of IP addresses for a large geographical area. ARIN controls the assignment of IP addresses for the Americas and Africa. For more information on the rules of IP addressing, visit www.ARIN.net.

Both methods of obtaining valid IP addresses will cost a company, and paying for an IP address ensures that an individual client on the network is the only one using it. Proxy Server provides an additional benefit in that it doesn't need valid IP addresses for internal clients. Because these addresses will never be used on the Internet, it really doesn't matter what range of IP addresses are used internally. Only the proxy server that sits on the edge of the network and that is connected to the Internet needs an address that is valid for use on the Internet. Clients on the internal network can be assigned a range of what are called *private IP addresses*. Any IP address that is not for use on the Internet needs to be unique for only the local network on which it resides. A company using Proxy Server needs to buy valid IP addresses for only the proxy servers that connect to the Internet.

Private Ranges of IP Addresses

Some ranges of IP addresses are reserved for internal use on networks, which means that these addresses cannot be used on the Internet. Network numbers such as 10.0.0.0 and 192.168.0.0 are examples of private addresses. The recommended setting for Proxy Server is that the internal network use a private range of IP addresses and that only the external connection(s) to the Internet need a valid IP address. This setting adds a measure of safety for the network. If one of the clients tries to connect directly to the Internet instead of through the Proxy Server, the invalid client IP address will prevent the connection.

Because Proxy Server drastically reduces the number of external IP addresses that are needed, you may need to reconsider the use of IP addresses on the network. A private range of addresses needs to be selected for internal use on the network, and you may find that you need only one external IP address. The exact use of IP addresses may be delayed until a network diagram allows a designer to see the needs of the network.

The Network Diagram

Networks are more complicated to design when WAN connections are involved. A network diagram reveals to the designer of network services how users are concentrated and interconnected. A simple network diagram for Proxy Server design should include the following elements:

- LANs
- WAN connections
- Number of users at each LAN

Figure 8.3 shows an example of a simple network diagram.

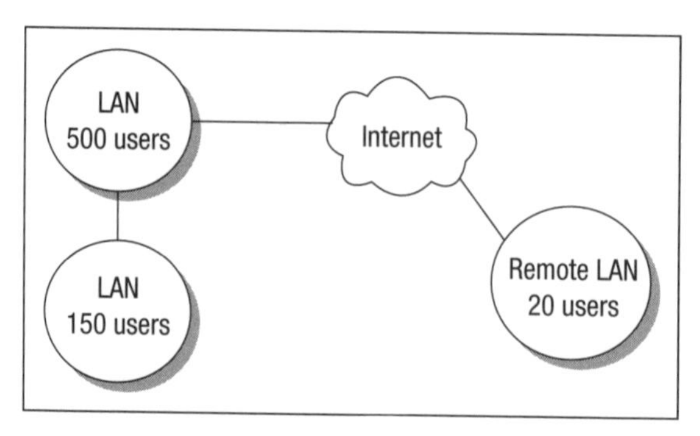

Figure 8.3 Use a network diagram before making decisions with a Proxy Server design.

Determining the Number of Proxy Servers

Depending on its size and geographic distribution, a network can implement one to several proxy servers. In a large network, an overburdened proxy server can act as a bottleneck for Internet traffic, slowing connections when it can't keep up with the demand. Determining the number of proxy servers can be a factor not only of the number of Internet users, but also in the type of Internet traffic and the size of downloaded files. A medium single network location of 500 users may work well with only one proxy server if Internet traffic is light, but that same network—if it uses the Internet heavily to transfer large files—may need a few proxy servers or even an array of proxy servers.

Microsoft recommends that each WAN location have one proxy server. This rule should be followed even if each WAN location does not have its own Internet connection. A proxy server does not necessarily have to be connected to the Internet or even have two network interfaces to be a part of a network design. A proxy server can provide caching services to a network even if it is not providing security services. Proxy servers can fill different roles on the network to help different network situations.

Chaining Proxy Server

Networks that have many locations but only one connection to the Internet can benefit by chaining proxy servers. Chaining proxy servers distributes their load across a network and allows them to check more than one cache before making a request on the Internet. Individual proxy servers or arrays can exist in a chain. Keep chains shallow: Fewer hops are best, because several hops can increase latency.

Upstream vs. Downstream

To design proxy server chains, it is important to understand the terms *upstream* and *downstream*. Going upstream means heading towards the Internet and away from the internal network, and going downstream means heading away from the Internet and towards the internal network. When designing chains, proxy servers will either be upstream or downstream from each other. Downstream proxy servers will pass a request upstream to other proxy servers, and each server will check its cache to try to fulfill the request before passing it upstream. The last upstream proxy server will make a request to the Internet for the requested page.

Proxy Server Routes

Setting up a chain of proxy servers involves configuring routes for the servers to follow when filling client Internet requests. Primary and alternate routes can be configured to provide for fault tolerance. In the event that the upstream proxy server is unavailable, the backup proxy server can be used instead. Proxy arrays work best in a chain of proxy servers. Several proxy servers on the edge of LANs can route to an upstream proxy array. This keeps the chain of proxy servers shallow and increases cache hits by providing a large cache in the array, while keeping the connection to the Internet just a few hops away. Figure 8.4 shows an example of Proxy Server routing. Proxy servers not connected to the Internet can be chained to the proxy servers that do have a connection to the Internet. The downstream proxy server in LAN2 will route Internet requests not fulfilled by cache to the upstream proxy array in LAN1.

Reverse Proxying

Some networks may want to provide Internet users with a Web site. Setting up a proxy server to protect your Web site is called *reverse proxying*. It is "reverse" because proxies normally protect internal clients from being exposed to the Internet. Reverse proxying allows external clients from the Internet to access Web services on an internal network. Proxy Server can be configured to help protect your Web site from this vulnerable situation of being exposed to an Internet connection.

Although Proxy Server must have IIS services loaded on the same server, do not place the Web site on the same server as Proxy Server. Proxy Server is vulnerable because it is on the Internet. Web sites need to be protected from malicious users who may want to break into a Web site and alter the contents of the Web pages. If a Web site and Proxy Server coexist on the same computer, then, when one is

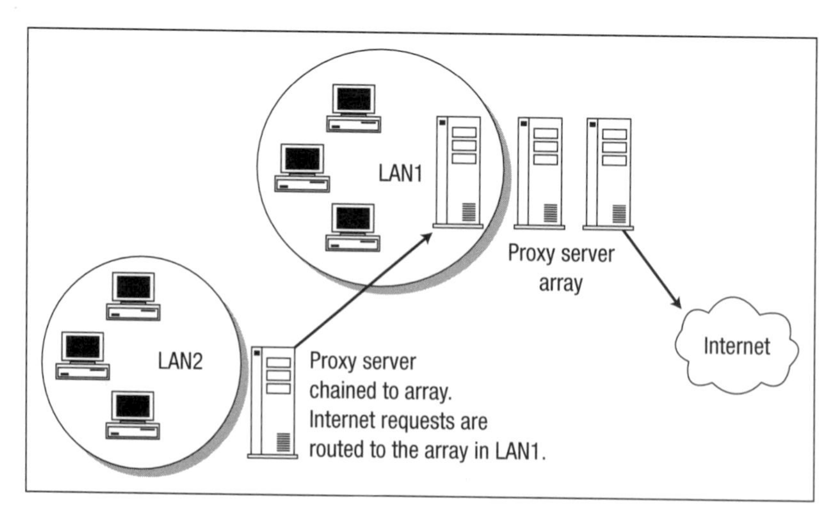

Figure 8.4 Proxy Server is useful for caching services on a network with just one connection to the Internet.

broken into, so is the other. Protect your Web sites by placing them on servers that are downstream of a server providing proxy services.

If security of data is a concern, then the Web server should be placed in a screened subnet that is separated from the rest of the internal network. Remember, any connection from the Internet into an internal network leaves that network vulnerable. An internal network with confidential information should not allow any inbound connections, and moving the Web server to a separate screened subnet with its own proxy server is the most secure solution.

Placing Proxy Servers on the Network

Once the network is diagrammed and Internet use is established, proxy servers can be correctly placed on the network. Proxy Server is not stringent on the types of interfaces with which it will work. Connections can be dial-up, persistent, or a combination of the two. Proxy Server allows for flexibility in selecting protocols from level 2, the data link layer, up to level 4, the transport layer.

Joining Dissimilar Networks with Proxy Server

One proxy server can be connected to networks using different access methods. If one network is using Ethernet and another is using Token Ring or Asynchronous Transfer Mode (ATM), Proxy Server just needs to have an adapter for each of these types of networks. This works because Proxy Server does not forward the requests between the networks. As you'll remember, if Proxy Server cannot fulfill the request from cache, it formulates a new request to pass it upstream to the Internet. No translation for the connections, such as a bridge, is needed.

Proxy Server can also be used on a network that uses IPX/SPX, Novell Netware's proprietary protocol stack, on the internal network. IPX/SPX can be implemented instead of the TCP/IP protocol stack on the internal computers. TCP/IP is required for only the external connection to the Internet.

External Connections

Just using proxy chains and arrays inside a network will not improve performance if there is still a bottleneck at the Internet connection. Proxy Server can allow a company to whittle its Internet connections down to one even if several WAN locations exist within the company. This may save money on the cost of Internet connections, but, if the one Internet connection is saturated, then more may be needed to accommodate the traffic. With this solution, caching throughout the network is maximized because different caches may be checked before sending a request to the Internet. If each WAN location has its own connection to the Internet, caching will be used less. If much of the information from the Internet contains secure or dynamic information, cache would not be as likely to fulfill the requests, and more Internet connections would be needed if a performance improvement is desired.

Ensuring That All Proxies Are Used Evenly

If more than one Internet connection accepts inbound client requests, two different methods may be used to ensure that all proxy servers are used evenly for Internet connections: multiple entries in DNS to create a round-robin effect, and network load balancing (NLB). Both methods ensure the distribution of incoming requests across all available proxy servers.

A DNS server containing records that have the same hostname mapped to different IP addresses will automatically resolve queries in a round-robin fashion. The first query is resolved with the first record in the list, and subsequent queries are resolved with the rest of the records, working down to the last entry then starting back at the top again. The following list shows how round-robin DNS entries work. These entries have the same hostname, but different IP addresses. DNS will start at the top of the list when resolving queries for **www.coriolis.com**. The first query will receive 192.168.0.5 as a response, and the next query will receive 192.168.0.6. DNS will continue to the bottom of the list and start back at the top, automatically load balancing incoming requests.

www.Coriolis.com	192.168.0.5
www.Coriolis.com	192.168.0.6
www.Coriolis.com	192.168.0.7
www.Coriolis.com	192.168.0.8

Installing the NLB service also distributes incoming requests across available proxy servers. Although round-robin DNS entries are a manual way to distribute traffic across available servers, NLB automatically distributes traffic across servers, like clustering. If one server is unavailable, DNS, using round-robin entries, will still send traffic to the unavailable server, whereas NLB will automatically adjust traffic until the unavailable server comes back online. The downside to NLB is that it has more CPU overhead than DNS round-robin entries. NLB is a better service to use if incoming connections must be serviced 24 hours a day with no exceptions.

NLB is not just for Proxy Server use. It is part of the Windows Clustering Service, and it allows incoming TCP/IP services to be distributed across multiple servers.

Review of Proxy Services

Now that you have learned of the services provided by Proxy Server, it is important to remember whether the service protects inbound or outbound connections. Remembering this will help keep the services straight when implementing them in a network solution. Figure 8.5 shows a list of inbound and outbound protection services provided by Proxy Server.

Setting up Proxy Clients

Proxy Server provides three different proxy services to the network. Web proxy has been discussed for most of this chapter, because it has the most features that can be set. WinSock and Socks proxy clients are used to connect computers using Web applications. Normally, the connection is made directly from client to server over the Internet, but, when a proxy server is used, the connection is made through the proxy server. Proxy clients must be aware of the proxy server and know how to use it in order for this connection to be successful.

Web Proxy Clients

Browsers making client requests to a Web proxy server need to be compliant with only the basic Web standards. This standard is from the Swiss Conseil European pour la Recherche Nucleair (CERN) (which translates as *European Laboratory for Particle Physics*). CERN is responsible for basic Internet protocol standards such as HTTP and the original idea for proxy servers. The most recent versions of Internet Explorer automatically detect a network's Web proxy server and use it with no configuration changes needed from a network administrator.

WinSock and Socks Proxy Clients

Unlike the Web proxy service, clients needing to connect to Web applications need some configuration changes in order to use the WinSock or Socks proxy

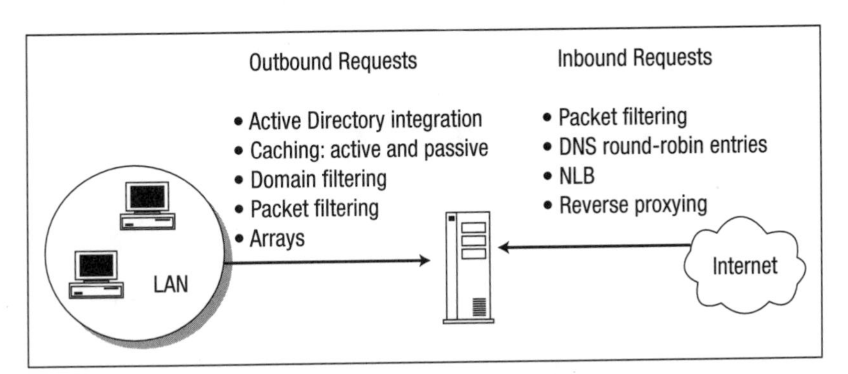

Figure 8.5 Inbound and outbound protection services provided by and used in conjunction with Proxy Server. Packet filtering is the only overlapping service.

service. Either the WinSock or Socks proxy service is needed, because they are designed for different types of clients. To connect to Web applications through a proxy server, Windows clients using the WinSock interface need the WinSock proxy, and non-Windows clients need the Socks proxy. During the installation of Proxy Server, a script is created that is used to configure WinSock proxy clients. WinSock clients need to connect to the Proxy Server to run the script in order to be configured to use the WinSock proxy service. The script will also configure the proxy clients to update their local LAT from a share on the proxy server. Socks client software does not come with Proxy Server but can be downloaded from **ftp://ftp.nec.com/pub/socks**. Remember to download version 4.3a, which is compatible with the Socks proxy service provided by Microsoft Proxy Server.

Practice Questions

Case Study

Hi-tech Company is located in San Diego, CA, and has 500 users. It would like to expand its presence on the Internet but know that this presents a security risk to its network. The company is looking for ways to secure and improve its Internet connections.

Current WAN Connectivity

Each user has his or her own connection to the Internet through a 56Kbps modem. Each user has a static IP address. The company is having difficulty controlling Internet connections and is wondering if this can be controlled.

Proposed WAN Connectivity

Hi-tech Company decides to simplify and centralize the connection to the Internet. Proxy Server has been suggested as a way to centralize the connection to the Internet and also provide control over the users' connections.

Future Internet Plans

Hi-tech would like to create a Web site for the company and host it from its own network.

Company Goal with Windows 2000

Since the network has been upgraded to Windows 2000 the company would like to take advantage of the new security features for Internet connections. The company would like to know which of these services is best for their network situation.

Question 1

What changes need to be made to the network to add a proxy server?

❍ a. Load a Web proxy client on the users' computers.

❍ b. Add routers to the network.

❍ c. Assign a private range of IP addresses to the internal network.

❍ d. Do nothing. The network is ready in its current state.

Answer c is correct. The network needs a private range of IP addresses assigned to the internal network. To keep users from making their own connection to the Internet a private range of IP addresses needs to be used for the internal network.

A private range of IP addresses will be a more secure solution for the network. A Web proxy client needs only to be a CERN-compliant browser to use a proxy server. More software is not needed. Routers will have no affect on a proxy server solution.

Question 2

How much hard disk space will be needed on the Proxy Server to adequately provide the clients with caching services?

- ❍ a. 100MB
- ❍ b. 250MB
- ❍ c. 350MB
- ❍ d. 500MB

Answer c is correct. Caching requires a lot of hard disk space. This network has 500 users and the recommended setting is 100MB of hard disk space plus 500K (0.5MB) for every supported user. 100 + (500 *0.5) = 350MB.

Question 3

A branch office with 50 users needs to be connected to the main office. The branch office is linked through a 56Kbps frame-relay connection. Without creating another connection to the Internet, how should this branch office be incorporated using a secure proxy server solution? [Check all correct answers]

- ❑ a. Add a proxy server to the branch office.
- ❑ b. Chain the branch office proxy server to the main office server.
- ❑ c. Implement NLB to ensure availability of the main office proxy server.
- ❑ d. Set up a backup route to the Internet for the branch office.

Answers a and b are correct. It is recommended that a proxy server be implemented at every WAN connection, even if it is not connected to the Internet. The proxy server at the branch location will provide a local cache for those users. Creating a proxy server chain will route Internet requests from the branch office to the main office and its connection to the Internet. NLB is for incoming requests from the Internet and not for internal requests. Answer d is a good answer if fault tolerance were an issue or if another connection to the Internet were part of the requirements.

Question 4

Due to the company's growth and increased Internet usage, performance to the Internet is too slow at the main location and the branch office. What proxy server solutions can help this situation? [Check all correct answers]

- ❑ a. Create a proxy array at the main location.
- ❑ b. Set up DNS for round-robin entries.
- ❑ c. Connect the proxy server at the branch office to the Internet.
- ❑ d. Enable packet filtering on the LAN proxy server.

Answers a and c are correct. A proxy array will improve caching of Web pages and improve performance for the large concentration of users at the main location. A separate Internet connection at the branch office will remove the burden off the main office proxy server. DNS round-robin entries work with only incoming packets, and this is not currently enabled for the network. Packet filtering is enabled by default and will not help to improve Internet connection performance.

Question 5

The company has just won a large contract for a project. Information regarding the project is available on a private Web site that can be accessed from the Internet. The site contains a Web application that users from the company need to use over the Internet. How can this be set up? [Check all correct answers]

- ❑ a. Set up a Socks proxy client software on each client.
- ❑ b. Run the WinSock proxy client script on each client.
- ❑ c. Configure each client as a Web proxy client.
- ❑ d. Do nothing. No configuration is needed.

Answer b is correct. During the installation of Proxy Server, a script is created to configure WinSock proxy clients. The script needs to be run on individual clients to configure the use of Web applications over the Internet. Socks proxy is only needed for non-Windows clients, and this network has Internet Explorer running on Windows 2000 Professional. Web proxies are only for Web pages and are not for connecting Web applications.

Question 6

An array has been set up at the main location. What performance enhancements does an array provide? [Check all correct answers]

- ❑ a. Filtering
- ❑ b. Caching
- ❑ c. Fault tolerance
- ❑ d. Chaining

Answers b and c are correct. Proxy arrays improve caching performance by allowing the caches on different proxy servers to act as one logical cache. Fault tolerance is also provided within an array. If one member fails, the others take over. Filtering is not a performance enhancement. It is a security enhancement. Chaining proxy servers is connecting proxy servers linearly and does not combine them logically into one unit.

Question 7

The company has decided to set up a Web site and host it at the main location. What service needs to be set up to allow this?

- ❍ a. Packet filtering
- ❍ b. Domain filtering
- ❍ c. Reverse proxying
- ❍ d. Network load balancing

Answer c is correct. Reverse proxying allows for Web publishing inside the screened subnet. It allows inbound requests from the Internet into the network to be serviced by the local Web server. Packet filtering stops incoming packets instead of allowing them in. Domain filtering is for outgoing connections only, and although NLB helps incoming connections, it is not required for these connections to work.

Question 8

Internet performance is still too slow and is causing delays in work performance. Most of the users are connecting to the project site and downloading secure pages. How can performance be improved?

- ❍ a. Add another proxy server with a separate Internet connection.
- ❍ b. Chain a downstream proxy server to the array.
- ❍ c. Use CARP as the caching protocol.
- ❍ d. Change passive caching to active.

Answer a is correct. Because most of the users are accessing secure Web pages, cache improvements will not help improve performance. Secure content cannot be cached. The only performance enhancement that will help the problem is another proxy server with another connection to the Internet. Answers b, c, and d all would improve caching performance, but because most of the pages are secure and therefore not being cached, cache enhancements will not help the problem of slow performance in this situation.

Question 9

The new project is causing security concerns. Information at the main office is confidential and needs to be protected. What security precautions can be taken to protect the information from inbound Internet traffic? [Check all correct answers]

- ❑ a. Use NLB.
- ❑ b. Implement domain filtering.
- ❑ c. Place the Web server in a screened subnet separated from the internal network.
- ❑ d. Enable dynamic packet filtering.
- ❑ e. Use packet filtering to close all inbound ports to the internal network.

Answers c, d, and e are correct. Currently, a Web server resides on the internal network, and reverse proxying allows inbound requests from the Internet to access it. The Web server needs to be placed in a screened subnet separated from the internal network. Dynamic filtering will add an extra measure of security by closing ports that are providing services when they are not active. NLB is for load balancing and not for security. Domain filtering blocks internal users from accessing certain Internet domains and does not help inbound traffic. Using packet filtering to close *all* inbound ports will not allow *any* connections to the internal network. Connections made to the Web server in the screened subnet in front of the internal network will be allowed, but traffic will be unable to continue on to the internal network.

Question 10

Packet filtering is enabled for the Web proxy service. As an added security precaution, the network administrator would also like to set up packet filtering for the WinSock proxy service. What needs to be done to enable this service? [Choose the best answer]

- ❍ a. Enable packet filtering in Internet Services Manager.
- ❍ b. Packet filtering is not available for WinSock proxy service.
- ❍ c. The WinSock proxy service uses domain filters instead.
- ❍ d. Do nothing. Packet filtering needs to be enabled on only one service.

Answer d is correct. Once packet filtering is enabled for one proxy service, it is enabled for all proxy services. Domain filters are used for outbound traffic to allow certain groups to use the proxy server to gain Internet access. Once packet filtering has been enabled for the Web proxy service, no other configurations are necessary to configure packet filtering for the WinSock proxy service.

Question 11

A private Web site in support of the project has been established in the company's main office. It is critical that the site be available at all times for external Internet access. What services are needed at the main office to ensure this happens? [Check all correct answers]

- ❑ a. Set up a proxy server array.
- ❑ b. Implement NLB with additional Web servers.
- ❑ c. Use active caching.
- ❑ d. Integrate Proxy Server with Active Directory.

Only answer b is correct. NLB with additional Web servers at the main office is the only option that will provide fault tolerance for incoming requests to the Web site. All other choices help fault tolerance or availability for outbound requests only.

Need to Know More?

Luotonen, Ari. *Web Proxy Servers.* Prentice-Hall, Inc., Upper Saddle River, NJ, 1998. ISBN 0-13-680612-0. Luotonen helped develop the original proxy software, and the book provides an overview of the development and inner workings of proxy servers.

www.microsoft.com/proxy/Support/win2kwizard.asp? *How to Install Proxy Server on Windows 2000.* Microsoft Corporation, Redmond, WA, 2000. This knowledge base article walks you through the process of installing Proxy Server on Windows 2000. A revised installation file needs to be downloaded from **www.microsoft.com/proxy**. This file does not contain Proxy Server installation files. Those files are included with BackOffice 4.0 and 4.5.

www.microsoft.com/ISN/whitepapers/network_load_balancing_win2k.asp *Network Load Balancing.* Microsoft Corporation, Redmond, WA, 2000. This Microsoft white paper explains the use of NLB service on a network.

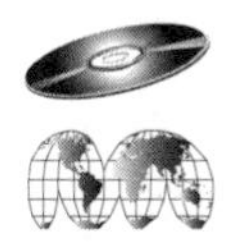

Search the TechNet CD (or its online version through **http://support.microsoft.com/directory**) and the *Windows 2000 Server Resource Kit* CD. First use the keyword "Proxy Server" and then, from that subset, search on "Windows 2000".

Routing in a Windows 2000 Environment

Terms you'll need to understand:

- ✓ Routing Information Protocol (RIP)
- ✓ Open Shortest Path First (OSPF)
- ✓ Unicast
- ✓ Broadcast
- ✓ Multicast
- ✓ Internet Group Management Protocol (IGMP)
- ✓ Hop
- ✓ Autonomous system
- ✓ Service Advertising Protocol (SAP)
- ✓ AppleTalk
- ✓ Channel Service Unit/Data Service Unit (CSU/DSU)

Techniques you'll need to master:

- ✓ Determining when routers are needed
- ✓ Selecting the right routing protocol
- ✓ Placing routers within a WAN environment
- ✓ Improving routing performance

This chapter teaches you how to implement routing in a Windows 2000 network infrastructure. Windows 2000 can work with third-party routers or provide its own routing services through the Routing and Remote Access Service (RRAS). You will need to learn which routing situation is most appropriate for a variety of different network configurations.

Routing Overview

Routing is defined as the procedure of finding a path from a source to a destination. The source and destination points can be any hardware interface on a network, whether a computer, printer, CD-ROM tower, or any similar devices.

Routing plays an important role in the function of wide area networks (WANs), which depend on routing to deliver packets from one local area network (LAN) to another. A *LAN* is defined as a network that covers a small geographical location, such as a single office building, and routing's mission is to deliver a packet of information from one LAN to another. It may help to compare the computers in a LAN to houses in a neighborhood. If you want to deliver a package to a house in your neighborhood, you can just take it yourself. Similarly, a computer that needs to deliver a packet to another computer in its own LAN can send the information directly to that computer. When you need to send a package outside of your own neighborhood, you take it to the post office. The package will be passed through other post offices until it reaches its destination. Computers don't know how to deliver packets outside of their local LAN, and so it simply sends the packet to the router instead. Regardless of whether this delivery is a long or short distance, it is the router's responsibility to start the delivery in the right direction. Because each LAN has a router, the routers simply pass the packet from router to router until it arrives at the correct LAN.

A router can be a physical piece of hardware that is dedicated to routing, or it can be software such as Windows 2000 Server running Routing and Remote Access Service (RRAS) with multiple network interface cards (NICs). A router is called a *gateway* because all packets leaving and entering the LAN must go through the router. When a computer on one LAN generates a packet that is destined for another LAN, the packet is forwarded to the gateway (or the router), which checks a table of available addresses and determines—based on the destination address—the best interface to send the packet out on. The router then forwards the packet to the appropriate LAN, where either one of two things occurs:

- The current LAN is the destination, and the packet is delivered to the destination computer; or
- The destination of the packet is another LAN, and the packet is sent to the next gateway to be forwarded until it reaches the destination LAN and computer.

Unfortunately, routers need to be told how a network of LANs is arrayed and what the best route is to choose. The best way to configure a router with this information depends on the complexity and size of the network.

Dynamic vs. Static Routing

Because a router's job is to deliver packets to their destinations by forwarding them to other routers, a router must build a table of information that it refers to when sending packets that are bound for different destination networks. This routing table can be built via different methods. A network administrator can enter in the routes manually or pick from different routing protocols to build the table automatically. Whatever method you choose depends on the design and goals of the network. The router refers to the routing table to decide which interface to send the packet out on and, if more than one route is available, which route is the best. A routing table determines the best route by comparing the routes' metrics, a value that is assigned to the route. Usually, the route with the lowest metric is the best.

Dynamic routing is implemented when a routing protocol is loaded onto a router. The routing protocol configures the routing table based on the rules of the protocol. Each routing protocol uses a unique set of rules to build the routing table and, if multiple routes are available, to determine which route is best. Routers using a routing protocol send information to each other that each uses to build the routing table. Windows 2000 RRAS supports some—but not all—of the currently popular routing protocols. Routing Information Protocol (RIP) in versions 1 and 2 and Open Shortest Path First (OSPF) are each supported by the RRAS service in Windows 2000.

Although the Windows 2000 RRAS service understands RIP version 1, only RIP version 2 can be selected as a routing protocol that can be loaded. RIP version 1 is not listed in the RRAS console.

Note: Interior Gateway Routing Protocol (IGRP) and Extended Interior Gateway Routing Protocol (EIGRP), both of which are popular routing protocols, are not supported by default by the RRAS service and will not be discussed as options in this chapter.

Static routing involves an administrator manually building the routing table. The administrator needs to determine which path, from router to router, that the packets should travel. Each router then needs to be programmed with the correct routing information. Static routers that do not have a routing protocol loaded follow the routes with which they are programmed and do not send information or communicate routing paths to other routers. Although performing these manual entries is difficult and time consuming in a large network, static routing can have advantages over dynamic routing. Because static routers do not communicate with each other, they do not add traffic to a network as dynamic routers do. Also, a static router can be integrated into a network that uses dynamic routing. Knowing the advantages and disadvantages of static and dynamic routing helps in deciding which is best to use when designing a network infrastructure.

Enabling Windows 2000 Routing

Although the routing service on a Windows 2000 server—RRAS—is installed automatically, it still needs to be enabled and configured, and this is done with the RRAS Management Console (MMC). You'll find it by going to Start|Programs|Administrative Tools|Routing And Remote Access.

To configure and enable RRAS, follow these steps:

1. Right-click on Routing and Remote Access in the left pane of the RRAS MMC and select Add Server.
2. Select This Computer and click on OK. In the left pane of the main console screen, highlight Server Status. You should now see other options that include the name of the local server.
3. Right-click on the server name and select Configure And Enable Routing And Remote Access.
4. Allow the wizard to guide you through the RRAS setup process. From the Common Configurations screen, select Network Router.
5. From the Routed Protocols screen, select the protocols that this server will use to communicate with connected LANs. (The protocols used for communication must be installed and bound to the appropriate interfaces.)
6. Specify whether to use demand-dial connections.
7. If you decide not to use demand-dial connections, the setup wizard will end. If you are going to use demand-dial connections, the wizard will ask you how you wish to assign IP addresses for incoming connections: by using DHCP or a newly specified range.
8. If you choose to make a new range of IP addresses, you will be prompted for the scope(s) to use. After entering this information, you'll select either Next or Finish to end the installation.

9. Once RRAS is installed, you need to enable routing on the local server. Click on Properties for the routing server in the RRAS MMC.
10. Under the General tab, check the Router box and select LAN or Demand-Dial Routing.

Unicasts, Broadcasts, and Multicasts

When computers send information to other computers, the information packets can be addressed to one or several computers. These types of transmission are unicasts, broadcasts, and multicasts, and each type has a different overhead and effect on the network. A unicast is a packet that is addressed to only one computer. In most network configurations, all computers see this packet, but, because it is specifically addressed to one computer, they ignore the packet. A broadcast packet, on the other hand, isn't addressed to any one computer in particular. Broadcast transmissions increase the network's workload because each computer must process all broadcast packets to see if the information is intended for them or another computer. Multicasts, however, are different from both unicasts and broadcasts, because they can be addressed to a specific group of computers. This capability helps to reduce network traffic. Unlike a broadcast, computers that do not belong to the multicast group can ignore the multicast just as they would a unicast. Also, instead of sending a separate unicast to each computer, a computer can send one set of packets for all computers in a multicast group.

RIP in versions 1 and 2 and OSPF are unicast routing protocols. By default, routers will pass unicasts that are intended for networks other than the one from which it originated. Routers will not, by default, pass broadcasts. If it is decided that the network needs to pass a certain type of broadcast, then the router can be set up to do so. An example of this is the DHCP service, which uses broadcasts. Loading the DHCP Relay Agent (also called BOOTP relay agent) on an RRAS router allows DHCP broadcasts to pass through that router.

IGMP

Multicasting requires the presence of multicasting protocols on the routers within the network. Although several such protocols are available, Microsoft Windows 2000 routing does not support any of them. However, Internet Group Management Protocol (IGMP) can allow multicast forwarding in a TCP/IP environment using Windows 2000 routing. The flexibility of multicasts is that multicast groups can be any size and that computers can join and leave groups at any time. IGMP keeps track of multicast group memberships. For IGMP to perform multicast forwarding, the network adapter must be able to go into multicast-promiscuous mode. Microsoft supports only one-hop forwarding with IGMP and not hopping through multiple routers in Windows 2000 routing.

Routing Information Protocol (RIP)

RIP uses a distance-vector algorithm that counts the number of hops to select the best route. RIP sends all or part of its routing table to its neighboring routers. It is also a single-path protocol, which means that it will have a preferred path to a destination. If two or more paths to a destination are possible, RIP always chooses the same one, provided the path is available. The type of RIP used depends on the protocol stack that is implemented in the network. TCP/IP uses RIP for IP, and NWLink—IPX/SPX in Novell Netware networks—uses RIP for IPX. Each has different implementation on a network, and the configuration for each will be covered later in this chapter.

RIP is best used in small to medium networks because of the way it builds its routing table and because of its hop limitation. RIP routers build their routing tables by broadcasting the networks and routes that they know about. Other RIP routers listen for these broadcasts and build their routing tables from the information contained within them. Each RIP router sends these broadcasts every 30 seconds by default, which can consume a lot of bandwidth on a large network.

Microsoft recommends that RIP be used only in networks with up to 50 subnets. Even with 50 subnets, the network must be designed so that all routes can be reached in 14 hops. While a packet is being routed, it is passed from one router to the next. Each of these passes is considered a hop. RIP normally has a hop limit of 15, but a Windows 2000 router assumes that all routes that aren't learned through a RIP broadcast have a hop count of two. Because none of a RIP router's own routes were learned from RIP, each RIP router gives its own routes a hop count of two. Thus, in Windows 2000 routing, a packet can travel through 14 routers to get to its destination, but, if it continues to a fifteenth router, it will be discarded.

Another reason why RIP cannot be used in large networks is that RIP uses the hop counts to determine the shortest path to a destination host. This may not always be the best path to the destination. In Figure 9.1, the shortest path (by hop count) is through the satellite connections at a speed of 1Mbps, and the longer path is through a T1 connection (1.544Mbps), which RIP will not use unless the satellite link is down. Other routing protocols (such as OSPF) that use more than just the number of hops to determine the best route may work better.

Comparing RIP Versions 1 and 2

You must understand the distinctions between the different versions of RIP. Because a Windows 2000 router will pass RIP v1 and RIP v2 packets, it can exist in a mixed environment of the two versions. RIP v1 does not accommodate flexibility in subnetting. If a network uses Classless Interdomain Routing (CIDR) with supernetting or variable-length subnet masks (VLSM), then only RIP v2 will

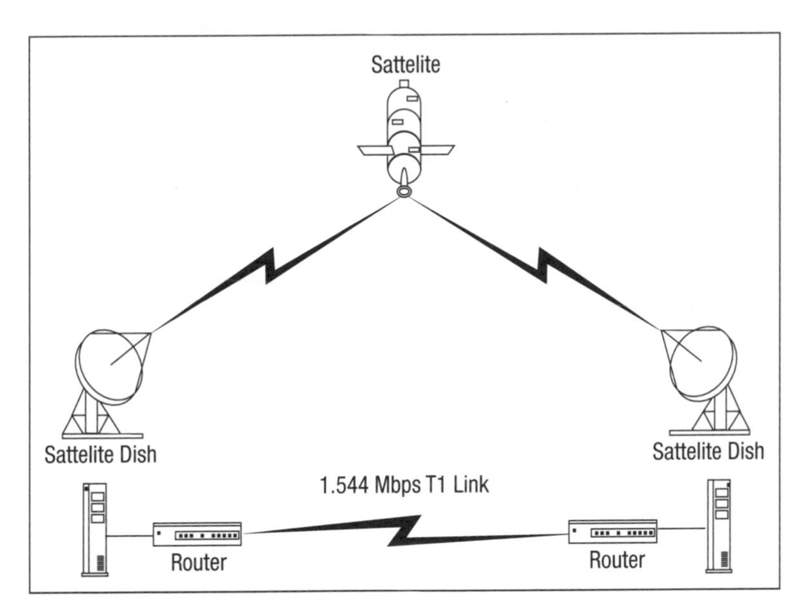

Figure 9.1 RIP hop-count costs.

support these. RIP v1 assumes that all subnet masks are the same across the network and doesn't even include subnet mask information in its routing table, whereas RIP v2 notes this information in the routing table.

In a network with identical network media types of the same speed, RIP is the best choice (provided the network has fewer than 50 subnets with no hop count exceeding 14). If the network media types are different and with differing speeds, OSPF is the best choice for a routing protocol. Although RIP can be used in IP and IPX environments, OSPF can be used only in an IP environment. We'll discuss it in the next section.

Note: Although more than one routing protocol is available, Microsoft recommends that each interface have only one routing protocol for a Windows 2000 router.

Routing in a TCP/IP Environment

In a TCP/IP environment, Windows 2000 RRAS offers two choices: RIP for IP and Open Shortest Path First (OSPF). We've already discussed RIP because it can be used in both a TCP/IP and IPX/SPX environment. The OSPF routing protocol, on the other hand, can be used in only a TCP/IP environment.

OSPF

The OSPF protocol is used in large to very large businesses. Indeed, Microsoft recommends using OSPF when a network has more than 50 subnets. The reason it is not recommended for small to medium networks is because its setup must be carefully planned and tested (which is time consuming). Unlike RIP, which uses a distance-vector algorithm for routing, OSPF uses the more complicated link-state protocol. OSPF routers actually build a map of the network, which is dynamically updated when changes occur. Because OSPF is a multiple-path protocol, it can send packets from the same transmission stream across different routes to the destination.

OSPF requires extensive planning and testing to implement it correctly. OSPF setup involves three levels.

- Autonomous system design
- Area design (within an autonomous system)
- Network design (within an area)

Because multinational companies can be quite large, OSPF designates autonomous systems (AS). Routing tables and maps maintained on the router can handle only so much information, so groups of routers can be designated as belonging to these individual autonomous systems. The routers on the interior of the AS are all a part of the same group and update each other. Border routers join autonomous systems, and all ASes are composed of areas that are connected by a backbone. (Each area that has no connections except to the backbone is called a *stub*.) Figure 9.2 shows four areas joined by a backbone to make one AS. In this diagram, all of the areas are stub networks. If area 4 were connected to area 3 instead of to the backbone, area 4 would be a stub and not area 3.

Routing in a Mixed Environment

Windows 2000 routing with RRAS can be integrated with the other routers. Also, other operating systems that use TCP/IP (such as Unix and Macintosh) can be clients of a Windows 2000 router. Unix uses TCP/IP and can be integrated into a RIP for IP or OSPF environment. AppleTalk routing for Macintosh clients is discussed later in this chapter.

Routing in a Novell Environment

Although new Novell systems use TCP/IP, this section refers to routing in a Novell environment in which IPX/SPX (or NWLink) is being used as the protocol stack for at least a portion of the network. In Windows 2000 routing, only one routing protocol supports this manner of routing: RIP for IPX. The setup for routing in a Novell environment is different than the setup using RIP in a TCP/IP environment.

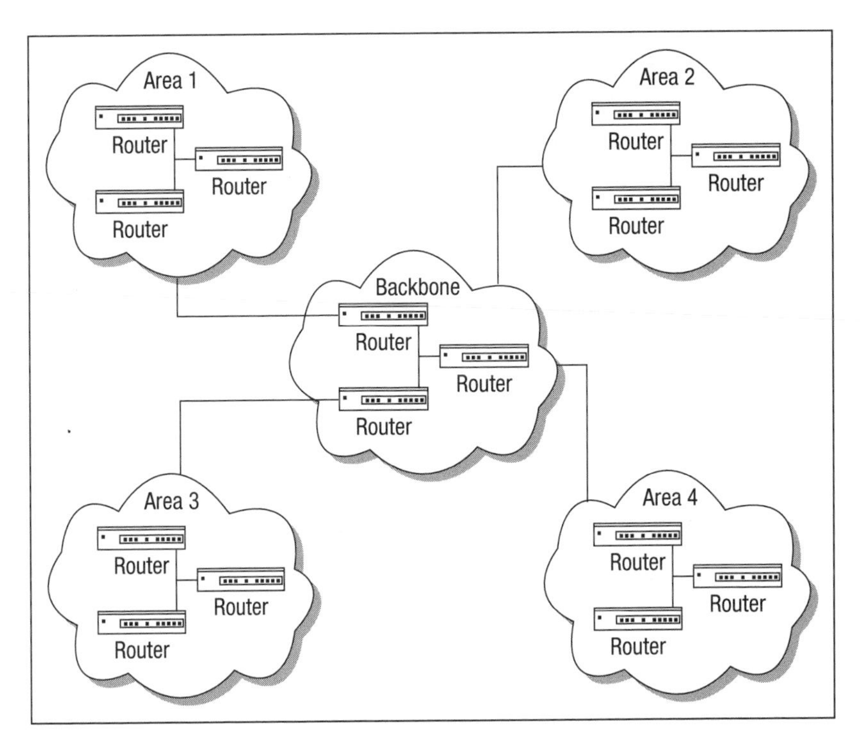

Figure 9.2 Autonomous system network.

Service Advertising Protocol (SAP)

Although it isn't a true routing protocol, SAP is an essential element when setting up routing for a Novell environment. Novell Netware servers can advertise services that they provide to the network with SAP. Netware clients can locate needed services by sending SAP requests. SAP allows the Windows 2000 RRAS server to keep a list of the servers and their services so that, when a client requests a service, the server (if on the local network segment) can acknowledge that it has the services requested. If the needed service is on another network segment, the router will acknowledge the server's existence for the client to communicate with the server. All routers that will be acknowledging these requests must have SAP enabled.

When a server comes on line, it broadcasts its service information, and these broadcasts are added to the router's SAP table, which is then broadcast to all networks to which the router is connected. This process continues across the whole network, until all SAP information is eventually propagated throughout the network.

AppleTalk Routing

Besides an IP and IPX router, the Windows 2000 RRAS service also supports AppleTalk routing for Macintosh clients. AppleTalk has two versions of networking: phase 1 and phase 2. Windows 2000 routing supports AppleTalk phase 2. AppleTalk also designates a *seed router* to broadcast routes for a network. (Windows 2000 routing can be a seed or non-seed router.)

Comparing Routing Protocols

As mentioned, each routing protocol has its benefits and drawbacks. Depending on the configuration and size of a given network, one protocol may be preferred—or even required—over another. Table 9.1 compares RIP and OSPF.

Convergence is the time that it takes for all routers in a WAN to update their routing tables with a route change. Although route changes can occur when a LAN is added or removed from the WAN, the main convergence issue is when a router malfunctions and the other routers must route packets around it. RIP updates are timed according to configuration settings, with the default being 30 seconds. When the table is updated, RIP broadcasts it in its entirety. OSPF, on the other hand, updates the routing tables only when a change is detected in the network topology. Further, OSPF broadcasts only the changes. These two features make OSPF's convergence time shorter than RIP's (and reduce the network traffic, also).

Routing in a WAN Environment

A network that contains WAN connections requires more configuration than those without WAN connections. Demand-dial connections and leased lines have required and optional settings for connectivity and security.

Table 9.1 Comparing RIP and OSPF.

Attribute	OSPF	RIP
Convergence	Converges faster	Converges slower
Hop-count limits	Has no limit	Has a hop limit of 15 (14 in Windows 2000)
Path-determination	Uses bandwidth to determine routes	Uses a hop count as its metric
Router table updates	Has optimized updates	Has unwieldy updates

Demand-Dial Connections

Demand-dial connections are controlled by placing routers on either side of the connection. RRAS allows for control of these connections with filters and time restrictions. The filters control which packets will be dropped and which packets are allowed to pass through the router. RRAS allows for packet filters that control which types of traffic are allowed, and these filters are applied to every type of connection including demand-dial connections because they are applied after the connection to the router is made. If you want to restrict just demand-dial connections, you can apply a demand-dial filter. A demand-dial filter is applied before the connection is made, so that the demand-dial connection won't even be used if the criteria are not met. Setting dial-out hours for users can also control demand-dial connections. With this setting, the administrator can set during which hours of the day that dial-in use is permitted. RRAS controls packet types and dial-out hours for the whole connection. If you want to control these settings by groups of users, then a remote-access policy is needed. When you are placing routers at demand-dial connections, Microsoft recommends that you configure static routes to reduce overhead for traffic and administration.

Note: Although demand-dial connections are often pay-per-use, they can also be persistent, as in the case with ISDN.

Leased Line Connections

When using leased lines, extra equipment is needed to adapt the signal. A Channel Service Unit/Data Service Unit (CSU/DSU) connects a T1 or T3 line to a network and is required for both sides of the connection. Routers are used in conjunction with the CSU/DSU to control traffic over the leased line. Figure 9.3 shows a network with a T1 connection that has CSU/DSUs and routers to make the WAN connection.

Integration

The routing features of RRAS integrate well with some Windows 2000 features to enhance the network.

Depending on the needs of the network, the following features may be implemented individually or together.

Internet Protocol Security (IPSec)

When used with RRAS, IPSec enables authentication and encryption between routers. So, not only does IPSec prevent unauthorized routers from being added to the network, it also uses encryption to keep routing information secure. Both of these options are useful when using the Internet as the backbone.

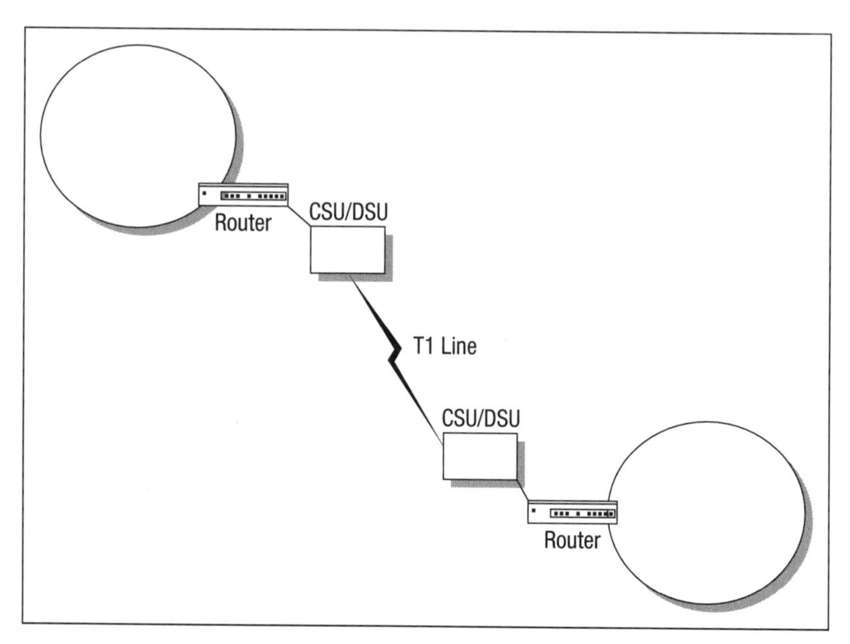

Figure 9.3 Routing with WAN connections (T1 with router).

Routing and Remote Access

Routing and remote access allows connections between routers to be dial-on-demand. This feature can be used with connection devices such as modems and ISDN adapters.

Active Directory

Active Directory allows certificates to be used to authenticate routers. This will be covered in more detail in the following section.

Security

Securing routers in a network is a task crucial to keeping the network safe from other network segments (which may include the Internet).

You have many options in securing routers, and deciding which to implement depends on your network and security needs.

Authentication

Windows can manage access authentication through Active Directory. To be able to communicate with another RRAS server in the group, the remote RRAS server must be a member of the RAS or IAS security group.

Authentication can be set through RADIUS, in which user credentials are used to verify the RRAS server.

Virtual Private Network (VPN)

VPNs can be established between routers to ensure that the transmissions among them are secure.

Through VPNs, security can be set using three possible types of protocols depending on existing architecture:

- *Point-to-Point Tunneling Protocol (PPTP)*—Used in networks that already have other Windows 2000 RRAS servers and any third-party routers that can support PPTP. If the network is already using Windows NT 4 RAS servers, then PPTP must be used (if security is needed).
- *Layer 2 Tunneling Protocol (L2TP)*—Used in networks that already have other Windows 2000 RRAS servers and any third-party routers that can support L2TP. Windows NT 4 does not support L2TP.
- *Internet Protocol Security (IPSec)*—Used in conjunction with L2TP to add authentication to L2TP. Certificates are required with IPSec, and these can be set under Group Policy or by using the Certificate Snap-in. Every RRAS server must have a certificate loaded for IPSec to work properly.

Availability

You can use many strategies to ensure that a RRAS server is available for constant use.

- Make sure that one RRAS server is dedicated to routing. Having a dedicated RRAS server prevents you from having to reboot the server whenever you add applications or change a configuration setting.
- Have multiple RRAS server connections in a mesh to provide redundant links to all of the network segments. This mesh will prevent any segment from becoming disconnected from the rest of the network.
- Have redundant RRAS servers to fill in for a failed RRAS server.
- Use persistent connections from the RRAS servers to keep the connections running at all times. This ensures availability between network segments.

Performance

Solutions to performance issues are somewhat the same as the solutions to availability problems.

- A RRAS server should be dedicated to its task to prevent its resources from being used by unimportant applications or services. This exclusivity improves routing performance by making sure the resources are available when needed.
- Have multiple RRAS server connections in a mesh to allow multiple paths to destinations. This option is extremely important with OSPF, which uses bandwidth as a metric to make path selection. These multiple connections prevent overutilized network segments from being swamped with traffic.
- Having multiple RRAS servers to distribute traffic is greatly preferred to having a single, central RRAS server that routes almost all of the traffic. (As stated previously, use multiple connections.)
- For better performance between network segments, use persistent connections from the RRAS servers to keep the connections running at all times. Having to establish connections takes time and decreases performance.

Practice Questions

Case Study

Current LAN/Network Structure

2Market currently has 10 branch offices with headquarters in Chicago, Illinois. The branch offices are located in the following cities:

Los Angeles, California

New York City, New York

Houston, Texas

Miami, Florida

Indianapolis, Indiana

Boston, Massachusetts

Salt Lake City, Utah

Nashville, Tennessee

Redmond, Washington

Aspen, Colorado

The branch offices are not currently connected in a network.

Proposed LAN/Network Structure

2Market wants to purchase a Web-based application for the branch managers to place orders and to see upcoming price specials.

Current WAN Connectivity

None at the current time.

Proposed WAN/Internet Connectivity

2Market wants to connect all branches through the Internet while still remaining isolated for security.

All branches will have access to not only resources on the Internet, but also to the Web-based application that is located at the headquarters in Chicago. Access to the Web-based application must be available 24 hours a day, 7 days a week.

Question 1

Which routing protocols could be used? [Check all correct answers]

- ❑ a. NetBEUI
- ❑ b. RIP for IP
- ❑ c. TCP/IP
- ❑ d. RIP for IPX
- ❑ e. OSPF
- ❑ f. IPX/SPX
- ❑ g. IGMP

The answers are b and e. Choices a, c, and f are routed protocols, not routing protocols. Choice d is incorrect because the Internet (which is TCP/IP-based) will be used as the backbone. IGMP is for multicasting purposes, which is not required. This leaves only the choices for RIP for IP and OSPF.

Question 2

If the branch offices had multiple connections to the Internet, with each being a different network media and speed, which routing protocol would be the best choice?

- ❍ a. RIP for IP
- ❍ b. RIP for IPX
- ❍ c. IGMP
- ❍ d. OSPF

The correct answer is d. OSPF's metric is based on bandwidth. If there were multiple routes with each a different speed, OSPF would be the best choice for selecting the best route.

Question 3

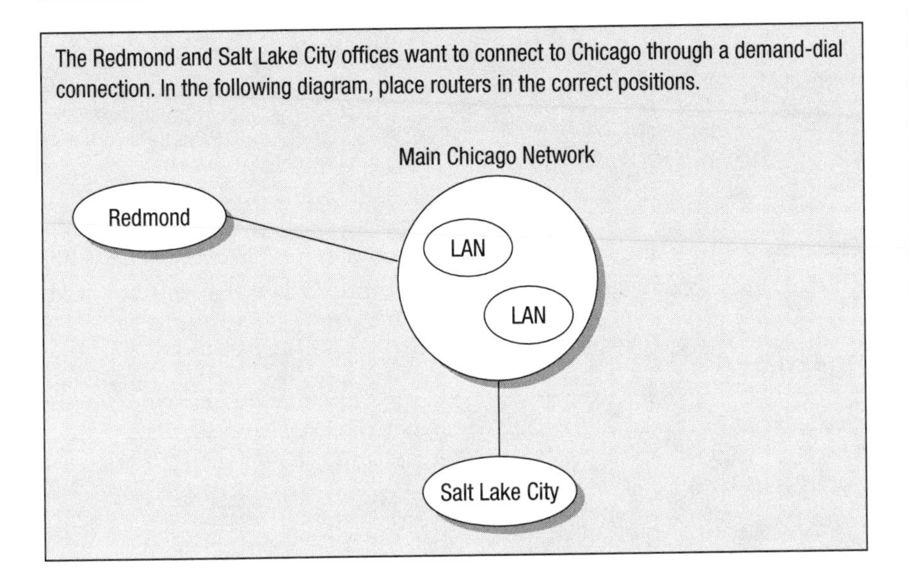

The Redmond and Salt Lake City offices want to connect to Chicago through a demand-dial connection. In the following diagram, place routers in the correct positions.
Main Chicago Network
Redmond
LAN
LAN
Salt Lake City

The answer is:

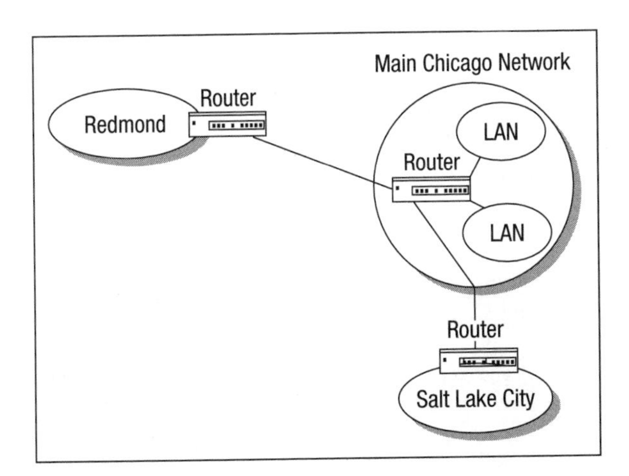

A router needs to be added at each of the remote locations. At least one router is needed at the Chicago office connecting the LANs at Chicago with the remote locations. More than one router can be used at the Chicago location.

Question 4

If demand-dial connections were used to connect all branch offices and only static routes were used instead of routing protocols, this design would improve performance.

- ❍ a. True
- ❍ b. False

The answer is a. Routing protocols will use resources and network bandwidth, which decreases performance. Static routes are preferred for their low overhead.

Question 5

The Miami office will have T1 connection. What connectivity device(s) is needed with this connection? [Check all correct answers]

- ❑ a. A router on either side of the connection.
- ❑ b. A router on one side of each connection.
- ❑ c. A CSU/DSU on either side of each connection.
- ❑ d. A CSU/DSU on one side of the connection.

The correct answers are a and c. A CSU/DSU at the T1 connection is required to connect the network with the T1 line. A router between the CSU/DSU and the network will control traffic over the WAN connection.

Question 6

Aspen to Chicago is a demand-dial connection. The network administrator wants to allow only TCP port 80 for access into Chicago from this connection and wants to allow users access only between 8 A.M. to 5 P.M. daily. He also wants administrators to be able to use the demand-dial connection 24 hours a day. What will he need to configure to accomplish these goals? [Check all correct answers]

- ❑ a. Demand-dial filter
- ❑ b. Proxy server
- ❑ c. Dial-in hours
- ❑ d. Remote access policy

The correct answers are a and d. A demand-dial filter will allow the administrator to close all ports except for port 80. Because this feature is available, the administrator does not need a proxy server. Configuring dial-in hours at the RRAS server will apply to all users including administrators. To apply dial-in hours to selective groups of people will require a remote access policy.

Question 7

If a 2Market branch had four connections to the Internet and OSPF were being used, which would be the chosen route?

❍ a. 28.8Kbps link

❍ b. 56Kbps link

❍ c. 2–56Kbps multilink

❍ d. 2–28.8Kbps multilink

The correct answer is c, which gives a total bandwidth of 102Kbps—the most of the available choices.

Question 8

If authentication and encryption were to be used over the VPN, which two options could be used in conjunction? [Choose the two that apply]

❑ a. IPSec

❑ b. PPTP

❑ c. PPP

❑ d. L2TP

The correct answers are a and d. IPSec and L2TP used together provide authentication and encryption. PPTP uses MPPE as its encryption protocol, and MPPE does not need to be selected seprately from PPTP. PPP is used for dial-up connections for remote access (See Chapter 11).

Need to Know More?

Microsoft Corporation. *Windows 2000 Server Resource Kit*. Microsoft Press, Redmond, WA, 2000. ISBN 1-57231-805-8. The *Internetworking Guide* provides useful information on routing and routing protocols.

Rees, Matthew, and Jeffrey Coe. *CCNA Routing and Switching Exam Cram*. The Coriolis Group, Scottsdale, AZ, 1999. ISBN 1-57610-434-6. This book covers basic routing concepts in depth.

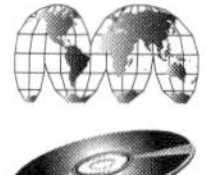

Search the TechNet CD (or its online version through **www.microsoft.com**) using the keyword "RRAS", "OSPF", or "RIP". Also, see the Windows 2000 Server or Advanced Server help.

Dfs

Terms you'll need to know:

- ✓ The Distributed File System (Dfs) tree
- ✓ Dfs root
- ✓ Domain-based root
- ✓ Standalone root
- ✓ The blob
- ✓ Dfs link
- ✓ Root replica
- ✓ Link replica

Techniques you'll need to master:

- ✓ Using the Dfs Administration MMC
- ✓ Creating the Dfs tree
- ✓ Creating a replica
- ✓ Ensuring fault tolerance and redundant links

In this chapter, you'll learn what the Distributed File System (Dfs) is and how it can be implemented in your environment. You'll become familiar with the capabilities of Dfs and the requirements for Windows 2000, Windows NT 4, and Windows 9x operating systems. We'll cover Dfs administration and design, along with some practical applications and examples. You'll be introduced to the installation procedure for Windows 2000, as either a Dfs server or client.

Dfs Overview

Microsoft Dfs was first released as an add-on for Microsoft Windows NT 4. In a large-enterprise environment, servers are replaced due to attrition faster than we would like. Moving shared data results in changes to profiles and logon scripts. Another downfall is the transfer sometimes causes mission-critical data to be unavailable for unacceptable lengths of time. Dfs acts like a file manager for your network shares. It allows administrators to create a directory tree that appears to be located on one server when, in actuality, the tree could contain shared folders from several different servers.

Dfs Capabilities

Dfs can make files stored on multiple servers appear to be located on a single server. For example, you have four servers in your LAN. One server is located in the accounting department, one in the sales department, one in the production department, and one in the administration department. All of the departments have shared directories with files that are accessed via drive mappings by all the other departments. With the current design, each client workstation will require four mappings to access the data. With Dfs, you can create a share that will incorporate all of the shared directories on the servers and give the users a single drive mapping. What's more, this can be done seamlessly, during production hours, and with no interruption of the users' access to the files. If you have used logon scripts to create the previous mappings, the process is further simplified. The administrator can simply change the **net use** command within the logon script to point to the new share. After the user reboots, the new share is available.

In addition, let's say that the shipping department has grown and is no longer able to use the production server. After the new server has been placed in the shipping department, you move its data files to the new shipping server. With Dfs, you can change the location of the directories, and the users will not notice the change. Dfs does not display the location of the linked files or rely on UNC (universal naming convention) for user navigation. Dfs can also provide fail-over redundancy for the files at all locations by using root or link replicas, which will be described later in this chapter.

With Dfs, you are no longer limited by the available disk space on a server. When space is needed for Dfs volumes, simply add another server to your Dfs tree. Because the process of adding additional servers is transparent to the clients, it prevents additional mappings or profile changes.

Common Uses

Dfs is most commonly used to provide centralized access to shared files. When creating a Dfs tree in an enterprise environment, the Dfs share becomes a centralized area for managing the shared directories.

By using the Dfs tree, you can add or remove servers or directories without changing the user's environment. For example, you have a tree that includes a directory called Focus on a server called Global. If the server becomes disabled, you can restore the Focus directory from a backup tape to another server and change the Dfs link to refer to the Focus directory on the replacement server. After the directory has been restored, the file is available again in its original context from within the Dfs root. All of these steps can be accomplished without changing the environment for the users. You can then restore the Global server as time allows.

Most enterprise networks use centralized backup, and you can better utilize a backup server by implementing a Dfs file structure in your network. You simply allow Dfs to manage the files. Windows 2000 backup is capable of backing up shared directories on remote servers. Dfs can simplify this process by managing the files and folders for you. Instead of browsing multiple servers and shares during the backup job creation, all you have to do is to select a single shared directory to back up. If you have created replicas of your links and one of the linked files is unavailable at the scheduled backup time, the backup agent will be directed to the replica and the backup will function as if the files were available.

The Dfs Tree

Dfs organizes your network files in a hierarchical structure referred to as the *tree*. The root is the top level of your Dfs tree, and shared folders added to the root are known as *leaf objects*. Leaf objects can be added to the root during or after its creation.

Dfs leaf objects have two limitations: They must reside in the same domain, and they cannot span multiple servers.

Active Directory Integration

Dfs is integrated with the Active Directory (AD) database and replicates between domain controllers. The AD database is used to store the topology information of the Dfs tree. The host domain controller stores the topology information known as the *blob* or Binary Large Object, and replicates this information to all other Dfs-enabled domain controllers. Before the replication is complete (which can take up to five minutes for local DCs), the controller's views of the Dfs tree may not be the same. This is because the blob does not replicate just the changes of the tree design. Instead, the entire blob will be replicated across the domain, which can cause latency and increased network traffic. If the controllers are located across slower WAN links, factor this into your blob replication time. While the replication is taking place, clients local to the DC—which is not synchronized with the hosting server—will also have a copy of the tree that is not current. To force synchronization after changes occur, use the refresh utility from within the Dfs administrator on the hosting DC.

Requirements for Windows 2000 Dfs

Windows 2000 has certain requirements for Dfs root servers to host a domain or standalone Dfs root. Table 10.1 lists the requirements for a Dfs root server in a Windows 2000 domain environment.

Although Windows 2000 can host a Dfs root as either a domain controller or a member server, you are limited to hosting one Dfs root on a server. You can have the root reside on an NTFS or FAT partition, and the advantages of the root residing on an NTFS partition are security and synchronization of shared folders.

Windows NT 4 can host a Dfs root as a member server only. This limitation is because of to the inability of the AD to fully integrate with the older flat-file account database that is incorporated into Windows NT 4.

Windows 2000 has certain requirements for clients to be able to access a Dfs tree or host a linked folder. Table 10.2 lists the requirements for a Dfs client in a Windows 2000 domain environment.

Dfs clients are able to browse the Dfs tree and host a shared file in the tree. Clients are limited to using Dfs from within the domain where they reside. Multiple-domain environments require a Dfs root in each domain that will be used by domain members. The clients cache a referral to a Dfs root or a Dfs link for a

Table 10.1 Requirements for a Dfs root server in a Windows 2000 domain environment.

Operating System	Other Requirements	Operations
Windows 2000		Can host Dfs root as DC or member server
Win NT 4	Service Pack 3 or higher	Can host Dfs root as a member server only

Table 10.2 Requirements for a Dfs client in a Windows 2000 domain environment.

Operating System	Other Requirements	Operations
Windows 2000 Professional		Able to host shared folders within a Dfs root
Windows NT 4 Server	Service Pack 3 or higher	Able to host shared folders within a Dfs root
Windows NT Workstation	Service Pack 3 or higher	Able to host shared folders within a Dfs root
Windows 98	Client for Dfs 4/5	Able to host shared folders within a Dfs root
Windows 95	Client for Dfs 4/5	Able to host shared folders within a Dfs root
DOS and Windows 3.1	Not supported	

specific time period, which is set by the administrator from within the Dfs administration MMC.

Installing Dfs Host Servers

The following sections detail the installation of the Dfs services that are needed to host the Dfs root.

Windows 2000

With the release of Windows 2000, Dfs is now integrated into the operating system, and you do not need to install any additional software or make any selections during the installation. If the administration tools have been installed on the server, you will find the Dfs administrator in Programs|Administrative Tools. If the administrative tools were either not installed or have been removed, you may install them from the administrative tools setup program located in the I386 directory on the Windows 2000 CD-ROM.

Windows NT 4

Because Windows NT 4 was released before Dfs, a working copy of Dfs was not included with Windows NT 4 Server, Workstation, or BackOffice. The software, however, is free and can be downloaded from Microsoft's Web site. The download file is a self-extracting executable that will expand the files in the appropriate directories when it is launched.

After installing the file, add the Dfs service from the network applet within the control panel. When this has been completed, a Configure Dfs dialog box is displayed. You'll be prompted to enter the name of the share (which will become your root), or you can choose to create a new share.

Client Software

Windows NT 4 requires client software to view Dfs shared trees. With the release of Windows 2000, Windows NT 4 and Windows 98 clients were able to browse and host shared directories without client software. Windows 95 requires a Dfs client 4/5. Windows for Workgroups, DOS, and NetWare servers are not able to either browse or host a Dfs folder.

Browsing a Dfs Tree

You can browse a Dfs tree just like any other shared directory with subdirectories. The root directory of the share is, of course, the Dfs root directory. The subdirectories are shared directories that can be located anywhere with your domain. The example in Figure 10.1 shows the Dfs root "Domain Root". Inside Domain Root, the folders Dfs 1 through 5 are visible. These folders are shares located on servers 2K01 and 2K02 within the domain. The folders Dfs2 and Dfs4 are located on 2K01, and Dfs1, Dfs3, and Dfs5 are located on 2K02. The folder Link On Win98 Client is a shared folder on the Windows 98 workstation Compaq. The Users folder is a subdirectory that resides inside the folder that was designated as the root. This folder is not shared, but, because it is inside the root folder, which is shared, it is also accessible by browsing the root.

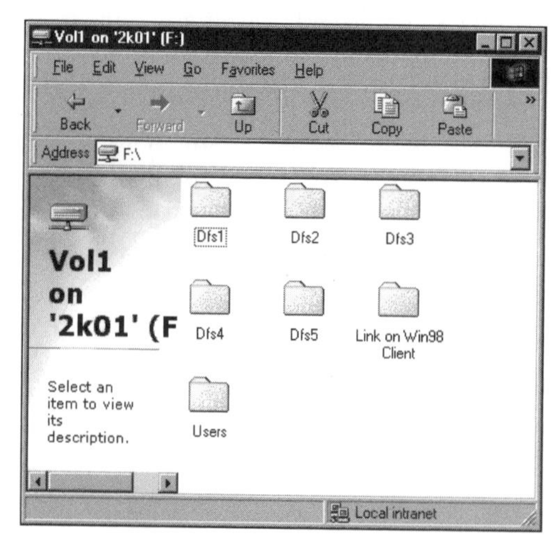

Figure 10.1 The Dfs root "Domain Root".

This example demonstrates the flexibility of the Dfs tree. In this example, you can see the ability to add folders from other servers and clients, and to place folders directly within the Dfs root directory to provide access to the users. The destination or link of the folder is not shown, which gives the users a seamless interface.

Planning is the important key when you build your tree. If you plan correctly, a logical order can be used to prevent users from accessing multiple drive mappings on different servers. Any modifications after the initial implementation will result in different views of the tree until replication has taken place and the workstation's cache has expired.

Administration Tools

Dfs is controlled from a server in your Windows 2000 network. (The server can be a DC or member server.) You can choose to create a Dfs root directory on the server you have accessed, or on another server within your domain, by using the administration tools. Figure 10.2 shows the Dfs administrator and the Dfs domain-based root used in the previous example.

When you launch the Distributed File System MMC from the administrative tools program group, two panes will be displayed. The left pane shows your tree design, and the right pane displays the details of the selected icon. This configuration is very similar to Windows Explorer or WinFile. When the Dfs administration program has been started, the MMC will display the Dfs root on that

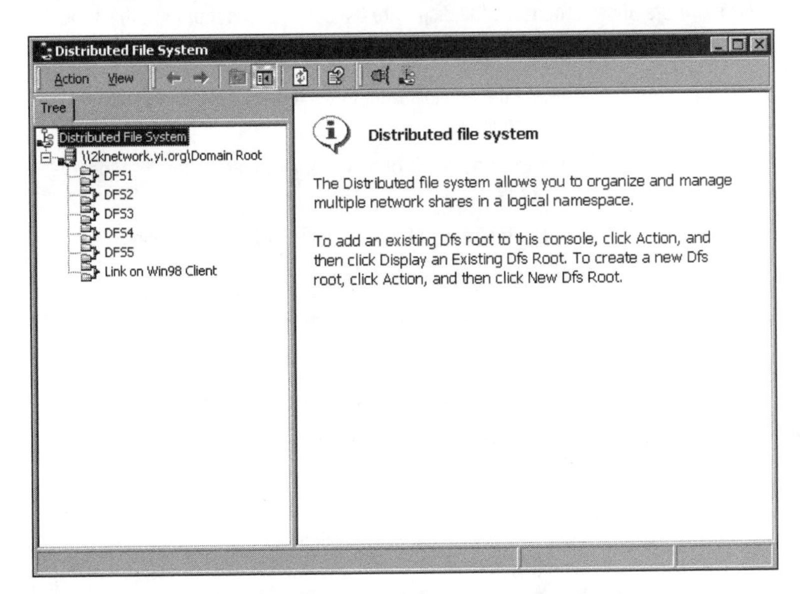

Figure 10.2 The Dfs administrator and the Dfs domain-based root.

server (if one has been created). If you do not have a root on this machine, you can connect and manage any root partition in the domain by right-clicking on the Distributed File System icon in the tree pane and choosing Display An Existing Dfs Root, or by using the action menu.

The toolbar buttons at the top of the MMC allow you to perform functions inside the console. If you click on the Create A New Dfs Root button, a wizard will guide you through the rest of the process.

After you have created the root, Dfs links will be added or deleted from this console. For redundancy, you can create replicas, which allow you to specify an additional directory that the users will be directed to if the primary shared folder becomes unavailable. You can also specify that changes within the replicated directory be duplicated on the replica. This is an extremely powerful tool, but you must be aware that, if you implement this on a large folder that is changed frequently, you will increase the traffic created by the changes. Table 10.3 lists all options available from within the Dfs administration program.

Table 10.3 Dfs administration program options.

Menu Item	Action
New Dfs Link	Creates a link or pointer to a shared directory.
New Root Replica	Replicates a copy of the root share to another server for fault tolerance. Not available on standalone Dfs root shares.
New Replica	Creates a replica of the selected link.
Remove Display Of Dfs Root	Removes the display of the selected Dfs root from the MMC.
Delete Dfs Root	Deletes the Dfs root.
Replication Policy	Allows the administrator to set the replica to automatic replication.
Check Status	Performs a check of the link destination for the specified object.
Open	Opens the selected link or root with Windows Explorer.
New	Another way to create a new link, root, or replica.
All Tasks	Shows the tasks that are available for the selected object.
View	Allows the administrator to customize the detail view.
Refresh	Refreshes the Dfs view or forces a replication of the blob.
Export	Allows the administrator to export the selected item's name and link type to a text file or comma-separated text file.
Properties	Allows the administrator to view the properties of the selected item. Share permissions can be made by selecting the Security tab.
Help	Allows the administrator to view the help files.

Creating a Dfs Root

To create a new Dfs root, first launch the wizard by right clicking on the Distributed File System icon in the tree pane of the Dfs MMC. The first window informs you that you have accessed the wizard and prompts you to click on Next to begin the creation. A dialog box then asks you if you would like to create a standalone or domain-based root. After you have made this decision, continue by clicking on Next. Now you will be prompted to enter the server location, or the server that will host the Dfs root. You can specify this either by typing in the server name, network name, and extension or by simply browsing and selecting it.

After you have entered the root location, you are asked to specify the root share, or the shared directory that will contain the pointers for the Dfs tree. You can use an existing network share or have the wizard create a new one. After you have entered a name for a new directory, the wizard asks you to enter a shared name for the directory and any comments that you would like to include. The next window that appears lists the parameters that you have entered during this process and prompts you to click on Finish to complete the process.

Dfs Fault Tolerance and Load Balancing

In a Windows 2000 environment, Dfs can integrate with Active Directory to provide fault-tolerant root shares. If you have multiple servers in your domain, any or all of the participating hosts can provide fault-tolerant Dfs root shares. Active Directory is used to ensure domain controllers in the domain share of a common Dfs architecture. This is implemented by choosing the domain-based root option during the root creation.

Likewise, you can create a standalone Dfs root, but doing so does not take advantage of Active Directory and does not provide the fault tolerance as with the domain-based option. A standalone Dfs root will, however, allow you to have an unlimited number of Dfs root shares in a domain.

With domain-based Dfs root topology, up to 32 DCs can host a single Dfs root and can have unlimited multiple Dfs root volumes within the domain. Use the new root replica on domain-based Dfs roots by right-clicking on the root and choosing New Root Replica from the drop-down menu.

Additional root or linked folders can provide load balancing by breaking up the shared data to several standalone Dfs root shares. As users request files from the node in the Dfs namespace, they randomly select one of the computers for the accessed node.

By using root and link replicas, you can create a virtual failover cluster for your file structure. If the shared directory is unavailable when a client tries to access it, the user is automatically directed to a replica of that file. This redirection is transparent to the user, occurring without their knowledge or interaction. Mission-critical files located within your Dfs root should be replicated to other servers. At this time, Microsoft's cluster server will not support Dfs topology. Replicas will be explained further in this chapter.

Dfs File System Security

You need to be a member of the administrators group to create a root partition; otherwise, Dfs does not implement any additional security features. For example, if you have created a Dfs link to a shared folder and your account has the appropriate permissions to access the shared directory, accessing through the Dfs root share will be possible.

To assign permissions to a Dfs folder, use My Computer or Windows Explorer. With the exception of the root, all folders will need to be shared before they are added to the tree. After your tree is constructed, you can change permissions using Windows Explorer or My Computer.

To take advantage of file system security, the Dfs root or linked folder must reside on an NTFS partition. FAT partitions provide only share-level security. Also, a Dfs root or shared folders must reside on an NTFS partition to take advantage of automatic replication.

Creating a New Link to a Shared Folder

Now that you have created your Dfs root, it is time to incorporate shared folders to complete your tree design. Like creating a root, pop-up dialog boxes will guide you through the addition of the new Dfs link. To begin the new Dfs link dialog box, right-click on your Dfs root in the left pane of the MMC. From the pop-up menu that appears, select New Dfs Link from the menu, and a Create A New Dfs Link dialog box appears.

Enter the name that you would like to be displayed from within the root share in the Link Name dialog box. Now specify the UNC path to the shared folder in the Send The User To This Shared Folder dialog box. The Comment dialog box allows you to add a comment to the link that will be visible when you right-click on the link and choose Properties.

The Clients Cache This Referral For dialog box allows you to specify the amount of time that the link will appear within the root if it has become unavailable. The default is 1,800 seconds (30 minutes). After you have entered this information and clicked on OK, the link will be added to your root. Figure 10.3 shows the Create A New Dfs Link dialog box.

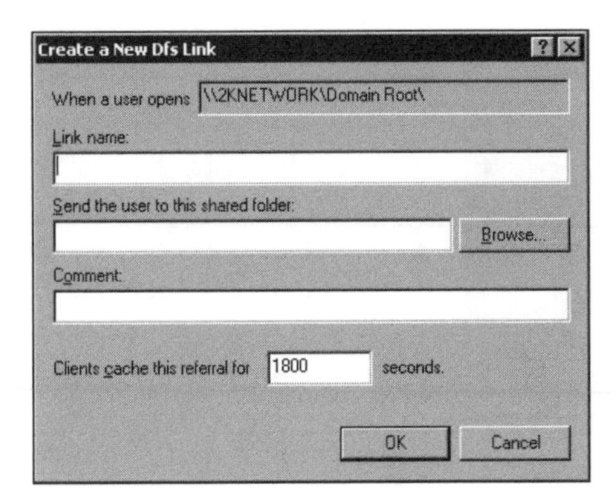

Figure 10.3 The Create A New Dfs Link dialog box.

Deleting a Link to a Shared Folder

Deleting a link is a very simple process. You simply right-click on the link name and choose Remove Dfs Link from the pop-up menu. This immediately deletes the link; however, the link remains visible to the client until the cache has expired.

Creating a Replica

Replicas of a Dfs root or leaf object can be created to provide fault tolerance. Both the primary and the destination of the replicated folder must reside on an NTFS partition to take advantage of automatic replication, which synchronizes the data and files located within these two directories. Doing this, however, increases the amount of traffic on your network. Replicas are better utilized on directories that do not change frequently. A good example is company-related forms that are utilized by departments to complete their daily work.

Banks and insurance companies utilize data normally provided on CD-ROM for value estimation. These files are normally copied from the CD to a network share for company-wide use. If you place this network share inside a Dfs root and use automatic replication, you will not only have redundant copies for fault tolerance, but you will need to update the primary folder with only the new files. The changes will be automatically propagated to replica directories for you.

To create a replica, right-click on the Dfs link or root from within the tree pane of the MMC and choose New Replica from the drop-down menu. This opens the New Replica window. Then send the user to this shared folder dialog box. Specify the destination directory by its UNC path or click the browse button. Now select either the Manual Replication radio button or the Automatic Replication dialog button from the replication policy options group. Manual replication provides no replication service to the destination directory. Any updates will

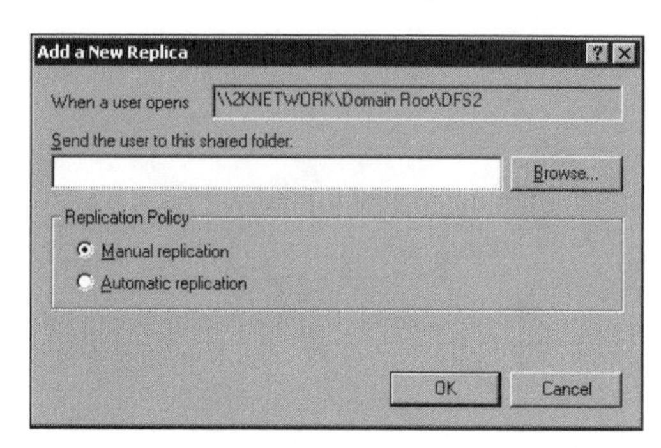

Figure 10.4 The Create New Replica dialog box.

need to be done by the administrator. The automatic replication option will synchronize the primary and destination folders behind the scenes. Figure 10.4 shows the Create New Replica dialog box.

To change the replication policy, right-click on the Dfs link in the tree pane of the MMC and choose Replication Properties from the drop-down menu. This opens the Replication Policy window, where you'll make changes to your configuration. You are also able to change the primary and destination directories.

Root replicas create a copy of the root share on another server for fault tolerance. This feature is available only on domain-based Dfs roots.

Deleting a Replica

Deleting a replica is a simple process. Simply click on the leaf object in the left pane of the MMC. The right pane of the MMC will now display the object and its replica. Now you can right-click on the replica and chose Remove Replica from the drop-down menu.

Dfs Command Index

Dfs supports command-line configuration and management. In most cases, these command-line options will be used in program files or from within a programmer's code. Custom-built applications can utilize the flexibility of the Dfs tree structure in enterprise applications. Table 10.4 lists the available commands and their function.

Optimizing Your Dfs Design

The previous topics of this chapter relate to the requirements and criteria for implementing Dfs in your Windows 2000 environment. This section describes a scenario and the ways to best optimize your Dfs design.

Command	Function
NetDfsAdd	Creates a new Dfs link or adds a share to an existing link
NetDfsAddStdRoot	Creates a new standard or standalone Dfs root
NetDfsAddStdRootForced	Creates a new standard or standalone Dfs root in a cluster environment, allowing an offline share to host the standalone Dfs root
NetDfsEnum	Enumerates all Dfs links in a named Dfs root
NetDfsGetClientInfo	Returns the client's cached information regarding a specific Dfs object
NetDfsGetInfo	Returns information about a Dfs link
NetDfsManagerInitialize	Reinitializes the Dfs service on a specified server
NetDfsRemove	Removes a share from a Dfs link; removes the Dfs link if the share is the last associated with the specified link
NetDfsRemoveFtRoot	Removes a server and share from a domain-based Dfs implementation; deletes the Dfs root if there are no more associated shares
NetDfsRemoveFtRootForced	Removes the specified server from a domain-based Dfs implementation even if the server is offline

Table 10.4 Available Dfs command index.

Let's say that you are designing a Dfs structure for a WAN that consists of three separate locations: A, B, and C, as shown in Figure 10.5.

Location A is the company headquarters, which houses the corporate officers and the IS staff. This location has two DCs, two member servers, and 150 hosts. One of the member servers is a backup server that uses a DLT drive to back up mission critical files. The DCs contain forms that are used in the company's daily operations. DC1 houses shared folders named Employee and Customers that are needed by all locations. DC2 houses a shared folder named Managers that should be available to the management staff at all locations.

Location B is where the marketing and sales headquarters are located. This location has two DCs, no member servers, and 100 hosts. DC3 houses a shared folder called Potential, and DC4 houses a shared folder called Forecast that should be available to all employees at all locations.

Location C is the production facility that has one DC and one member server. The member server contains a shared folder called Production that needs to be accessed by the administrators and sales team at the other locations.

All of the shared folders are located on NTFS partitions. You are responsible for creating a solution for a centralized backup using the standard NT backup, as

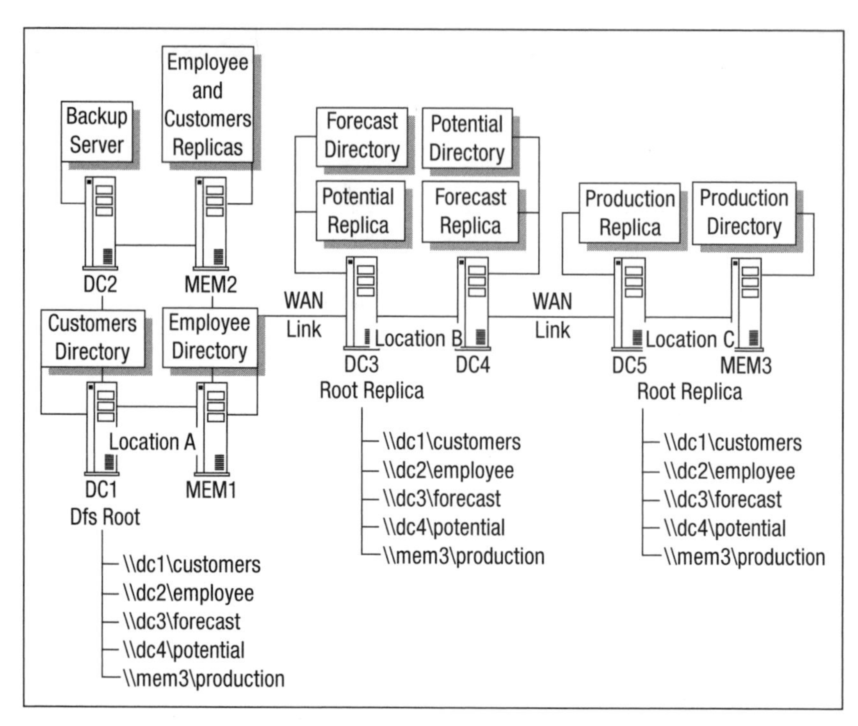

Figure 10.5 The sample Dfs structure for a WAN.

well as a seamless interface to the corporate shared files. Because these files are mission critical, your design should provide redundancy.

You have decided that you will create a domain Dfs root. You will create the root for the shared folders on MEM1 at location A and name it Corpshare. After you have created the root, you add the pointers to the shared folders Customers and Employees at location A. Now, you add the links for the shared folders Forecast and Potential at location B. You then add a link to the shared directory Production at location C.

The folders currently have the correct security permissions, so no changes are needed. Now edit the logon script for the users to point to the DC1 server's Corpshare folder. From the Dfs administrator, right-click on the Dfs root that you created, and choose New Root Replica. Place the replicas on DC3 at location B and MEM3 at location C. This allows the users to access the root if DC1 or a WAN connection becomes disabled.

Now, to provide redundancy of the links, place replicas of the Customers and Employees shared folders on MEM02 at location A. Replicas of the Forecast and Potential shares are located on the servers at locations opposite of which they reside. A replica of the production link is placed on DC05 at location C. All of the root and link replicas have been set to update automatically. This will keep the data in the primary and replicated directories synchronized. Because the locations are geographically separated to minimize the replication traffic, with the exception of the root directories, the replicas have been placed with the subnet. If a WAN link goes down, users will be able to access the shared files local to their subnet and the servers at whichever of the two links has not been disabled.

The backup server is able to access the shared directories from one location provided by the Dfs root. This requires the selection of only one shared directory when the backup job is defined in Windows 2000 Backup.

Practice Questions

Case Study

VirtuCon is a manufacturer of hi-tech equipment, based in Carson City, Nevada. It has a manufacturing plant in Indianapolis, IN, and a distribution facility in Louisville, KY. The corporate offices in Carson City have 150 hosts. The manufacturing plant in Indianapolis has 300 hosts, and the distribution center has 120 hosts. The network infrastructure was recently upgraded. All network cards, hubs, and switches are 10/100. Management has assigned you to design a new file structure that will provide load balancing and failover redundancy.

Current WAN Structure

VirtuCon is currently using Windows 2000 servers at all locations. The client workstations are running Windows 95, Windows 98, Windows NT 4 Workstation, and Windows 2000 Professional.

Carson City has two DCs and one member server. DC1 houses a shared folder named Policies. Mem1 has a DLT drive installed for centralized backup. Indianapolis has one DC and one member server. The DC contains a shared folder named Customers, and the member server contains a realtime job tracking database. Louisville has one DC with a shared folder called Shipping Info. Currently the users have multiple drive mappings to provide access to the files at all locations, and there is no redundancy.

The locations have T1 connections from Carson City to Indianapolis and from Indianapolis to Louisville. The routers have been replaced in the past year and are QoS aware.

The Owners have begun negotiations to purchase a small firm in Evansville, IN. This firm has an existing infrastructure in place that utilizes Windows NT 4 Server. Because this purchase is still in negotiations, further details are not available.

Current WAN Connectivity

The locations have T1 connections from Carson City to Indianapolis and from Indianapolis to Louisville. The routers have been replaced in the past year and are QoS aware.

Proposed WAN Connectivity

There are currently no plans to change your WAN design. However if the ownership purchases the company in Evansville, your design should provide the best integration possible.

Directory Design Commentary

VirtuCon's current password policies will be duplicated on the Windows 2000 servers.

Current Internet Positioning

VirtuCon currently accesses the Internet from all locations using a single leased IP address at the Indianapolis location. This location has an IP Proxy and firewall to protect the network and provide access.

A Web-hosting firm hosts the company Web site. The firewall server at the Indianapolis site provides a Web-based email client for remote access to email to all remote employees.

Future Internet Plans

Eventually, VirtuCon would like to host its own site and provide remote users with Web-based access to its intranet mail.

Company Goal with the Proposed Upgrade

You are a network administrator for VirtuCon. Management has asked you to implement a file management structure that will provide redundancy for mission-critical shared files. The redundancy will need to provide access to all users in the event of a server or WAN link failure. You would also like to provide a more efficient way to utilize the DLT drive on the member server at the Carson City location to back up all of the shared files.

The administrators at all locations would like more efficient access to the CD-ROMs on servers. They use the CD-ROMs to access program installation files and utilities when supporting clients and servers.

Question 1

Considering the case study, which type of Dfs root will provide the appropriate level of redundancy for the shared data files?

❍ a. Domain-based Dfs root

❍ b. Standalone Dfs root

❍ c. Dfs leaf object replicas

❍ d. Standalone Dfs root with a root replica

Answer a is correct. A domain-based Dfs root can provide redundancy of the root by using the root replica option. Standalone Dfs roots cannot be replicated to other servers so answers b and d are incorrect. Dfs leaf objects do not provide redundancy to the Dfs root, so answer c is incorrect.

Question 2

Considering the case study, which type of Dfs root will provide the appropriate level of redundancy for the CD-ROM shared folders?

- ❍ a. Domain-based Dfs root
- ❍ b. Standalone Dfs root
- ❍ c. Dfs leaf object replicas
- ❍ d. Standalone Dfs root with a root replica

Answer b is correct. Since redundancy of the tools and utilities was not a requirement of the case study, a standalone root will be sufficient. None of the other options are necessary.

Question 3

Considering the case study, which servers or workstations will be eligible to host the required Dfs root or roots needed? [Check all correct answers]

- ❑ a. Windows 2000
- ❑ b. Windows 2000 Professional
- ❑ c. Windows 98 clients
- ❑ d. Windows NT Workstation

Answers a, b, and d are correct. With the Windows 2000 implementation of Dfs, Windows 2000, Windows 2000 Professional, Windows NT Server, and Windows NT Workstation can host Dfs roots. Windows 98 clients cannot host Dfs roots.

Question 4

Considering the case study, which clients will require the Dfs client 4/5 to browse the Dfs root or host a Dfs leaf object?

- ❍ a. Windows 95
- ❍ b. Windows 98
- ❍ c. Windows 2000
- ❍ d. Windows 2000 Professional

Answer a is correct. The Windows 2000 implementation of Dfs only requires Windows 95 clients to use Dfs client software.

Question 5

Considering the case study, what should be created to provide redundancy for the shared data files? [Check all correct answers]

- ❑ a. Two or more identical standalone roots
- ❑ b. A single domain-based root with replicas at each location
- ❑ c. Replicas of the Dfs leaf objects at each location
- ❑ d. None of the above

Answers b and c are correct. In order for the mission-critical files to be redundant, a single domain-based root should be created and a replica placed at each location. The replicas will ensure that the root share will be available if the WAN link is disabled. Replicas of the remote shared files should also be stored on servers at each physical location, since bandwidth is not a limiting factor.

Question 6

Considering the case study, where would you place root and link replicas to provide the proper fault tolerance?

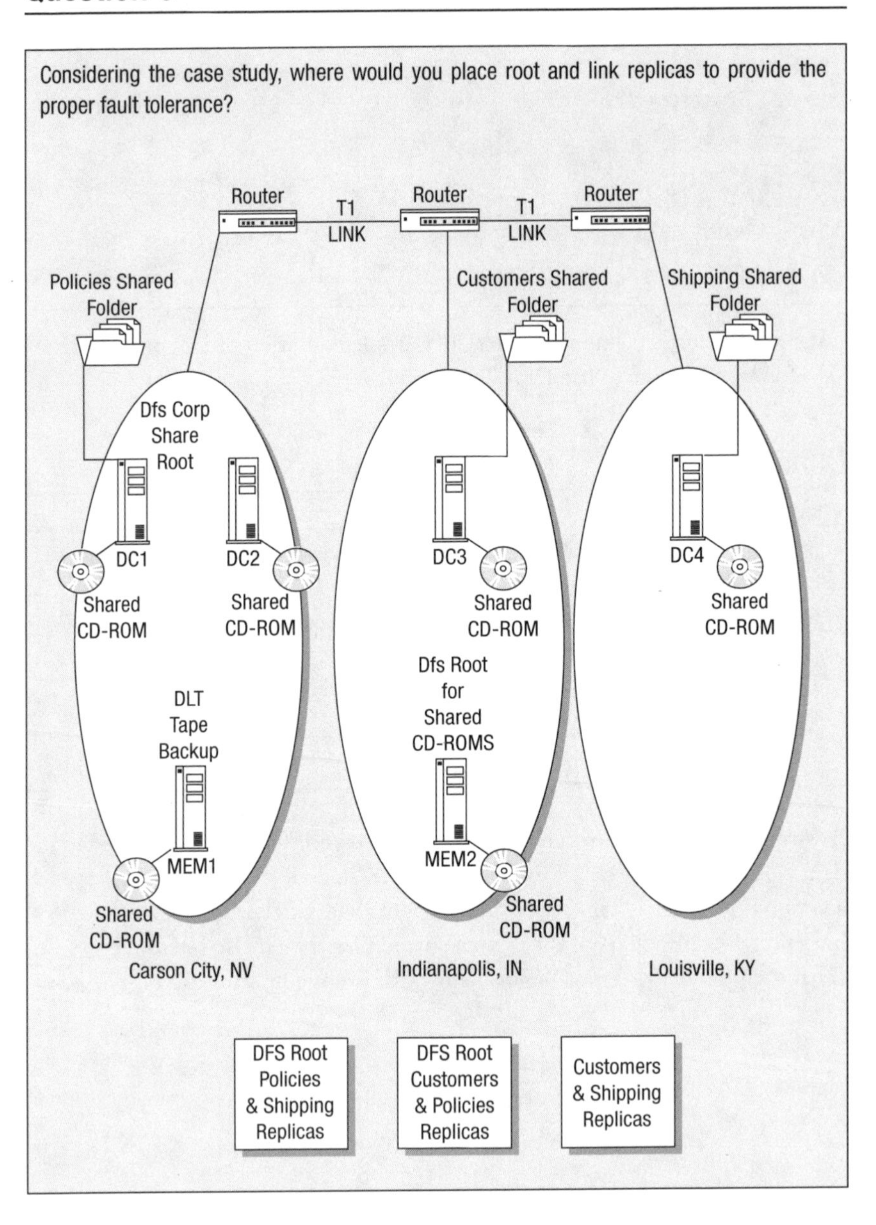

Answer:

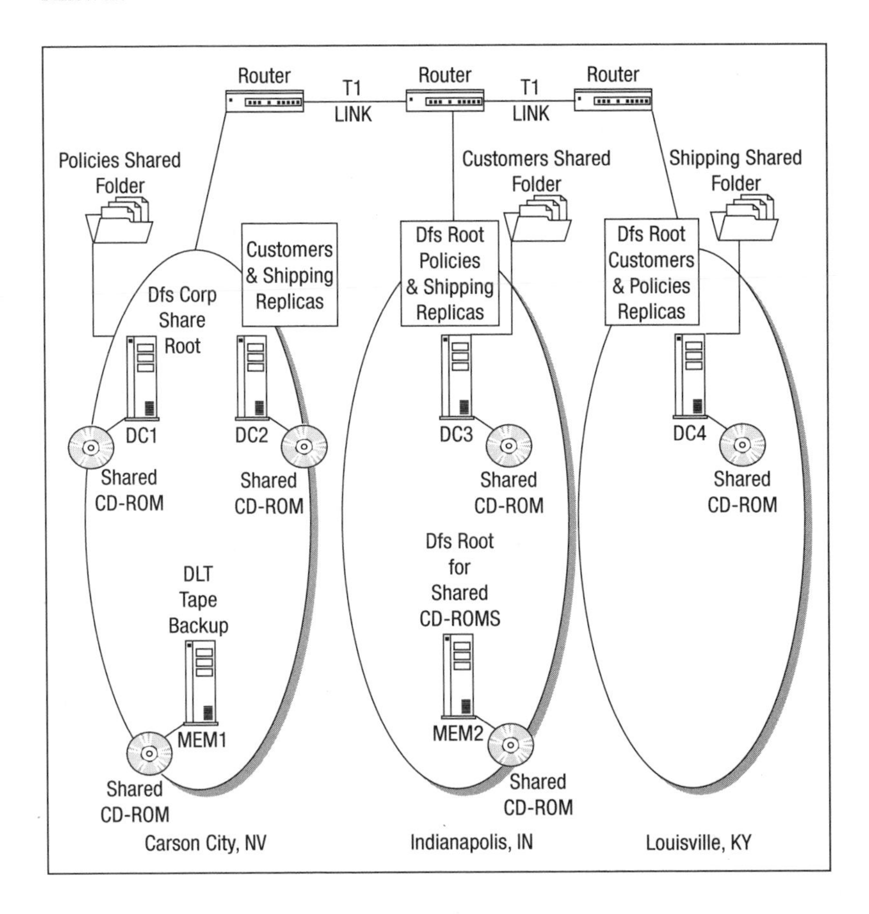

By placing the replicas in this manner, all of the data will be available in the event of a server crash or a temporary interruption of the T1 link. By placing the CD-ROM Dfs root at the Indianapolis location, a WAN link failure will be limited to the failed subnet. For example, if the link between Carson City and Indianapolis fails, both Indianapolis and Louisville will still have access to the CD-ROM Dfs root. If the CD-ROM root was located at the Carson City location and the link failed between Carson City and Indianapolis, only the Carson City location will have access to the CD-ROM Dfs root.

Question 7

Considering the case study, what additional permissions need to be set to allow the users who currently have access to the shared folders to connect to the same folders though the Dfs root?

❍ a. Security permissions should be set through the Dfs administrator program

❍ b. Security permissions should be set through My Computer

❍ c. Security permissions should be set through the Windows Explorer

❍ d. None

Answer d is correct. The case study mentions that the users are currently accessing the files through multiple drive mappings. This means that the proper security permissions are already set. Dfs does not implement any additional security.

Need to Know More?

Alexander, Geoffry, Anoop Jalan and Joseph Alexander. *MCSE Windows 2000 Network Design Exam Prep.* The Coriolis Group, Scottsdale, AZ, 2000. ISBN 1-57610-725-6. See chapter 20 for a discussion of Dfs.

For more information on the subjects covered in this chapter, read the following TechNet article available at **www.microsoft.com**.

TechNet Article Q241452. "How to Install Distributed File System (Dfs) on Windows 2000."

Search the TechNet CD (or its online version through **www. microsoft. com)** using the keyword "Dfs".

Remote Access in a Windows 2000 Environment

Terms you'll need to understand:

- ✓ Dial-up
- ✓ Virtual Private Network (VPN)
- ✓ Remote Access Policy
- ✓ Point-to-Point Protocol (PPP)
- ✓ Point-to-Point Tunneling Protocol (PPTP)
- ✓ Microsoft Point-to-Point Encryption (MPPE)
- ✓ Layer 2 Tunneling Protocol (L2TP)
- ✓ Internet Protocol Security (IPSec)
- ✓ Tunneling
- ✓ System Network Architecture (SNA)

Techniques you'll need to master:

- ✓ Determining how to implement remote access
- ✓ Using remote-access techniques
- ✓ Implementing remote-access security
- ✓ Improving remote-access performance
- ✓ Making remote access available

This chapter teaches you how to implement remote access in a Windows 2000 network infrastructure. You'll learn how to design a network using remote access to enhance and secure the Windows 2000 infrastructure.

Remote Access Overview

Remote access allows users to dial into a Routing and Remote Access Server (RRAS) from a remote location. Using a modem, the user can access the office network as if he or she were sitting in the office (Figure 11.1). Remote access can also be a dial-up connection to the office through the user's Internet Service Provider (ISP) (Figure 11.2). Remote access can also be used to connect multiple remote sites in a WAN, using either direct dial from one site to another or connecting through the Internet (Figure 11.3).

If users connect to the Internet through their ISP, they can use a Virtual Private Network (VPN) to connect to their company's network through the company's

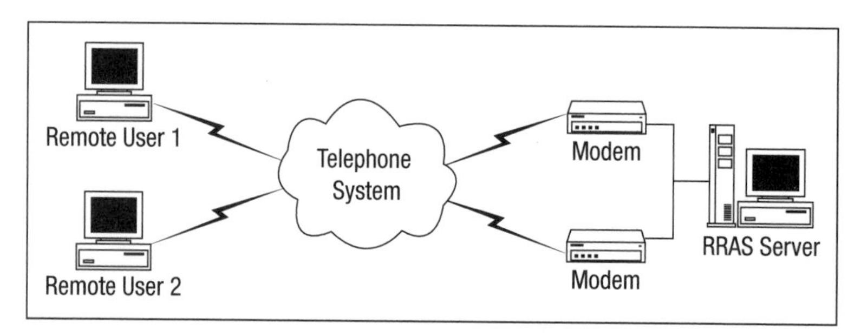

Figure 11.1 Remote telephone dial-up.

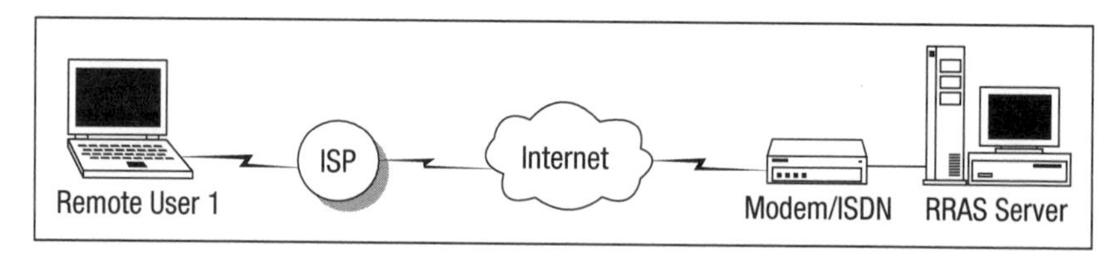

Figure 11.2 Remote ISP dial-up.

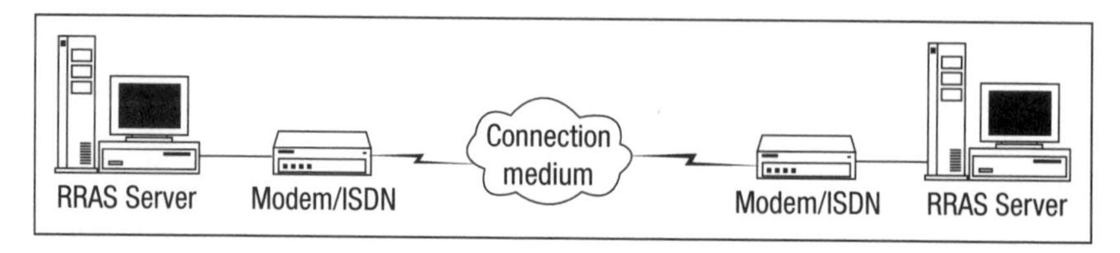

Figure 11.3 Remote site-to-site dial-up.

Internet connection. Remote offices can also use VPNs to connect to one another through the Internet as well.

All of these connections can use various protocols and connection mediums.

Remote Access Implementation

Remote access is enabled when the RRAS service is enabled and configured. By default, remote-access clients have no access unless they are given specific dial-in permissions. These permissions are assigned in the user properties under Active Directory Users And Computers on the Dial-In tab (Figure 11.4).

To specify user dial-in access, change the option under the Remote Access Permission (Dial-in or VPN) section from Deny Access to Allow Access.

Callback options can be set to No Callback, which has no security enforcement. Once a user connects, they are prompted for a username and password, which then allows them access to the network according to their rights and permissions.

When Set By Caller is enabled, the user is prompted to enter a username and password. Once authenticated, the user is then prompted for a phone number, which the RRAS server (after disconnecting) uses to call the user back. This callback allows the remote user to avoid the long-distance charges, which will be billed to the company where the RRAS server is located. The user pays only a

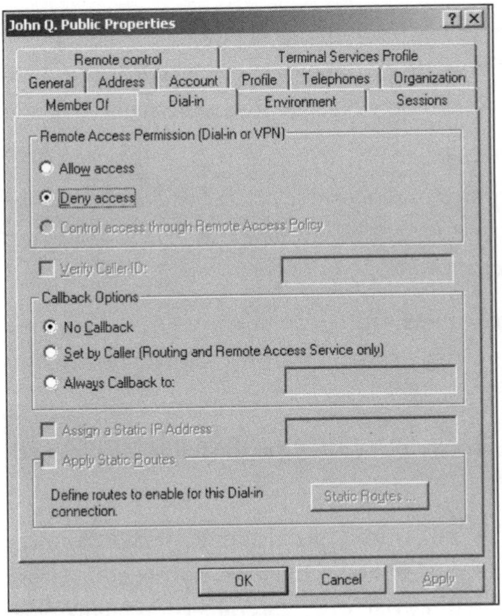

Figure 11.4 Dial-in user properties.

small toll for the initial, brief connection to enter username, password, and call-back phone number.

For a dial-in connection that is more secure, select the option Always Callback To and enter a phone number for the specified user account. By disallowing a user from logging in from locations other than the one specified, this option protects the data from being accessed from an unsecure location. With this option, the user connects from the specified number and is prompted for their username and password. Once the user is authenticated, the RRAS server disconnects and calls the user back at the specified phone number.

Although this type of security is perfectly adequate for a small number of dial-in users, a larger number of users is best handled by implementing policies to assign privileges to groups of users. To implement dial-in policies, select Start|Programs|Administrative Tools|Routing and Remote Access.

Once Routing and Remote Access services are enabled (see Chapter 9), select the local server name in the left pane. In the right pane, double click Remote Access Policies. In the right pane, right-click on an open area and select New Remote Access Policy to start the Remote Access wizard.

To configure the policy, the wizard will go through the following steps:

1. The first screen asks for a policy name. Enter an easily remembered name in the space provided.

2. In the next screen, options can be set to determine whether specifications are to be used for a connection. These are such things as tunnel-type, Windows groups that the user belongs to, protocol type, service being requested, and time and day.

3. The next screen pertains to the previous option selected. For example, on the Time And Day option, you can specify which hours of which day that a group will be permitted or denied access.

4. After all of the conditions are entered, the next screen gives you the option to specify (if the conditions are met) whether the user will be permitted or denied access.

5. The next option is to edit the profile. The profile has the following tabs with the indicated options:

   - *Dial-in constraints*—Set disconnect time, set maximum session connection time, restrict access to specified hours and days, restrict access from a specified phone number, and restrict access by connection media type.

- *IP*—Set IP assignment (manual, DHCP, and so forth) and IP filters to and from the RRAS server.
- *Multilink*—Specify dial-in client to be permitted to use a specified number of ports; specify to drop a multilink port if bandwidth falls below a certain percentage for a specified amount of time.
- *Authentication*—Specify to use the Extensible Authentication Protocol (EAP), for use when using smart-card security. Specify other authentication protocols such as MSCHAP, CHAP, or no authentication. EAP is used for hardware authentication such as smart cards, retina-scan devices, and other hardware security implementations.
- *Encryption*—Specify the type of encryption to be used by the remote client. These include None, Basic, and Strong.
- *Advanced*—Specify additional options sent to the RRAS server by the client on connection (such as the IP address of the RRAS server that the client wants to log into for authentication).

6. Once you click on the Finish button, the wizard will end and the policy will be listed in the right pane. Once the policies are listed in this pane, you can arrange them in any order—which is important because the policies are applied to the dial-in connections from top to bottom.

Virtual Private Network (VPN)

With the Internet's popularity has come its increasing use as a backbone to connect multiple sites or to connect on a user-by-user basis.

VPNs comprise multiple components (Figure 11.5). These components include:

- *Client*—The system that is connecting to the network to use its resources.
- *Server*—The RRAS system that is receiving the connection request from the client to connect to the resources on the resource network.

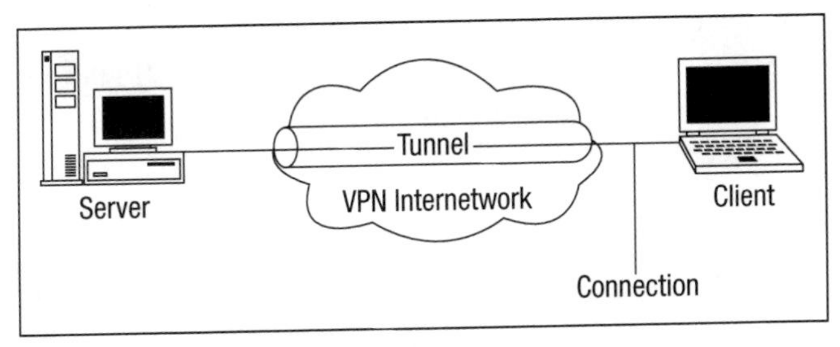

Figure 11.5 VPN component diagram.

- *Tunnel*—Where the data is encapsulated through the connection.
- *Connection*—Where the data is encrypted through the connection.
- *Tunneled data*—Data sent over a point-to-point connection.
- *Tunneling protocols*—Used to manage tunnels and data.
- *VPN internetwork*—Network media connection between client and server.

Note: For a VPN, data must be tunneled and encrypted.

VPNs can be used between remote connections and also routers (see Chapter 9). VPNs feature three major properties: encapsulation, data encryption, and authentication.

Encapsulation

With a VPN network's encapsulation (or *tunneling*), you can transmit private data over a public network. This is possible because encapsulated frames have a special header that allows them to be routed over the public network.

This special header has the information for routing through the VPN internetwork. Once the packet has reached the endpoint of the VPN, the special header is removed (de-encapsulated), and the packet is then sent to its final destination on the private network. The path that the encapsulated packet takes is the tunnel.

The following sections describe some common types of encapsulation:

Point-to-Point Tunneling Protocol (PPTP)

PPTP allows IP, IPX, or NetBEUI to be tunneled with an IP header for transmission over a TCP/IP network. PPTP uses a Microsoft proprietary encryption protocol called Microsoft Point-to-Point Encryption (MPPE). To encrypt data with PPTP (and MPPE), MSCHAP (version 1 or 2), and EAP are the only user authentication protocols that can be used. When using PPTP for a VPN over an Internet connection, the encryption is only between the ISP and the VPN server at the corporate private server. For example: A user dials in to the ISP and the ISP (acting as the VPN client) connects through the Internet to the corporate VPN server. The encryption works in connection between the ISP VPN client and the VPN corporate server. The connection from the remote client to the ISP is not encrypted.

PPTP encapsulation is created by the following means:

1. The data frame is encrypted with a Point-to-Point Protocol (PPP) header.
2. The PPP frame is then encapsulated with a Generic Routing Encapsulation (GRE) header.

3. The GRE packet is then encapsulated with a header containing the server and client addresses.
4. A final IP header and trailer are added for routing purposes on the VPN network. This is the full PPTP packet.

Layer 2 Tunneling Protocol (L2TP)

L2TP allows IP, IPX, or NetBEUI to be encrypted and sent over a PPP connection. PPP connections are possible over such media types as PSTN, X.25, ISDN, Frame Relay, and ATM using IP, which is the only transport protocol that L2TP currently supports.

L2TP supports not only encryption of frames, but also compression. Each L2TP tunnel can support multiple calls at once.

Unlike PPTP, L2TP works with all user authentication protocols, such as SPAP, PAP, EAP, CHAP, and MSCHAP. Also, L2TP uses IPSec as its authentication protocol, which is an open Internet standard and not proprietary. An L2TP VPN working through an ISP will start encryption from the remote user's computer instead of at the ISP. For these reasons, L2TP is considered to be the stronger protocol for security when compared to PPTP.

IP Security (IPSec) Tunneling Protocol

With IPSec, the data is encrypted and then encapsulated for transmission. The receiving end will de-encapsulate the encrypted data and then decrypt the data for use.

IPX Tunneling

IPX Tunneling is used when the private-network protocol is IPX/SPX, but the IPX/SPX packets will be encapsulated to be sent over a TCP/IP public network.

The encapsulated data is sent as User Datagram Protocol (UDP) packets.

Note: UDP packets are connectionless, which means that they are unreliable as to whether they arrive at the destination.

System Network Architecture (SNA) Tunneling

SNA Tunneling is used to encapsulate SNA packets for transmission over a VPN using TCP/IP.

SNA integrates IBM mainframes with other computer systems such as the PC, Macintosh, Unix, and operating systems such as Windows, OS/2, and DOS.

An SNA server acts as a gateway between the mainframes and the client systems. The SNA server can communicate with the client computers using protocols such as TCP/IP, IPX/SPX, NetBEUI, Banyan VINES IP, AppleTalk, and RRAS. Once requests are received at the SNA server, these packets are converted to SNA packets and sent to the mainframe. The connection between the client and SNA server are physical units (PUs), and the connection from the SNA server to the mainframe are logical units (LUs).

SNA Tunneling allows a private network with a mainframe to be accessed from remote locations over a public network.

Data Encryption

Data encryption is the process by which the encapsulated data is changed by an algorithm (encryption key) to obscure the data content.

Note: The more data that is encrypted, the easier it is to decrypt the data and find the key that decrypts all of the data that uses the same encryption algorithm.

Authentication

The two types of VPN authentication—*user* and *data*—are explained as follows:

- *User authentication*—The server authenticates the client when connecting to the server. If mutual user authentication is used, the client and server authenticate each other when connections are initiated.

- *Data authentication*—The server verifies that the data is not corrupted and that it is actually being sent from the specified client.

Features

Remote access supports many different connection types, and the protocols and security measures that you use depend upon the connection type.

Dial-in access is used by clients using point-to-point connections using the PPP or MS-RAS protocol.

Dial-in connections allow protocols such as TCP/IP, IPX/SPX (NWLink), NetBEUI, and AppleTalk. Both the server and client must have the same protocol to be able to communicate.

Dial-in connections are not permanent connections, but are initiated on command by using modems, ISDN, and X.25 connections.

Integration

RRAS can be integrated with Windows 2000 network services and be placed in a LAN or WAN. Depending on how a network is or will be set up can determine which options will be integrated with RRAS.

2000 Services

RRAS integrates with other Windows 2000 services to extend capabilities for client use. This integration also helps reduce management overhead for administrators.

Integration with such services as DHCP, DNS, WINS, Active Directory, and RADIUS will help reduce administrative overhead and still allow a remote client full network functionality.

DHCP Integration

Integrating DHCP with remote-access clients allows automatic updates of IP information to the client. These automatic updates eliminate the errors that would result if the IP information were entered manually on the client computers.

DHCP leases 10 IP addresses at a time for client systems. When the addresses are no longer needed, they are returned to the DHCP pool for use by other clients (see Chapter 4). If more than 10 users are connecting to a RRAS server, the RRAS server will lease another 10 addresses. When only 10 clients or fewer are connected to the RRAS server, it will drop the additional 10 addresses and have only 10 addresses at a given time.

DHCP Relay Agent must be configured on the RRAS server to be able to issue more TCP/IP information than just the IP address and subnet mask to the remote clients.

For performance reasons, DHCP services should not be installed on the RRAS server. Only Relay Agent should be installed for the purposes of the RRAS clients.

DNS Integration

RRAS integration with the DNS server allows dynamic updates of the DNS database by the RRAS clients.

Thus, the remote clients will have their names resolved in the same manner as all of the local clients when using DNS.

When the client disconnects, the client will de-register its DNS account entry.

WINS Integration

Similarly, RRAS integration with the WINS server allows dynamic updates of the WINS database by the RRAS clients.

Thus, the remote clients will have their names resolved in the same manner as all of the local clients when using WINS.

Active Directory Integration

RRAS integration with Active Directory in native mode allows policies to be administered through the Active Directory services for remote clients.

RRAS integration with Active Directory in non-native mode will not allow policies to be administered through the Active Directory services for remote clients.

RADIUS Integration

RADIUS integration allows central management of RRAS servers to manage policies and keep logs of client authentication.

RADIUS can be specified as the authentication provider for remote clients. (See Chapter 12.)

LAN Integration

Using remote access for a LAN provides for centralized connections for the clients. A benefit of this integration is that it allows central management for the administrator.

An administrator can allow access by the usernames and also by creating a policy for groups of users. If more connections are required, more dial-in services can be added to give the required bandwidth needed.

WAN Integration

Because most networks are WANs, this is where more consideration can affect the design. Whether the integration is with a LAN or WAN, identical protocols must be enabled for both the RRAS server and the client.

Clients can access a network (LAN or WAN) in two ways: one uses VPNs (which were discussed earlier in this chapter) and the other uses dial-in access.

Dial-in connections let an administrator specify the maximum number of remote clients that will be supported at one time. This is determined by the number of modems on the RRAS server to accept calls from the clients.

The administrator can also specify which users or groups have access to the network from a remote location. These policies or rights can be set to allow specific times when connections are allowed.

Remote Access Placement

Placement of the remote access server can affect network security when using a VPN.

If the RRAS server is inside the firewall (between the company network and the firewall) and cannot be compromised, confidential data may be stored on it for remote use. In this situation, you need a firewall to protect the RRAS server from illegal access from the Internet.

If the RRAS server does not contain any important data, it can be placed outside the firewall, between the firewall and the Internet. Placing the server here allows only VPN connections from the RRAS server to go through the firewall.

Note: See Chapter 7 for limitations on using VPN protocols with NAT.

Security

We've previously discussed security options for keeping remote access secure—such as setting dial-in permissions for a user in Active Directory Users and Computers. The other options for access will be restricted by a remote-access policy. RADIUS can also be used for remote access authentication (see Chapter 12).

In situations where remote access connections need high security, smart cards offer the strongest type of user authentication that is available with Windows 2000. Each smart card user needs a smart card reader and smart card with a certificate preloaded by an administrator. After smart card logon has been enabled for a domain, a Windows 2000 user can log on with a PIN number instead of username and password. Smart cards can be used across VPNs as long as a certificate has been loaded on the VPN router and the smart card authentication has been enabled for the VPN. For networks needing high security, remote access policies can be set to require remote users to log on only with smart cards.

Availability

For redundancy, you can use more than one RRAS server or VPN connection. Having an extra server or connection allows remote services to be available if a server or connection should fail.

Similarly, each remote client should have multiple phone numbers to dial into the RRAS server if one modem or phone line should fail.

In the case of multiple sites connected in a WAN, multiple RRAS servers and connections should also be available.

With VPNs, each RRAS server should have a round-robin DNS entry to ensure that, when one server goes down, the VPN uses the next server in the list.

Network load balancing can be used if using a cluster. Clusters provide fail-over for the VPN services if one server should fail. All RRAS servers in the cluster need persistent connections for remote users.

Performance

Set specific phone numbers to clients so that a specific node is dedicated to them when they connect to a RRAS server by phone.

RRAS servers should be placed on the network segment that contains the resources that need to be accessed by the remote clients. If needed, add a RRAS server on each network segment or, specifically, each remote site.

Adding multiple VPN servers will increase the resources to handle bandwidth.

Because RRAS services support multiple CPUs in a server, this helps to process the client requests. Multiple modems can be used to increase bandwidth. If connection bandwidth is greater then network bandwidth, upgrade the network cards in the RRAS server to handle the load. With any service on a Windows server, increase memory to reduce the drive swapping that is associated with virtual memory. Also make sure that the disk drives in the RRAS server are fast enough to handle the file access and virtual memory swapping. Use Performance Monitor to check the performance of the memory, CPU, and network card to look for bottlenecks.

RRAS servers should be dedicated to their task of handling remote-access clients.

For VPNs, upgrade the connection to achieve greater bandwidth for the remote clients who use the Internet to tunnel into the company network. Use permanent connections because non-permanent connections take time to dial and connect, which will decrease performance.

Practice Questions

Case Study

Current LAN/Network Structure

2Market currently has 10 branch offices and headquarters in Chicago, Illinois. Its branch offices are located in the following cities:

Los Angeles, California

New York City, New York

Houston, Texas

Miami, Florida

Indianapolis, Indiana

Boston, Massachusetts

Salt Lake City, Utah

Nashville, Tennessee

Redmond, Washington

Aspen, Colorado

The branch offices are not currently connected to headquarters in a WAN.

Proposed LAN/Network Structure

2Market wants to improve communications among branches. All "paperwork" must be approved through headquarters, but sending mail and faxes is too slow and expensive.

2Market is also starting a research-and-development (R&D) department that is considered a highly secure area where only specific employees are allowed. The R&D department will have its own building that will be on the other side of Chicago from the headquarters.

Current WAN Connectivity

2Market has an Internet presence as 2Market.com. The company currently hosts its own Web servers in the IT department at headquarters.

Proposed WAN/Internet Connectivity

2Market wants to connect all offices through the Internet. Sales people at all offices need access to the network not only from home, but also from various remote locations. Some sales personnel have Internet access at home, and some do not.

Question 1

The Windows 2000 network uses Active Directory. The R&D office needs to authenticate users to their accounts in Active Directory. What protocol can be used to implement a retina scanner at the R&D office, but be authenticated at headquarters?

❍ a. IP

❍ b. IPX

❍ c. PPP

❍ d. EAP

The correct answer is d. EAP is used for hardware devices connected to the network. IP and IPX are standard protocols, which would encapsulate the EAP protocol; so choices a and b are incorrect. PPP is a dial-in protocol for accessing a network remotely with a modem through a RRAS server, making choice c incorrect.

Question 2

What is the economical way to connect all of the offices?

❍ a. Connect the sites directly using multiple links for redundancy.

❍ b. Connect all offices through the Internet using VPNs.

❍ c. Each site will use a direct-dial connection to the nearest site and create a "linear" link between all of the sites.

❍ d. Use a dial-on-demand connection from each site to headquarters.

The correct answer is b. Every site connects to a local ISP for access to the Internet, and VPNs are set up between all sites. This will be the cheapest option. All other connections would require a long-distance connection that would cost a lot.

Question 3

What is required to allow the sales staff of all of the offices to connect to the network from remote locations or from their homes? [Check all correct answers]

❑ a. Modems

❑ b. Connection to ISP

❑ c. Hub

❑ d. Switch

The correct answers are a and b. Each sales person will need a modem and (possibly) access to the Internet through an ISP. VPNs can be created from their laptop to the company RRAS server. Or, a sales person could direct dial into the RRAS server if modems were added on the RRAS server to direct dial connections.

A hub and switch would be used in the company network, but not by the sales personnel from their homes or other remote locations. The sales personnel will not need any additional hardware.

Question 4

With security enabled for dial-in access, would a user dialing in have access if the user had the following allowable times in group policies and the user belonged to all four groups?

Group1 access permitted Monday–Friday 8:00 A.M. to 5:00 P.M.

Group2 access permitted Monday–Friday 8:00 A.M. to 12:00 P.M.

Group3 access permitted Monday–Saturday 8:00 A.M. to 5:00 P.M.

Group4 access denied Saturday–Sunday all hours

The administrator denies dial-in connections on the users properties. Will the user have access on Monday morning at 9:30 A.M.?

❍ a. Yes

❍ b. No

The correct answer is b. If the user properties is set to deny dial-in connections, this setting overrides all policies that could permit the user to dial in at certain times.

Question 5

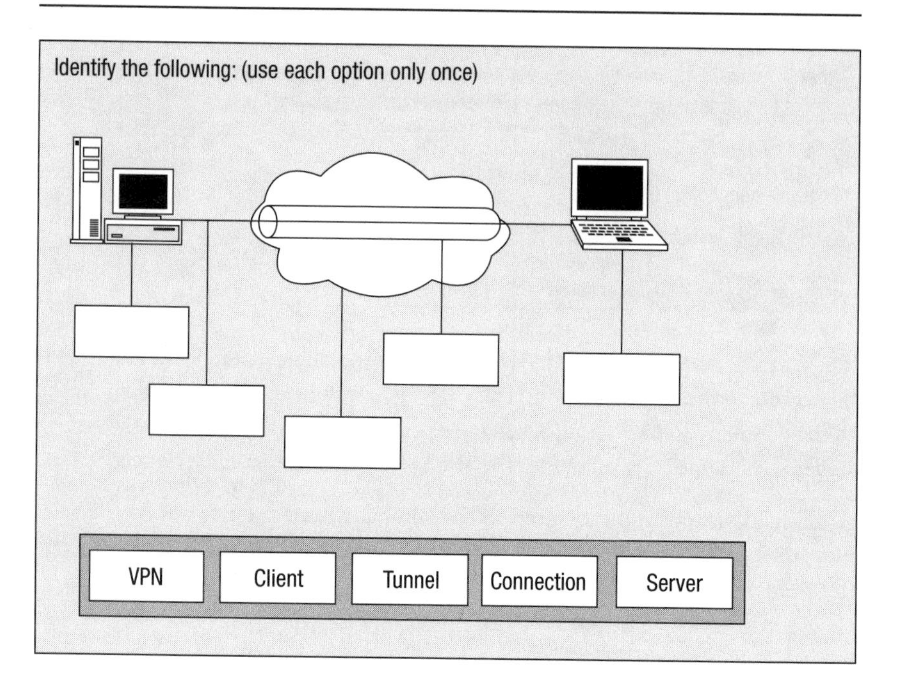

The answer is shown in the following diagram. See Figure 11.5 in this chapter for more information.

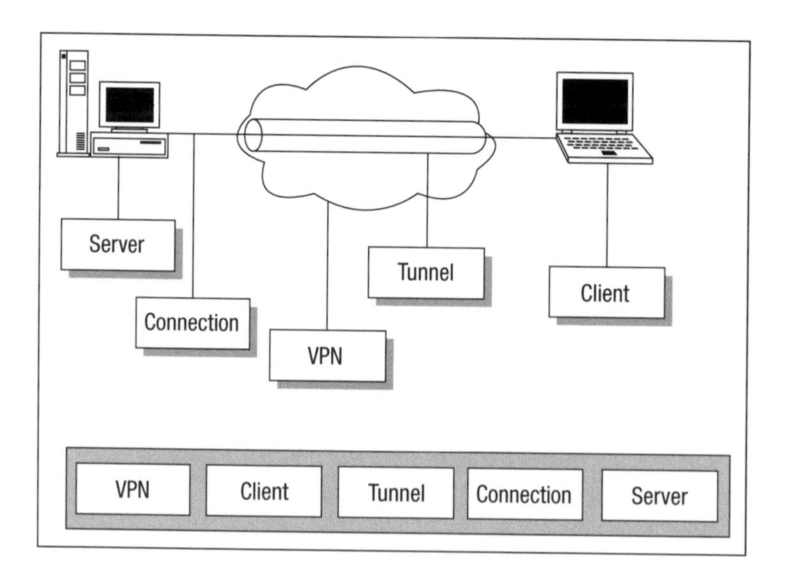

Question 6

Which of the following are connection protocols? [Check all correct answers]

- ❑ a. PPP
- ❑ b. L2TP
- ❑ c. MS-RAS
- ❑ d. IPSec

The correct answers are a and c. Choices b and d are security encapsulation used in VPNs. PPP and MS-RAS are used as dial-in connection protocols.

Question 7

For best performance and security, which of the following offices should have a RRAS server for remote users to connect to? [Check all correct answers]

- ❑ a. Headquarters in Chicago, Illinois
- ❑ b. Los Angeles, California
- ❑ c. New York City, New York
- ❑ d. Houston, Texas
- ❑ e. Miami, Florida
- ❑ f. Indianapolis, Indiana
- ❑ g. Boston, Massachusetts
- ❑ h. Salt Lake City, Utah
- ❑ i. Nashville, Tennessee
- ❑ j. Redmond, Washington
- ❑ k. Aspen, Colorado
- ❑ l. R&D in Chicago, Illinois

The correct answers are a, b, c, d, e, f, g, h, i, j, and k.

All offices should have their own RRAS server for performance improvements. This will prevent a high load of VPN traffic if all users connect to one office and then tunnel to all of the other offices. If every office has its own RRAS server, then most traffic would be limited to its local network.

For security reasons, the R&D office should not have its own RRAS server to better prevent unauthorized access attempts. The office can also filter out any RRAS connections to pass over the VPN to the R&D network.

Question 8

The IT manager wants to set up the VPN on the RRAS server at headquarters on clustered servers for redundancy. The IT manager also wants this implemented for sharing the VPN traffic to improve performance. This implementation will work for redundancy and performance.

❍ a. True

❍ b. False

The correct answer is b. Network load balancing must also be enabled to balance the load between the PPTP links.

Question 9

2Market has no important data stored on the RRAS server at the Indianapolis office, but, at the Houston office, the RRAS server doubles as an SQL server. Where should the RRAS servers be placed in the following diagram? [Use each option twice]

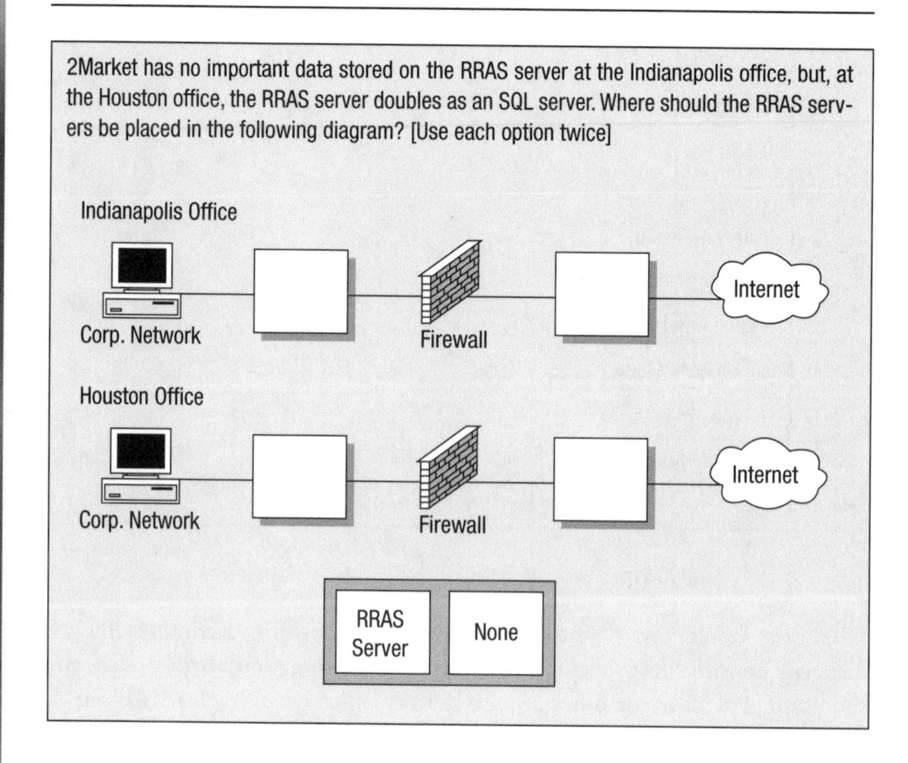

The correct answer is

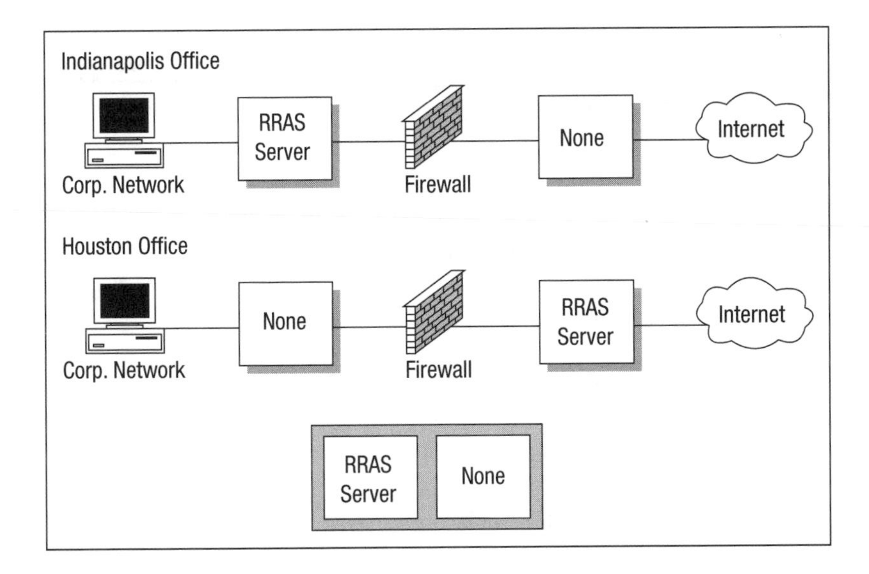

Because the Indianapolis server has important data on it, it needs to be placed behind the firewall for more protection. The Houston office is the opposite.

Question 10

The IT manager wants to increase performance for the remote clients. She wants to implement DHCP on the RRAS server to reduce network traffic on the dial-in clients. This implementation will improve performance.

❍ a. True

❍ b. False

The correct answer is b. DHCP services should not be run on the RRAS server; it should run only DHCP Relay Agent.

Need to Know More?

Charles, Kackie. *Windows 2000 Routing and Remote Access Services.* Macmillan Technical Publishing, Indianapolis, IN, 2000. ISBN 0-73570-951-3. This guide to RRAS service offers more in-depth detail about installing and configuring the RRAS service.

Goncalves, Marcus. *Implementing Remote Access Services with Microsoft Windows 2000.* Que, Indianapolis, IN, 2000. ISBN 0-78972-138-4. This book covers the implementation of remote-access services, with detailed information on configuration and implementation.

Microsoft Corporation. *Windows 2000 Server Resource Kit.* Microsoft Press, Redmond, WA, 2000. ISBN 1-57231-805-8. Contains chapters dedicated to setting up VPNs and RRAS for remote connectivity.

Search the TechNet CD (or its online version through **www.microsoft.com**) using the keyword “Remote Access”. Also, see the Windows 2000 Server or Advanced Server help.

Understanding RADIUS

Terms you'll need to understand:

- ✓ Internet Authentication Services (IAS)
- ✓ Remote Authentication Dial-In Service (RADIUS)
- ✓ Routing and Remote Access Service (RRAS)
- ✓ Realm
- ✓ Network Access Server (NAS)
- ✓ Point-to-Point Protocol (PPP)
- ✓ Shared secret
- ✓ Points of Presence (POP)
- ✓ Remote access policy

Techniques you'll need to master:

- ✓ Differentiating between the different components of RADIUS
- ✓ Understanding how RADIUS fits into a RAS solution
- ✓ Determining placement of the RADIUS client and server
- ✓ Improving security and availability in a RADIUS solution

As discussed in previous chapters, Windows 2000 includes many services that allow long-distance connections to a network. As networks grow, so does the need for connections between geographically diverse locations. One problem that has plagued network administrators is how to connect remote users—and especially those who roam among a variety of remote locations—to the network. Remote connections jeopardize the security of a network by their very nature. Yet, in today's network environment, users need access to private network resources regardless of where they are physically located.

What Is RADIUS?

RADIUS (Remote Authentication Dial-In User Service) provides three services to a network: authentication, authorization, and accounting. For a number of reasons, it can be quite difficult to secure a network that has many remote users. Such a network may need to allow remote connections from other locations in the network or from users who are dialing in from home or even while traveling. This last group—roaming users—poses a network's largest security risk. Allowing users to connect from any location makes it difficult to maintain control over incoming connections to the private network. The purpose of RADIUS is to control the actions of remote and roaming users without allowing sensitive network information like usernames and passwords out of the private network. RADIUS does this by using a client/server architecture that is specifically designed for a geographically dispersed environment.

It is important to remember that RADIUS is not a full remote-access solution. It merely adds security and accounting to a remote-access design for a network. RADIUS protects a private network by isolating authentication of remote users from the rest of the data exchange that occurs over lines that are not secure. In a traditional remote-access solution, the RAS server connects users to the network, and all data transfer occurs through the RAS server including authentication and accounting information such as transaction logging. In a RAS solution that uses RADIUS, the RAS server still controls the transfer of data between the remote client and the private network, but it passes to the RADIUS service the responsibility of authenticating the user, authorizing user actions, and tracking remote user actions.

Tracking Remote Connections with RADIUS Accounting

The accounting service provided by RADIUS increases control over remote connections. Because RADIUS can log remote connections to a network, such network usage can be monitored. The accounting service can log the IP address of the computer that requests authentication, the time of the call, the call status (such as success or failure), which RADIUS client sent the request and which RADIUS server accepted the request. This accounting service, which is separate from the authentication and authorization services provided by RADIUS, can also be used for billing or security purposes. Later in this chapter, we'll see how Internet Service Providers (ISPs) can use the accounting feature to charge for RADIUS services that are provided to a network.

RADIUS Service Basics

Although RADIUS is a service supported in Windows 2000, the term *RADIUS* can also refer to a protocol because networking services are often named after the protocol that runs the service. (Just like the FTP service is run by the FTP protocol, the RADIUS service is run by the RADIUS protocol.) Support for RADIUS was first introduced in later versions of the Windows NT 4 Option Pack, and it is integrated into the Routing and Remote Access Service (RRAS) service and the Internet Authentication Service (IAS) in Windows 2000. Before learning about the RADIUS service, it is important to have an overview of the RRAS service, which is provided in Chapter 9.

The standards for implementing RADIUS are currently being determined by the Internet Engineering Task Force (IETF). RFCs 2138 and 2139 describe how the RADIUS service and its accounting features work. Because it is to be an open standard, the Windows 2000 RADIUS service can be integrated into a heterogeneous network with different operating systems such as Unix and Novell Netware.

Instead of using TCP, RADIUS uses UDP as its transport level protocol. UDP provides connectionless, or *not guaranteed*, service—which means that there isn't as much checking to make sure that the information made it to its destination. UDP makes sense because RADIUS is a supporting service on the network. TCP is used when data such as Web pages or files is being transferred. As a transport protocol, UDP requires less traffic and keeps the service lightweight.

When RADIUS was first introduced, the ports used were 1645 for authorization and 1646 for accounting. Because these ports conflicted with another service, the ports have recently been changed to 1812 for authentication and 1813 for accounting. Although either set of ports will still work, all computers involved in the RADIUS process must use the same ports to communicate. If you experience any trouble with connections, check the port settings on each of the machines to ensure that they are the same.

Components in a RADIUS Solution

To design a RADIUS solution, you must understand the different roles that need to be filled. Because RADIUS is designed to be an open standard, it uses generic terms for the different components that are needed to set up the service. So, for a good RADIUS design, you must know the generic terms as well as the specific Windows 2000 service that fills the generic role. The generic terms allow different vendors to supply different RADIUS components, while still ensuring that they operate with each other because the vendors followed the same RADIUS standard.

RADIUS centralizes the authentication process by using a client/server architecture for the service. This architecture allows RADIUS clients to be located in any remote location. These RADIUS clients accept authentication requests from RAS clients and pass them on to a RADIUS server. The RADIUS service does not provide authentication to the client, but instead passes the authentication request in a secure manner from a remote client to the authentication server. Figure 12.1 shows the process that the RADIUS service uses to get the RAS client authenticated onto the private network. In Figure 12.1, a RADIUS client is located at the remote LAN. The RADIUS client accepts authentication requests from RAS clients on the local network. The RADIUS client forwards the requests to the RADIUS server located at the main network location, and the RADIUS server forwards the authentication request to the authentication server on the local network. A successful authentication will be passed back to the RADIUS client and on to the RAS client.

Realms

In a Windows 2000 network, user accounts are authenticated on a domain controller. So, *authentication server* is a generic term in RADIUS, and *domain controller* is the corresponding specific authentication server used in Windows 2000. Similarly, *realm* is another generic term in the RADIUS standard that needs to be mapped to a specific Windows 2000 service. A realm contains the information that is needed to authenticate users onto the network; the RADIUS service uses realms to differentiate between groups of users. The realm used in a Windows 2000 RADIUS service is the Active Directory domain, and the realm in a Novell Netware network would be within Netware Directory Services (NDS). A

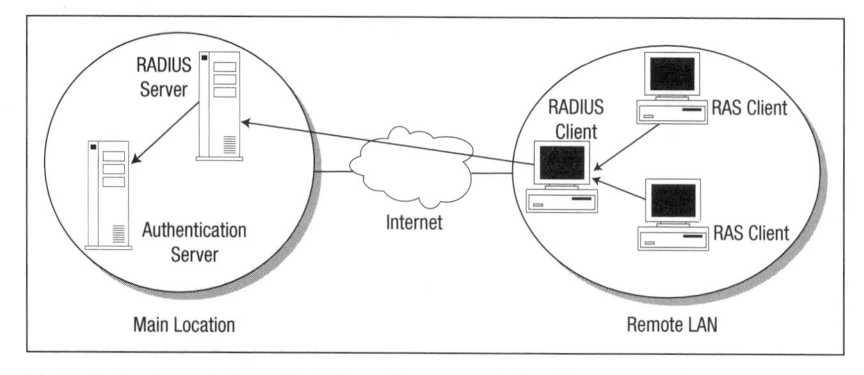

Figure 12.1 A simple RADIUS solution with one remote location.

RADIUS authentication packet specifies the realm for which it is intended. For a Microsoft implementation of RADIUS, Windows NT 4 domains and Windows 2000 Active Directory domains can be used as realms in the RADIUS service.

RADIUS Servers

In Windows 2000, the RADIUS server component is called the Internet Authentication Service (IAS). Installing the IAS service creates a RADIUS server on a Windows 2000 server. Authentication of user accounts between a RADIUS server and an authenticating server within a realm should be within a private network. This means a RADIUS server needs to be located on a local network with the authentication realm. Translating these generic RADIUS terms into terms used by Windows 2000 means that the server with the IAS service loaded (making it a RADIUS server) must be on the same local network as the domain controller that provides authentication for the RADIUS service.

RADIUS Clients

As shown in Figure 12.1, a RADIUS client accepts a request for authentication and passes the request to the RADIUS server. The authentication requests that a RADIUS client receives are from a RAS client, and these clients should be located on the local network with the RADIUS client. The RADIUS service defines a RADIUS client as a Network Access Server (NAS), one that provides a connection to a remote network. In Windows 2000, the RRAS service fulfills the role of an NAS server in the RADIUS standard. This means that a RADIUS client is a RRAS server in the Windows 2000 implementation of RADIUS. The NAS server then, acting as a RADIUS client, passes the authentication request to the RADIUS server.

To centralize and control the remote connections, RADIUS places the local RADIUS client with the RAS clients and the local RADIUS server with the authentication service. This way only the RADIUS client and server are passing sensitive authentication information over WAN connections. The alternative would be for each RAS client to authenticate itself. A RRAS server acting as a RADIUS client centralizes RADIUS requests, which makes the authentication process more secure.

As a review, Table 12.1 lists the generic RADIUS component (as listed in the RADIUS standard) along with the component that fulfills that role in a Windows 2000 RADIUS solution.

Shared Secret

The purpose of having RADIUS clients and servers is to centralize and secure the authentication of remote users. Instead of allowing all remote clients to send

Table 12.1 Generic RADIUS components and their Windows 2000 equivalent.

Generic RADIUS Component	Windows 2000 RADIUS Component
RADIUS client	RRAS server
Network Access Server (NAS)	RRAS server
RADIUS server	Internet Authentication Service (IAS)
Realm	Windows 2000 Active Directory domain

a RADIUS request to a RADIUS server, only a small number of RADIUS clients are authorized. Yet, even this reduced number of RADIUS clients still allows the possibility of someone attempting to impersonate a RADIUS client when communicating with a RADIUS server. To thwart such an attempt, the administrator sets a password—called a *shared secret*—during the configuration of RADIUS. Both the RADIUS client and server know the shared secret, but it is never sent over the network. Instead, the service uses a hashing system to verify the shared secret. Also, the location of each RADIUS client that will be sending authentication packets is specified to the RADIUS server, and only these specified RADIUS clients can forward authentication packets to a RADIUS server.

The shared secret is not used between just the RADIUS client and server. The shared secret is also used during the encryption process for a RAS client's password. This means that a shared secret needs to always be included in a RADIUS solution and that the shared secret needs to be a password that is difficult to guess. Like any password, a shared secret is case-sensitive and must match exactly on RADIUS clients and servers. Microsoft's IAS service allows for the shared secret to be up to 16 characters long, a mixture of upper- and lowercase letters as well as numbers and special characters (such as !, #, %, and so on). Other operating systems' implementation of RADIUS may only allow up to 10 characters and may not allow special characters. Because the shared secret must match exactly between the RADIUS client and server then these differences are important. It's best to use at the maximum characters allowed for a shared-secret password when implementing RADIUS.

Network Diagram

To design an effective RADIUS solution, you'll need a network diagram similar to those used to design other services. To construct such a diagram, use the following steps and add each of the items to the diagram:

1. Draw in the WAN locations.

2. At each WAN location, fill in the number of remote users.

3. Label the type of connection between the WAN locations. Dial-in lines that have a direct connection into the network need a different design than do lines that connect through the Internet.
4. Mark whether the Internet connections are serviced by an ISP or by the local network.
5. Add the locations of domain controllers that can authenticate RADIUS requests.
6. Add the current location of RAS servers that need to be integrated into a RADIUS solution.
7. If users will be roaming and connections to the network are from unknown or several locations that are not marked on the network diagram, then note that a roaming user solution is needed.
8. Note the UDP ports used by the authenticating service and also the accounting service (if it is being used).

Several network services affect the design of a RADIUS solution. Once the basic elements are on the network diagram, you'll need to add some extra information.

Authentication Protocol

When a remote user is authenticated onto a network, the username and password passed between the RADIUS client and server are encrypted. The Windows 2000 RRAS and RADIUS services support six different authentication protocols, each of which is best used with a different type of client operating system. Table 12.2 shows Microsoft's recommendations for which authentication protocol should be used with what remote client operating system. Two authentication protocols are versions of the Microsoft Challenge Handshake Authentication Protocol (MSCHAP), which is Microsoft's version of another accepted authentication protocol (CHAP). Because MSCHAP is a Microsoft-specific protocol, only Microsoft clients can use it. If RAS clients are other than Microsoft operating systems,

Table 12.2 Authentication protocols and recommended client usage.

Authentication Protocol	Recommended Client Usage
MSCHAP version 2	Windows 2000
MSCHAP	Other Windows clients
CHAP	Macintosh, Unix
EAP	Clients using smart cards
Shiva (SPAP)	Shiva LAN Rover
PAP	When the client will accept no other authentication protocol

MSCHAP will not work as the authentication protocol. The network diagram needs to note what authentication protocol is used.

Data Encryption

Authentication is not the only information that needs to be encrypted in a remote-access solution. The data that passes between the user and the private network should also be encrypted by setting up a Virtual Private Network (VPN). Your biggest decision is where the VPN—and therefore the encryption—will begin. Later in the chapter, we will discuss security in a RADIUS solution that includes Internet connections.

Transport Protocols

Both the RRAS and the RADIUS services support more than just TCP/IP as the transport protocol for the networks that they connect. IPX/SPX and AppleTalk are also supported. Because transport protocols are based upon the needs of the clients that RADIUS will connect, you should mark on the network diagram what transport protocols need to be supported at each WAN connection.

Connection Methods

The RRAS service in Windows 2000 allows users to connect to the network using their choice of many different methods. Thus, part of a RADIUS solution involves documenting the types of incoming remote connections.

Of the different ways to connect to the network, dial-in lines have a disadvantage if remote users are outside the local calling area and need to make long-distance connections to the private network. Although connecting to the Internet is a cheaper solution than leasing dial-in lines, the Internet connection causes more concern because private company information is passed over what is essentially a public network. If the Internet is chosen as a connection alternative, then encryption through a VPN is needed.

The next choice to make is whether a network will set up a private connection to the Internet or use an ISP to connect to the Internet. Mark this choice on the diagram, because RADIUS settings are affected. Later in the chapter, we'll cover RADIUS solutions that include ISP connections.

Persistence and Data Rate for Connections

The last thing that needs to be added on the network diagram is whether the connections are persistent and what data rate they can handle. A connection can be either demand-dial, which means that it is used only when a remote connection is in progress, or persistent, which means that it is always available. In Figure 12.2,

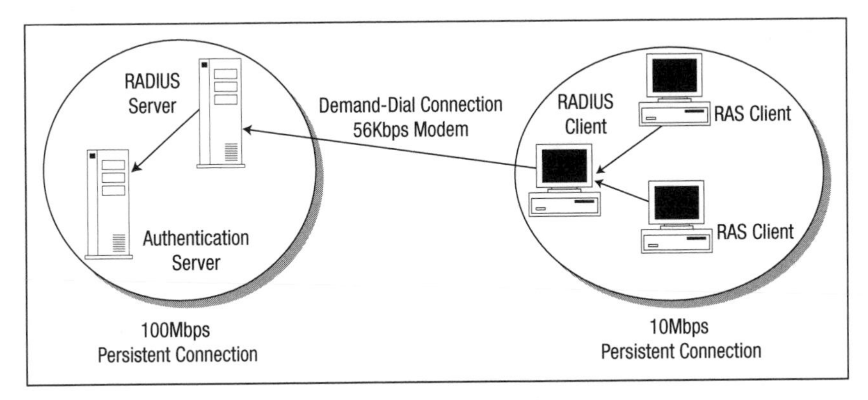

Figure 12.2 A network diagram showing that the persistence of connections can change between different components in a RADIUS solution.

the connection between the RAS client and the RADIUS client is persistent. It is a demand-dial modem connection between the RADIUS client and the RADIUS server, but back to a persistent connection on the private LAN between the RADIUS server and the authentication server. A data rate can be set on a persistent connection to allow the RADIUS service to predict how long a RADIUS component will take to respond.

Placing RADIUS Components

Once the network diagram includes the basic information, the next step is to decide where to place the RADIUS servers. The servers need to be placed on the same network as the domain controllers to which they'll pass authentication requests. This is usually at a central location on the LAN, such as the main office. Locating RADIUS servers with authenticating domain controllers keeps the database of user accounts, and the traffic to and from it, within the protected private network.

RADIUS Clients

The design of RADIUS encourages placing the RADIUS client locally with the RAS clients that need authentication. By placing RADIUS clients on the local network with the RAS clients and placing RADIUS servers on the same local network as the authenticating servers, you'll reduce the amount of sensitive authentication traffic over unsecure connections. The RADIUS service is designed to keep sensitive authentication and authorization traffic just between RADIUS clients and RADIUS servers over WAN connections.

Outsourcing RAS Connections

A company can save money on roaming connections by using a national or global ISP. With an ISP, a roaming user can simply call a local access number, connect to the Internet, and then navigate to the private network. A direct connection to the private network through dial-in lines without going through the Internet involves long-distance telephone charges. Using an ISP adds an additional element to the RADIUS design, because some RADIUS components need to be located at the ISP. This situation points directly to the reason why the RADIUS service was created: A company using an ISP needs the ISP to be a part of the authenticating process, but locating an authentication server at the ISP will make it difficult to maintain control over its security. Using the RADIUS service, an ISP simply needs to install a RADIUS client. A roaming user will connect to the ISP, and the local RADIUS client at the ISP will pass the authentication request to the RADIUS server located on the private network. No authentication information such as user accounts need be given to the ISP, allowing for a secure and a much less expensive connection for roaming users. To ensure the security of the connection, all data needs to be encrypted with the use of a VPN when using Internet connections. This configuration is shown in Figure 12.3.

Connecting Roaming Users through an ISP

Instead of a company maintaining its own connection to the Internet, many choose to go through an ISP. Using an ISP removes the burden of obtaining IP addresses and maintaining an often-expensive connection to the Internet. If a company chooses to use an ISP to connect to the Internet, then the RADIUS service is

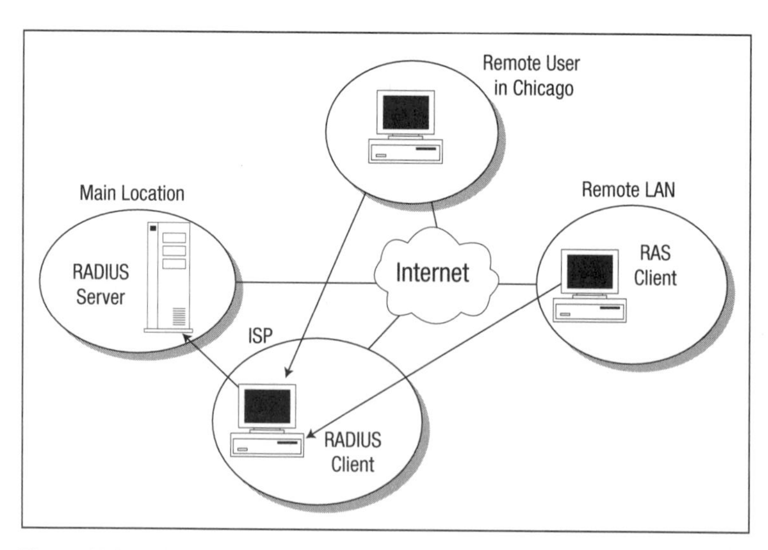

Figure 12.3 A RADIUS client located at the ISP passes authentication requests to the RADIUS server in the private network.

still a secure choice for roaming users and even remote offices to connect to the private network. A national or global ISP uses local Points of Presence (POPs) that let users connect to the Internet with just a local call, wherever they roam. After connecting to a local POP server, the user then needs to access the Internet and, in a RADIUS solution, to connect to a RADIUS client to get to the RADIUS server on the private network. An ISP can locate RADIUS clients configured to pass authentication packets onto a company's RADIUS server at a central location physically near the company that they support. The only problem is that a RADIUS client is normally located in the same physical network as the RAS client. In this case, the roaming RAS client is communicating with the RAS client over the Internet. The secure solution in this case is to implement a VPN between the roaming RAS client and the RADIUS client located at the ISP. Figure 12.4 shows the network configuration when using ISPs to outsource Internet connections.

Using the Accounting Feature for Billing

RADIUS accounting comes with an accounting start and stop feature. An ISP can use this feature to log when remote users place calls and need connections to the RADIUS server in the company network. The ISP can then charge by usage of the service that it provides to the company network. Because the accounting

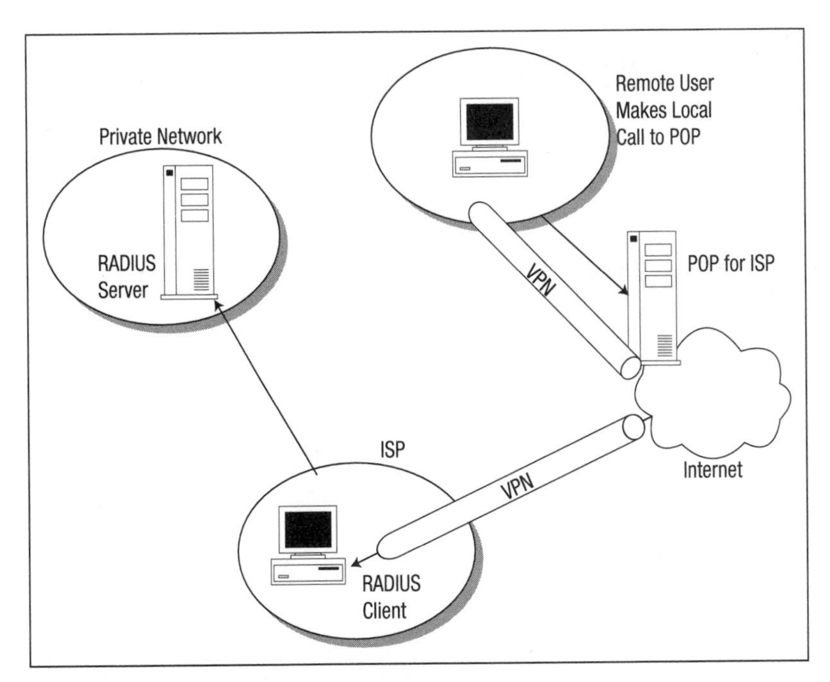

Figure 12.4 RAS client with local connection to POP for ISP using a VPN to securely connect to RADIUS client. RADIUS client at ISP connecting to RADIUS server at company.

feature in the RADIUS server is an open standard, the accounting features need not be provided by the same operating system as the rest of the RADIUS components. The company and ISP can interoperate using the RADIUS service even if only one of them is using Microsoft's implementation of the RADIUS service.

Ensuring Security in a RADIUS Solution

Security can be increased by combining it with other services on a network (just like many of the services in Windows 2000 RADIUS can work in an environment that uses a screened subnet). Also, RADIUS automatically looks to apply remote-access policies to incoming RAS client connections. These policies allow for finer control, such as restricting remote connections by computer name, username, IP address, and/or time of day.

Screened Subnets

RADIUS can work within a network environment that uses screened subnets—also known as DMZs. In such an environment, the RADIUS service needs specific settings on the firewall to allow passage of packets using the RADIUS service. First, make sure that the firewall allows packets that use the correct UDP ports to pass through. As discussed earlier, the UDP ports used by the RADIUS service can vary. Next, to create a secure solution, allow packets to pass through the firewall only to and from specific remote RADIUS clients. The RADIUS servers should be placed inside the screened subnet, and the authenticating domain controller should be inside the private network to protect the user account information. Figure 12.5 shows an example of a RADIUS server inside a screened subnet with only UDP ports 1812 and 1813 open to allow RADIUS authentication and accounting packets to be passed from the outside to the screened subnet.

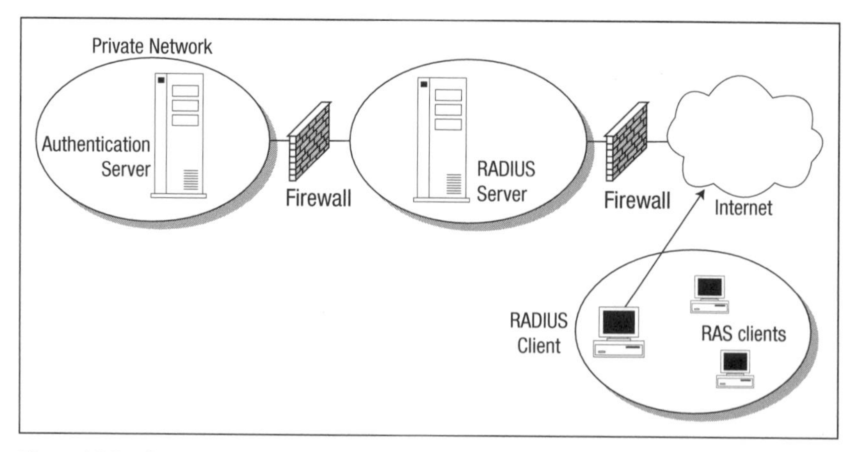

Figure 12.5 Screened subnet with RADIUS server inside and RADIUS client outside.

Remote-Access Policies

In previous versions of Windows, dial-in connections had a simple system of control. The permission to dial in to a network was granted on an all-or-nothing basis. When the user is allowed to enter the network through a remote connection, no extra control is allowed over the connection.

To allow for better control over users who connect from remote locations, Windows 2000 uses remote-access policies. With a remote-access policy, an administrator can set conditions to control what a dial-in user must do to be authenticated to a network. Instead of granting a blanket right to dial in, as in previous versions of Remote Access in Windows, remote-access policies allow a finer level of control. A remote-access policy allows an administrator to assign different permissions to different sets of users. Remote users accessing the network through a VPN can be assigned different conditions than a user accessing the network through a dial-in connection. Conditions can also include the vendor of the RADIUS client, the IP address of the connecting computer, the group to which the user must belong, and the time and day that remote connections can be used. Assigning multiple conditions can better control what connections will be accepted into the network.

The RADIUS service checks for remote-access policies for all incoming users. Every user requesting a remote connection to a network must have at least one remote-access policy that applies to the user's account. If no policy applies to the user (or if the user is not following the guidelines set in a policy that does apply), access will be denied.

The RRAS service without a remote-access policy can set the same restrictions on a remote connection, such as time of day connection is allowed and types of packets allowed and disallowed, and can even set different settings for traffic entering through a dial-in rather than persistent connection. The difference between remote-access policies and RRAS restrictions is that the latter apply to all connecting users. Remote-access policies can apply restrictions to select groups of users and even to individual user accounts.

Increasing RADIUS Availability

Just as with many other services, fault tolerance can be an issue. Although only one RADIUS server is needed to create a RADIUS solution, backup servers may be needed to ensure that the service is available all of the time. IAS has features that make it easy to add fault tolerance to the RADIUS service.

Configuring Backup IAS Servers

IAS allows the configuration of one RADIUS server to be copied to another. When fault tolerance is included in the design of a RADIUS solution, this feature makes it easy to create backup IAS RADIUS servers. Copying the IAS configuration copies all of the IAS settings also, including registry settings, logging settings, and remote-access policies. Thus, with this feature, you really need to configure only one IAS server, even if more than one IAS server is needed in the RADIUS service design. RADIUS clients can then be configured to try the backup IAS server if the primary RADIUS server is down.

Optimizing the Logging Feature

Because the RADIUS accounting feature involves logging activity, using it may cause a burden on the logging server. Although logging provides the ability to examine remote connection activity (which is useful for checking the security of the service and billing companies or departments for their usage), the overhead of the service needs to be weighed against the needs of the company. For optimized performance, you should log only those settings that are needed. For example, if you are using the logging feature for security, you likely don't need to log successful connections. In this case, you'd be most interested in only those connections that failed, as these may show if someone is trying to break into the network through remote connections.

Practice Questions

Case Study

ABC Company provides telephone customer service support and currently has a main location and a remote location. Due to a large amount of growth and employee requests, the company has decided to allow employees to work from home. However, because of security concerns, company management wants to develop a plan for remote access that makes the connections secure. The decision is to use RADIUS for secure authentication and authorization for remote users.

Current WAN Connectivity

The main LAN and the remote location are connected by a 56Kbps Frame Relay connection.

Proposed WAN Connectivity

Remote users at home will use dial-in lines and locally loaded modems to connect to the main location.

Current Internet Connectivity

This network currently has no Internet connection.

Proposed Internet Connectivity

No Internet connection is planned due to security concerns about private company information on a public network.

Company Goal with Windows 2000

The company is currently upgrading to a Windows 2000 network. The transition is scheduled over the next year.

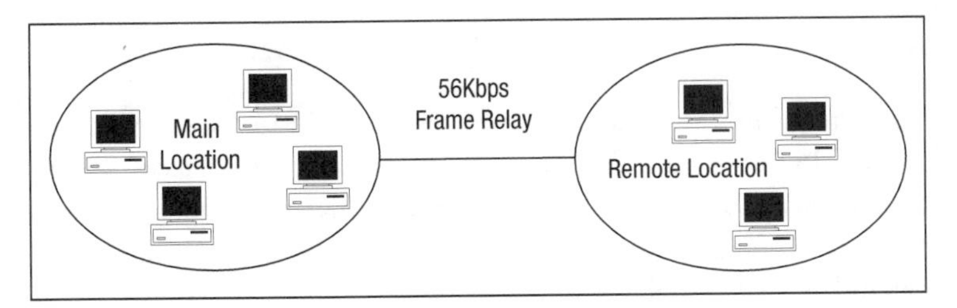

Figure 12.6 The current state of the ABC Company network.

Question 1

The servers at the main location have been upgraded to Windows 2000 and also upgraded to domain controllers using Active Directory. One Active Directory domain has been created. Based on Figure 12.6, where is the best place to locate the RADIUS server?

The correct answer is:

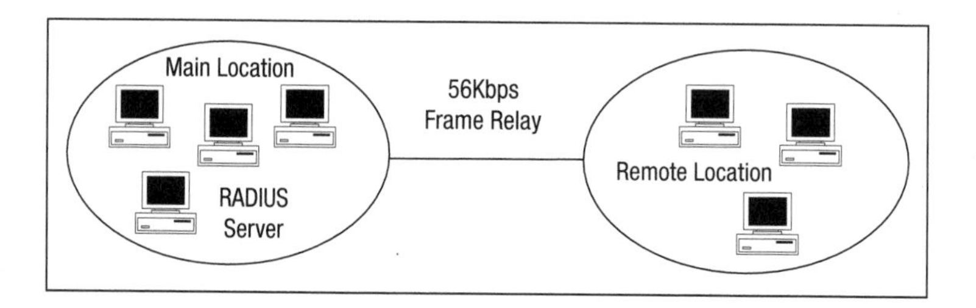

The RADIUS server needs to be placed on the LAN with the authentication server. This allows for the highest amount of security for the authentication information sent between the authentication server and the RADIUS server.

Question 2

Which service will need to be loaded on the RADIUS server?

- ❍ a. NAS
- ❍ b. CHAP
- ❍ c. IAS
- ❍ d. POP

Answer c is correct. Internet Authentication Service (IAS) is the service that loads the RADIUS server on a Windows 2000 server. Network Access Server (NAS) is a generic RADIUS term for a RAS server. Challenge Handshake Protocol (CHAP) is used for authentication encryption, and Point of Presence (POP) is a server at an ISP that accepts client connections.

Question 3

Remote users from home will be using Windows 98, Windows NT 4 Workstation, and Windows 2000 Professional. What authentication encryption protocols are needed for users to securely authenticate with the RADIUS server? [Check all correct answers]

- ❑ a. CHAP
- ❑ b. MSCHAP
- ❑ c. MSCHAP version 2
- ❑ d. EAP
- ❑ e. SPAP
- ❑ f. PAP

Answers b and c are correct. A Microsoft version of CHAP called MSCHAP is designed for encryption of authentication for Microsoft clients. MSCHAP version 2 is for Windows 2000 clients. MSCHAP (before version 2) is used by Microsoft clients other than Windows 2000. CHAP, not in the Microsoft version, is for other clients such as Macintosh and Unix. EAP is used to encrypt authentication for clients using smart cards, and SPAP is used in with clients in a Shiva LAN Rover network. PAP, because of its weak security, is used for clients that accept no other authentication encryption protocol.

Question 4

How many realms will this network be using?

- ❍ a. 0
- ❍ b. 1
- ❍ c. 2
- ❍ d. 3

Answer b is correct. *Realm* is the generic RADIUS standard term for a group used for authentication. In a Windows 2000 environment, a domain is a RADIUS realm. The network has only one Active Directory domain and that will be used as the realm for the RADIUS service.

Question 5

The company is trying to decide on the best way to provide a connection to the main location from the remote users' homes. The two ideas are a modem bank at the main office using dial-in lines or an Internet connection and an ISP. An Internet connection has never been used at the company, and company management would like to know what the advantages are to using an ISP and Internet connection instead of a modem bank. What are the advantages? [Check all correct answers]

- ❑ a. If users are outside the local calling area, an Internet connection will be cheaper.
- ❑ b. If users are outside the local calling area, an Internet connection will be more costly.
- ❑ c. An Internet connection is faster.
- ❑ d. An Internet connection is slower.

Answers a and c are correct. An Internet connection is cheaper if the users are outside the local calling area. An Internet connection would allow a local telephone call and connection instead of a long-distance one. An Internet connection is faster than a pure modem connection, because the fastest modems are capable of a maximum connection speed of only 56Kbps. Although a signal would leave the remote user's computer at 56Kbps, it would speed up from the ISP through the Internet. A modem-only connection to the private network would allow only a 56Kbps connection.

Question 6

The company has decided to go with an Internet connection. Figure 12.6 shows the network in its current state. Where would the RADIUS clients need to be located?

The correct answer is:

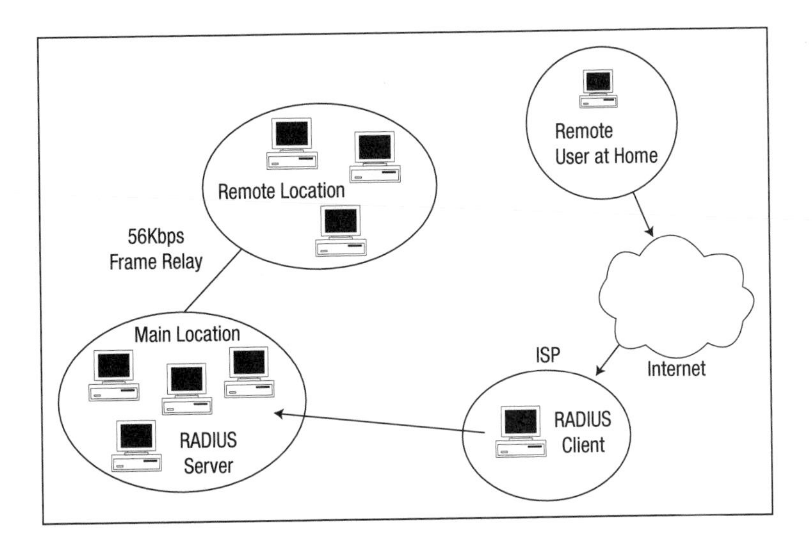

The RADIUS clients need to be placed at the ISP to allow the remote users to connect to the RADIUS client and then be authenticated onto the private network at the main location.

Question 7

How can the connection through the Internet from the remote users to the RADIUS clients be secured?

- ❍ a. Authentication encryption
- ❍ b. A screened subnet
- ❍ c. A firewall
- ❍ d. A VPN

Answer d is correct. A Virtual Private Network (VPN) will encrypt all data from the home user to the RADIUS client. Authentication encryption will encrypt only the username and password information. A firewall would create a screened subnet but would not encrypt the information over the Internet.

Question 8

Now that a connection to the private network exists, what is the best way to increase security so that only specified users can access the network and only during work hours?

- ❍ a. A remote-access policy
- ❍ b. Turn off the service during off peak hours
- ❍ c. A screened subnet
- ❍ d. User profiles

Answer a is correct. A remote-access policy allows administrators of the RADIUS service to control which groups of users can use the RADIUS service. The policy can set times that the RADIUS service will accept connections, as well. Turning the service off is unnecessary when a remote-access policy is used. Although a screened subnet protects a private network, it does not turn the RADIUS service off. User profiles set desktop settings and are not related to the RADIUS service.

Question 9

The ISP needs help deploying the RADIUS service. It has servers that use Windows NT 4, Windows 2000, and Novell Netware 5.x. Which servers can be used as a RADIUS client?

- ❍ a. None
- ❍ b. Windows NT 4
- ❍ c. Windows 2000
- ❍ d. Novell Netware 5.x
- ❍ e. Any will work

Answer e is correct because RADIUS is an open standard. Windows NT 4 and Windows 2000 support this standard. Other operating systems like Netware and Unix also support the RADIUS standard and can be used in a Windows 2000 RADIUS solution.

Question 10

The ISP chose to use Windows 2000 for its RADIUS clients. What service needs to be installed in order to set up the RADIUS clients?

❍ a. Remote-access policy service

❍ b. RRAS

❍ c. IAS

❍ d. NAS

Answer b is correct. A RADIUS client needs to have the RRAS service loaded. There is no such thing as a "remote-access policy service." The Internet Authentication Service (IAS) is for the RADIUS server service. The Network Access Service (NAS) is a generic RADIUS term for a RAS server, and does not specify a specific service in Windows 2000.

Question 11

The RADIUS servers were set up at the main location of the private network. Now the ISP is setting up the RADIUS clients. How should they set up the shared secret? [Choose the best answer]

❍ a. Make it a combination of upper- and lowercase letters as well as numbers and special characters.

❍ b. Make it at least 16 characters.

❍ c. Make it identical to the shared secret on the RADIUS server.

❍ d. Make it difficult to guess.

Answer c is correct. A shared secret needs to be identical on the RADIUS client and server. It is recommended that the shared secret be a combination of upper- and lowercase letters, including numbers and special characters. It is also recommended that the shared secret be at least 16 characters long. A shared-secret password should also be difficult to guess. However, unless the shared secret is identical to the one on the RADIUS server, a connection will not be allowed between the two.

Question 12

If the company starts to hire people all over the world, what RADIUS and remote-access solution will work best for it? [Check all correct answers]

- ❑ a. The ISP will need local POP that remote users can use to connect.
- ❑ b. The ISP will need to be global.
- ❑ c. An ISP cannot be used in this situation.
- ❑ d. The current remote solution will work.

Answers a and b are correct. The current situation will need some adjustment in order for the solution to be a global one for remote users. The ISP will need to have a global presence to be practical. The ISP will need local Points of Presence (POP) that will allow global users to make a local telephone call to get connected to the private network through the Internet.

Need to Know More?

RFC 2138 Remote Authentication Dial-In User Service (RADIUS), at **http://ietf.org/rfc/rfc2138.txt?number=2138**. Basic information about the RADIUS service and standard.

RFC 2139 RADIUS Accounting, at **http://ietf.org/rfc/rfc2139.txt?number=2139**. Discusses standards for the RADIUS accounting feature.

Open Help from the Internet Authentication Service. Because this is a newly supported service, not much documentation is available on it. Help includes explanations of how the IAS service works as well as steps for installation. Troubleshooting information includes specific errors that can occur and fixes for each.

Search the TechNet CD (or its online version through **support.microsoft.com/directory**) and the *Windows 2000 Server Resource Kit* CD using the keywords "RADIUS", "RRAS", and "IAS".

Managing Network Services

Terms you'll need to know:

- ✓ Management strategies
- ✓ Service interruptions
- ✓ Network status monitoring
- ✓ Data collection
- ✓ Distributed data collection
- ✓ Centralized data collection

Techniques you'll need to master:

- ✓ Using monitoring tools
- ✓ Using the system console
- ✓ Using logs and alerts

In this chapter, you'll learn about managing networking services. You'll become familiar with effective management plans that will incorporate security, availability, and performance into your design.

Planning Management Strategies

A good management plan will use strategies and processes to detect changes in your network and will also incorporate an initial course of action whenever such changes are detected. But a network management plan is not the only management strategy that should be in place by the IT staff and its management. A larger plan should include your network management plan and the applications that your network supports. This plan must outline how all of the other management strategies will work together when the unthinkable happens. Your management plan must contain these actions and the processes and procedures used to detect them, with a list of the responsible people (or groups of people) that it will integrate to resolve any issues when the need arises.

The main goal of the management plan should be to prevent problems and to detect and respond to critical events—such as interruption of service or total network failures—due to any number of internal or external forces. For example, redundancy of communications links and data-loss prevention should be included in your total management plan.

Your management plan should include strategies to:

- Respond to service interruptions and changes
- Ensure the current environment coincides with the design criteria
- Meet the future needs for the network services (planned expansion)
- Institute processes and procedures to monitor the network and analyze the collected data

Responding to Service Interruptions and Changes

Before resolving interruptions, you must first detect them. Your resolution strategy should define the process to automatically correct the interruption (such as a redundant link) or to notify responsible personnel of the interruption (if it requires manual correction). If possible, these processes should be initiated before the service becomes disabled so that corrections are made with minimal effect on the network.

Processes should be in place to provide detection and responses for:

- Services or server faults
- Failure of the network to fill client requests

- When predefined service values do not meet the minimum requirements
- When calculated values are not within working parameters

When notified of these events, the IS support staff needs to take action, following the steps outlined in the management plan, to minimize the effects of the interruptions on the clients. If you have implemented automated responses to events such as these, the IS staff should be notified to ensure that further action or monitoring is not needed or that services have been returned to their normal operating state.

Ensuring That the Current Environment Meets the Design Criteria

Of course, if your current environment does not meet the design criteria, monitoring for failures is pointless. Also, you will not have a baseline to define the criteria needed to detect failures. If the design goals that were planned are not correctly implemented, the required security, availability, and performance are also not within your design parameters.

A design should allow for fluctuations in the daily operations that are needed to service the clients. A conservative design provides for daily fluctuations and helps your network remain operational when faults occur. You can verify that parameters are within the design criteria either manually or automatically. To ensure that the network is operating within the design criteria, it will be necessary to capture and analyze network data against your predefined baseline. Only then will you be able to tell whether the network is operating within normal parameters. Table 13.1 lists testing methods and brief descriptions.

Table 13.1 Testing methods.

Testing Method	Description
Manual Testing	Certain components of your network may require physical interaction to determine their compliance, such as redundancy links or failover server redundancy.
Schedule Audits	Security and access adjustments are often made. Scheduled audits will help ensure compliance with your intended security and access requirements.
Monitoring	Monitor uptime, service performance, and service to interaction time to ensure compliance.

Planned Expansion to Meet Future Needs for the Network Services

Over time, the requirements of the infrastructure—and the infrastructure itself—can change. For example, the speed at which a server is able to satisfy client's requests degrades with increased client pressure. Day-to-day operations can require changes to the original design that can seem minor at the time, but, when these small changes are compounded by other required changes, redesign can become necessary.

Your management strategies should include provisions for future needs, as well as long-term processes to detect the evolution of the network. These strategies should contain procedures to accumulate data that will track the resource consumption. The data can then be evaluated to plan for future changes.

As an example, with the current popularity of Web-based applications, your IS staff can detect the current Internet information servers that are operating outside the design parameters, because some of your company's applications have been converted to Web-based applications. Monitored data will show a decline in performance of the servers and implement your management policy to facilitate additions or upgrades.

Implementing Network Status Monitoring

Your management plan must have processes in place to detect the status of your network. For example, if a service fails, the responsible parties must be notified immediately to reduce the failure's effects on the clients. Your monitoring process should be able to:

- Determine the current state of the network services and infrastructure
- Detect trends from collected data
- Verify compliance with the network design
- Respond to service interruptions and bring performance back within the design parameters

Some companies introduce management software that can provide the network with automated monitoring and management of the network infrastructure. These management applications can significantly reduce the cost of ownership (the total dollars used to purchase and support a network resource). Windows 2000 can be monitored and managed using Microsoft Systems Management Server or other third-party management applications.

Getting Information on the Status of Services

When getting information on the status of services, the status of individual services must be included along with the status of the network as a whole. The detection of parameters outside the design goals can be accomplished by the following:

- Data collection
- Tools and utilities
- Performance logs
- Alerts
- The simple network management protocol (SNMP)
- Event logs
- Scripting tools
- Programming languages
- Management instrumentation

Data Collection

Collecting status information is necessary to the monitoring process. Monitoring a network is an intensive operation that can create large amounts of data. Using an event signal can reduce the amount of stored data, because the event signal notifies the responsible party that a preset threshold has been reached. This notification can also serve as a prompt for action that includes the monitoring of network resources. Notifications can be generated from unprocessed data to determine the status of the network, and events can be generated by tools, utilities, and automated monitors.

The two major data-collection strategies are distributed and centralized. Both methods can employ in-band or out-of-band data collection to generate automated or manual event notification. In-band and out-of-band collection will be explained in detail later in this chapter.

Distributed Data Collection

With a distributed collection strategy, data is monitored and collected from several points within your network infrastructure. With this strategy, responses and the analysis of the collected data can be decentralized to several locations, although, in most instances, the collected data is analyzed and processed at a central management point, such as a call center or help desk.

Centralized Data Collection

With a centralized point for collection and analysis, data is accumulated and analyzed from a single location. In most cases, the central point is also a centralized management station, such as a help desk or a node within a larger management system, such as a technology asset management center. Centralized monitoring can increase traffic on a local segment, and a centralized monitoring center does not provide redundant monitoring points. For instance, if the local network segment or the host(s) responsible for monitoring the network becomes disabled, the current state of the network will not be available.

To design a centralized collection strategy to be available, a path for the collection of data must be available to the monitoring point. There are two strategies for providing a path for the collected data:

- *In-band data collection*—With this strategy, the collected monitoring data travels on the same physical infrastructure that provides service to your clients. This means that the monitoring will generate an increase in network traffic. If a failure of the network services occurs and no redundant links are available, no transport service will be available for the collected data.
- *Out-of-band data collection*—An alternate path will be used to transmit the monitored data to the centralized management point such as an ISDN or modem connection. If you do not have redundant links built into your network infrastructure, it will be necessary to use an alternate path for monitoring and notification. Otherwise, if a total failure occurs, the centralized management point will not be notified of the failure.

Note: Use the in-band data collection strategy if redundant links are built into your network infrastructure. Use the out-of-band collection strategy if redundant links are not built into your network infrastructure.

Generated Events

Event notification requires that the current state of the network be available to the monitoring-service personnel or software. Software can actively monitor the current status of the network. When predefined thresholds are reached, the software will generate an event that can be used to notify responsible personnel that manual action is needed. In some cases, the event can be used to automatically restart the failed service.

Responsible personnel can use the notifications of service restart to deduce whether further action is needed. If frequent automatic actions are occurring, the design should be reviewed for problems.

Monitoring Tools Used to Generate Events

Many tools and software utilities can generate events when thresholds are reached. The following utilities are some of the more commonly used:

- *System Monitor*—Allows events to be logged to a log file when a threshold is exceeded. Notification is displayed as an error that prompts the system administrator to use the event view for further information. Most administrators are familiar with this tool.
- *Service Monitor*—Allows events to be available depending on the options that are selected during the installation of Windows 2000. Service recovery and monitoring are a part of the Windows 2000 operating system and is also provided by some BackOffice applications. Microsoft Exchange Server services can provide notification and monitoring of links from within the Exchange Administrator. These notification events can be sent to designated personnel via email or by the message utility built into Windows 2000.
- *SNMP (Simple Network Management Protocol)*—An additional TCP/IP utility that can be installed on a Windows 2000 computer. With SNMP, you can create traps that capture data for analysis. SNMP traps may be generated based on the events written to the event log and defined in the Management Information Base (MIB) for a particular service.

Note: To determine whether the SNMP service has been installed, look at the installed services by accessing the services administration tool from within the Windows 2000 administration tools. To add this service, access the network properties by right-clicking on My Network Places and choosing Properties. This opens the Network and Dial-Up Connections window. Now, right-click on the Local Area Network connection that you wish to add the service to and choose Properties. This opens the Local Area Network window. Now click on Install, and the Select Network Component window opens. From within this window, select Service to open the Add Service window. You can now select the SNMP service and click on OK to install the service.

Network Monitor

Network Monitor is used to gather statistics on frames and packets sent through your network. Although Network Monitor will not generate a notification event, it can be used to identify problems and track variations in the quality of service.

Command-Line Monitoring Tools

Command-line monitoring tools can be used to interactively view the current status of the network or to capture data to a file for later review. These tools help administrators to analyze whether the network services are operating within predefined parameters, as well as detect variations in the network's performance.

Following are some of the commonly used command-line monitoring tools and utilities:

- *Netdiag*—Performs a series of tests that are local to the host and used to determine the current state of the network client, including the availability of the WINS, DNS, and default gateway. This is a quick way to achieve several tests with one command.

Note: Netdiag is a utility that is added when you install the Windows 2000 Support Tools from the installation disk. The Support Tools installation program is located in the Tools subdirectory of the Support directory. When you install the Support Tools, an icon to launch the command interpreter is placed within the Support Tools folder on the Start menu.

- *Ping*—A utility that is used to check connectivity. It sends packets to a host and waits to receive a reply. You can specify the packet size, how many packets to send, whether to record the route used, what Time-to-live (TTL) value to use, or whether to set the "don't fragment" flag. When the response is received from the sending host, the maximum roundtrip time (RTT) is displayed. You can use the results of the RTT to determine whether the path between the two hosts is performing within the network management specifications.

- *Tracert*—A utility to discover the route used between two communicating hosts. Tracert uses the IP TTL field in the Internet Control Message Protocol (ICMP) to provide the route information.

- *Pathping*—Similar to both ping and tracert. However, pathping is a better diagnostic tool to troubleshoot router congestion, because it tests the path for 125 seconds. The statistics that pathping delivers show the number of packets that have been lost, thus providing the user with the ability to find routers that are not performing within parameters. Pathping is a new tool released with Windows 2000, and it is not supported by Windows 98.

- *Nslookup*—Provides an interactive means to check a DNS server resolution. This utility displays the hostname and IP address of the DNS server.

- *Netstat*—Displays protocol statistics and current TCP/IP network connections. This utility also displays the currently active ports and their states, such as "listening" or "established".

- *Nbtstat*—Displays the NetBIOS of TCP/IP statistics for troubleshooting networks that have clients other than Windows 2000. This tells administrators whether the WINS server or broadcast messages have been used to provide name resolution.

Using Monitoring Tools

Windows 2000 provides several tools to monitor your network. The most widely used monitoring tools are Performance Microsoft Management Console (MMC) and Event Viewer. The monitoring of TCP/IP statistics with Performance MMC requires that the SNMP services be installed on the Windows 2000 host. This section reviews Performance MMC, Event Viewer, and the SNMP protocol. Figure 13.1 shows Performance MMC. The Performance MMC is located in the Administrative tools program group.

The System Console

The system console, which is located within Performance MMC, allows administrators to view graphs of data or collect the data in log files. Graphs are useful for short-term, realtime monitoring of the performance statistics of either local or remote computers. Logs allow you to capture data over a period of time and view the data with graphs and line charts to discover trends. You can also use log alerts to see if the predefined thresholds have been reached. To do this, specify a counter on the local and remote computers. To create log alerts, set triggers on the counter and specify a value to trigger the process.

The counters can monitor system resources and network usage, such as memory and processor usage or network counters like current bandwidth usage. The performance counters can be set to track the local machine or multiple remote machines.

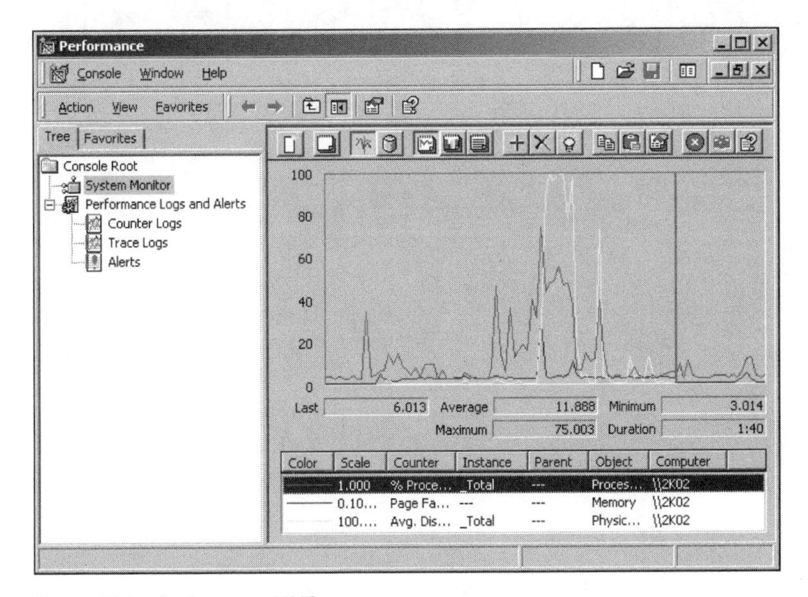

Figure 13.1 Performance MMC.

The counter can also be scheduled to track network or system performance at designated times and for a given period of time.

Using the System Console

The system console monitors performance counters that you designate by adding the counter to the system console. To add a performance counter, open the system console and either right-click in the graph area of the system counter or click on the plus sign on the tool bar. This opens the Add Counters window. To add counters for local system monitoring, click on the Use Local Computer Counters radio button. To monitor a remote system, click on the Select Counter for Computer radio button. If you selected the Use Local Computer Counters button, you can specify the UNC name for the machine you wish to monitor. If you did not select this option, the box will be ghosted.

The performance object is the type of counter that you want to monitor. The processor object allows you to monitor the current status of certain processor counters. After you have selected the type of object, such as processor, memory, or physical disk, that you wish to monitor, add the performance counters to monitor specific types of usage. For example, if you want to evaluate the performance of an application server, select %Processor Time. Microsoft has three counters that are considered important in monitoring server performance. Table 13.2 lists these counters and their descriptions.

Table 13.2 Counters and descriptions.

Performance Object Type	Counter Name	Application
Processor	%Processor Time	This counter indicates the percentage of time that the processor is executing a non-idle thread, a primary indicator of processor activity. This statistic is calculated by monitoring the time the service was inactive and then subtracting that value from 100%.
Physical Disk	Average Disk Queue Length	This statistic is the average number of both read and write requests that were queued for the selected disk during the sample interval.
Memory	Pages/Sec	This is the number of pages read from or written to disk to resolve hard-page faults. (Hard-page faults occur when a process requires code or data that is not in its working set nor elsewhere in physical memory and must be retrieved from disk.) This counter was designed as a primary indicator of the kinds of faults that cause system-wide delays.

Windows 2000 Active Directory uses DNS to resolve hostnames to logical IP addresses. To monitor name resolution, use the DNS counters to monitor specific actions that relate to hostname resolution, dynamic DNS updates, and zone transfers. For example, you can monitor counters that relate to query, zone, and secure update failures to indicate a failure of DNS to resolve hostnames.

When you are deciding on the appropriate counters to monitor your network, you can view a description of the counter monitors by clicking the Explain button in the Add Counters window. The explain text window will open to describe the usage of the selected counter.

Using Logs and Alerts

Logs and alerts work in much the same way as the system console. Counters are added to monitor statistics on specific resources and to generate logs or alerts, or to perform an action.

Counter Logs

Counter logs gather data and record the captured statistics to a log file, which is later viewed from the system console. Whereas the system console shows live, realtime status of the selected counters, log files capture data at specific intervals to evaluate long-term trends. For example, you can use a counter log to monitor the %Processor Time counter on an application server for 24 hours to evaluate at what time the server was under the heaviest processing load. With this information, you can decide whether the server is capable of handling the utilization, and then plan for upgrades, if they are needed.

To create a new counter log, expand the Performance Logs and Alerts object by clicking on the "+" sign. After the expansion, you will notice the counter logs icon in the tree pane of Performance MMC. Right-click on the counter logs icon, and choose New Log Settings from the drop-down menu, or select New Log Settings from the action menu. A new log-setting dialog box appears. Enter the name for your new log and clicked on the OK button; the properties box will appear for your new log. The properties box has three tabs, General, Log Files, and Schedule.

The General tab allows you to specify the counters to track, and the interval and units. You now add the counter to capture statistics and set the interval at which the counter is monitored. For example, to monitor the processor utilization every 15 minutes, select the %Processor Time counter and specify "15" in the interval dialog box. Then select "minutes" from the unit's drop-down box.

The Log Files tab allows you to specify the name and location of the log file, the characters that designate uniqueness of the log file names, the type of file that is to be created, a descriptive comment for your counter log, and size limitations. The default name of the log file is the name that was given to the counter log. You can use the end names with the drop-down box to create unique file names, if the counter is scheduled to run at designated times. For example, if you scheduled a counter to run manually (by clicking the counter log icon and designating "nnnnnn" in the End File Names With dialog box, the name file will be "your_log_file_name_000001.blg" the first time it is run. The second time it is run, it will be "your_log_file_name_000002.blg" and will increment by one each time it is run.

Although you can save log files as text or binary files, you should choose binary to reduce the file size. If you choose binary circular file and specify a size limitation of the file, the file will be overwritten when the size limit is reached—which can cause you to lose valuable information. Binary files can be viewed only from within the system console, but text files can be opened with many word processor and spreadsheet applications.

Microsoft recommends that you always save logs as binary files to reduce the amount of disk space used to store the file.

The Schedule tab allows administrators to schedule the counter log to run at designated times or upon clicking on the counter's icon. Within the schedule, you can also specify a stop time for the counter log and a command to be run. For example, you can use the **net send** command to notify you when the log is completed, or you can use the **copy** command to place a copy of the file at an administrative station, such as the help desk.

Trace Logs

Trace logs record data collected by the operating system provider or one or more nonsystem providers, such as programmers. A new trace log is created in the same manner as a counter log. The Log Properties dialog box has one additional tab, Advanced. The General tab allows you to select the system and nonsystem providers that you wish to monitor. The Log File and Schedule tabs are identical, with exception of the log file type drop-down list in the Log File tab. With a trace log, your log types are sequential and circular. Circular trace logs will overwrite the entries when the specified maximum size has been reached.

Alerts

Alerts prompt an action when a threshold is reached on a counter. The Alert Properties dialog box has three tabs: General, Action, and Schedule. The General tab allows administrators to add a descriptive comment, the counters to be monitored, at what threshold value to trigger the event, and the sample interval and units.

The Alert When Value Is drop-down box allows you to specify whether the trigger will be activated when the threshold value is over or under the value in the Limit Dialog box. For example, you can add the Errors Logon counter from the server object to alert you if the number of failed logon attempts to the server exceeds a certain threshold. This can indicate whether password-guessing programs are being used to crack the security on the server.

The Action tab is where you'll utilize the full power of alerts. You can choose to log an alert in the event viewer, send a network message, start a performance log, and run a program or specify command-line arguments, or any combination of these events, when a threshold is reached. For example, if our Errors Logon counter threshold was reached, we can verify that a message is sent to certain computers, that a performance log is started, that the netlogon service was stopped via the **net stop** command, and that the message contained the variables in the text message and command arguments. Figure 13.2 shows the Action tab of the Alerts utility.

Using the Event Viewer

The Event Viewer server notifies when errors occur in the system, security, application, directory service, DNS server, and file-replication services. This notification is postmortem, meaning that Event Viewer is capable of showing errors only after they occur. Unlike Performance Monitor, Event Viewer does not allow

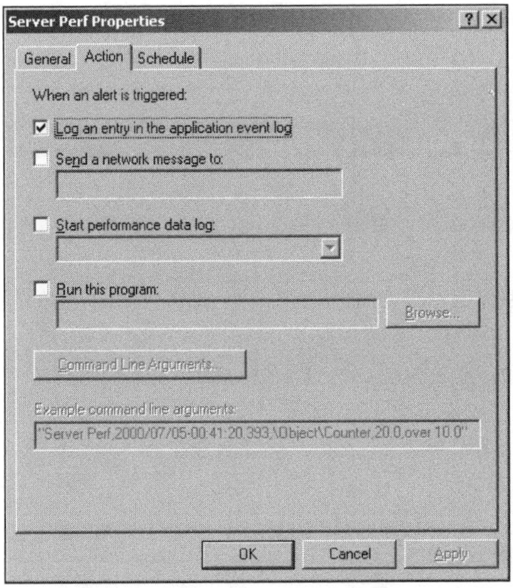

Figure 13.2 The Action tab of the Alerts utility.

the administrator to view the current status of the network or services. It also doesn't provide any ability to capture statistics. However, Event Viewer does keep log files that list all errors, their type, and when they occurred. Figure 13.3 shows Event Viewer.

You can use the filter options inside Event Viewer to filter out log entries that are not needed for your current task. The types of events that are entered into the error log are categorized, and each event type has a descriptive message and a colorful icon to help in quickly locating error messages that indicate possible disruptions of service. Table 13.3 lists the event type and its description.

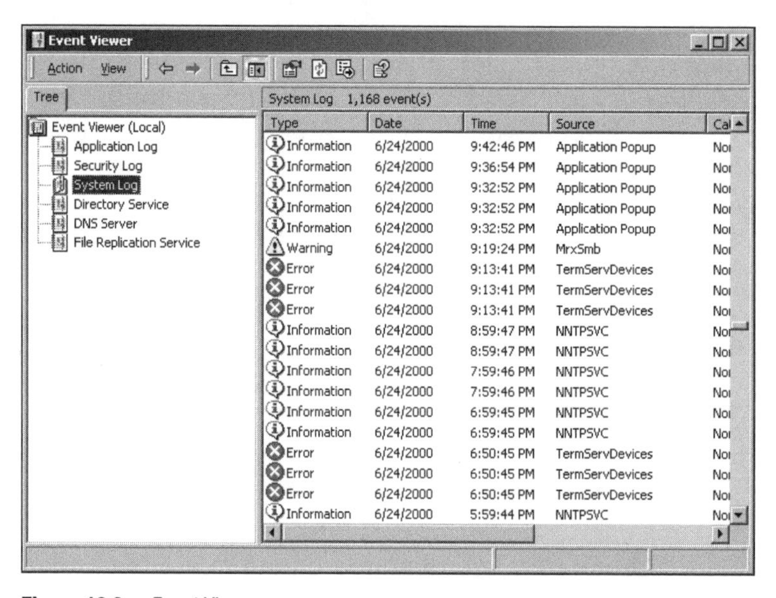

Figure 13.3 Event Viewer.

Table 13.3 Event types and descriptions.

Event Type	Event Description
Error	An event has occurred that may cause an interruption of the service that is listed in the log.
Warning	An event has occurred that may cause a future interruption of service, for example, when disk space is getting low.
Information	An event has occurred that indicates that the driver or service has been successfully started.
Success Audit	An event has occurred that indicates that an audited security event has successfully been accessed.
Failure Audit	An event has occurred that indicates that an audited security event has failed to grant access.

Windows 2000 Support for SNMP

The Windows 2000 TCP/IP stack supports the Simple Network Management Protocol (SNMP), and you can use SNMP to monitor the status of the hosts in a TCP/IP network. For TCP/IP counters to be used within the Performance Monitor, the SNMP service must be installed. If you have routers, switches, and hubs that are managed and configured by SNMP, you need SNMP installed to access the support services for these devices.

The SNMP service is used to remotely configure devices and services, monitor network services and performance, and detect network faults. Software components and services using SNMP are referred to as SNMP agents and have a defined management information base (MIB). Reading the MIB can provide status information, and writing to the MIB reconfigures elements of a component service.

Getting Statistics with Scripting and Programming Tools

Windows 2000 allows administrators to gather network statistics using programming and scripting. To provide for the automated running of scripts and programs to collect data and perform other tasks, Windows 2000 administrators can use the AT command or the Window Script Host to set automated processes.

Windows Script Host

The Windows Script Host can automatically run script files for logon scripts, and administrative and automated tasks. Scripts can be written in several languages, and the most commonly used are Microsoft Visual Basic Script Editing (VBScript) and Microsoft Jscripts. Windows Script Host also supports other languages, like Perl.

Windows Script Host can be run from within Windows or from the command prompt. To run it from within Windows, use the **Run** command to launch Wscript.exe or, from the command prompt, type "Cscript", followed by the script name and any command-line arguments.

Note: You can type "Cscript" from the command prompt, and the available options will be displayed.

Custom Applications

Applications can be written in languages like Microsoft Visual Basic or Microsoft Visual C++ to gather network statistics and implement a partial or complete solution to the network event. You can create applications that act as separate executable files or that can be accessed from within MMC.

Windows Management Instrumentation (WMI)

WMI is an interface that programmers can use to create custom applications that monitor the status of services. These applications can acquire the status of a service from local and remote Windows 2000 computers using scripts that access a WMI repository or provider.

WMI is started automatically by Windows during its boot process. Windows 9x products also support this programming interface, but the service must be manually started. WMI, which is referred to as the Common Information Model (CIM), is a Microsoft implementation of Web-based Enterprise Management (WBEM). This management architecture was designed by the Distributed Management Interface (DMI) and CIM to provide an extension of management protocols such as SNMP. You can use WMI to provide network statistics automatically using Windows Script Host.

Analyzing Collected Data

You can determine the current status of the network by viewing realtime statistics, logged statistics, and calculated analysis. You must use the collected statistics to create a set of results. The results will be analyzed to look for trends in portions of your network that are not working within the designed parameters. To obtain a result set, you must analyze all of the collected data.

Analysis

Analyzing data involves comparing the collected data to your expected results and the original design parameters to determine the state of the network. You can use any of several techniques to determine the state of the network.

Data can be analyzed manually or by using applications to aid in the process. MS Excel, Access, or SQL Server can be used to not only log the statistics and determine the results, but also to provide recommendations for responses (if they are required). Custom-built applications and third-party software can also be used, and such implementations are often a part of a larger management plan.

Point-in-time analysis of data will alert the administrators to conditions like service or network failures, as well as network operations that are outside the designed parameters. You can use trend analysis to predict possible future variations in your network services, as well as to indicate areas of growth that will require a redesign. You can use one of two types of analysis to determine your network state: manual and automated.

Manual Analysis

Manual analysis is most often used for point-in-time analysis of the network. You use this type of analysis to prompt the pertinent parties to respond to variations in the network. For example, if the disk space on a server is low, the administrators can analyze the current available space, on a daily or weekly database, to predict when the situation will require action.

Automated Analysis

Automated analysis is used when automated responses correct the network variance. Normally, these responses provide an alternate path for the network traffic, such as redundant WAN connections.

Response Strategies

Response strategies are processes that occur when the network service reaches a point at which an action needs to be taken to correct or circumvent a problem. Response strategies fall into two categories: proactive and reactive.

Proactive Response Strategies

Proactive responses to network problems require that trend analysis be used to predict possible failures and growth or variances that will place the network service in a state that does not meet the design requirements. Proactive responses can better serve a network that has requirements of minimal downtime and warnings of capacity limitations. You will find that nearly every network has these expectations and that few ever reach their design goals. With proper monitoring and planning, as well as a conservative design, this is an obtainable goal.

Reactive Response

In the real world, this is the way that variations respond. Even with monitoring, these are the best results you can expect without good trend analysis and planning. With good monitoring, you can minimize the effect of service failures with proper notification and response strategies. For example, if a monitoring tool reports a status failure, it will be resolved much quicker if you have a plan for responding to the failure. In large companies, sometimes the failure of the service is amplified by the time it takes to get approval to restore the service. If your plan was defined before the event and approval for action was already granted, the correction of the service can be accomplished much quicker.

Events that can trigger a reactive response include status logs, email notifications, help desk calls, and monitoring services. The reactive response strategy can be used if some downtime is expected or if redundancy of network services is built into your design. Redundancy of network services can minimize the effect of the failure on the clients and allow the response to be activated promptly.

Practice Questions

Case Study

VirtuCon is a manufacturer of high-tech equipment. Based in Carson City, Nevada, the company has a manufacturing plant in Indianapolis, Indiana, and a distribution facility in Louisville, Kentucky, as shown in Figure 13.4. The corporate offices in Carson City have 150 hosts; the manufacturing plant in Indianapolis has 300 hosts; and the distribution center in Louisville has 120 hosts. The network infrastructure was recently upgraded, and all network cards, hubs, and switches are 10/100. The management staff has assigned you to design a new file structure that will provide load balancing and failover redundancy.

Current WAN Structure

VirtuCon currently uses Windows 2000 servers at all locations. The client workstations currently run Windows 95, Windows 98, Windows NT 4 Workstation, and Windows 2000 Professional.

Carson City has two DCs and one member server. Indianapolis has one DC and one member server. Louisville has one DC. Each location contains a shared folder that needs to be accessible to all users. Currently, the users have multiple drive mappings to provide access to the files at all locations. There is no redundancy.

The locations have redundant T1 connections from Carson City to Indianapolis and from Indianapolis to Louisville. The routers have been replaced in the past year and are QoS aware.

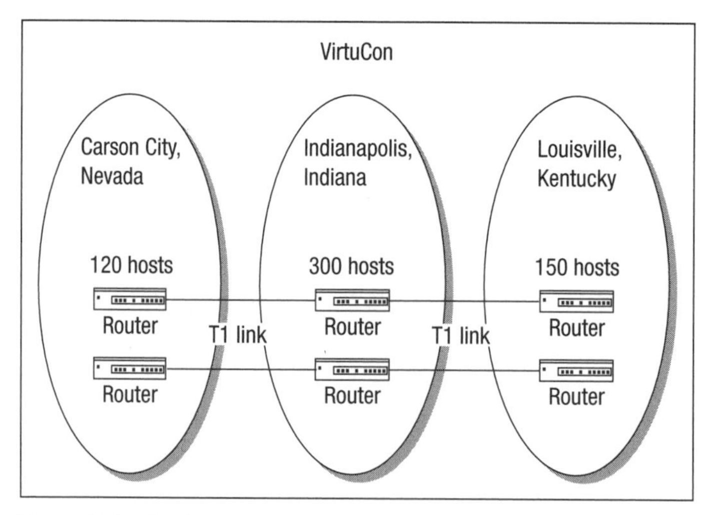

Figure 13.4 VirtuCon WAN.

The owners have begun negotiations to purchase a small firm in Evansville, Indiana. This firm has an existing infrastructure that utilizes Windows NT 4 servers. Because this process is still in negotiations, further details are not available.

Current WAN Connectivity

The locations have redundant T1 connections from Carson City to Indianapolis and from Indianapolis to Louisville. The routers have been replaced in the past year and are QoS aware.

Proposed WAN Connectivity

The company currently has no plans to change its WAN design. However, if the company in Evansville is purchased, your design should provide the best integration possible.

Directory Design Commentary

VirtuCon's current password policies will be duplicated on the Windows 2000 servers.

Current Internet Positioning

VirtuCon currently accesses the Internet from all locations using a single leased IP address at the Indianapolis location. This location has an IP proxy and firewall to protect the network and provide access.

A Web-hosting firm hosts the company Web site. The firewall server at the Indianapolis site provides a Web-based email client for mail access for all employees.

Future Internet Plans

Eventually, VirtuCon would like to host its own site and provide remote users with Web-based access to their intranet mail.

Company Goal for the Network Infrastructure and Responses to Events

Your management plan will use strategies and processes to detect changes in your network, as well as to incorporate an initial course of action, when your network changes.

VirtuCon uses an application that tracks an order from the sales desk to the shipping department. The management staff at your company has placed an emphasis on zero down time to prevent late shipping dates to your customers.

Question 1

Considering the case study, which type of data-collection strategy would best suite your WAN links?

❍ a. In-band data collection

❍ b. Out-of-band data collection

❍ c. Manual data collection

❍ d. Automatic data collection

Answer a is correct. Considering that you have redundant WAN links, an in-band collection strategy will provide network statistics, even in the event that one of the WAN links becomes unavailable. Out-of-band collection requires additional connections to the network. Since you have redundant links this would result in unnecessary costs. Manual and Automatic are types of collection that are automatically or manually monitored; they do not require the consideration of WAN links. Both manual and automated data collection can be used in either in-band, or out-of-band collection.

Question 2

Considering the case study, how would you implement a distributed data-collection strategy?

❍ a. Configure monitoring on one server.

❍ b. Configure monitoring on the Windows 2000 clients only.

❍ c. Configure monitoring on the Windows 98 clients only.

❍ d. Configure monitoring on several hosts in your domain.

Answer d is correct. To implement distributed data collection, monitoring is done at several hosts on the network. A certain type of host may or may not provide the services needed to gather information.

Question 3

Considering the case study, which of the following would be applicable as tools to monitor your network's status? [Choose all correct answers]

- ❑ a. System monitor
- ❑ b. Service monitor
- ❑ c. SNMP
- ❑ d. DHCP

Answers a and c are correct. The system monitor and SNMP can be used to monitor the network. To use the service monitor, Microsoft Exchange needs to be installed and service monitors must be defined. In the case study, company mail is accessed via an Internet mail application based in Indianapolis. DHCP provides dynamic IP allocation to TCP/IP hosts and cannot be used to monitor network statistics.

Question 4

Considering the case study, which of the following command-line utilities could be used to evaluate the network status?

- ❍ a. Pathping
- ❍ b. Nslookup
- ❍ c. Netstat
- ❍ d. All of the above

Answer d is correct. Pathping, nslookup, and netstat are command-line utilities that you can use to evaluate the current state of the network.

Question 5

Considering the case study, what graphical utility will be best for viewing a realtime chart of the network services?

- ❍ a. System console
- ❍ b. Network monitor
- ❍ c. Event Viewer
- ❍ d. Windows Script Host

Answer a is correct. The system console can provide a realtime status of your network resources in a line chart format. Network monitor provides network statistics in an information console format. Event Viewer display's post mortem information on failed services in a graphical format. Windows Script Host is used to create custom applications that can monitor or act upon network statistics.

Question 6

Considering the case study, in what format would you save log files to reduce the disk space required by the log files?

- ❍ a. Binary
- ❍ b. Text file
- ❍ c. ASCI
- ❍ d. None of the above

Answer a is correct. Microsoft recommends that all log files be saved in binary format to limit the space needed by the log files. The other options will not save space.

Question 7

Considering the case study, what interface can programmers utilize to create custom applications that monitor the status of services?

- ❍ a. Windows Management Interface
- ❍ b. Windows Script Host
- ❍ c. Application Programming Interface (API)
- ❍ d. SMNP

Answer a is correct. WMI is an interface that programmers can use to create custom applications that monitor the status of services. These applications can acquire the status of a service from local and remote Windows 2000 computers using scripts that access a WMI repository or provider.Windows Script Host is used for non-interactive scripting needs, such as logon scripts, administrative scripting, and automated tasks. The API is used by programmers to integrate with Windows 2000 utilities. SMNP is part of the TCP/IP stack and allows the monitoring of network statistics.

Need to Know More?

Anderson, Duncan, Thomas W. Shinder, Syngress Media. *MCSE Windows 2000 Certification Head Start.* Osborne McGraw-Hill, Berkley, CA, 1999. ISBN 0-07-212250-1. Pages 657-662 overview monitoring tools.

Microsoft Corporation. *Windows 2000 Server Resource Kit.* Microsoft Press, Redmond, WA, 2000. ISBN 1-57231-805-8. Chapter 8 of the *Development Planning Guide* volume provides some guidelines used for monitoring.

Spalding, George. *Windows 2000 Administration.* Osborne McGraw-Hill, Berkley, CA, 2000. ISBN 0-07-882582-2. Page 138 provides an overview of the performance console.

Combining Network Services

Terms you'll need to understand:

- ✓ Routing and Remote Access Service (RRAS)
- ✓ Proxy server
- ✓ Network Address Translation (NAT)
- ✓ Remote Authentication Dail-In User Service (RADIUS)
- ✓ Virtual Private Network (VPN)
- ✓ Internet Service Provider (ISP)
- ✓ Active Directory
- ✓ Windows Internet Naming Service (WINS)
- ✓ Domain Name Service (DNS)
- ✓ Internet Authentication Services (IAS)
- ✓ Network Basic Input/Output System (NetBIOS)

Techniques you'll need to master:

- ✓ Determining the resource usage of network services
- ✓ Combining network services for efficient server use
- ✓ Determining the sensitivity of data used by network services
- ✓ Balancing security with performance in network services

Each service in this book is discussed separately to provide an understanding of what the service is and what it adds to the network. After gaining an understanding of each of the services individually, we need to find ways to combine the services. To load each service on a separate server would require an unnecessarily high number of servers on a network—which also would increase the cost and complication of the network design. The best solution is to combine the network services onto one server. Because many of the services also need to communicate with each other, this solution has the added benefit of helping to reduce network traffic by allowing the services to communicate locally instead of over the network. However, the difficulty in combining services is that no one solution fits all networks. Although some services combine well, others work best on their own. In general, the services that are used most often on a network won't combine as well as those services that are used less. Ultimately, the best way to combine network services depends on the needs of each network.

Goals of Combining Network Services

Deciding which network services will work for a network is just the first step in designing a network infrastructure. Determining how to place the services throughout the network requires much more information and effort, because so many factors affect the decision. The goals of combining network services include reducing administration and network traffic to make the network more efficient. Another goal is to increase fault tolerance and security on the network. These goals do not always work well together and oftentimes work against each other. The best way to increase the efficiency of the network is to pare the services down so that the network contains as few servers as possible. However, adding fault tolerance to a service means adding redundancy, and security usually creates extra traffic. This apparent contradiction does not mean that these goals are not attainable. But, when combining services on a network, the designer needs to know which goals are most important—and therefore which should be emphasized when making design decisions.

Design decisions are also affected by other factors, such as hardware resource usage, the number of supported users, and WAN connections. Adding these factors to the goals of combining network services keeps the process from being exact. A network service designer first needs to decide which services are needed on the network. A network overview is then needed so that all of the information is available when making service placement decisions. Network services can be combined to increase the efficiency of the network, even if redundancy and security are needed.

Combining Network Diagrams

A good network overview allows a designer of network services to see what effect placing services in different areas will have. Network diagrams for each network service have some common basic components necessary for design decisions for all network services. These basic components include each network location, concentration of users at each location, bandwidth of WAN connections, and WAN connectivity devices. Some services need extra information, also. Understanding what information is needed to get an accurate picture is important when building a network diagram. Figure 14.1 shows the basic components needed in a network diagram.

Network Diagram Additions

Each service may require additional information on the network diagram, because not every user on the network uses every available service. So, although the basic network diagram shows the total number of users on the network, the number of users of some services may need to be adjusted. Some services such as DNS and DHCP will be needed by nearly all computers in a Windows 2000 network. Services that provide remote connections need information only on the number of users who need a remote connection. Table 14.1 shows additional information needed by each service.

Also, the network may have operating systems other than Windows 2000. The network may be in transition while upgrading to Windows 2000, or it may need to integrate other operating systems into the network. To keep the network diagram

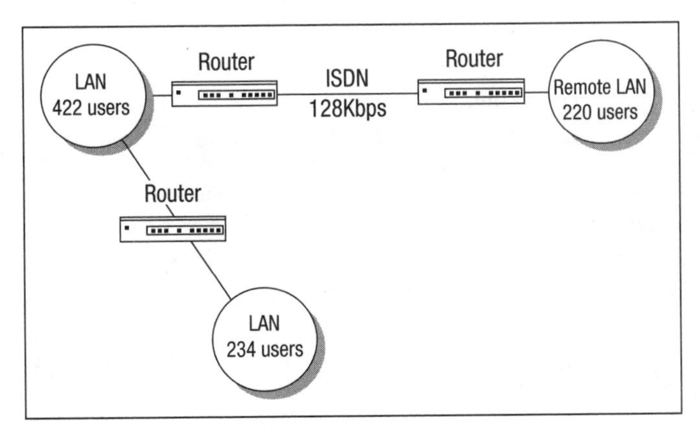

Figure 14.1 Network diagram with basic components, including each of the three network locations, number of users at each location, bandwidth between WAN locations and connectivity devices such as routers, switches, or bridges.

Table 14.1 Network diagram additions.

Service	Extra Information Needed on the Network Diagram
DHCP	Location of DHCP servers
DNS	Location of DNS servers
IAS	Locations of domain controllers
NAT	Location of remote connection into the network
Proxy Server	Location of Internet connection
RRAS (Remote Access)	Number of remote users, connection to ISP (if used)
RRAS (Routing)	Number of users in each subnet
VPN	Location of Internet connection, connection to ISP (if used)
WINS	Location of NetBIOS clients

from becoming too complex, the designer should assume that all computers are Windows 2000 unless otherwise marked. Clients such as Macintosh, Unix, Novell, and Windows operating systems that are other than Windows 2000 need to be marked.

Internet Connections

The biggest change in Windows 2000 is the addition of services that add security to outside connections. We know that the Internet is not a secure connection because it is open to the public, and that connecting a private network to the Internet opens the network up to attack. Services like Routing and Remote Access Service (RRAS), proxy servers, Network Address Translation (NAT), and Remote Authentication Dial-In User Service (RADIUS)—as well as the implementation of virtual private networks (VPNs)—are designed to protect networks from the Internet. With the added security of a combination of these services, a company can choose to use the Internet as a less expensive connection between WAN locations.

The use of an Internet Service Provider (ISP) has a large effect on the placement of Internet-related services. In particular, the inclusion of an ISP in the network design greatly affects NAT, RRAS, and RADIUS designs, and these services may need to be located at the ISP instead of at the remote or private network. Although relocating these servers adds more servers to the network design, it also adds security.

As a last addition to the network diagram, note how many users at each location need the service. Some of the LANs in the whole network may not need the service, or only a few users on a particular LAN may need the service. Services are more easily combined onto one server if they support fewer users. Noting the number of users will help in deciding how many services a single server can support.

Making Service Decisions

Because the goals of combining network services are not often complementary, it's best to try to accomplish them one at a time. First, make the network more efficient by combining the right services onto fewer servers. Then, add fault tolerance and security as needed for your particular network. The servers that are freed up by making the network more efficient can be used to increase fault tolerance and security if these services are needed. To reduce the number of servers, a network designer needs to know what resources each network service uses and how many are needed to support the workload.

Although many services are available in a Windows 2000 network, not every network needs every available service. Designing a network infrastructure involves deciding which services are needed for a network and which services can be left out. Focusing on providing support for the users on your network should help in making your decisions for what services are needed. The number of users that need to be supported for each service can vary. The number of users who need DNS support is probably different than the number of users who need RRAS support. Using only the services needed will reduce the network's administrative overhead and keep the design simple.

Hardware Resources

Services can be loaded onto the same server if the hardware resources on the server can handle the workload. The four main hardware resources are processor, disk, memory, and network. Because most network services do not heavily use all four, one of the tricks to combining network services is to evenly use hardware resources. If one service heavily uses the memory and disk, then it can be combined onto the same server with a service that heavily uses the network or processor. Table 14.2 shows a list of the network services and the hardware resources

Table 14.2 Hardware resources used by network services.

Service	Most-Used Hardware Resources
DHCP	Processor, disk
DNS	Memory, disk
IAS	Memory
NAT	Processor, memory, network
Proxy Server	Processor, memory, disk, network
RRAS (Remote Access)	Processor, memory, network
VPN	Processor
WINS	Disk

that are heavily used by that service. It does not mean that other unlisted hardware resources aren't used. The resources listed are just those the service uses most heavily.

If services that all use the same resource need to be used together, then that resource may need to be increased. If a server's resources are overused, the performance can be enhanced by adding another processor or a more powerful processor, a disk that has better read and write performance, more memory, or more or better-performing network adapters.

Applications on a Server

Network services are not all that gets loaded on a server. Applications that support the network will also use hardware resources when loaded on a server. Application servers on a network can also have network services loaded on them as long as they can still function well. Some applications are so resource intensive that they are best left alone on a server. Applications like SQL Server and Exchange Server work best if they are all that a server supports. Adding a network service on the same server most likely results in poor performance for the network service and the application. However, other applications that are less resource intensive can coexist on one network server with other services.

When loading applications, make sure that they are approved by Microsoft to work with Windows 2000. With Windows 2000, Microsoft differentiates between approved and unapproved software by using digital signatures, which is given to software when it is approved. Windows 2000 checks for this digital signature when software is loaded, and a warning will appear if it is not present. The purpose is to let an administrator loading the software know if it has been tested and is stable on Windows 2000. If a network service that needs to be available as much as possible coexists on a server with unsigned software, then Microsoft warns of the possibility that the unsigned software may crash the server—making the Microsoft network service loaded on the server temporarily unavailable.

Using Fewer Servers

As a general rule, services should be combined onto as few servers as possible. However, this rule is not as simple as it sounds. Separations by WAN connections and limitations of hardware resources will cause the need for services to be spread throughout the network. Even with these obstacles at this stage of design, your emphasis should still be on keeping the network design simple and lowering administrative overhead.

Although some services can be combined, doing so still depends on what is needed for the users of the network. Combinations of services that increase security are different than combinations that increase availability or performance. Now that you've looked at the network diagram for ways to reduce the number of servers, you will need to add more servers for the services based on security and fault tolerance.

Combinations to Increase Security

Some services should be combined, and others—like security when remote and/or Internet connections are used—should remain on separate servers. The creation of screened subnets prompts a need for a separation of services and very often requires the addition of several servers.

Some services contain sensitive information. For example, information contained on a domain controller includes usernames, passwords, and user account information as well as service information if the services are Active Directory-integrated. When combining services, you must evaluate whether the information will be vulnerable when you place it on certain servers. For example, a screened subnet exists outside of the private network and usually allows incoming requests from the Internet. Such a place is a vulnerable place for sensitive information. If the information is of a sensitive nature, it should be kept separate and removed from the Internet connection.

Adding Screened Subnets to a Network

A screened subnet can be created with the Proxy Server or NAT service. Each service protects the internal network by controlling connections from an external network, such as the Internet. Screened subnets are set up between a private network and the (public) Internet to separate the two, because a connection to the Internet is a possible connection to all users—authorized and unauthorized. Companies still set up connections to the Internet, even though it makes their networks more vulnerable, because it is a less expensive and easier way to create a connection for remote users. If set up in a secure manner, a private network can be protected from the Internet and still allow authorized access. Figure 14.2 shows

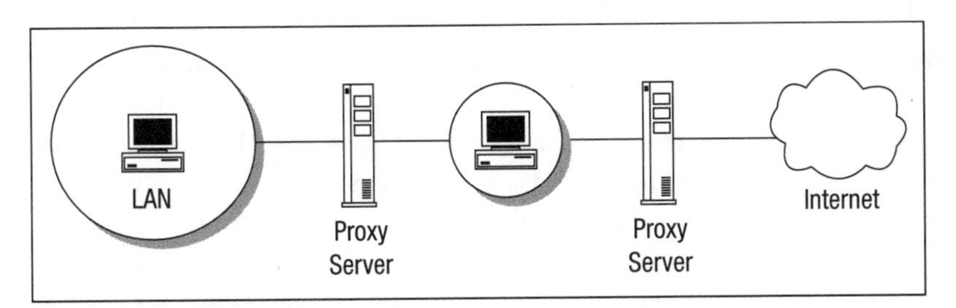

Figure 14.2 A server inside the screened subnet allows access to it from the Internet but also protects the internal network.

a proxy server setup to create a screened subnet and separate the internal network. This effectively separates the public-access network and an internal network for private use.

The service that creates the screened subnet is the most vulnerable. Proxy Server or the NAT service is placed on the Internet to protect the private network, but no service protects the server that creates the screened subnet. Thus, no other service should be placed on a server that is creating the screened subnet, simply because it is the most likely server to have a break-in attempt. When creating a screened subnet, choose a server that will create the screened subnet, and load only the services that are required to create the screened subnet. No other services should be loaded on the server that sits between the public and private network. For Proxy Server, the required services are Internet Information Server and the Proxy Server service. For NAT, the required service is RRAS.

Even services located inside the screened subnet are vulnerable, although less so than the server creating the screened subnet. The service creating the screened subnet must let some traffic in so that Internet users can get to the services inside the screened subnet. Remember that services acting as firewalls close ports so that connections to the services inside the screened subnet are limited. Only the ports that are needed to allow connections to specific services are opened. Connections coming in from the Internet to the private network should all be refused. Allow only connections from the private network out to the screened subnet, so that the information on the servers in the screened subnet can be refreshed from the internal network.

Screened subnets can also be used to isolate services that are needed by remote users coming in over the Internet. Services that are located within the screened subnet should be there only if Internet users need the information. A Web server intended for public access should be in a screened subnet. Internet users will be allowed to access this Web server, but access to other than Web services will be denied to try to protect it. A second proxy server between the Web server and the private network will prevent any incoming connections into the private network, thus protecting it from outside access.

Before placing a service inside a screened subnet, you have to evaluate the sensitivity of the data. A domain controller is a good example of a service that should not be inside a screened subnet nor should WINS and DNS services, which include databases of IP addresses and computer names. If the design of the network must include these services in the screened subnet, then the replication must be tightly controlled. The most secure way to accomplish this replication is a one-way exchange from the private network to the screened subnet. Communication from the screened subnet to the internal network should not be allowed.

Remote Access Connections

A server that creates a screened subnet is not the only type of server that is vulnerable. Any server that is at the edge of a network and open to a public connection is susceptible to attack via that public connection. Even remote access servers with the RRAS service should be isolated because of their connection to an outside network. So, for the sake of security, an RRAS server should have only those services that are needed for the remote clients to connect to the private network.

Combinations to Increase Performance

The ability to increase performance on a network is directly related to individual services being able to complete their tasks in the least amount of time possible. Even though security increases the amount of traffic and the number of servers on a network, this doesn't mean that the service's performance can't be improved. We've already discussed the effect of hardware on a server's performance, which can be measured with monitors and analyzers. These tools can tell you how the server is handling the load placed on it. If the server is overburdened, the solution may be to move services to less-stressed servers or to add more or better-performing hardware to the server.

Reducing Network Traffic

Performance can also be improved by designing the network infrastructure so that it is less burdensome. Some services, such as DNS and DHCP, need to communicate and share information. If services are combined for performance, then it's a good idea to place services that need to share information on the same server. Doing so also reduces network traffic. In general, services do not tend to use as much network bandwidth as application or file traffic. Still, you should try to arrange services around the network so that they can communicate without ever causing any network traffic.

Combinations to Increase Availability

Increasing a service's availability means providing fault tolerance for it. Fault tolerance provides redundancy to a service so that, if a failure occurs on the server on which the service is loaded, the clients have an alternative server. Combining network services onto fewer servers helps make the network perform more efficiently. The goal of adding fault tolerance is not to make the network more efficient, but to keep it working even though a failure has occurred. If some services are deemed to be mission critical or needed 24 hours a day, then that service needs fault tolerance. If such availability is not an issue, then a network will work more efficiently without fault tolerance for the services.

Although fault tolerance can be set up in different ways for different services, it usually means loading the service on a different server and designating a primary and a backup for the client to go to when it needs to use the service. If the designated primary server does not respond to calls from the client, the secondary server (or servers) is contacted. The primary/secondary method is often recommended for services, but other methods are also available, such as using Windows Clustering.

Windows Clustering

Windows Clustering actually comprises two services: Cluster Service and Network Load Balancing. Cluster Service—which is available for use on only Windows 2000 Advance Server and Datacenter Server—can help to provide fault tolerance to services within a network. Cluster Service allows a group of individual servers to act as a larger server, operating as a server cluster. The point of using Cluster Service is to provide fault tolerance for the services loaded in the cluster. It is an alternative to providing fault tolerance for individual services that allows for the use of fewer servers.

Applications loaded on a cluster are either cluster-aware or cluster-unaware. Only large applications like the Enterprise versions of Exchange Server and SQL Server are actually cluster-aware. Network services such as the ones we are planning are often cluster-unaware. This doesn't mean that they can't be used with Cluster Service; it just means that they are not aware that clustering is happening.

Microsoft provides a terminal emulator called Terminal Services. When loaded on a server, Terminal Services allows a client to remotely connect to a server, run services and applications from the server, and receive the Windows 2000 Professional desktop, even though they are running a legacy operating system. Terminal Services should not be loaded on a server that is configured as a domain controller, and it should be installed on a server before loading any of the applications that will use it.

Terminal Services can be loaded onto more than one server and combined with the Windows Clustering service Network Load Balancing to balance incoming requests.

Practice Questions

Case Study

The We Transport company is currently a large operation with one location: Bloomington, Illinois. The company provides delivery services for packages, and, although the industry has experienced much recent growth, the company isn't growing at the same rate. Company management has decided that this lack of growth is due to outdated technology being used to ship and deliver packages. The company needs to expand by adding small remote locations. Also, the company needs to upgrade its network infrastructure to take advantage of new, less expensive connection technologies. Establishing a Web presence is also a top priority. The company would like to learn of connectivity possibilities as well as security solutions. Figure 14.3 shows the current state of the network.

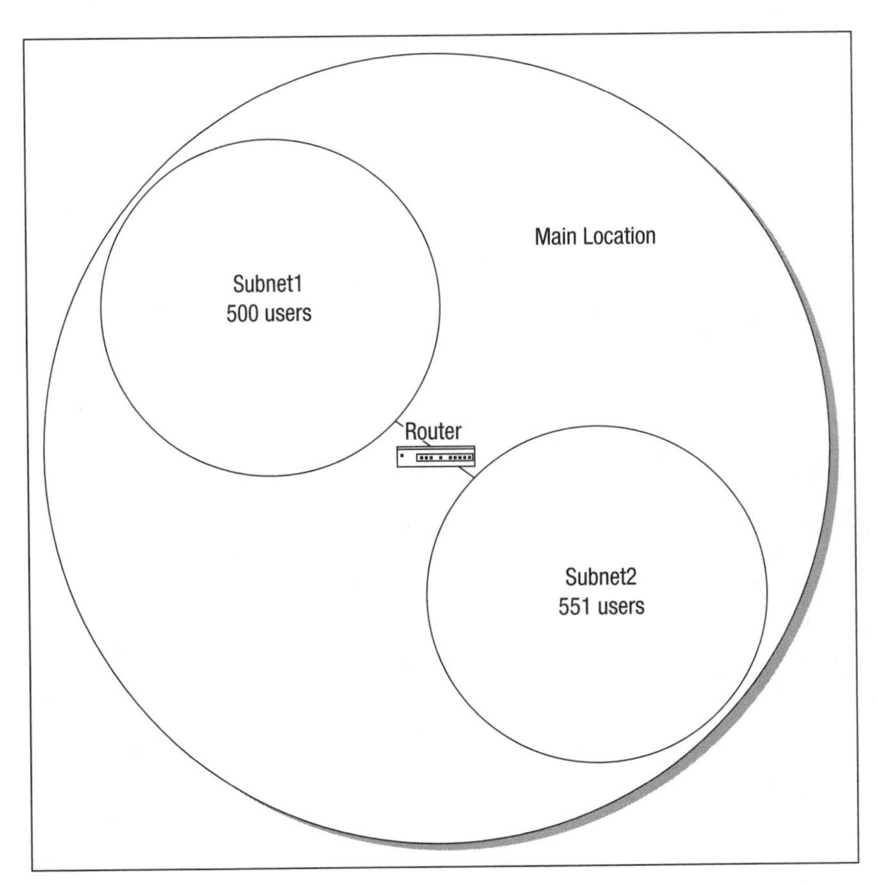

Figure 14.3 The current state of the network includes 1,051 users in a single location. A router divides the network into two subnets of 500 and 551 users each.

Current WAN Connectivity

The company currently has only one main location with no connectivity to the outside world.

Proposed WAN Connectivity

The company has plans for remote locations starting with all major cities. These locations need to be connected in an inexpensive yet secure manner.

Current Internet Connectivity

The network currently has no Internet connection.

Proposed Internet Connectivity

A connection to the Internet will connect the main office to the proposed new remote offices. Also, a new Web site with commerce abilities will be located at the main office.

Company Goal with Windows 2000

The company would like to simplify the network design and lessen administrative overhead. To support the new network infrastructure, Windows 2000 has been chosen as the new operating system. The main office is currently upgrading. Remote offices will be set up with Windows 2000 as the computers are installed.

Question 1

The following diagram shows the network at the main location and the servers in each subnet.

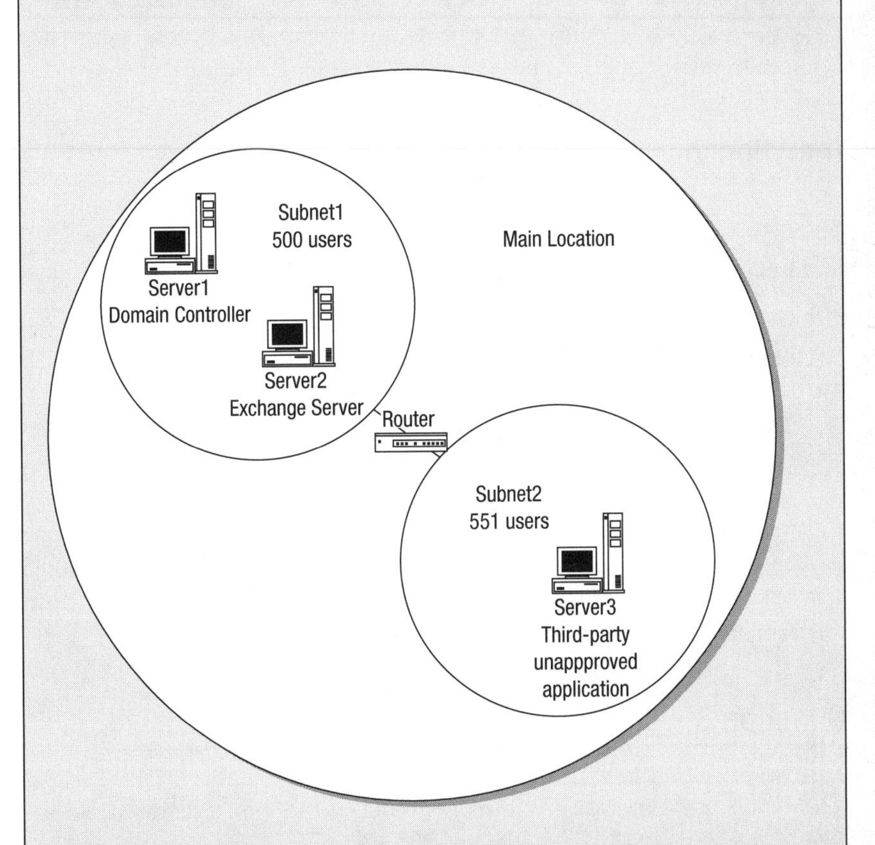

The following list of services has been discussed as possibilities for the main location. Currently, no remote locations are ready to connect to the main network location. Which services are needed for the main location only? [Check all correct answers]

- ❑ a. WINS
- ❑ b. DNS
- ❑ c. DHCP
- ❑ d. NAT
- ❑ e. Proxy Server
- ❑ f. RADIUS
- ❑ g. RRAS

Answers a, b, and c are correct. With no remote connections and no Internet connection, only WINS, DNS, and DHCP are needed. Because the company has stated that it would like to lessen administrative overhead, each of these services are appropriate for the network. Proxy Server, NAT, RRAS, and RADIUS all provide or protect connectivity to outside networks and, because no outside connection exists, there is no need to install these services at this time.

Question 2

How many servers are needed to provide the users in the main network location with the services selected in the previous question?

- a. One
- b. Two
- c. Three
- d. Four

Answer a is correct. Fault tolerance is not an issue in this question so only one incidence of each service is needed to support the users in this network. All of the services can be combined onto one server and still support the number of users in this network.

Question 3

Based on the network configuration shown in Figure 14.4, on which of the currently available servers is it best to load the WINS, DNS, and DHCP services?

- a. Server1
- b. Server2
- c. Server3
- d. No current server will work

Answer a is correct. By process of elimination Server1 is the best choice to load the services on. Server2 is eliminated because it is an Exchange server and should not have any other services loaded on it. Server3 has a third-party unapproved application. Because the WINS, DNS, and DHCP services currently have no fault tolerance, an unapproved application may cause that server to become unstable, making these services unavailable if it crashes.

Question 4

The remote location in Denver, Colorado, is ready to connect to the main location in Bloomington, Illinois. Users from the remote network need access to resources inside the network at the main location. Until an Internet solution is implemented, the remote location is temporarily connected with an ISDN line at 128Kbps. Will any new servers be needed to support this connection?

- ❍ a. Yes
- ❍ b. No

Answer a is correct. A server with the RRAS service loaded is needed to set up remote access from the remote location to the main office. Because the users need access to resources inside the main location, the remote-access service on the RRAS server should be isolated. RRAS should be the only service loaded on the server that accepts remote connections into the network.

Question 5

How many new servers are needed to support the additional service in the preceding question?

- ❍ a. One
- ❍ b. Two
- ❍ c. Three
- ❍ d. Four

Answer b is correct. With only one ISDN line, an RRAS server at each end of the connection will centralize and control access to the remote connection. Only one server would have to be at the main location to accept connections. Three and four servers are unnecessary.

Question 6

Two more remote locations are now ready to be added to the network. Now that three remote locations are connected to the main network, company management feels that the use of an ISP would help to more quickly and less expensively connect these and other remote locations to the network. Which services are needed to make the connection to the ISP and main network location secure? [Check all correct answers]

- ❏ a. WINS
- ❏ b. DNS
- ❏ c. DHCP
- ❏ d. VPN
- ❏ e. RADIUS
- ❏ f. RRAS

Answers d, e, and f are correct. RRAS will provide the connection to the main network and RADIUS will provide authentication services. A VPN will provide encryption for the information being passed over the Internet. WINS, DNS, and DHCP are not needed to establish a secure remote connection between the networks.

Question 7

In the following diagram, place on the servers the services that would best provide security and efficiency for the network.

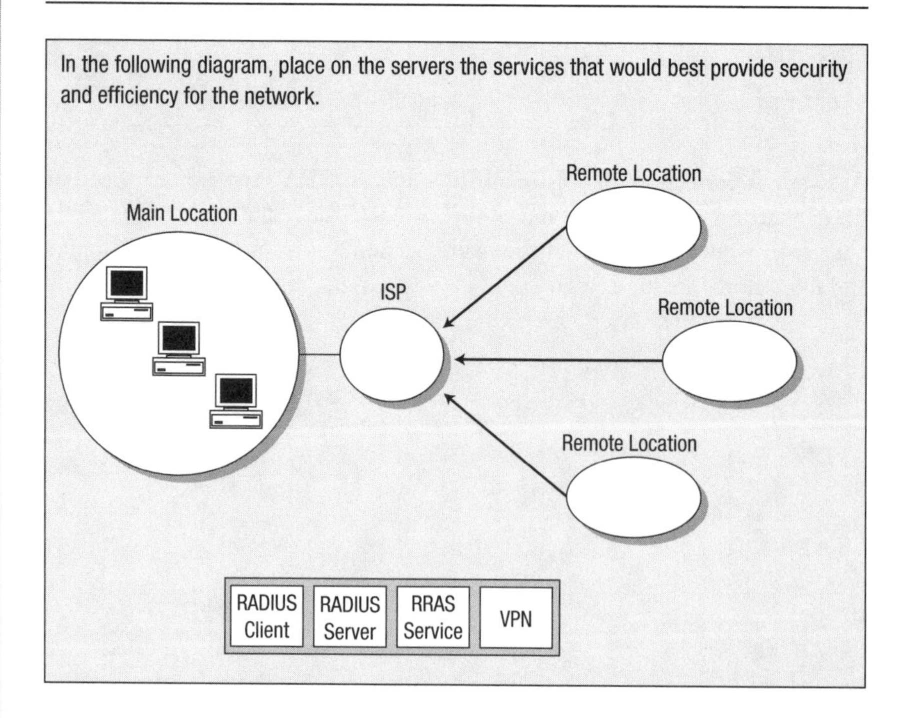

The answer is:

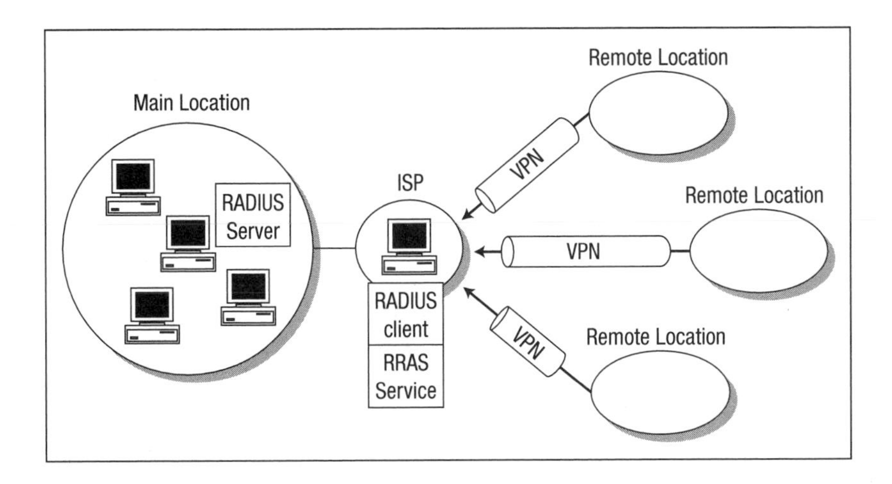

Because the RRAS service is required for the RADIUS client, both services need to be loaded on the same server. These should be located at the ISP. The RRAS service should also be loaded at the remote locations so that the RAS clients can make a centralized connection to the ISP. The RADIUS server needs to be loaded at the main location where the domain controller is located. A VPN needs to be set up between the RAS clients and the RADIUS client.

Question 8

The company is now ready to add a Web site at its location. What service is needed to keep the Web site separate and secure from the main network?

- ❍ a. DNS
- ❍ b. NAT
- ❍ c. Proxy Server
- ❍ d. RADIUS

Answer c is correct. The addition of Proxy Server will create a screened subnet to protect the internal network from the incoming Internet requests. Proxy Server can implement reverse proxying to allow incoming requests into the screened subnet. NAT is for smaller networks and does not work with the WINS, DNS, or DHCP services. Because the Web site will be for public use, no authentication service such as RADIUS is needed. DNS is needed to connect to the Web site, but it is not used for the security of a Web site.

Question 9

How many servers will be needed to provide the most security to the main network?

- ❍ a. No additional servers are needed
- ❍ b. One additional server
- ❍ c. Two additional servers
- ❍ d. Three additional servers

Answer d is correct. The most secure solution involves setting up a screened subnet with two proxy servers. The Web server should be placed inside the screened subnet between the two proxy servers. This protects the Web server from most incoming traffic from the Internet. Because the Web server provides Web services, this type of traffic needs to be allowed into the Web server by the proxy server. To protect the internal network, the second proxy server blocks all incoming traffic. Users from inside the main network can update the Web site, because this type of outgoing traffic can be allowed. The following diagram shows the most secure solution for this situation.

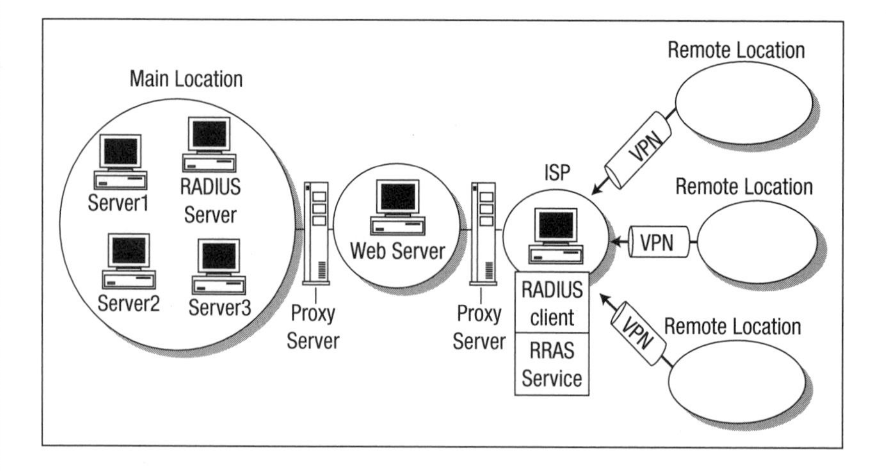

Question 10

The company thinks three servers (as arrived at in the previous question) is too many. Can some or all of the services be combined and still provide a secure solution for the network?

- ❍ a. Yes
- ❍ b. No

Answer b is correct. Each of the three servers is needed for a secure solution. The proxy server cannot protect the Web server if it is located on the server that provides the proxy service. Proxy Server can protect only what is behind it. Also, without the second proxy server, incoming Internet connections will be allowed into the private network, providing an opening into the private main location that jeopardizes the security of the network.

Question 11

The company now wishes to add e-commerce ability to its Web site, so client requests can be processed online. To add these capabilities, an SQL server is added to the network to hold client information. Of the servers currently being used, on which server is it best to load this new service?

❍ a. Server1

❍ b. Server2

❍ c. Server3

❍ d. None of the servers listed

Answer d is correct. SQL Server is a resource-intensive application and should not be loaded on any existing servers. All of the existing servers on the network already have services or applications loaded on them. SQL needs to be loaded on a new server.

Need to Know More?

Smith, David. *Managing Windows 2000 Network Services.* Syngress Media, Rockland, MD, 2000. ISBN 1-928994-06-7. This book focuses on network services, including the implementation and overview of the services.

www.microsoft.com/windows2000/library/howitworks/cluster/introcluster.asp. *Introducing Windows 2000 Clustering Technologies. Cluster Server Architecture.* Microsoft Corporation, Redmond, WA, 2000. This white paper describes the Clustering Service that is part of Windows Clustering. It serves as an overview of how the service works and provides fault tolerance for services on the network.

In the Books Online that come with Windows 2000, read the chapters on monitoring and diagnostic tools, networking, and disaster protection. Just click F1 when at the desktop to find Books Online, and then select the "contents" tab.

Search the TechNet CD (or its online version through **support.Microsoft.com/directory**) and the *Windows 2000 Server Resource Kit* CD using the keywords "Proxy Server", "Windows 2000", "performance", "VPN", "security", and "availability".

Putting It All Together

Terms you'll need to understand:

- ✓ Active Directory
- ✓ Domain Name Service (DNS)
- ✓ Windows Internet Naming Service (WINS)
- ✓ Routing and Remote Access Service (RRAS)
- ✓ Internet Service Provider (ISP)
- ✓ Network Address Translation (NAT)
- ✓ Remote Authentication Dial-In User Service (RADIUS)
- ✓ Proxy Server
- ✓ Virtual Private Network (VPN)

Techniques you'll need to master:

- ✓ Choosing appropriate network services based on a given scenario
- ✓ Selecting suitable network service options
- ✓ Improving security in a network design
- ✓ Improving availability and performance in a network design
- ✓ Recommending network design changes based on a given scenario

Now that you've learned about the services that are an integral part of a Windows 2000 network, all that remains is putting it all together and designing a network infrastructure. The design process includes evaluating, selecting, placing, and combining services. In the 70-221 exam, case study scenarios provide all of the information you need to make the right design decisions. Each scenario can emphasize different needs for a network that will affect design decisions. For example, if security were a prime concern, this prompts a designer to make different decisions than if performance were the main factor. Searching for and using the right clues in the scenario will lead you to the right design decisions.

Remember that you are not changing the network based on what you think it needs, but based on what the case study says is important.

Evaluating Existing Network Infrastructure

Network infrastructure design decisions start with an evaluation of the current network infrastructure. Study the current network to see why the infrastructure needs to be upgraded. Will the protocols and current structure need to be changed to support additions to the network? What are the network's limitations that may hinder the upgrade? Also take a look at the applications that are currently in the network. Can these applications stay, or do they need to be expanded throughout the network? If additional locations are being added, will the current main location be able to handle the increased traffic? Even connectivity devices like routers may need to be upgraded to handle the load of more traffic (or of a different type of traffic). Keep in mind which Windows 2000 network services can help to solve some of these problems. Understanding the current state of the network allows a designer to see how changes will affect it and to see what upgrades are needed, but knowing how the company would like to change the network is equally important.

Selecting Appropriate Network Services

Even networks that start in the same configuration can have different issues and goals. To be able to make the correct design decisions, a network designer needs a clear definition of what a company wants. What does the company hope to accomplish with a network infrastructure upgrade? Because some design goals do not work well together, it's important to establish a priority of the company's goals for the network. For instance, security and performance are two goals that work against each other. Because a network designed for security will not have performance as high as one with less security, the company needs to decide which should be more emphasized within the design. A designer needs to establish a balance between performance, connection of remote locations, security, and availability of services. How this balance is found depends on which goals are more important to the company.

Selecting Services

Evaluating the current infrastructure and company goals for the network allows a designer to see problems that need to be addressed. Having done this, the designer can begin to select services that deal with the identified problems and the needed upgrades. Selection of services is only done at this point because evaluation of the current infrastructure and goals of the company provides the designer with a starting point. A designer should try to keep the network design simple by selecting only the services needed on the network. If a service is not specifically needed, it should not be added to the network. Table 15.1 shows network requirements that can be filled with a particular service.

Selecting Appropriate Service Options

Once the services are selected, the next step is to decide which options need to be configured on each service. Options for a service include the different ways that the service can be implemented. The RRAS service can be implemented as a firewall that blocks incoming packets from the Internet or as a RADIUS client that authenticates users onto the network from a remote location. Each setting is a different option that can be set within the RRAS service. Even a DNS server can be set up with different zones and zone types that affect how the service runs. Network services are versatile and have many options that change what they can offer to the network. Selecting the right options puts the services in line with the goals of the company.

Server Placement

The next step is to place the services on servers and in the right location on the network. Too many servers on a network cause a strain on the services and the network as a whole. Careful planning of service placement within the network allows each one to work more effectively. Simply placing more incidences of services on more servers isn't often the best method. When it comes to placing services, a lean design is frequently better. The one exception to this rule is caused

Table 15.1 Network requirements filled by services.

Network Requirement	Service
All Windows 2000 network	DNS
Mix of Windows operating systems	WINS
Security for remote connections	RRAS
Security for internal Web services	Proxy Server, RRAS
Connecting to external resources	NAT for a small network

by a company's need to emphasize security. Implementing a secure solution—especially for remote or Internet users—will necessitate the placement of servers on the network with just one or a few services loaded on them. RRAS, RADIUS, and Proxy Server are examples of services that may need to be loaded alone or with only supporting services to keep a network secure. Also, the use of an ISP to provide Internet connections may also create a need for more servers, even if they are located at the ISP's location.

The lean approach is best used on services that work internally in a network such as DHCP, DNS, and WINS. Often, one incidence of each of these services is placed per location, even if it is subnetted. A design decision that needs to be made is which subnet to load the service on. Simply put, the service should be loaded on the subnet with the most users. Figure 15.1 shows a network with one physical location that has two subnets. WINS, DNS, and DHCP are all placed on one server on the A subnet, simply because it has more users than subnet B. This method allows for the largest concentration of users to have the shortest distance and time to get to the service.

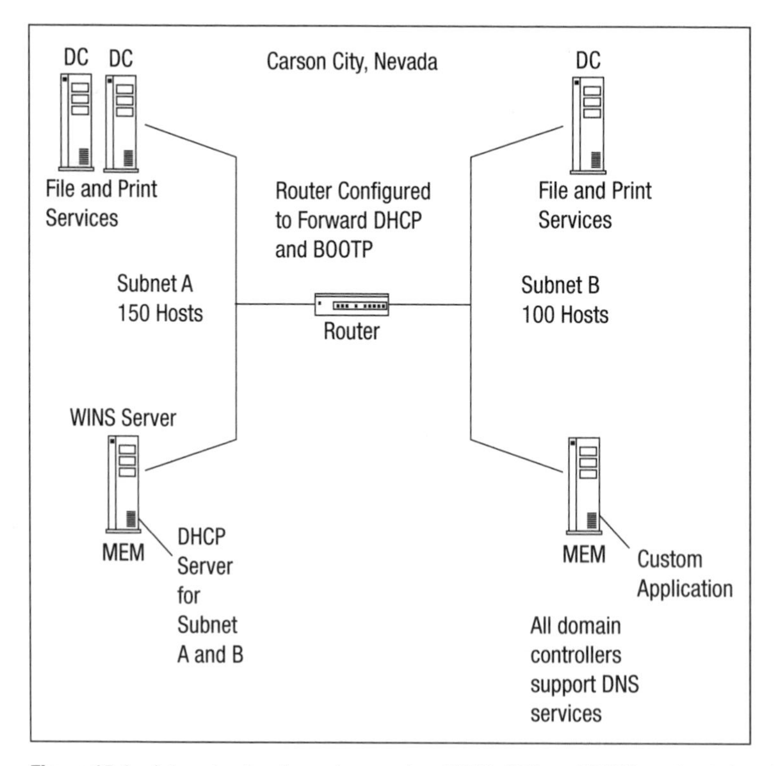

Figure 15.1 Internal network services such as WINS, DNS, and DHCP are best placed with one at each physical location. Within the location, place the services on the subnet with the most users.

Creating a Secure Network Design

Every designer needs to try to identify possible security risks within a network. These risks can vary from unsecured network connections to sensitive data that needs to be protected. Even if security is not considered a primary design objective, the security of the network still needs to be examined. Studying the network design can reveal possible problems. For instance, connections that are open to public networks, such as remote or Internet connections, are not secure. A network can be protected from these connections by separating it from them and adding extra services to ensure that only authorized users are allowed access. Data traveling over a public network is completely exposed unless encryption services such as those used in a VPN are implemented. However, data is not vulnerable only when it is transmitted over a public network. Data of a particularly sensitive nature—such as personal data on employees or customers—may need to be protected even within a private network.

Identifying the possible security risks helps a designer decide what services can help reduce these risks. When choosing services that reduce security risks, a designer needs to balance the benefits of implementing the service with the other goals of the network. Will the security benefit outweigh the decreased performance or other loss?

Enhancing Availability

The availability of a service has to do with how much it is accessible to the user. Services that are deemed to be mission-critical need to be available 24 hours a day, 7 days a week. It is not likely that any service is unimportant, but the designer needs to look into what will happen when a service goes down, even for only a short period. Is the loss of a service a minor inconvenience, or does the business of the company come to a halt? The setup for a mission-critical service is different than the setup for a service that can be unavailable for a short period of time. Microsoft suggests that Cluster Server be used to add fault tolerance to services, so this is a possibility that needs to be understood. Fault tolerance for each service can also be achieved by adding more incidences of a service so that another is available in case one goes down. The use of Cluster Server can reduce the overall number of servers that are needed, and it can also simplify the network design. Microsoft also recommends running multiple instances of services within a cluster.

Enhancing Performance

Designing for performance is different then designing for availability or security. Performance is often not the top priority, because designing for availability and security will usually detract from the network's performance. This does not mean, however, that performance is not a factor when designing a network infrastructure.

Even when security and availability of services is integrated into a design, performance can be improved. The key lies in finding a balance among these goals.

Ensuring that servers have adequate hardware to support the users helps performance. Combining the services so that no hardware resource is overused helps a server better support all of the services that are loaded on it. It may be better to add more or better hardware resources if the number of users or services loaded on it causes any one resource to be overburdened.

Identifying Network Services

To design and implement an effective network infrastructure, you must first identify the correct service for your requirements. Another important point is to make sure that your design has the ability to scale up or down to the changing needs. The layout of the services will be the foundation that allows the network to operate within the design goals. If the services are not planned correctly, not only could the original goals be missed, but the redesign could also prove to be extremely costly, as well as limiting the functionality of the network while the corrections are made.

Windows 2000 services should be included in the design of the physical layout. During the planning, it's important to plan strategic locations for these services to properly serve the clients. A good network schematic outlines and documents the Windows 2000 service and the proposed service to the clients. Table 15.2 lists some of the Windows 2000 services that can be included in your design schematic.

Including Services in Your Design

During your planning stage, your schematic is drawn and the services are placed and outlined. For example, let's say that you have been employed by a company called VirtuCon to design its network infrastructure. VirtuCon is a new startup company, founded in Carson City, Nevada. It currently has a production facility being built in Indianapolis, Indiana, and a distribution center in Louisville, Kentucky. Your assignment is to incorporate the existing infrastructure in Carson City and provide new infrastructure for Indianapolis and Louisville.

Carson City

The Carson City location currently has 250 hosts on two subnets, which are connected by a router. Subnet A has 150 hosts, and subnet B has 100 hosts. The backbone that will connect all of the physical locations will reside on a new subnet that you will implement by adding another router and a T1 connection to the Indianapolis and Louisville sites. Your goal at this location is to use the current

Table 15.2 Windows 2000 services for network design.

Windows 2000 Service	Functionality
TCP/IP	Provides a common transmission protocol suite that will allow seamless Internet connectivity
DHCP	Automatically assigns IP addresses to DHCP or BOOTP clients, as well as other configuration parameters, such as the default gateway, DNS servers search order, and WINS server address
DNS	Provides name resolution of fully qualified domain names to IP addresses
WINS	Provides name resolution of NetBIOS names to IP addresses for clients not running Windows 2000
Microsoft Proxy Server	Provides security by isolating your internal network addresses from the Internet; it requires a single registered IP address to provide connectivity to clients
Routing and Remote Access	Provides connectivity to the different geographical locations of your network and allows you to create Virtual Private Networks by using inexpensive Internet connections

infrastructure, which consists of three domain controllers and two member servers, as illustrated in Figure 15.1. Subnet A contains two domain controllers that provide authentication and file and print services. The member server has DHCP service installed to automatically assign IP addresses to the clients.

Subnet B contains one DC and one member server. The domain controller is used for authentication, file, and print services. The member server has a custom-designed application that tracks daily operations, such as sales, marketing, production, and shipping at all locations.

To minimize network traffic and speed the boot process, you will place one DHCP-enabled server at each physical location. In this case, you will minimize the load on both of the servers on subnet B, while still providing automatic TCP/IP addressing for the hosts on subnet B. To provide this service to the hosts, configure the routers on subnet A and B to forward DHCP requests to the hosts.

Your domain controllers are currently configured to resolve fully qualified domain names for the virtucon.com zone and to automatically update with the DHCP server leases. The hosts at both locations are a mixture of Windows 2000 and Windows 9x clients. To provide NetBIOS name resolution, the member server on subnet A is configured as a WINS server, and all clients on both subnet A and subnet B receive the IP address of the member server from the DHCP server. The DHCP server also specifies the default gateway for the subnets.

You must redesign this existing structure to include connectivity to the backbone for connection to the sites that are currently under construction. Your first order will be to create subnet C. Subnet C will provide a new connection for the WAN link while still allowing subnet A and B to exist in their current states and reduce the interruption of service for its implementation. Subnet C will have three hosts that consist of routers to connect subnet A to subnet C and subnet B to subnet C. By using this model, the change can be made with little interruption of service to the current infrastructure. To accomplish this, two additional routers will be used, as shown in Figure 15.2. The static routing tables will also need to be configured. Router C, which connects the backbone, will not forward DHCP requests, thus preventing clients at the other physical locations from receiving an IP address outside their current scope.

Indianapolis

The Indianapolis, Indiana location production facility will require connection to the backbone and support for 150 hosts. You expect a dramatic increase in the amount of hosts and calculate that with the available resources, an additional subnet will be needed in the next year to provide the required performance. To handle the requirements for the site, your current plan is to implement two subnets. One subnet will connect all of the hosts to the second subnet, while the other subnet will connect to a WAN link. This design will mirror Carson City when the expected growth requires an additional subnet. Your design goal is to incorporate these considerations. As with Carson City, to speed the boot process and

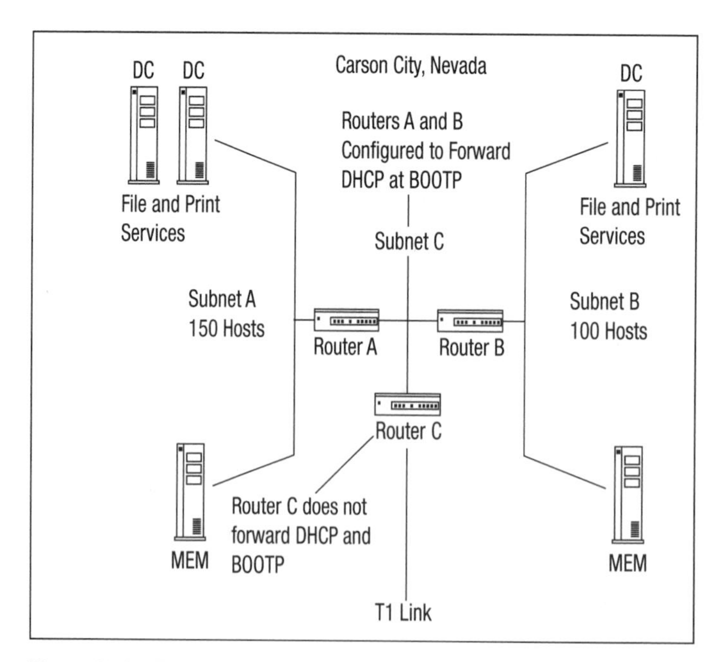

Figure 15.2 The current infrastructure of the Carson City location.

maximize the available bandwidth for intersite communications and the custom application, you will need to provide automatic IP addressing to the initial hosts, as well as plan for the expansion of the additional subnet.

All of the hosts at this location will be Windows 2000 based. This means that NetBIOS name resolution will not be an issue; however, the domain controllers must automatically update the DNS entries and use DHCP to specify the DNS server addresses for the child domain production.virtucon.com. VirtuCon currently has placed orders for two servers, and you will implement these servers to provide the best performance possible. You can configure one server as a domain controller to provide local authentication. This server will also provide DNS services for the production subnet virtucon.com zone. The member server will act as the DHCP servers.

Routing tables will need to be configured on both routers C and D. The routers will not pass DHCP/BOOTP requests, thus preventing clients from receiving IP addresses that are outside of their subnet. Figure 15.3 shows the proposed infrastructure for Indianapolis.

Louisville

The distribution center in Louisville, Kentucky, will support 50 hosts and require connection to Indianapolis and Carson City. Because you do not expect a

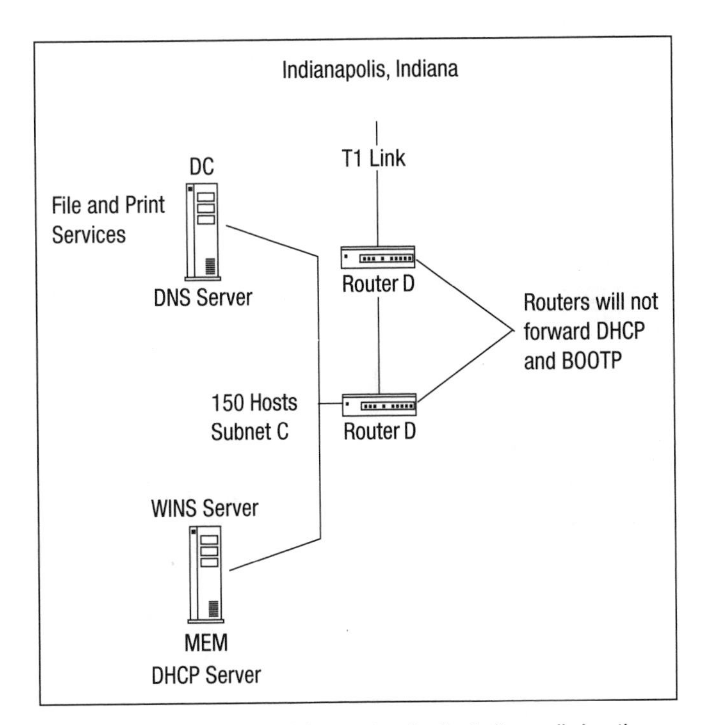

Figure 15.3 The proposed infrastructure for the Indianapolis location

dramatic increase in the amount of hosts, you calculate that, with the available resources, a single subnet will be needed to connect the hosts to the WAN link. Your design goal is to incorporate these considerations. As with Carson City, to speed the boot process and maximize the available bandwidth to intersite communications and the custom application, you will need to provide automatic IP addressing to the hosts.

All of the hosts at this location will be Windows 2000 based. Again, this means that NetBIOS name resolution will not be an issue, but the domain controllers must automatically update the DNS entries and use DHCP to specify the DNS server addresses for the child domain production.virtucon.com. VirtuCon currently has placed orders for one server, which you will implement to provide the best performance possible. You can configure the server as a domain controller to provide local authentication. This server will also provide DNS services for the distribution, virtucon.com zone, and act as the DHCP server.

Routing tables will need to be configured on router E. This router will not pass DHCP/BOOTP requests, and this prevents clients from receiving IP addresses that are outside of their subnet. Figure 15.4 shows the proposed infrastructure for the Louisville location.

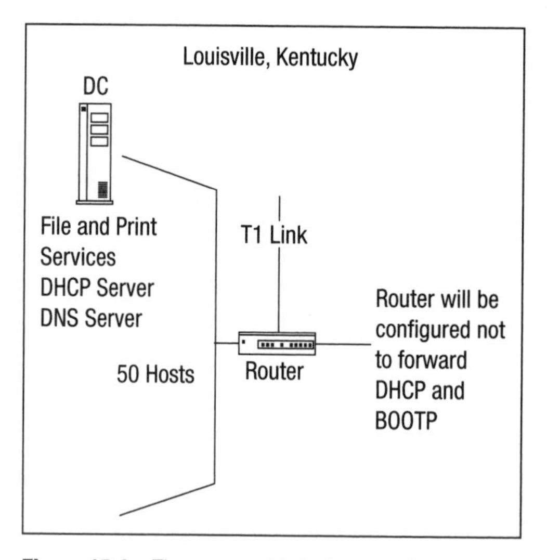

Figure 15.4 The proposed infrastructure for the Louisville location.

Practice Questions

Case Study

VirtuCon, a manufacturer based in Carson City, Nevada, has had significant growth over the past years. The owners have recently acquired an engineering firm in Evansville, Indiana, to reduce the amount of outsourced engineering costs. The engineering firm currently has an outdated network that will need to be incorporated into the VirtuCon infrastructure.

Due to greater competition in the Evansville area, the cost of high-speed Internet connections is significantly less than it is in the other cities, and management would like to provide Internet access to designated users at all locations. The engineers at the Evansville location would like to access the Internet by connecting to a modem pool at the Evansville office. See Figure 15.5.

Current WAN Connectivity

Currently, leased T1 lines connect Carson City, Indianapolis, and Louisville.

Proposed WAN Connectivity

Incorporate Evansville into the VirtuCon infrastructure, using a high speed T1 connection. Incorporate Internet connectivity into the VirtuCon network and provide dial-up connections for the engineers.

Current Internet Connectivity

This network currently has no Internet connection.

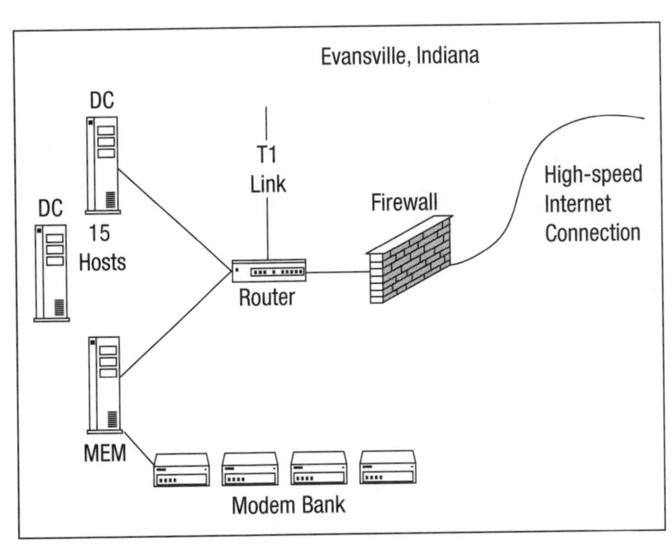

Figure 15.5 Proposed changes to the Evansville site.

Proposed Internet Connectivity

The Evansville location will use a connection to the Internet to provide access to designated users at all locations through the T1 connections.

Company Goal with Windows 2000

The company would like to incorporate the Evansville location into the existing Windows 2000 company network. The Evansville location is currently upgrading from Microsoft Windows NT 3.51.

Question 1

Refer to Figure 15.5 showing the network at the Evansville location and the proposed servers. Which of the following services could be used to automatically configure the clients to resolve fully qualified domain names at the Evansville location?

❍ a. WINS

❍ b. DNS

❍ c. DHCP

❍ d. NAT

Answer c is correct. DHCP scope or global options allow administrators to automatically configure BOOTP or DHCP clients to resolve fully qualified domain names to DNS servers.

Question 2

Considering the proposed Internet connectivity, which service could be utilized to control access to the Internet?

❍ a. DNS

❍ b. DHCP

❍ c. WINS

❍ d. Proxy Server

Answer d is correct. Proxy Server allows control over Internet connections. DHCP provides IP addressing to clients; DNS and WINS provide name resolution services for clients.

Question 3

Considering the answer to Question 2, how many registered IP addresses will be required for VirtuCon?

- a. 1
- b. 2
- c. 3
- d. 0

Answer a is correct. Microsoft Proxy Server requires one registered IP address for the connection to the Internet. For connections to the internal network, private ranges of IP addresses should be used.

Question 4

Considering the client type at the Evansville location, what service will be needed for NetBIOS name resolution?

- a. WINS
- b. DHCP
- c. DNS
- d. None of the above

Answer d is correct. Because all of the hosts in the Evansville location are Windows 2000 based, NetBIOS name resolution will not be needed.

Question 5

Considering that the clients will have their IP addresses configured automatically using DHCP, how will you configure DHCP to prevent address resolution problems?

- a. Allow dynamic updates
- b. Allow secured updates only
- c. Automatically update DHCP client information in DNS
- d. None of the above

Answer c is correct. DHCP can be configured to automatically update DHCP client information in DNS. Configuring dynamic and secure updates is done in DNS rather that DHCP.

Question 6

Which options should be set within the Evansville DHCP server to ensure connectivity when the existing infrastructure is achieved? [Check all correct answers]

- ❑ a. WINS server address
- ❑ b. DNS server address
- ❑ c. DHCP servers
- ❑ d. Default gateway

Answers b and d are correct. The default gateway allows users to access resources not in the Evansville location. The DNS server resolves the IP address to fully qualified domain names for name resolution. WINS is not needed at the Evansville location, because all the clients are Windows 2000 and a DHCP server option does not exist.

Question 7

What service should be used to provide the dial-up connections for the engineers at the Evansville location?

- ❍ a. RADIUS client
- ❍ b. RADIUS server
- ❍ c. RRAS service
- ❍ d. VPN

Answer c is correct. RRAS should be used to provide dial-up connectivity for the Evansville engineering staff. The RADIUS service and VPNs provide security for existing RAS connections.

Need to Know More?

Smith, David. *Managing Windows 2000 Network Services*. Syngress Media, Rockland, MD, 2000. ISBN 1-928994-06-7. This book focuses on network services, including the implementation and overview of the services.

www.microsoft.com/windows2000/library/howitworks/cluster/introcluster.asp. *Introducing Windows 2000 Clustering Technologies*. Microsoft Corporation, Redmond, WA, 2000. This white paper describes Cluster Service, which is part of Windows Clustering. It is an overview of how the service works and provides fault tolerance for services on the network.

In the Online Books that come with Windows 2000, read the chapters "Monitoring And Diagnostic Tools" and "Networking And Disaster Protection".

Search the TechNet CD (or its online version through **support.Microsoft.com/directory**) and the *Windows 2000 Server Resource Kit* CD using the keywords "Proxy Server", "Windows 2000", "performance", "VPN", "security", and "availability".

Sample Test

Case Study 1

The headquarters of Quick Ride Bus Depot—a small bus company with three bus depots—is located in Los Angeles, California. The company transports passengers between these three sites and also leases a bus and driver for group trips.

Current LAN/Network Structure

Quick Ride Bus Depot currently runs an IBM mainframe with every site running dumb terminals. The other sites are located in:

Las Vegas, Nevada

Redmond, Washington

All of the sites are currently connected using Frame Relay.

Proposed LAN/Network Structure

All current dumb terminals will be replaced with Windows 2000 workstations. The mainframe will be replaced with a Windows 2000 server running SQL.

Current business has improved greatly, and the owner wants to implement a new network with Internet connectivity for a Web site that customers can visit to reserve bus tickets, check on time schedules, and even reserve hotel rooms.

All sites will be connected through the Internet, and the Frame Relay will be removed.

All buildings are to be remodeled and each will include 20 network connections in the lobby of the bus station. Passengers will use these terminals to access the

Internet, so they can check on current time schedules, reserve bus tickets, and reserve hotel rooms at their final destination.

Los Angeles will host the SQL database for all of the information for each depot. No data should be stored locally at any site except Los Angeles.

The network on which the employees connect should be separate from the network that the passengers can use from the lobby of the bus depots.

Current WAN Connectivity

Frame Relay connectivity between Las Vegas, Redmond, and Los Angeles.

Proposed WAN Connectivity

Frame Relay will be removed and replaced with Internet connections. Future plans include the purchase of three new bus depots in the following cities:

Houston, Texas

Phoenix, Arizona

Boise, Idaho

All routers will be BOOTP enabled throughout the entire WAN. (Although the router types have not been determined, they will support BOOTP.)

Current Internet Positioning

Quick Ride Bus Depot is registered as QRBD.COM., with the Web server hosted at headquarters.

Future Internet Plans

No changes in the current structure are proposed at this time.

Future Miscellaneous Plans

Each bus will feature a low-powered device that emits a unique frequency, so that when a bus enters a bus depot it will be registered as arriving and all time schedules will be changed accordingly.

Question 1.1

For redundancy and performance, what should be done with the SQL server in Los Angeles on the proposed network?

❍ a. One SQL server

❍ b. Two SQL servers with no replication

❍ c. Two SQL servers with replication

❍ d. Clustered SQL servers

Question 1.2

If Internet private addresses were used on the private network for the employees network (Class A) and a different one for the passengers network (Class B), what scopes would be used for the Los Angeles depot? [Check all correct answers]

❑ a. 10.0.1.0/16

❑ b. 10.1.0.0/16

❑ c. 10.2.0.0/16

❑ d. 10.3.0.0/16

❑ e. 192.168.1.0/24

❑ f. 192.168.2.0/24

❑ g. 192.168.3.0/24

Question 1.3

What is required to set up the passenger connections to the Los Angeles depot from the Las Vegas depot? [Check all correct answers]

❑ a. Router

❑ b. Hub

❑ c. WINS

❑ d. DNS

❑ e. DHCP

❑ f. Proxy Server

Question 1.4

Which protocol will be used by the devices that detect the transmissions of the low-powered devices installed on each bus?

❍ a. BAP

❍ b. EAP

❍ c. IPX/SPX

❍ d. TCP/IP

Question 1.5

How should DHCP servers be implemented for the proposed network?

❍ a. One DHCP server at Los Angeles with six scopes.

❍ b. One DHCP server at every depot with two scopes enabled on each.

❍ c. Two DHCP servers at every site with one scope enabled on each.

❍ d. One DHCP server at Los Angeles with 20 percent of the scope for all depots and 70 percent of its own scope. One DHCP server at the other depots with 80 percent of its scope and 10 percent of the Los Angeles scope.

Question 1.6

The company buys an existing bus depot in Houston, Texas, that has an existing connection to the Internet that uses an older router that isn't BOOTP compatible. What services would be required in the Houston depot if it were set up like all other sites? [Check all correct answers]

❑ a. Router

❑ b. Hub

❑ c. WINS

❑ d. DNS

❑ e. DHCP

❑ f. Proxy Server

❑ g. DHCP Relay Agent

Question 1.7

Considering the scenario in Question 1.6 and the following depots:

Los Angeles

Houston

Redmond

Which of the following should be used in each location? [Some items will be used more than once, and not all items will be used]

DHCP server

NAT server

RRAS server

SQL server

DHCP Relay Agent

Proxy Server

Hub

WINS server

DNS server

Dfs root directory

Question 1.8

If the implementation of the proposed network took months to finish, with the data conversion from the mainframe to the SQL server also taking several weeks, how would the dumb terminals still contact the mainframe if needed?

- ❍ a. Keep the Frame Relay connections as long as needed.
- ❍ b. Install a Windows terminal server at each site.
- ❍ c. Let SNA be encapsulated and sent over the VPN.
- ❍ d. Install a mainframe at each site with data replication.

Question 1.9

If Quick Ride Bus Depot acquired a large number of bus depots and had approximately 5,000 employees and bus drivers, and this growth caused unforeseen network traffic involved in accessing the Internet, what steps could be taken to improve performance? [Check all correct answers]

- ❑ a. Add a proxy server array at each site with the unacceptable performance.
- ❑ b. Change the network to Token Ring.
- ❑ c. Upgrade the Internet browser to a newer version.
- ❑ d. Upgrade the Internet connections at all sites that have unacceptable performance.

Question 1.10

If the performance has declined for access to the Web server from the Internet, but internal access is still more than acceptable, what could improve the performance?

- ❍ a. Add a proxy server array at Los Angeles.
- ❍ b. Upgrade the Internet connections at all depots.
- ❍ c. Upgrade the Internet browser to a newer version at the Los Angeles depot.
- ❍ d. Upgrade the Internet connection at the Los Angeles depot.

Case Study 2

Fudd Fire Extinguisher Company has three buildings, all located in a three-block area. The company manufactures, repairs, and refurbishes fire extinguishers. The following diagram shows the company's building layout.

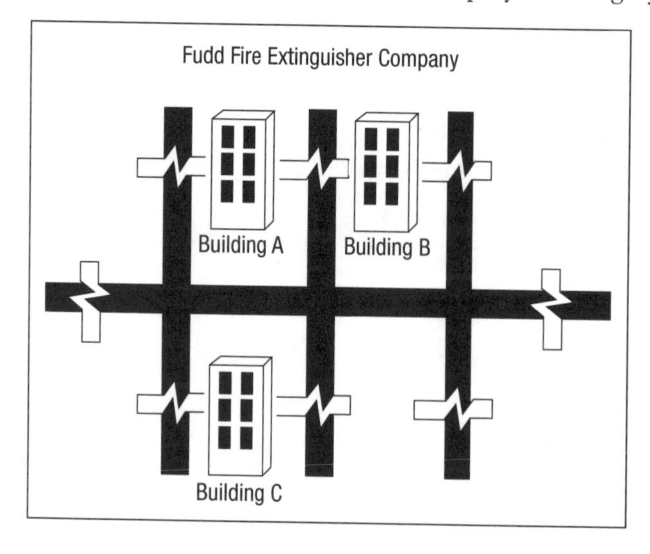

Current LAN/Network Structure

Building A has the administrative, human resource, sales, and accounting departments.

Building B has the marketing, research and development, and IT departments.

Buildings C has the repair and refurbishment department, as well as the storage room for stock.

Buildings A and B have 200 employees, and Building C has 75 employees.

All buildings are connected with bridges: an NT 4 PDC in Building B, and an NT 4 BDC in Building A and C. The PDC runs the Exchange services for the whole company. Building A has SQL running on its BDC to host the customer and sales databases.

All workstations are running Windows 95 or Windows for Workgroups using NetBEUI.

Proposed LAN/Network Structure

All systems will be upgraded to Windows 2000, and 25 dial-up connections will be added for traveling sales people.

Current WAN Connectivity

Each building is connected with fiber-optic cables. Building A is connected to Building B, and Building B is connected to Building C.

Proposed WAN Connectivity

All links will remain, but the bridges will be replaced with routers.

Current Internet Positioning

None at the current time.

Future Internet Plans

An Internet connection will be implemented for remote connectivity for employees to check their mail from home. This implementation will not happen for three to five years. The design must take into account future plans proposed for the WAN.

Question 2.1

How many WINS servers should be implemented at the current time?

- ❍ a. 0
- ❍ b. 1
- ❍ c. 2
- ❍ d. 3

Question 2.2

How many WINS servers should be implemented when the proposed network is completed?

- ❍ a. 0
- ❍ b. 1
- ❍ c. 2
- ❍ d. 3

Question 2.3

Once the proposed network is in place, how should the routers be set up?

- ❍ a. Using RIP version 1
- ❍ b. Using RIP version 2
- ❍ c. Using OSPF
- ❍ d. Using static routes
- ❍ e. Using IGMP
- ❍ f. Using VPNs
- ❍ g. Using IGRP

Question 2.4

Services are needed to be redundant in the proposed network. What option should be implemented for DHCP?

- ❍ a. A DHCP server in Building B
- ❍ b. Three DHCP servers in Building B
- ❍ c. A DHCP server in each building with one scope
- ❍ d. A DHCP server in each building with two scopes
- ❍ e. A DHCP server in each building with three scopes

Question 2.5

For the three buildings:

Building A

Building B

Building C

Match the following services that would be needed at each building in the proposed network. [Some items may be used more than once, and some items may not be used]

DHCP service

WINS service

DNS service

Dial-up service

Proxy service

Dfs service

NAT service

DHCP Relay Agent service

Question 2.6

For complete fault tolerance of the network topology, what should be implemented? (The implementation should also consider cost.)

- ❍ a. Connect Building A and C with a fiber connection
- ❍ b. Extra routers
- ❍ c. VPNs
- ❍ d. Microwave antennae on each building for a backup

Question 2.7

How can a dial-up service in Building A be made secure? Use the following diagram to place objects where they should go. [Options may be used more than once]

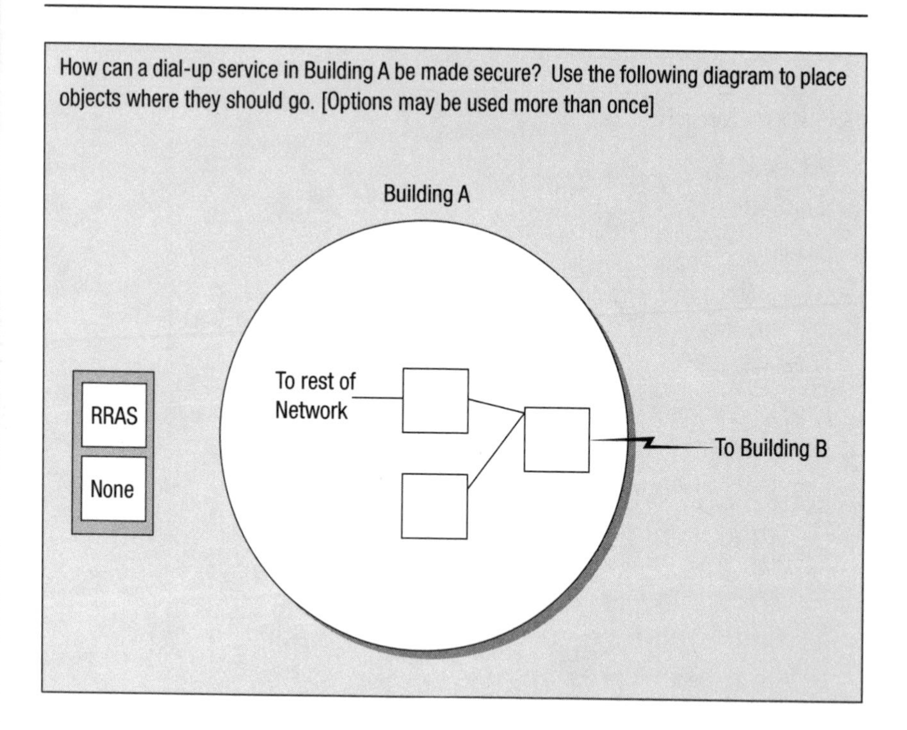

Question 2.8

How could the SQL server and Exchange server be made redundant?

❍ a. Have each server replicate its services and databases to the other server for the other server to act as a backup if one server should fail.

❍ b. Have each server replicate its services and databases to the server in Building C for that server to act as a failover if one of the other two servers should fail.

❍ c. Add a second server to Building A and B, and implement a cluster in each building.

❍ d. Add a second server to Building A and B, and implement a cluster in each building and have all services and data replicated to the other cluster.

Question 2.9

Arrange the following steps in the recommended order to implement the proposed network:

Upgrade workstations

Upgrade bridges with routers

Add dial-up server in Building A

Change network to TCP/IP

Upgrade servers

Question 2.10

In the next few years, when Internet access is added and a Web site is being hosted onsite, which building should have the Web server and Internet connectivity directly connected?

❍ a. Building A

❍ b. Building B

❍ c. Building C

❍ d. Buildings A and B

Case Study 3

Mercury Bike Company is a custom bicycle manufacturer located in Nashville, Tennessee. Mercury's management staff has asked you to change the current structure of the network to increase file access and provide load balancing. Your solution should also simplify the logon scripts and reduce the drive mappings needed at the fabrication facility in Nashville and the retail stores in Chattanooga, Tennessee; Denver, Colorado; Bonham, Georgia; and Grand Ledge, Michigan.

Current LAN/Network Structure

The manufacturing and assembly facility in Nashville has recently upgraded to Windows 2000. This location has two DCs, one member server, and 75 client workstations. All of the retail sites currently use Windows NT 4 servers and workstations and access a point-of-sale program from the member server at the fabrication and assembly facility. Each site has a single server and five workstations.

All of the sites share information and have drive mappings for the shared folders at each location. The shared folders contain an employee schedule and a time-clock application that allows the payroll staff at the Nashville location to extract the employee's hours for weekly payroll.

Proposed LAN/Network Structure

The LAN structure will not be modified.

Current WAN Connectivity

Each location is connected with dual-channel ISDN connections.

Proposed WAN Connectivity

No changes will be made at this time.

Current Internet Positioning

All locations have access to the Internet by using a net appliance located in Nashville.

Future Internet Plans

No changes are planned at this time.

Question 3.1

Which location would provide the best placement for the Dfs root?

❍ a. Nashville

❍ b. Chattanooga

❍ c. Grand Ledge

❍ d. Bonham

Question 3.2

You would like the Dfs root to be protected in case of failure of the main-office server on which it resides. Where would you place the Dfs root replica to protect file access in the event of a server failure?

❍ a. Nashville

❍ b. At one of the retail outlets

❍ c. At each retail outlets

❍ d. None of the above

Question 3.3

Which type of Dfs root will be required at the Nashville location to allow a Dfs root replica to be created?

❍ a. Standalone

❍ b. Domain-based

❍ c. Active Directory

❍ d. None of the above

Question 3.4

After the root has been created, what is added to create the Dfs tree?

❍ a. Replicas

❍ b. Leaf object

❍ c. Dfs link

❍ d. A binary large object

Question 3.5

You would like to create a redundant copy of the shared directory at each location. How would you accomplish this and not affect the utilization of the WAN links?

- ❍ a. This cannot be done.
- ❍ b. Create replicas on the servers at each location.
- ❍ c. Create replicas at the Nashville site.
- ❍ d. Create a link replica and place it on one of the workstations at each retail site.

Question 3.6

Considering that Service Pack 6a has been installed on all of the Windows NT 4 machines, what additional client software will be needed to browse the Dfs tree?

- ❍ a. Dfs client 4/5
- ❍ b. Third-party software
- ❍ c. No additional software is needed
- ❍ d. Windows NT 4 is not compatible with Windows 2000 Dfs

Question 3.7

What services can the replicas at the retail locations provide? [Check all correct answers]

- ❑ a. Fault tolerance
- ❑ b. Load balancing
- ❑ c. Redundant login
- ❑ d. Centralized backup point

Question 3.8

What additional security will Dfs provide for the files in the Dfs tree?

- ❍ a. Dfs will require authentication by the Dfs root server.
- ❍ b. You can specify additional file level control.
- ❍ c. To browse the tree, you must have the browse right to the Dfs root.
- ❍ d. None.

Question 3.9

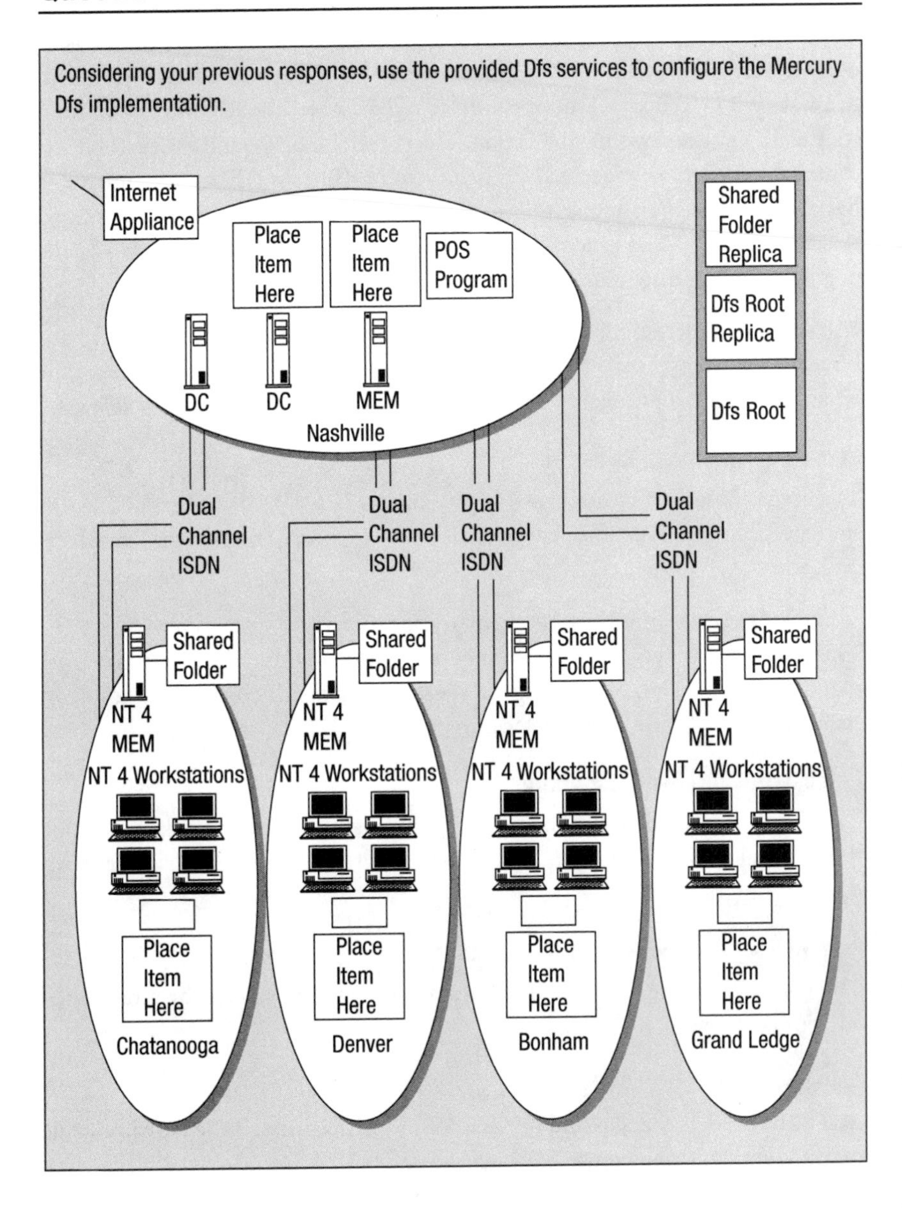
Considering your previous responses, use the provided Dfs services to configure the Mercury Dfs implementation.
Internet Appliance
Place Item Here
Place Item Here
POS Program
DC
DC
MEM
Nashville
Shared Folder Replica
Dfs Root Replica
Dfs Root
Dual Channel ISDN
Dual Channel ISDN
Dual Channel ISDN
Dual Channel ISDN
Shared Folder
NT 4 MEM
NT 4 Workstations
Place Item Here
Chatanooga
Shared Folder
NT 4 MEM
NT 4 Workstations
Place Item Here
Denver
Shared Folder
NT 4 MEM
NT 4 Workstations
Place Item Here
Bonham
Shared Folder
NT 4 MEM
NT 4 Workstations
Place Item Here
Grand Ledge

Case Study 4

Fuzzy Fruit is a produce grower in Atlanta, Georgia. Its corporate office is in downtown Atlanta, and the distribution center is on Peachtree Drive just north of the city limits. Fuzzy Fruit recently added 30 new employees to its existing staff of 195 at the downtown location. The corporate office and the distribution center are currently connected by a dedicated 56Kbps line. The corporate office has also purchased an application to track shipments for billing customers, and this application will be located at the corporate office and will be accessed by the employees at the distribution center to enter shipment information.

You are a contract engineer for a local Microsoft solutions provider and have been contracted by Fuzzy Fruit to upgrade its network to accommodate the new employees and to optimize the performance of the shipment-tracking software.

Current LAN/Network Structure

The corporate office is currently using Windows NT 4 on its servers and workstations. The corporate office has purchased two new servers with Windows 2000 preloaded.

The distribution center has 15 client workstations and one server. When the application was tested, the software vendor reported that the application's performance was poor. The cost of a higher-speed connection is significant because of the distribution center's remote location.

Proposed LAN/Network Structure

The IT personnel would like to improve performance of the network by dividing the physical network into two logical networks to improve the performance of the application.

Current WAN Connectivity

The corporate office and the distribution center are connected by a dedicated 56Kbps connection.

Proposed WAN Connectivity

Make any needed changes and provide additional security on the network while maximizing the shipping application.

Current Internet Positioning

Fuzzy Fruit has an Internet connection that is used only by employees to access the Internet (very seldom). The Internet connection is ISDN BRI.

Future Internet Plans

No changes are planned at this time.

Question 4.1

Considering that the current network IP address is 190.65.12.0, what subnet mask could be used to logically separate the network at the corporate office into two subnets and provide the most host IP addresses?

❍ a. 255.255.192.0

❍ b. 255.255.253.0

❍ c. 255.255.248.0

❍ d. 255.255.255.248

Question 4.2

What could be implemented to provide security between network hosts?

❍ a. QoS

❍ b. Packet filtering

❍ c. MS CHAP challenge response authentication

❍ d. IPSec

Question 4.3

What Windows 2000 TCP/IP enhancement could help prevent the unnecessary retransmission of data over the slow WAN link?

❍ a. QoS

❍ b. IPSec

❍ c. DHCP

❍ d. SACK

Question 4.4

Which IPSec predefined policy would prevent nonsecured communications between the network hosts?

❍ a. Client

❍ b. Server

❍ c. Secured Server

❍ d. ISAKMP/Oakley

Question 4.5

What configuration would need to be made to the routers to allow seamless routing of IPSec? [Check all correct answers]

❑ a. Header Traffic Protocol ID 51 (0x33)

❑ b. IMAP4 protocol on port 110

❑ c. ESP Protocol ID 50 (0x32)

❑ d. SNMP protocol on port 25

Question 4.6

What could be used to guarantee bandwidth for the shipping application?

❍ a. IPSec

❍ b. WINS

❍ c. DNS

❍ d. QoS

Question 4.7

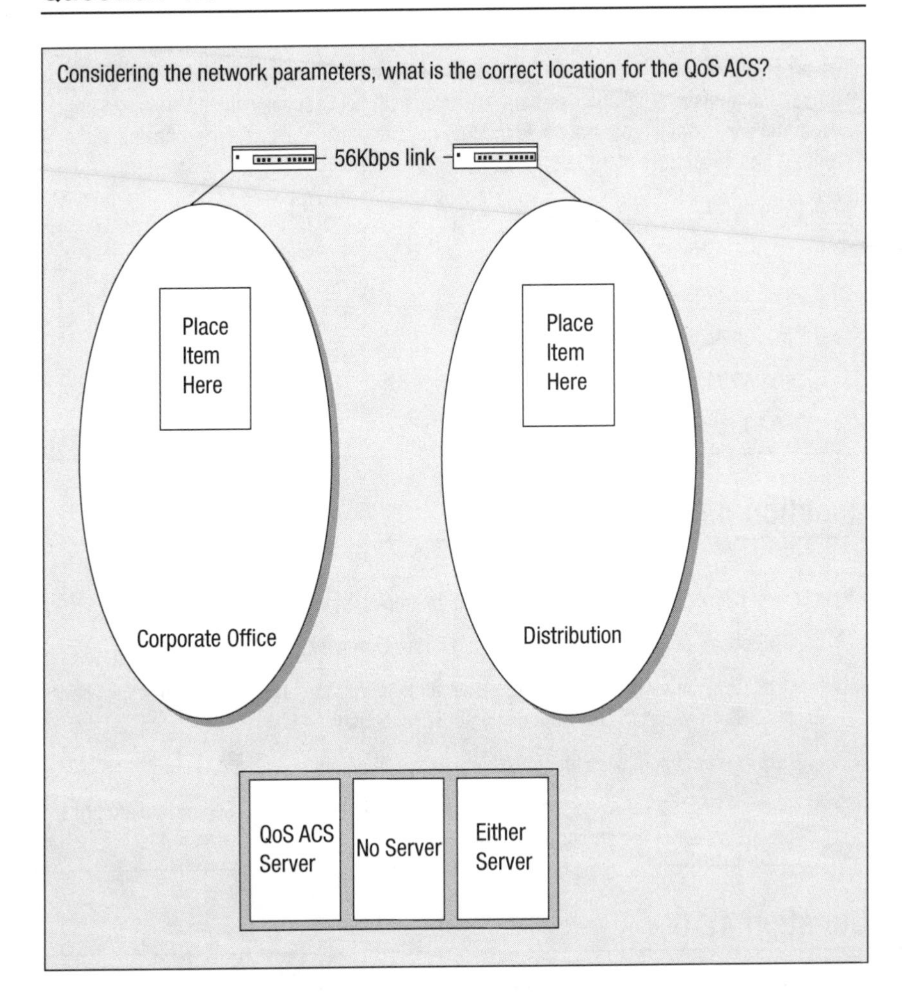
Considering the network parameters, what is the correct location for the QoS ACS?
56Kbps link
Place Item Here
Place Item Here
Corporate Office
Distribution
QoS ACS Server
No Server
Either Server

Question 4.8

The proxy server at the corporate office has an external address of 38.10.74.150 and 190.65.12.5 for its internal address. If an employee at the distribution center were accessing an Internet site, what IP address would the Internet site register the person as having, if the client PC had an address of 190.65.12.250?

- ❍ a. 190.65.12.5
- ❍ b. 38.10.74.150
- ❍ c. 190.65.12.250
- ❍ d. 38.10.74.250
- ❍ e. 192.65.12.150
- ❍ f. 38.10.74.5

Question 4.9

With little network bandwidth, how should DNS be implemented?

- ❍ a. DNS server at corporate integrated with Active Directory.
- ❍ b. DNS server at each site. The DNS server at the corporate office is the primary, while the DNS server at the distribution center is secondary.
- ❍ c. DNS server at both sites integrated into Active Directory.
- ❍ d. Primary DNS server at each site with the distribution center DNS server forwarding to DNS server at the corporate office.

Question 4.10

If all systems except the NT 4 servers were to be upgraded to Windows 2000, what services are required at each location?

Locations

Corporate office

Distribution center

Services

RRAS

WINS

DNS

Dfs

DHCP

Answer Key

For asterisked items, please see the textual representation of the answer on the appropriate page of this chapter.

1.1	d	2.4	e	3.7	a, b
1.2	b, e	2.5	*	3.8	d
1.3	a, b, d, e, and f	2.6	a	3.9	*
1.4	b	2.7	*	4.1	a
1.5	d	2.8	c	4.2	d
1.6	a, b, d, e, and f	2.9	*	4.3	d
1.7	*	2.10	b	4.4	c
1.8	c	3.1	a	4.5	a, c
1.9	a, d	3.2	a	4.6	d
1.10	d	3.3	b	4.7	*
2.1	b	3.4	c	4.8	b
2.2	a	3.5	d	4.9	c
2.3	d	3.6	c	4.10	*

Question 1.1

The correct answer is d. To cluster the SQL servers would allow both servers to send and receive information at one time and to have the other server available if one server should fail.

One SQL server by itself would provide no performance increase or fault tolerance in case of failure. Having two SQL servers with no replication would provide some performance increase if the database were split into two separate databases, but there would be no redundancy. Two SQL servers with replication would provide a performance increase, because either server could handle information requests from a client, but still no fault tolerance is implemented.

Question 1.2

The correct answers are b and e. Because Los Angeles will be the central connection point for all sites, it should be the first range of addresses (for best practice). So the employees would use the 10.1.0.0/16 subnet, while the passengers would use the 192.168.1.0/24 subnet.

Choice a is incorrect because it is an invalid subnet. Choices c, d, f, and g are not the first subnets. These subnets would make the network functional, but the best practice is to use lower-numbered subnets for the main subnets.

Question 1.3

The correct answers are a, b, d, e, and f. All choices can be implemented for functionality (except WINS). For multiple connections in the lobby for passenger use, a hub is needed to bring all connections together to one point. A proxy server can be implemented to help performance by caching Web pages. The router would be implemented to connect Las Vegas to Los Angeles through a Virtual Private Network (VPN). DNS would be required on the network for Internet name resolution. (For redundancy, a DNS server should be at Las Vegas in case the Internet connection failed between Las Vegas and Los Angeles. This would allow the passengers at Las Vegas to still have name-resolution capabilities.) DHCP would be required for the passengers to receive an IP address for use on the private network (clients must be configured as DHCP clients).

WINS is not required because no NetBIOS name resolution will be required, but WINS will not hinder performance.

Question 1.4

The correct answer is b. EAP is an authentication protocol that is used with hardware devices such as retina scanners and other such devices. The frequency-emitting device could be used as an authentication device to authenticate which bus is arriving at a depot.

BAP is the bandwidth allocation protocol that is used to specify the amount of bandwidth required by an application over dial-up links.

Using the Internet as a backbone, TCP/IP will be used—but only to encapsulate the EAP packets for transmission to Los Angeles from Las Vegas. IPX/SPX is not an option because it does not need to be implemented at all in the scenario.

Question 1.5

The correct answer is d. All options would be functional for the scenario. With each site having two subnets—one for the employees and one for the passengers—each site requires two scopes.

Choice a would have no redundancy, and performance would be based on the bandwidth between a depot and the Los Angeles depot and would have no redundancy if the DHCP server or a connection should fail between a depot and Los Angeles.

Choice b would have excellent performance, but no redundancy if a DHCP server would fail.

Choice c would have excellent performance because it also wouldn't need to send traffic out of the site for DHCP requests. Again, no redundancy is provided if a server failed. This choice also has the cost factor of buying two servers for each depot just to manage DHCP.

Choice d gives excellent performance and is also redundant if a server should fail. If a connection should fail between depots, DHCP requests can still be acknowledged. If a server fails at any depot, another server will be able to answer requests for DHCP (because there are two DHCP servers with a portion of any given scope).

Question 1.6

The correct answers are a, b, d, e, and f. All choices can be implemented for functionality (except WINS). For multiple connections in the lobby for passenger use, a hub is needed to bring all connections together to one point. A proxy server can be implemented to help performance by caching Web pages. The router would be implemented to connect Houston to Los Angeles through a Virtual Private Network (VPN). DNS would be required on the network for Internet name resolution. (For redundancy, a DNS server should be at Houston in case the Internet connection failed between Houston and Los Angeles. This would allow the passengers at Houston to still have name-resolution capabilities.) DHCP would be required for the passengers to receive an IP address for use on the private network (clients must be configured as DHCP clients).

WINS is not required because no NetBIOS name resolution will be required, but WINS will not hinder performance.

DHCP Relay Agent should not be used, because it provides no redundancy. If the network link between Houston and Los Angeles fails, no IP addresses will be assigned to computers. In this scenario, two DHCP servers should be implemented and share a scope, with 50 percent of the scope on each computer. If both DHCP servers should fail, then no addresses would be assigned. These DHCP servers would not be able to provide redundancy for the Los Angeles subnet like the other sites as stated in the answer for Question 1.3. Redundancy could be achieved by having two DHCP relay agents, but, if the link between Houston and Los Angeles were to fail, the DHCP relay agents would be useless.

Question 1.7

The correct answer is:

Los Angeles

- Hub
- RRAS
- DHCP server
- SQL server
- DNS server
- Proxy server

Houston

- Hub
- DHCP server
- DNS server
- Proxy server

Redmond

Hub

RRAS

DHCP server

DNS server

Proxy Server

Question 1.8

The correct answer is c. SNA can be encapsulated in TCP/IP packets and sent over a TCP/IP network (in this case, the VPN over the Internet). SNA tunneling must be enabled to encapsulate the SNA packets.

Keeping the Frame Relay connections as long as possible would not be cost effective and would be getting the network closer to the proposed LAN/WAN configuration. Installing a Windows terminal server at each depot would not do anything for the dumb terminals to connect to the mainframe. A terminal server only allows a Windows server to act as a central processor for clients to run applications. Installing a mainframe at each site is not cost effective.

Question 1.9

The correct answers are a and d. Adding proxy arrays will improve performance by caching more sites and helping with some load balancing between the two servers. Upgrading the Internet connection at the depots will increase bandwidth to the Internet at each site and allow better performance.

Changing the network to a Token Ring topology will have little change if going from a 10MB Ethernet network to a 16MB Token Ring network, and would be adversely affected if going from 100MB Ethernet to 16MB Token Ring topology.

Upgrading to newer versions of the Internet browsers used at the depots will have little noticeable effect on performance.

Question 1.10

The correct answer is d. The only area that has access from the Internet to the Web server is the Los Angeles Internet connection. This is the only link that requires an upgrade for increasing performance for access to the Web server.

Question 2.1

The correct answer is b. At the current time, one WINS server is required because there are non-Windows 2000 systems that require a WINS server for better performance. Only one is required because the network has fewer than 10,000 systems.

Question 2.2

The correct answer is a. After the proposed network is in place, no WINS server will be required because all systems will be Windows 2000 based.

Question 2.3

The correct answer is d. In the case of such a small number of sites connected by routers, static routes should be implemented to cut down on overhead of routing protocols. Once the routers are configured, everything should be done. There are no plans for growth in the business (at least for adding sites), and a business can always expect to add a few employees if needed.

Question 2.4

The correct answer is e. Putting a DHCP server in each building with three scopes, using 80 percent of the scope for its subnet and 10 percent of each of the other two building's scopes. This lets a scope manage its own subnet and also a portion of the other two subnets if one of the other DHCP servers should fail. All routers should be BOOTP-enabled to make this work.

Question 2.5

The correct answer is:

Building A

DHCP service

DNS service

Dial-up service

Building B

DHCP service

DNS service

Building C

DHCP service

DNS service

Question 2.6

The correct answer is a. If there were another connection between Building A and C, then there would be another route to each building if a fiber connection should fail. This solution is cheaper than adding microwave antennae for backup. The other options do not provide any fault tolerance.

Question 2.7

The correct answer is:

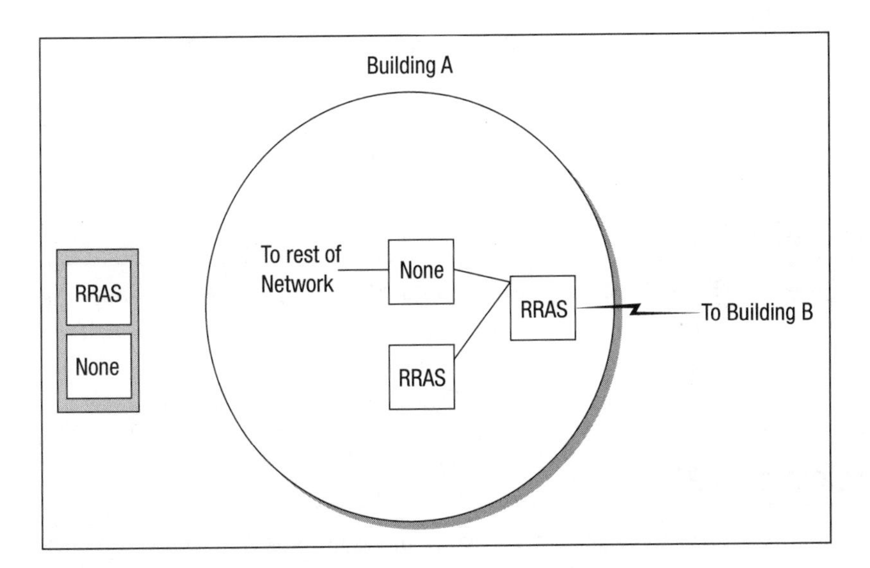

A RRAS server will be used for routing from Building A to Building B with routing services enabled. Another RRAS server will be on its own subnet separate from the rest of the network for better security to provide remote-access services.

Question 2.8

The correct answer is c. The SQL and Exchange server should be clustered for fault tolerance. To replicate databases anywhere would just make a backup of the data.

Question 2.9

The correct answer is:

Change network to TCP/IP

Upgrade bridges with routers

Upgrade servers

Upgrade workstations

Add dial-up server in Building A

Question 2.10

The correct answer is b. The main purpose stated was for employees to access email remotely over the Internet. The Exchange server is located in Building B, so the connections should be placed closest to the service to prevent more network traffic. If remote access were needed to the data on the SQL server, then the SQL server could be moved to Building B, or the Exchange server and Internet connection could go to Building A. (This would be the best choice if Buildings A and C were also connected by a fiber connection.)

Question 3.1

Answer a is correct. By placing the root at the Nashville location, you reduce the impact on all of the retail stores if one of the WAN links becomes disabled. If the root were placed at a retail location, other sites would not have access if the link between the retail store and the Nashville location were disabled.

Question 3.2

Answer a is correct. To protect file access in case of a server failure, a replica should be placed at the Nashville location. This would protect file access if the hosting server fails, and it doesn't increase the network traffic between the Nashville location and the retail stores.

Question 3.3

Answer b is correct. To create a Dfs root replica, a domain-based root must be created. Standalone Dfs roots are not capable of being replicated. Active Directory is not a valid type of Dfs root.

Question 3.4

Answer c is correct. After the root has been created, Dfs links are added that specify the destination of the pointer. After the links are created, they are referred to as Dfs leaf objects. Replicaas re created to rprovide redundancy and load balancing by making a coyp of the shared folder. A binary large object or blob stores the Dfs topology of the Dfs root.

Question 3.5

Answer d is correct. Replicas can be placed on the client workstations. With this design, if the server became disabled, the client could still log on to the domain over the WAN link. The Dfs root is located at the Nashville location, which means it would still be available. If the local Dfs leaf object were replicated to a workstation, the retail store could continue normal operations in the event of a server failure.

Question 3.6

Answer c is correct. Windows NT 4 has the ability to browse the Dfs root and host Dfs leaf objects if Service Pack 3 or higher has been installed.

Question 3.7

Answers a and b are correct. The Dfs link replicas will provide fault tolerance and load balancing at the retail location. The Dfs root would provide a centralized backup point. Dfs does not requite or provide any additional authentication security.

Question 3.8

Answer d is correct. Dfs supplies no additional tools to secure files or directories.

Question 3.9

The correct answer is:

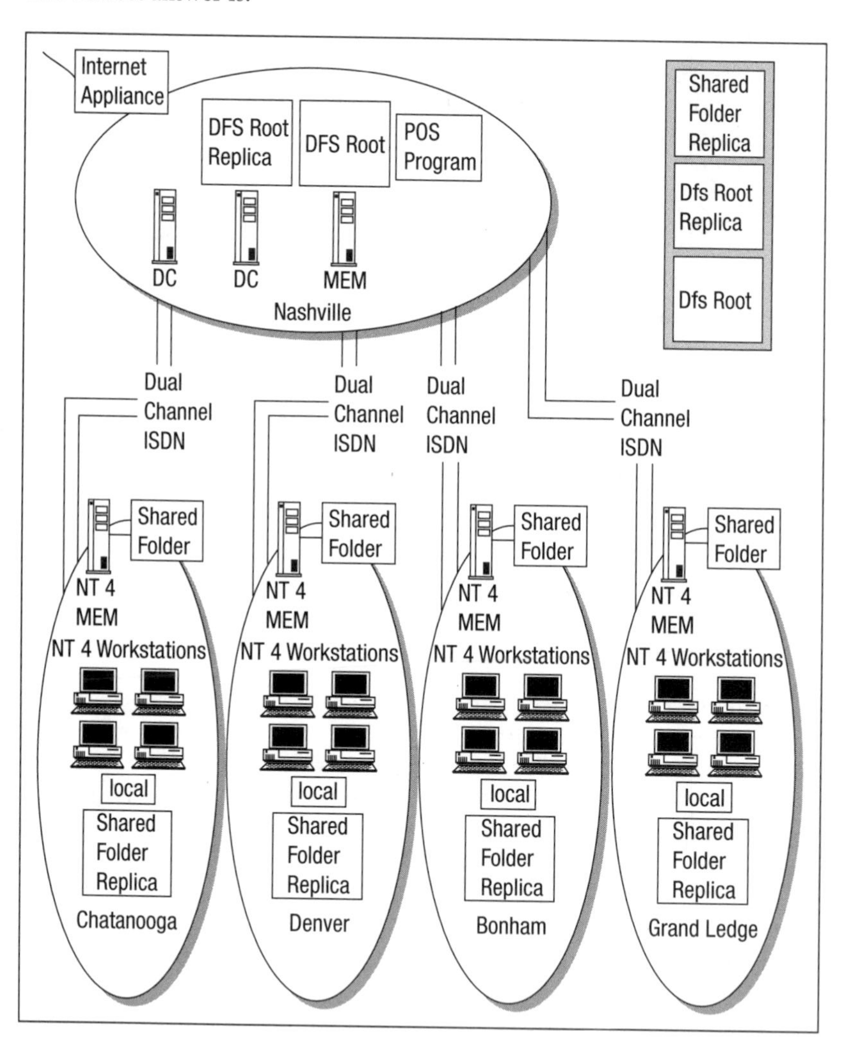

Question 4.1

Answer a is correct. By using 255.255.192.0 as the subnet address, the network could be separated into two logical networks and would provide for 16,382 host IP addresses.

Question 4.2

Answer d is correct. IPSec encrypts TCP/IP communications between hosts. QoS guarantees available bandwidth to QoS applications. Packet filtering can restrict access by a certain type of traffic to a specific TCP/IP port. MSCHAP is a logon challenge authentication protocol that helps prevent unauthorized access but does not provide secure communications between the hosts after the authentication process.

Question 4.3

Answer d is correct. SACK or TCP Selective Acknowledgment reads all data in the TCP window and requests only the retransmission of those packets that have not been correctly received within the TCP window. QoS guarantees the availability of bandwidth for a QoS enabled application. IPSec encrypts communications between hosts. DHCP provides automatic IP addressing for DHCP and BOOTP-enabled clients.

Question 4.4

Answer c is correct. Secured Server requires secured communication. Any requests to send using unsecured communications are rejected. Both client and server will allow unsecured communications. ISAKMP/Oakley is a protocol used for authentication; it does not define the type of communication allowed by either host.

Question 4.5

Answers a and c are correct. IPSec Header Traffic Protocol ID 51 (0x33) and IPSec ESP Protocol ID 50 (0x32) need to be enabled on the router to support IPSec routing. IMAP4 is used by email clients, and ESP headers are used for encryption security.

Question 4.6

Answer d is correct. QoS (Quality of Service) provides a routing mechanism that can guarantee delivery of data for a certain application. Paths for traffic flows are determined based on some knowledge of resource availability in the network. WINS and DNS are used to resolve names to IP addresses. IPSec provides encryption between TCP/IP hosts.

Question 4.7

The correct answer is:

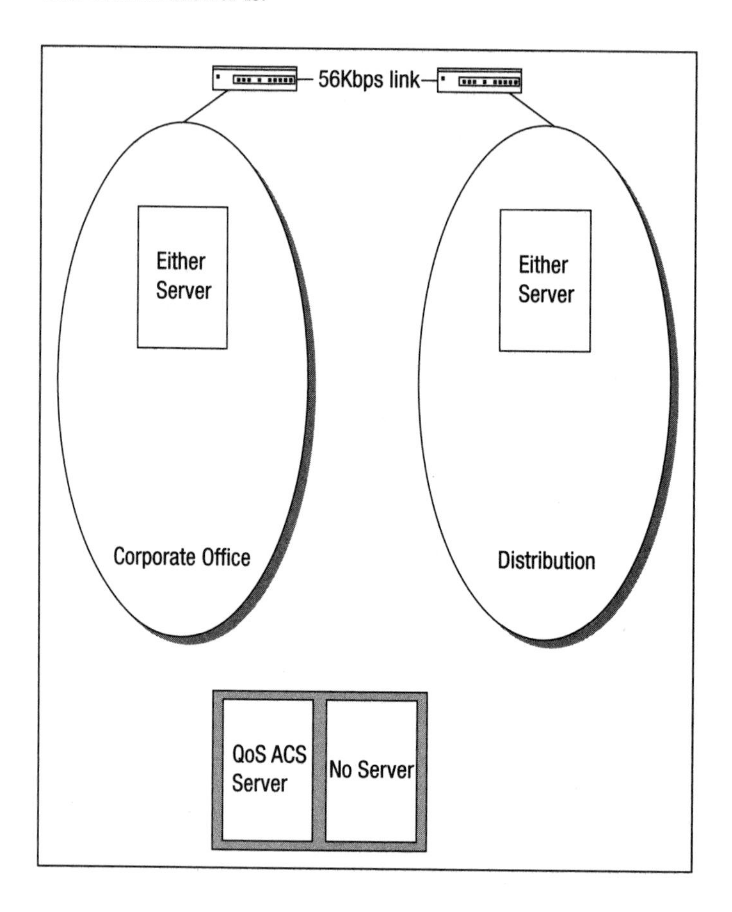

You should place the QoS ACS server on overpopulated segments. Because the 56Kbps link is the limiting factor in this scenario, the ACS server could be placed at either location.

Question 4.8

The correct answer is b. All IP packets will be sent from the proxy server to the Internet. The requests are actually generated by the proxy server with the address of 38.10.74.150.

Question 4.9

The correct answer is c. Because bandwidth is at a minimum, using Active Directory will cause a little less overhead and allow all DNS tables to be synchronized identically. Using forwarders will cause more overhead and consume more bandwidth.

Question 4.10

Corporate office

RRAS

WINS

DNS

Dfs

DHCP

Distribution center

RRAS

DNS

Dfs

DHCP

RRAS would be needed at each site if physical routers were not purchased. WINS would be required because an NT 4 system would still be in place. The WINS system should be placed on the same subnet as the location of the most non-Windows 2000 systems, which would be the corporate office. DNS servers are required for Windows 2000 name resolution. Dfs services would be required for the Dfs tree. DHCP services would be required to assign IP addresses. Because the IP addresses are subnetted, it would be best to use DHCP in case the subnet is changed again. For redundancy, a DHCP server should be at each location in case the 56Kbps link were to fail between the sites.

Glossary

Access control list (ACL)
A table listing what actions a user is allowed to perform on network resources.

Active Directory
Windows 2000 directory service to store network object information.

Active Directory-integrated zone
A type of DNS zone that is Microsoft-specific. Integrates with Active Directory.

Alert
Notification of problems on a computer. An alert causes an action to take place when a threshold is reached on a counter.

AppleTalk
Native network architecture used by Macintosh computers.

Application layer
The top or highest layer of the OSI model. The Application Program Interface (API) uses this layer to access program utilities such as file and print services.

ARIN (American Registry of Internet Numbers)
An organization that administers and controls the registration of IP addresses.

ARPANET (Advanced Research Projects Agency Network)
The world's first packet-switching network.

AS (autonomous system)
A group of routers exchanging routing information.

ASP (active server pages)
A set of technologies often used in Web pages for the purpose of creating dynamic content on a Web site.

Authentication
A method to validate log-on information.

Automated Analysis
The use of automated responses to correct the network variance.

Automatic Private Addressing

IP autoconfiguration, or automatic private IP addressing, is a new feature that uses discovery packets to assign a unique IP address if no manual or BOOTP/DHCP configuration is available. Also referred to as Automatic private IP addressing (APIPA).

BackOffice

A suite of server applications designed to provide all the services a company requires for a network.

Bandwidth

The difference between the highest and lowest frequency available over a connection that can be used to transfer information.

BIND (Berkeley Internet Name Domain)

An implementation of DNS server designed by the University of California at Berkeley.

BOOTP (Boot Protocol)

The protocol for a system to obtain boot information. Also defines if a router is BOOTP-enabled to allow DHCP broadcasts to pass through it.

Bottleneck

A situation in which a resource is unable to keep up with required use, such as a hard drive that cannot write data as fast as it needs to be written.

Broadcast

In regards to networking, refers to a packet that is not addressed to any one computer but a group of computers.

Cache

A buffer used to store information for quicker access than without a buffer.

Cache hit ratio

The percentage of Web requests that a proxy server can fulfill from cache instead of having to retrieve the page from the Internet.

CARP (Cache Array Routing Protocol)

A protocol to compute on which single server in a proxy array a Web page should be cached.

Centralized data collection

A process by which there is a centralized point for collection and analysis; data is accumulated and analyzed at a central location.

CERN (Conseil European pour la Reserche Nucleair)

The particle physics lab in Switzerland that created the Web and the first proxy servers.

Chaining

Configuring proxy servers to route their client requests to other upstream proxy servers instead of sending them directly out to the Internet.

CHAP (Challenge Handshake Authentication Protocol)

Protocol used to authenticate usernames and passwords. Encrypts the information for transport over a network.

Client

A device on a network that uses resources from a server to accomplish a task.

Cluster

A combining of two physical hardware computer systems to act as a single logical unit until one fails and the other system will still function for redundancy.

Convergence
Stabilization of routing tables when network topology changes.

Convergence time
When used in reference to the WINS service, convergence time is the time it takes to copy a change to the WINS database to all other WINS replication partners.

Counter logs
Logs used to gather data and record the captured statistics to a log file. The log file is later viewed from the system console.

Data collection
The collecting of statistics to determine the state of a resource or service.

Data link layer
The layer directly above the physical layer. This layer assembles the bits into recognizable data called *frames*.

DES (Data Encryption Standard)
These standards describe data encryption from 40-bit DES to 128-bit Triple DES (3DES).

Dfs (Distributed File System)
A chain of shared folders that can be accessed from one share point to provide a way to centrally manage a group of network shared folders.

Dfs client
A machine that requests Dfs services from a hosting Dfs server.

Dfs leaf object
The name of a link to a shared resource in a Dfs tree.

Dfs replica
Replicas of a Dfs root or leaf object created to provide fault tolerance.

Dfs root server
A server that hosts a Dfs root.

Dfs tree
The hierarchical structure that Dfs uses to organize your network files.

DHCP (Dynamic Host Configuration Protocol)
Protocol used to automate the assignment of IP addresses and other TCP/IP options like IP address, Subnet Mask, Gateway, and others.

DHCP Relay Agent
A service used to act as a “middle man” between clients on a subnet that cannot communicate with a DHCP server on another subnet because the subnets are connected by a non-BOOTP router.

Dial-up
A network connection that is typically open only when in use. When not in use, the connection is closed.

Digital signature
A piece of code that allows someone to sign and therefore authenticate a document electronically for two people to exchange encrypted information.

Directory services
A set of services in a network operating system (NOS) that governs how users can access resources on the network.

Disk subsystem
Any hardware pertaining to hard drives, such as hard drive controllers and hard drives.

Distributed data collection
A strategy that utilizes more than one collection point for network statistics.

DNS (Domain Name System)
A service to resolve a computer host name (or NetBIOS name) to its IP address.

Domain controller
The server that authenticates user logon. Part of Active Directory.

Domain filter
A filter based on the Internet domain to which a packet is connecting.

Downlevel
Refers to earlier versions of a service or operating system.

EAP (Extensible Authentication Protocol)
Extension of PPP allowing user authentication.

Encapsulation
The method used to pass data from one network to another when both networks use different protocols.

Encryption
The method to disguise data and hide its content.

Event Viewer
A service that notifies when errors occur in the system, security, application, directory service, DNS server, and file-replication services.

Exchange Server
Part of the Microsoft BackOffice suite of products. Provides email and communication services to a network.

Failover
The process by which services on one system take over when a cluster fails.

Fault tolerance
The ability of a system to keep working even though a failure has occurred on a clustered system.

Filter
The set of rules that specify whether a packet is permitted to pass from one subnet to another.

Filtering
Allowing only those packets that meet a certain criteria.

Firewall
A system that protects the internal network by closing ports and preventing incoming connections from the public-access network.

Forwarder
A DNS server that directs a query to another DNS server when the query cannot be resolved locally.

Frame Relay
A protocol used in packet-switching networks to provide WAN connections at varying speeds.

Gateway
The service that sends from one subnet the protocols that are destined for another subnet.

GUI (graphical user interface)
A program interface that allows users to click on graphics when they want to perform an action, instead of requiring the user to type in commands.

Hop count
The number of routers that a packet travels through from its source to its destination.

Host
A name that refers to a node on a TCP/IP network.

HTTP (Hypertext Transfer Protocol)
The high-level protocol used by the Web. Part of the TCP/IP suite of protocols.

IAS (Internet Authentication Services)
Service in Windows 2000 that includes the RADIUS server component.

ICMP (Internet Control Message Protocol)
A protocol that allows the gateway to be discovered without an entry using router discovery messages called *router advertisements* and *router solicitations*.

IETF (Internet Engineering Task Force)
Internet Engineering Task Force. The body responsible for posting RFCs.

IGMP (Internet Group Management Protocol)
A list of members that are to receive multicast packets.

IIS (Internet Information Server)
Part of the Microsoft BackOffice suite of products. Provides Web, FTP, and other Web-related services to a network.

In-band data collection
A strategy in which the collected monitoring data travels on the same physical infrastructure that provides service to your clients.

Interface
The device that is used to connect something to a network.

IP addressing
The addressing scheme of four numbers (from 0 to 255) that is a numeric representation of a system on a network.

IPSec (Internet Protocol Security)
A set of protocols that provide data integrity and data encryption in your Windows 2000 network.

IPX/SPX
The transport protocol commonly used by Novell.

ISAKMP/Oakley
A protocol that allows the receiver to verify the sender's identity using X.509 digital certificates.

ISDN (integrated services digital network)
Digital communication for data and voice with speeds of 64 or 128Kbps.

ISP (Internet Service Provider)
A company that provides access to the Internet.

L2TP (Layer 2 Tunneling Protocol)
The method of encapsulating IP, IPX, SNA, or NetBEUI.

LAN (local area network)
The portion of a single network in a small geographical area, such as a building.

Latency
The period of time that one component or computer waits for another to respond.

Lease
The set amount of time that a computer is able to use its assigned IP address before it has to renew the address.

Legacy
Describes an older, usually out-of-date application, hardware, or operating system that is considered necessary to a network that needs to be connected to and integrated into a network.

Lightweight
When used in reference to bandwidth and networking, refers to a protocol or service that is designed to generate little network traffic.

Link state
Router requirement to send routing information from one router to all routers on a network.

Linux
An open-source network operating system.

MAC (media access control) address
The hard-coded physical address that is given to a network interface card by the manufacturer.

Macintosh
A line of Apple computers or their GUI operating system.

MADCAP (Multicast Address Dynamic Client Allocation Protocol)
A protocol that distributes multicast address configuration.

Management strategy
A plan that details the proposed responses to network and application resource variances due to failures and projected growth.

Manual analysis
A technique used for point-in-time analysis of the network.

Manual testing
Testing that requires physical action from the responsible parties.

Master
A server that sends information to another (slave) and which is the only source of that information.

MD5 (Message Digest 5)
Protocol that operates over the entire data packet, including the header, to provide 128-bit authentication with random keys.

Metric
The value of distance through routers from source to destination.

MMC (Microsoft Management Console)
A management tool to control applications and services in Windows 2000.

Modem pool
A set of multiple modems.

MS-CHAP (Microsoft Challenge Handshake Authentication Protocol)
Authentication protocol for dial-up connections to a remote-access server.

Multicast
To send information over a network to multiple systems at once.

Multilink
Using multiple connections to act as one connection.

Namespace
A set of rules that govern the creation of computer names.

NAS (network access server)
A generic RADIUS term referring to the server that acts as the RADIUS client that accepts local RAS client requests and forwards them to the RADIUS server. In Windows 2000, the RRAS service acts as the NAS.

NAT (network address translation)
Translation of IP addresses to other addresses for use on the Internet or other public networks when the original IP addresses need to remain hidden.

NetBT (NetBIOS over TCP/IP)
A protocol, used at the session layer, that is required when protocols in the TCP/IP stack use NetBIOS at the session layer.

Nbtstat
Nbtstat displays the NetBIOS of TCP/IP statistics for troubleshooting networks that have clients other than Windows 2000.

NDS (Novell Directory Services)
The directory services provided by Novell Netware.

NetBIOS (Network Basic Input/Output)
The session layer network designed by API to provide a connection between computers in a LAN environment.

Netdiag
Netdiag performs a series of tests that are local to the host and used to determine the current state of the network client, including the availability of the WINS, DNS, and default gateway.

Netstat
Netstat displays protocol statistics and current TCP/IP network connections.

Network layer
The third layer of the OSI model. This layer provides addressing, routing, and traffic management for transmissions between nodes.

Network Monitor
A monitoring utility to track statistics on network resources and services.

NIC (network interface card)
The hardware peripheral card that allows a computer to be connected to a network.

NLB (network load balancing)
Part of Microsoft's Windows clustering service. Distributes client requests across available servers.

Node
A computer or device connected to a network.

NOS (network operating system)
An operating system that provides services that allow control over a network of users and computers.

Novell Netware
Novell corporation's network operating system (NOS).

Nslookup
Nslookup provides an interactive way to check DNS server resolution. This utility displays the hostname and IP address of the DNS server.

NWLink
Microsoft's version of IPX/SPX.

Option Pack
A set of Web applications and supporting software from Microsoft that are all a part of Internet Information Server. Also called the Windows NT 4.0 Option Pack.

OSI (Open Systems Interconnection) model
A seven-layer model created by the International Standards Organization (ISO) that defines a standard for network communications.

OSPF (Open Shortest Path First)
The protocol used to transmit routing information between routers.

Out-of-band collection
An alternate path will be used to transmit the monitored data to the centralized management point.

Packet filter
A filter based on the protocol and destination port of a packet.

Packets
A collection of data that is transmitted from one computer to another.

PAP (Password Authentication Protocol)
Protocol used to authenticate username and passwords.

Pathping
Does not actually encrypt the username and password over a network. Although similar to both ping and tracert, pathping provides a better diagnostic tool to troubleshoot router congestion by testing the path for 125 seconds.

Performance object
A type of counter associated with a resource that is to be monitored for certain performance values..

Persistent
A network connection that is always open.

Physical layer
The lowest layer of the OSI model. This layer defines architecture standards and is responsible for the transfer of binary data.

Ping (Packet Internet Groper)
A utility that can be used to check connectivity.

POP (point of presence)
A device that will accept a user's connection and allow the user to access an ISP's network.

Ports
The TCP/IP method to determine the program that is sending or receiving data.

PPP (Point-to-Point Protocol)
A protocol used to connect remote clients to a network.

PPTP (Point-to-Point Tunneling Protocol)
The method of encapsulating IP, IPX, SNA, or NetBEUI inside IP packets.

Presentation layer
The sixth layer of the OSI model. This layer provides standards for encoding and encryption across a network. This layer acts as negotiator for the rest of the protocol stack and is responsible for making the protocol stack network independent.

Primary zone
A DNS zone that is authoritative.

Private network
A network to which only certain users have access, such as a corporate LAN.

Proactive response strategies
A strategy requiring that trend analysis be used to predict possible failures and growth or variances that will place the network service in a state such that the service no longer meets the design requirements.

Proxy array
A group of proxy servers that can combine their cache to act as one.

Proxy Server
Part of Microsoft's BackOffice suite. A server used to protect internal network clients by making Internet requests for them and improving performance by caching data.

Public network
A network to which anyone has access, such as the Internet.

Pull replication
A type of WINS replication that uses time as the replication trigger to get the WINS table from replication partners.

Push replication
A type of WINS replication that uses a set number of changes as the replication trigger to send the WINS table to replication partners.

QoS (Quality of Service)
A routing mechanism that can guarantee data delivery for a certain application. Paths for traffic flows are determined based on some knowledge of resource availability in the network.

RADIUS (Remote Authentication Dial-In User Service)
The service used to authenticate remote users onto a network.

Reactive response
This response strategy describes action after the event has occurred.

Realm
A generic RADIUS term that refers to what will authenticate the incoming RADIUS request. In Windows 2000, Active Directory acts as the realm for RADIUS.

Redundancy
The provision of a backup in the event that a service fails.

Replication
When used in reference to the WINS service, replication is the copying of WINS database changes between WINS servers.

Resolver
A client in the DNS system that is trying to resolve a name by querying a DNS server.

Resource record
Individual records in a DNS zone file that map a computer name to an IP address or a computer to some resource type.

Response strategies
Processes that occur when the network service reaches a point at which an action needs to be undertaken to correct or circumvent a problem.

Reverse proxy
A service provided on a proxy server that maps incoming Web requests to an internal Web server.

RFC (Request for Comment)
The documents that specify TCP/IP details.

RIP (Routing Information Protocol)
A protocol used to transmit routing information between routers.

Rogue servers
A DHCP server that is activated on a network but is not authorized to be running.

Router
The device used to forward a packet from one subnet to its destination subnet.

Routing
The process of determining a path over routers for a packet to be sent from one subnet to another.

RRAS (Routing and Remote Access Service)
The service to specify routing and remote-access configuration.

SACK
TCP selective acknowledgment.

SAM (Security Access Manager)
A database of user and computer accounts in Windows NT used as part of directory services.

SAP (Service Advertising Protocol)
The protocol used to advertise resources available on a server.

Scope
A range of IP addresses and options for a DHCP server to assign to DHCP clients.

Screened subnet
A part of a network that is separated from the internal network by a device using packet filtering.

Secondary zone
A DNS zone that is copied from another DNS server.

Server
A device on a network that satisfies the requests of a client.

Session layer
The fifth layer of the OSI model. This layer defines the management of individual network sessions. It establishes, maintains, and ends sessions between nodes.

SHA
A 160-bit authenticator to provide data-origin authentication.

Shared folder
A folder that is shared to allow access by clients.

Shared secret
The password used to authenticate the connection from a RADIUS client to a RADIUS server.

Slave
A DNS server that can send unresolved queries to only a forwarder. It is not allowed to send the query to the Internet.

Smart card
A small device that can be programmed for a range of functions when connected to a computer.

SNMP (Simple Network Management Protocol)
An additional TCP/IP utility that can be installed on a Windows 2000-based computer to allow management of systems and services remotely by using the SNMP protocol.

Socket
A connection between a client and a server that works at the session layer. Created by the combination of an IP address and port, such as 192.168.1.1 port 80.

SOCKS
An IETF standard that allows proxy servers to connect clients to Internet applications.

SOCKS proxy
A service provided on Microsoft Proxy Server that connects non-Windows clients to Web applications.

Spoke and hub
Refers to the way in which WINS servers should be physically set up for replication. One server should be selected as the center (hub) from which all updates will be replicated to other servers, like the spokes in a wheel.

SQL Server
Part of the Microsoft BackOffice suite of products. A database management product providing database services to a network.

SSL (Secure Socket Layer)
A protocol that works at the Session layer of the OSI model. Used to provide secure Web connections by encrypting Web pages.

Streaming video
Video images that are sent from one system to another or multiple computers over the network.

Subnet
A portion of a TCP/IP network.

Subnet mask
A filter that designates which portion of the 32-bit TCP/IP address relates to network identification and which relates to the actual host ID.

Supernetting
A process by which two or more small subnets are combined.

Superscope
Multiple scopes defined on a DHCP server.

System console
The MMC with the appropriate snap-in to provide management for a specific service.

System Monitor
A utility program that allows the viewing of live or realtime network resource statistics.

T1
A high-speed digital link of 24 64Kbps channels, totaling 1.544Mbps.

T3
A high-speed digital link of 28 T1 lines, totaling 44.736Mbps.

TCP (Transmission Control Protocol)
Transport layer protocol in the TCP/IP stack. Guarantees delivery of packets.

TCP window size
The size of the receiving window determines how many packets can be received before an acknowledgment is sent to the sending host.

TCP/IP (Transmission Control Protocol/Internet Protocol)
The most commonly used suite of protocols in today's networks.

TCP/IP stack
The common term used for the TCP/IP suite of protocols.

Tombstoning
Specifying a record in a WINS database for deletion and allowing it to replicate to all WINS databases. If a simple deletion is done, the record may be replicated back to the database where it was deleted from originally and made active.

Trace logs
Logs that record data collected by the operating system provider or one or more non-system providers, such as programmers.

Tracert
A utility to discover the route used between two communicating hosts.

Transparent
In a network environment, describes a service that works without the user becoming aware of it.

Transport layer
The fourth layer of the OSI model. This layer is responsible for making sure that the data was received without errors.

TTL (Time To Live)
Information used by protocols and services to require that packets be discarded after a set amount of activity on a network.

UDP (User Datagram Protocol)
Transport layer protocol in the TCP/IP stack. Does not guarantee delivery of packets.

UNC (Universal Naming Convention)
A standard used to reference shared resources on a network.

Unix
An operating system that uses a command-line interface and TCP/IP as its networking protocol.

URL (uniform resource locater)
A standard format for specifying an address to a Web page.

Variable length subnet mask (VLSM)
A method to further break down a subnet. An existing subnet mask is subdivided in a hierarchical fashion.

Vendor options
DHCP configuration for specific hardware vendor types.

VPN (Virtual Private Network)
A connection that allows remote access to a private network over a public network.

VPN client
The computer using a VPN to access resources on a VPN server.

VPN connection
The physical link on which a VPN is created.

VPN server
The computer sharing resources through a VPN by VPN clients.

VPN tunnel
The logical connection between VPN server and a VPN client where data transferred is encapsulated and or encrypted.

VPN Tunneled Data
Information transferred between the VPN client and VPN server.

VPN Tunneling Protocols
Protocol used to encapsulate and or encrypt tunneled data.

WAN (wide area network)
Collection of LANs over a wide geographical area.

Web proxy
A service that allows a Web client to connect to a proxy server when requesting a Web page instead of connecting directly to the Internet.

Windows Clustering
A Microsoft service that allows individual servers to act as a group. It includes the Microsoft Cluster Server and Network Load Balancing services.

Windows Management Instrumentation
An interface that programmers can use to create custom applications that monitor the status of services.

Windows Script Host
A service that can automatically run script files for logon scripts, administrative, and automated tasks.

WINS (Windows Internet Naming Service)
A service that resolves a NetBIOS computer's name to IP addresses.

WinSock proxy
A service provided on Microsoft Proxy Server that connects Windows clients to Web applications.

wizard
Setup screen that asks for information to perform the actual configuration for which the wizard is designed.

zone
A portion of the distributed DNS database contained in one file.

Index

Bold page numbers indicate sample exam questions.

D

E

I

N

Q

R

V

W

Z